THE BIRTH
TO PRESENCE

MERIDIAN

Crossing Aesthetics

Werner Hamacher
& David E. Wellbery
Editors

Translated by
Brian Holmes
& others

Stanford
University
Press

———

Stanford
California
1993

THE BIRTH
TO PRESENCE

Jean-Luc Nancy

Stanford University Press
Stanford, California

© 1993 by the Board of Trustees of the
Leland Stanford Junior University

Printed in the United States of America

CIP data are at the end of the book

Acknowledgments

I warmly thank everyone who helped in the birth of this book. First, Helen Tartar, Humanities Editor of Stanford University Press, by whose invitation—at the suggestion of David Wellbery—the idea for this collection was born. Her help has been precious and precise during the whole process. Then, Brian Holmes, who played the role of editor for the translation. He coordinated the work of the different translators, suggesting changes within the texts, as well as in the choice of texts. And, with him, all the translators and editors, whose job, I know, was not easy: Xavier Callahan, David Carroll, Mary Ann and Peter Caws, Thomas Harrison, Nathalia King, Christine Laennec, Katherine Lydon, Juliet Flower MacCannell, Emily McVarish, Paula Moddel, Avital Ronell, Claudette Sartiliot, Michael Syrotinski, Rodney Trumble, and David Wellbery. Then, the publishers of the first versions of the texts, in French or in English, who kindly gave their permission to reprint or translate the essays: *Alea, Cahiers de l'Herne, Critique*, Columbia University Press, Duke University Press, Editions Galilée, Flammarion, The Johns Hopkins University Press, *Po&sie, Revue des Sciences Humaines, Social Research, Stanford Italian Review* and Anma Libri, Sud, University of Wisconsin Press, and *Yale French Studies*. Finally, my friends and colleagues Philippe Lacoue-Labarthe and Ann Smock, who agreed to publish here two dialogs they wrote with me.

Full bibliographical data for a certain number of references are missing in this volume. I am responsible for that. After hard and dedicated work by the translators in locating the quotes, Helen Tartar, who did a meticulous general revision of the manuscript, asked me to help fill in the remaining references. In some cases, however, it has been impossible to do so. Some readers may take this to be oversight or a blameworthy hastiness, even if the reference is to a well-known text. ("What is 'well-known' isn't known at all," writes Hegel; I know this sentence well, but I don't know where to locate it in the *Phenomenology of Mind.*) Maybe some French have a certain lack of philological seriousness. But, without trying to make excuses, one should also take into account a Nietzschean heritage of rebellion against a certain philology. Therefore, the omission was sometimes done deliberately from the outset: I wanted to let some citations stand by themselves (in their proper value), out of their initial context, because for me their usage didn't implicate any reference to the context. Thereby the sentence is given as much value as the information it carries. You sometimes have to take books out of libraries, and sentences out of books; that's a way of giving them another chance or letting them run another risk. Some texts in this collection have been deliberately conceived that way (e.g., the first part of "Exscription").

J.-L. N.

§ On the Collection As Such

A collection is not a pure aggregation of different pieces. It builds a whole, if not a system (but, why not?), at least a coordination of themes. What perhaps is more, it makes sensible an insistence, if not an obsession (but, why not?), in a certain way of thinking.

Here, this is clearly a thinking of "presence." Not the firmly standing presence, immobile and impassive, of a platonic Idea. But presence as a to-be-here, or to-be-there, as a come-to-here, or there, of somebody. Some *body*: an existence, a being in the world, being given to the world. No more, no less, than *everybody*, everyday, everywhere. No more, no less than the *finitude* of this existence, which means: the matter of fact that it does not have its sense in any Idea (in any achievement of "sense"), but does have it in being exposed to this presence that comes, and only comes. As when we are born—an event that lasts all our lives. Coming (being in the birth, being a birth), existence misses sense as meaningful "sense." But this missing makes itself sense, and makes sense, our sense, the sense of exposed beings.

Hence, the two parts of this book: "Existence," which comprises texts on finitude, on different points of view; and "Poetry," whose concern is the presentation of presence. "Poetry" means, not a literary genre as such, but the limit of "literature," of "writing," where nothing is written but the coming of a presence, a coming

that can never be written or presented in any way. The edge on
which writing writes only its own limit, exposed to . . . .
. . . .
. . . .
. . . .

Contents

THE BIRTH
TO PRESENCE

§ Introduction:
The Birth to Presence

The epoch of representation is as old as the West. It is not certain that "the West" itself is not a single, unique "epoch," coextensive with humanity ever since "homo" became *homo* (whether *habilis*, *faber*, or *sapiens*, we need not examine here). This means that the end is not in sight, even if humanity's self-suppression is now a possibility in humanity's general program. And, consequently, the end of representation is not in sight. There is, perhaps, no humanity (and, perhaps, no animality) that does not include representation—although representation may not exhaust what, in man, passes infinitely beyond man.

Yet this also means that the limit of the West is ceaselessly in sight: "the West" is precisely what designates itself as limit, as demarcation, even when it ceaselessly pushes back the frontiers of its imperium. By the turn of a singular paradox, the West appears as what has as its planetary, galactic, universal vocation limitlessly to extend its own delimitation. It opens the world to the closure that it is.

This closure is named in many ways (appropriation, fulfillment, signification, destination, etc.); in particular, it is named "representation." Representation is what determines itself by its own limit. It is the delimitation for a subject, and by this subject, of what "in itself" would be neither represented nor representable.

But the irrepresentable, pure presence or pure absence, is also an

effect of representation (just as "the East," or "the Other World,"
are effects of "the West"). The subject of representation even
represents to itself, as a blinding sun, the pure object of knowledge
and desire that absolutely given Presence would necessarily be.

The characteristic of representational thought is: to represent,
for itself, both itself *and* its outside, the outside of its limit. To cut
out a form upon the fundament, *and* to cut out a form of the
fundament. Thereafter, nothing more can come, nothing more can
come forth or be born from any fundament.

It is different for whoever comes after the subject, whoever
succeeds to the West. He *comes*, does nothing but come, and for
him, presence in its entirety is coming: which means, not "having
come" (past participle), but a *coming* (the action of coming, arriving). Presence is what is born, and does not cease being born. Of it
and to it there is birth, and only birth. This is the presence of
whoever, for whomever *comes*: who succeeds the "subject" of the
West, who succeeds the West—this coming of another that the
West always demands, and always forecloses.

~

Not form and fundament, but the pace, the passage, the coming
in which nothing is distinguished, and everything is unbound.
What is born has no form, nor is it the fundament that is born.
"To be born" is rather to transform, transport, and entrance all
determinations.

To be born is not to have been born, and to have been born. It is
the same with all verbs: to think is not yet to have thought, and
already to have thought. Thus "to be born" is the verb of all verbs:
the "in the midst of taking place" that has neither beginning nor
end. The verb without a presence of coming to presence. The
unique "form" and the unique "fundament" of being. "To be" is
not yet to have been, and already to have been. To be born is the
name of being, and it is precisely not a name.

Since the dawn of contemporary thought, since Hegel (it suffices
to reread the preface of the *Phenomenology*), "birth" has been used
to speak of what is absolutely in excess of representation. Already
Hegel grasps essential knowledge—which will *engender* absolute

knowledge—as this movement of arising *and negating any representation given with this rising*, as well as any representation *of* this rising. Hegel names this "the experience of consciousness." *Experience*: traversal to the limits, traversal as knowledge, and no knowledge of the traversal if not that formed by "traversing" itself.

Presence is only given in this arising and in this stepping beyond, which accedes to nothing but its own movement. One can of course say "I = I," but the *I* will not have preexisted birth, nor will it emerge from birth, either: it will be born to its own death.

Can I think that "death" will be *born* in me? That it is always being born? Assuredly, I cannot think anything else.

Nothing will have preexisted birth, and nothing will have succeeded it. It always "is," it never "is." To be born is the name of being.

~

If death has fascinated Western thought, it is to the degree that Western thought believed itself capable of constructing upon death its dialectical paradigm of pure presence and absence. *Death* is the absolute signified, the sealing off of sense. It is the *name*, but "to be born" is the verb.

It is certainly neither false nor excessive to say that all production of sense—of a sense making sense *in this sense*—is a deathwork. It is thus with all "ideals," with all "works," and it is also thus, remarkably, with all philosophies. Philosophy distinguishes itself by the unique way it profits from death—which is also a way of assuring its own perdurability. Philosophy is ignorant of true mourning. True mourning has nothing to do with the "work of mourning": the "work of mourning," an elaboration concerned with fending off the incoporation of the dead, is very much the work of philosophy, *it is the very work of representation*. In the end, the dead will be represented, thus held at bay.

But mourning is without limits and without representation. It is tears and ashes. It is: to recuperate nothing, to represent nothing. And thus it is also: to be born to this un-represented of the dead, of death.

To be born: to find ourselves exposed, to *ex-ist*. Existence is an imminence of existence. Each day, each instant exposes us to its necessity, its law, its caprice. Existence *is* not; rather, it is the existing of being, to which all ontology finally boils down.

Thought is poor. It is this poverty that we must think. Thought is this: merely to be born to presence, and not to represent its presentation, or its absentation. Thought is poor, insofar as birth is thought.

The poverty of thought is imposed, in the face of philosophy and against it (even in the bosom of philosophy itself), by "literature," or "poetry," or "art" in general. *On the condition that these are not already replete with philosophy*, which occurs much more often than it might seem, for this is a matter neither of "genre" nor of "style." It goes much further. It is, quite simply, a question of knowing, in a voice, in a tone, in a writing, whether a thought is being born, or dying: opening sense, ex-posing it, or sealing it off (and wishing to impose it).

At issue is this: either a discourse *names*, or a writing is traced by its *verb*.

This is often, perhaps always, indiscernible. But *in experience*, it suffers no hesitation. Experience is just this, being born to the presence of a sense, a presence itself nascent, and only nascent. Such is the destitution, such the freedom of experience.

~

Before all representational grasp, before a consciousness and its subject, before science, and theology, and philosophy, there is that: the *that* of, precisely, *there is*. But "there is" *is* not itself a presence, to which our signs, our demonstrations, and our monstrations might refer. One cannot "refer" to it or "return" to it: it is always, already, there, but neither in the mode of "being" (as a substance) nor in that of "there" (as a presence). It is there in the mode of being born: to the degree that it occurs, birth effaces itself, *and* brings itself indefinitely back. Birth is this slipping away of presence through which everything comes to presence.

This coming is also a "going away." Presence does not come

without effacing the Presence that representation would like to designate (its fundament, its origin, its subject). The coming is a "coming and going." It is a back and forth, which nowhere exceeds the world in the direction of a Principle or an End. For this back and forth contained within the limit of the world is the world itself, is its coming, is our coming to it, in it.

Back and forth from birth to birth, from sex to sex, from mouth to word, from thought to thought.

Thus, presence is not "for" a subject, and is not "for" itself. Presence itself is birth, the coming that effaces itself and brings itself back. Always further behind, always in advance of itself. When an earlier thought said "the Idea!," or when it said, "praxis!," or when it said, "to the things themselves!," it meant to say only this. Only this birth, this "nativeness" that is not a signification, but the coming of a world to the world.

A moment arrives when one can no longer feel anything but anger, an absolute anger, against so many discourses, so many texts that have no other care than to make a little more sense, to redo or perfect delicate works of signification. That is why, if I speak here of birth, I will not try to make it into one more accretion of sense. I will rather leave it, if this is possible, as the lack of "sense" that it "is." I will leave it exposed, abandoned.

Joy, *jouissance, to come,* have the sense of birth: the sense of the inexhaustible imminence of sense. When it has not passed over into ornamentation or into the repetition of philosophy, "poetry" has never sought to create anything else. The coming and going of imminence.

"The delight of presence" is the mystical formula par excellence. It is even the formula of mysticism in general, that is to say, of the metaphysics present in all mysticism. *Presentia frui.* But at present it is a question of what has no "fruition," nor any "fruit," whose consumption or consummation is impossible. Or rather, and more precisely, it is a question of what in the "fruit" itself *makes* the fruit: its coming, its birth in flower, always renewed. It is a question of the pre-venience of the flower in the fruit. There is no mysticism in this. It merely invites a simple thought, withdrawn and coming forth, careful, graceful, attentive: pre-venient. It is a question of preventing philosophies, of preventing appropriative thinking—it is a question of this *jouissance*, of this "grander" rejoicing that Dante invokes at the end of his poem.

TRANSLATED BY BRIAN HOLMES

PART ONE

Existence

§ Identity and Trembling

Indifferent Identity

"Identity, as self-consciousness, is what distinguishes man from nature, particularly from the brutes, which never reach the point of comprehending themselves as 'I,' that is, pure self-contained unity."[1]

Such is the identity of what we call, in any possible sense, a subject or *the* subject—which is, always and in the last analysis, the philosophical subject. This identity is not the simple abstract position of a thing as immediately what it is and only what it is; rather, it actualizes itself as a grasping of itself by the unity that I am in myself: an Ego, an irreducible kernel of self-constitution. Whoever says "subject" presupposes this self-constituted Ego, however attenuated or remote it may be. Even the psychoanalytical subject still presupposes the philosophical subject—at least in terms of the practical prescription (which cannot avoid a stake in theory) whereby analysis splits off from hypnosis (and from seduction, as Freud made clear to Ferenczi). Like the Kantian *I*, and regardless of any splitting of his ego, the analysand, being a conscious speaker, must be able to accompany all his representations. The same goes for the analyst.[2]

The subject's identity is related to difference in three ways. It is *opposed* to difference in general, insofar as difference creates the disparity or exteriority of being-outside-the-self, or insofar as it posits that otherness with respect to which the identical pulls itself together from itself and upon itself. But identity, while pulling itself together, *assumes* and resorbs within itself the differences that constitute it: both its difference from the other, whom it posits as such, and its difference from itself, simultaneously implied and abolished in the movement of "grasping itself." In this way, finally, identity *makes difference*: it presents itself as preeminently different from all other identity and from all nonidentity; relating itself to itself, it relegates the other to a self (or to an absence of self) that is different. Being the very movement proper to self-consciousness, identity—or the Self that identifies itself—therefore makes difference itself, difference *proper*: and this property designates or denotes itself as "man."

Where does this difference of self-consciousness come from? How does man attain what the animals, according to Hegel, do not? Man's "humanity" cannot explain this, as long as that humanity has not been determined as, precisely, self-consciousness and identity. "Man" attains what the animals do not only because identity, in him, has preceded and established humanity in its very difference: "*Identity, as* self-consciousness, is what distinguishes man."[3]

Before difference, then, before all difference posited as such (which cannot be difference except through the identical), there is identity itself, difference *proper*, which will constitute the difference of "man" as much as of every "individual." (But why is there more than one individual? And why doesn't Identity constitute the difference of a single individual and a single man by contrast with Nature and the Animal? It is precisely this question that overtaxes the system of identity. That system offers no tidy way to account for the difference of the collectivity or for that between the sexes. Thus, as we continue here, this will be our only real topic.)

On that score, identity itself, the identity that alone can differentiate the identical from what is without identity, is indifferent identity. Only an identity without difference can constitute and determine an identity as difference proper, different from difference. The first identity is indifferent in two senses. It is identically valid for all individual identities, among which, on these grounds, it does not differentiate (thus individuals are indifferent differences), and it includes within itself the indifference to self and to itself: indeed, only a self already *one* and *the same* can later relate itself to itself. One cannot posit A = A unless A is identical to itself in the first place. No matter how this indifferent identity (whose history runs from Fichte to Hegel) *originarily* divides itself (*sich urteilen*, which is also to say "judges itself"), *it* divides *it*self. By itself, the indifferent abolishes its own negation and engenders the different as the reversal of this negation in affirmation of the identity between different identities. The true *plural* is excluded on principle. The path of self-consciousness can easily lead through desire and recognition of the other, but it is traced beforehand as the circular process of the Self of this consciousness.

> The life of spirit is not one that shuns death, and keeps clear of destruction; it endures death and in death maintains its being.[4]

The life of spirit is indifferent identity, which does not tremble before its own differentiation, not even in death, for there too it maintains *itself*.

The dialectic of the subject—the dialectic, the subject—has two sides, however. It contains its death, it has it only as a *moment*, but it does have that moment, the moment of gaping difference. The subject contains its difference from itself. The subject not only has this difference, it *is* this difference. If the subject did not differ from itself, it would not be what it is: a subject *relating* itself to itself. A = A signifies that A *in itself* is its difference from itself, and that it derives its equality, its being-equal to itself, only from this difference. (It must be understood what A means. It is not a logical symbol; it is the initial of every initial: it is a proper name, a face, a voice. Perhaps it is not, properly speaking, an individual, since it is divided by its equality and by difference from that equality, but it is a singularity. The A of speculative idealism is both the first notation of an algebra of ontological identity and the name of the singular in its singularity.)

A carries its difference within itself. Hegel (in opposition to Fichte) knew that; he knew only that. The whole *Phenomenology* is the vertiginous exposition of this knowledge, and the prodigious effort to render it equivalent to its object: to see difference open up as such. And, indeed, difference as such is exposed. But *as such*: it is therefore identified, and identified as the very difference of indifferent identity.

From where, then, can difference come to identity, if as difference it must not let itself be identified *as such*, that is, as the difference of identity, itself possessing its identity through the indifference that it divides and equalizes within itself? To put the question another way, where can a *different* identity come from? From where can B come to A? Or again, what can make A tremble? Hegel, of necessity, also knew this question, which the dialectical subject simultaneously uncovers and covers up again. But Hegel knew it, as we shall see, by way of a defective knowledge, a knowledge withdrawn to the extreme margins of the dialectic and of self-consciousness, by way of a knowledge that was, so to speak, somnambulistic.

Thanatos, Genesis, Hypnos

No more than it can die—no more than it can "seriously" die, if we can say that with a straight face—can the subject be born, or can it sleep. Immortal, unengendered, and insomniac: this is the triple negation over which the life of spirit rises, imperturbably adult and awake.

Spirit's steadfast preservation in death puts death itself to death and stitches up its "absolute rending" wherein spirit "finds itself again." That is why death is always *past* for the spirit. In death, nothing is strictly mortal except "immediate singularity" (*my* identity, *yours*): the "abstract term, the *death of the natural.*" What is abolished is the "being outside the other" of nature, but this is how "the subjectivity which is, in the idea of life, the concept" reaches the state of "concrete universality." Thus "the concept . . . has become *for itself.*"[5] The subject has become: it will, as subject, always have *become*. It will always have had the end of its natural identity (and, e.g., the end of the animal's) behind it. It does not pass on, its death is already past. It contains its death as the abolition of its own difference, as the abolition of the other identity, of its difference, of its exteriority.

Likewise, it has its birth as the past of its differentiation. It is not born, it *is* not, in it is born, in the movement, the delay, and the incompletion of being born. Rather, it *was* born. The passage of birth counts only as the instant of a completed rupture, beyond which the subject makes its first appearance:

> But it is here as in the case of the birth of a child; after a long period of nutrition in silence, the continuity of the gradual growth in size, of quantitative change, is suddenly cut short by the first breath drawn—there is a break in the process, a qualitative change—and the child is born.[6]

The child is born, not: the child *is born*. It is hardly possible to know the extent to which the child preceded itself in the womb, that place of simple feeding and quantitative growth. Access to the qualitative requires no passage, but takes place after passage—after anxiety—in and because of the free aerial element. The child as such, the subject in its first moment, will always already have been born. It will have passed; it does not pass; and it will no longer pass. Thus it will have put an end, within itself, to finitude, for "the finite *is* not, that is, it is not that which is true, but simply a mere *passing over*."[7]

The subject has differentiated itself from itself, from its quantitative state, from its indifference, and *is* only in having differentiated itself—which means that it has acquired *for* itself the infinite indifference that it was *in* itself.

Birth and death are a past difference, always already past—passed over, passed away. Sleep, symmetrical, is the past of indifference without identity. Insofar as the subject is the realized difference of identity with no difference from itself, it has always already slept. It has already passed through the night of its own subjectivity. (Sleep, perhaps, has never been philosophical. Descartes has this famous sentence: "To live with closed eyes, never trying to open them, is what it means to live without philosophizing."[8])

This sleep is no doubt that of the subject: it is *its own*, wherein it returns "from the world of *determinateness* . . . into the universal essence of subjectivity."[9] But this somnolent essence is nothing other than the *dreamy* essence of a subjectivity stripped of any relation to the objectivity of representation, without which there is no *consciousness*. Sleepy, dreamy subjectivity remains at the stage of the abstract universality of representation, as a "tableau of mere images," and does not grasp the "concrete totality of determinations." Thus the subject as such can consist only in "the being-for-self of the waking soul." Not only *has* it already *slept* (and dreamed), but it is *already* awake, or rather has already awakened *itself*. "The awakening of the soul" is the first true originary division, the immediate "originary-impartation" (*Ur-teil*),[10] before which there was no subject but only the lethargic essence of subjectivity.

Nevertheless, the awakening of the soul is only partially the awakening of the soul *itself*.

On the one hand, it is indeed the soul that has awakened itself. It has left "its still undifferentiated universality" and has become itself; that is, it has become the subject in the absolutely immediate form where it does not yet have the "self-identity of being-for-self" and does not relate itself to any objectivity in front of it. The difference between this state and that of undifferentiated universality consists only in the fact that "all determinateness"—which before was not the *soul*'s determinateness (that of a *certain* soul, of yours or of mine) but remained in the simple exteriority of nature—will from now on be posited as spirit's own, *proper* determinateness, as "its most particularized and characteristic natural property." The soul is the immediately selfsame [*propre*] spirit, with no process of appropriation for itself, and thus is placed in the element of *sensation* (common to man and the animals). In the awakening of sensation, the subject has still only simply and passively *found* itself in what is most characteristically its own.

On the other hand, "generally, the waking state includes all the self-conscious and rational *activity* of spirit's distinguishing itself as a being-for-self." Thus the motif of awakening initially appears, in the general presentation of "The Subjective Spirit," only with respect to consciousness: "*Consciousness awakens* in *the soul. It posits itself as reason,* which is immediately aroused into self-knowing reason."[11] What has, properly speaking, awakened itself and has always already ceased to sleep can only be consciousness. Only consciousness—to which "soul or natural spirit" by itself still has no access—can be the waking state as knowledge of itself *and* of the sleep that has preceded it. Only consciousness is in the element of spirit's manifestation—the object of its "phenomenology," while the soul remains the object of an "anthropology."

The first aspect of awakening, or the awakening of the soul as such, is therefore only a getting up on the wrong side of the bed, a scarcely awakening, the merely half-awake persistence of a stupor consubstantial to natural spirit. The morning of the soul is not the clear dawn of the day of consciousness. It is not even a simple sleeping-in. It is at most the somnolent prelude to an evening that carries the soul back to sleep—whereas, for consciousness, the lamps illuminating the labor of the concept are lighted at the hour when Minerva's owl takes flight.

The difference posited here is not that of consciousness; rather, it is the irresolvable difference of the alternation, in an "infinite progression," between waking and sleep as two states, the first of which offers to the soul, "for itself," "the content-determinatenesses of its dormant nature." The waking soul relates itself to nothing but its own sleep. It is the subject, but only as subject of its somnolence. Thus, in sensation, the determinatenesses that affect me are those "of my whole being-for-self, benumbed though it may be"; and "for itself, this stage is that of the darkness of spirit."

Hypnosis

Consciousness, therefore, is consciousness only in having *been* born, dead, and in having awakened itself from this double indifference. (But to what extent is it double? To what extent is death already determined as the negative moment of [re]birth?) Consciousness as such has never slept. But the soul where it awakens, or the soul that it wakes up *from*—where, as if by an awakening of awakening itself, it awakens the whole of reason—this soul, whose consciousness is, in one sense, the only genuine awakening, has nevertheless already known, by itself and for itself, its own, "proper" awakening.

Moreover, it has known it so well that awakening as such, despite its apparently exclusive assignment to consciousness, "properly" takes place at first only for the soul. The soul alone genuinely *emerges* from sleep in an alternation of states. It alone *is* not simply because it *has slept* but rather because it *passes* from sleep to waking. Without the awakening that the soul, as it were, communicates to consciousness, the latter would never awaken: it would simply be *(a) being-awakened* (yet consciousness is essentially the process of becoming self-consciousness; to such a *becoming* belongs, but without belonging to it, the movement of awakening, not just a being already awake). The originary-impartation of (the subject's) consciousness detaches itself from the still more originary impartation of the soul's awakening. It distinguishes itself from that awakening and proceeds from it. The fully realized impartation of consciousness proceeds from the soul's impartation in progress. The waking state proceeds from awakening, but in waking there is no more awakening—or rather, awakening no longer *passes*, no longer *comes to pass*. Its finitude is finished: waking is infinite.

In Hegel's vocabulary, the awakening of the soul borders on tautology. Not only is the soul alone in "genuinely" awakening, but awakening is its property—however strange this "property," which does not detach itself from what it leaves behind and has no access to what it opens. The soul is awakening—but awakening, strictly speaking, is only the subject floating up to the surface of sleep, passing along the surface of sleep; or, again, it is only sleep itself taking the figure—barely figurable—of the subject.

In this floating that passes along, by means of this quasi-configuration, the soul no longer experiences only sensation; it also experiences feeling. It is no longer offered only to the determination of sensation; it feels *within itself.* "In that it feels, the soul is inwardly and no longer merely naturally individualized." This primary and "*simple inwardness* constitutes individuality, and it persists throughout all the determinateness and mediation of consciousness subsequently posited within it." Individual identity does not yet constitute the identity of the subject; it is not the fully realized identity of A that *knows itself* to be A and develops this equivalence in the difference of consciousness. The soul is *simply* A, without which there could be neither equivalence nor difference between A and A. The soul is the individual identity that has not acquired or conquered or produced its identity—and that will nevertheless *endure* throughout the whole process of the subject. The soul is not the identity-in-difference of consciousness, and it is not indifferent identity, being neither anterior to the originary-impartation nor posterior and consequent to its development and sublation. The soul is simply A (your name, mine), individual identity simply imparted, as such.

The soul is simply this impartation of a simple interiority: it is the awakening that takes place in sleep itself, or it is sleep itself, that return "into the universal essence of subjectivity," *as an individual.* A sleeps being A himself, who is for himself while sleeping. This is called hypnosis.

Hypnosis, in the form that Hegel, in the language of his time, calls "*magnetic somnabulism*," defines the first stage, or the immediate moment, of the soul in the element of feeling—before this feeling becomes, in a second moment, feeling-of-self (in which once more—or properly—*awakening* and the differentiation of self take place: there is no end to awakening's "properly" taking place).

Hypnosis is not an image. It is the truth of the soul immersed in "the stupor of the life of feeling," the soul that does not emerge from its stupor, the soul for which this state constitutes precisely its first emergence as a soul endowed with feeling (that is, as a soul susceptible to being affected). Now, the first state of a being susceptible to affection cannot be any active disposition, not even any faculty of affectability. Such a "faculty," if we wished to suppose it, would be confused with simple passivity. But passivity cannot possibly be "simple": it cannot be determined as some "power" to receive and to be affected; it can be determined only in the very fact of *being* affected. The soul is not so much the affectable as the always already affected. The soul begins, if it properly begins, in an affection confounded with the soul. Affection is nothing but the possession of alteration as a property. Already, before feeling, sensation forms nothing but the fashion, for any determinateness, of belonging to the soul's "most particularized and characteristic natural property." But what is thus most proper to the soul—nothing other than "the content-determinatenesses of its dormant nature"—is precisely nothing but this property of being affected by sensations that are its *own*. The "self" of this "own" does not preexist sensation: its most particularized property confounds itself with its affection.

No doubt there is a being-for-itself of the soul. But in its immediacy—in its sleep—this being-for-itself *is* only the *felt* alteration, not the sensation of the alteration. Here, "I" *is* affected, it is through affection, or rather it is "pure" affection. I sleep, and I am the exterior that affects me. If I am for myself in this affection, it is because I am, right at my-self[12] in my very selfsameness, "a reflective totality of sensing." But this reflection is not that of a consciousness. It is what makes itself felt in its totality as the most characteristic property. Thus this property is not my own, it is not that of an *I*. It is *property*, absolutely, as the simple interiority of *feeling*. Feeling does not make *me* a subject, it makes the soul total affection, for itself, but only as a "selfsameness." The self*same* of the affective soul is this sleeping same that confounds itself—because it has never distinguished itself, never having *been*—with the totality of the other that affects it. Thus it knows neither the exterior as such nor limitation. "The soul, just in itself, is the totality of nature." But also: "The soul is the *existent* concept, the existence of the speculative." The concept says here *ego patior, ego existo*, or "I sleep, I exist."

The concept speaks as a sleepwalker, as one who is magnetized. The *sensible* world works out the truth of speculation—that is, the unity of opposites, of the in-itself and the for-itself—by hypnotizing the concept, affecting it and thereby making it exist.

Hypnotism

But "for itself, this stage is that of the darkness of spirit"—that is, scarcely a stage: spirit dark to itself is not spirit. In the stage of sleep, of the pulse of sleep and waking, and of affection as the unique— but absolutely characteristic—property of affected being, spirit in general and consciousness in particular can be posited only by way of anticipation.[13] This stage, as such, remains merely "formal." It takes on "particular interest" only "insofar as it has being as *form*, and so appears as a *state*." To speak in absolute terms, hypnotic existence is formless (precisely because it designates only a "formal" stage, not an actual state). It counts for something and is properly discerned only when it takes form in or from conscious being. It then offers itself as a relapse or regression of consciousness. The hypnotized subject has its lucid consciousness outside itself, "in a subjectivity that differs from it," in the magnetizer. As for "him," the sleepwalker, the magnetized subject, he is *diseased*: "As a *form*, as a *state* of the self-conscious, cultured, self-possessed person, the life of feeling is a disease."

Affected being (as its name, after all, indicates) can be recognized only in pathological states. Affection takes form, or gives the subject its form of affection, only as a *pathos*. Hypnosis is a diseased state. It provides the matrix, and perhaps even the essence, of psychic disease, which is "the truer form of spirit existing in a sub- ordinate and more abstract form": thus, self-consciousness *within* magnetic sleep. A pure and simple stupor of the soul could not be recognized as a state. But consciousness, sinking into stupor and thus differing from itself, reveals stupor and, so to speak, posits stupor for itself. This is hypnosis, and this is disease. Just as sleep and waking precede consciousness, madness precedes sense—but they are recognizable as states only in their regression from the superior state.[14]

Here, the logic of spirit is subject to a singularly pathological constraint. On the one hand, and as a matter of course, spirit will always have *been mad*, just as it will have slept, will have been born, and will have died. Not one of these darkling stages will have properly constituted a state of the spirit—even though spirit offers, in these stages, the extreme particularity of its property (but offers it to nothing and to no one, not even to itself, lost and benumbed in its own existence). In other words, spirit will always already have *existed*, existed immediately, nature and concept, to become what it is: the activity of the subject and the freedom of the "objective spirit." Becoming what it is, it nevertheless presents and causes recognition of the truth, forever past and passed over, of what it will always have *been* or of what it will have *passed* through: it presents truth as disease, which is no longer a stage but the state of "inadequation" of consciousness to its own life of feeling, into which it "sinks." And this presentation takes place through hypnosis or, more precisely, through hypnotism.

Hypnotism forms that circumstance in which one consciousness can plunge another into the "remarkable state" of "magnetic somnambulism." The possibility of hypnotism exists in fact and has been witnessed. That possibility does not inscribe itself in any natural necessity or in the becoming of spirit as such. It constitutes, as it were, an accidental but real after-the-fact of what will have always been but will, finally, never have existed as such. Hypnotism is the existence, pathological and surprising, of the soul's property, which consciousness, ever since its awakening, will never have had as its own property. Hypnotism's strangeness makes it an object of suspicion: it is considered "delusion and trickery." But it does exist; Hegel says so very emphatically (even though he does not have the leisure, in his "encyclopedic exposition," to consider its "factual aspect"). Besides, those who have already decreed that magnetizers are charlatans would never be convinced. Here, the conviction and, even more, the conception of what is at stake require escape from the slavery of the categories of the understanding. Hypnotism and its strangeness are, strictly speaking, the business of *reason*. The disease of affected being reveals what it is only to speculative spirit.

Hegel had already announced, well beforehand, the need for a "speculative consideration" of animal magnetism. He indicated then that this need is only a particular case—and particularly remarkable, by reason of the objects of experience that it offers—of the speculation required, in a very general way, by the contradiction between "the *freedom* of the spirit and its *being* determined."[15] What the speculative spirit must grasp, wherever determinations of the understanding are "discredited," is the determined existence of freedom, which is also to say the *finite* existence of spirit. Now, in this moment when spirit itself is barely awakening, everything happens as if the Spirit of the world were not yet there to ensure its self-determination as the veritable process of its freedom. It is assuredly there, since one can appeal to comprehension, or to speculative contemplation. But it cannot be *there*, in this sleep *that is its own* and that cannot, on principle, be *its own*.

The freedom that speculative spirit grasps is self-determined, and so sublates all determination. Yet determination *itself* is first grasped not in autonomy but in heteronomy. Could freedom, like magnetic sleep, be given by another? Speculative spirit prefers not to think so, cannot think so. It designates heteronomy as pathology. But in pathology, an insurmountable—and perhaps constitutive—affection of its own freedom stymies it, fascinates it.

Not that hypnotism should be thought of as a liberating force . . . But this means that philosophical speculation about "pathology," and the general determination of affected being as "pathology," both depend directly on thinking of freedom as the pure self-positing and pure self-production of waking consciousness. Ultimately, the soul's sleep would require another thinking of freedom.

Nevertheless, hypnotism is not the sole possible province of this pathology. It also affects, and is also the affection of, those who pine away or die after the death of a loved one, of those in the grip of homesickness, catalepsy, and "other morbid states, such as those that attend development in women, the approach of death, et-cetera." But the common feature of these states is the "stupor" or "sleep" of the individual's soul "immersed" in the "form of feeling." All these states have a hypnotic nature. But hypnotism, at best, lays bare the "essential determination" of these states, which is to be "a *passive state*." The *state* of passivity has the remarkable character of no longer being, or of barely, marginally being a state *of* the subject. "The diseased subject passes and remains *under the power of another subject*, the magnetizer." In this state, the diseased subject is "selfless": which is as much as to say that there is no subject, that this state is not *its own*. It is certainly a "being-for-self, but it is vacant, and to itself it is devoid of presence and actuality." The quality of self-presence is not, for the subject, one quality among others. It is not even the subject's quality; it is its essence, its nature, its structure. Not only is the subject present to itself, but presence in general occurs only by way of and for the sake of this presence of the subject.

In the hypnotized subject, it is the very present of its presence that is suspended. The subject is indeed *there*, it exists, it is *Da-sein* (in fact, it is nothing but . . .), yet it is elsewhere, in the "subjective consciousness" of the other. If in this way it is presence, it is as a pure presence, which for itself has no present and neither presents nor represents anything to itself, but is merely offered to the other's representation. This subject is no longer the subject of representation: it is no longer *the* subject. If, in spite of everything, it exists thus as a "formal self," it is because the *da* of its existence, in its material concreteness, is also the immaterial *da* of the soul. Indeed, in this "substantial identity" with others, the soul reveals that it "is truly immaterial, even in its concreteness."

Yet the opposition of the concrete and the material must still be clearly understood. It is not the opposition of two synonyms, as ordinary speech would have it. The Hegelian concrete is opposed to the abstract in that the abstract is only the unilaterality of one moment or of one element (the material moment, in isolation, is thus itself abstract), while the concrete is the actualized unity of opposed determinations: the concrete is the actualized concept.[16] If the immateriality of the soul therefore seems to oppose its concreteness, or to mark it with some kind of excess, it is to the degree that this soul, in order to be a subject, would have to be the unity of its material determination and of its spirituality: something like the speculative elevation of the substantial unity of soul and body in Descartes. But this union, determined as *mine* and as essentially mine in Descartes, here oversteps its boundaries in a substantial identity with another. The soul's immateriality is therefore not an abstract moment, but rather belongs to its concrete actuality in that the soul is also (or initially, or in affection) *itself in the other*. It is in the other or through the other that the *da* of the soul *takes place*, and to the extent that the soul is its body.

As in death—that is, always, in the death of the individual—what is withdrawn here from the soul is only its immediate and natural singularity, and with it the soul's abstract individuality. In hypnosis, the soul is a body offered up to existence within others. But individuality is withdrawn without this body's immediate existence being abolished. Hypnosis is an immobilized death in the *Dasein* of the soul, not a death sublated into universality. This death does not pass on to another life, it carries over to the life of another, it affects the soul in its own body with the soul of another. It is the soul's impartation.

The Knowledge of Affection

Here, death borders on birth. Not on the birth that has always already taken place, but on the birth that is happening. In hypnosis, death and birth are not past (they are not *present* as what has passed); rather, they come to pass.

The essential determination of the state of passivity has a model itself, more than a model, in fact: the state of the child in the body of its mother. It is the same, Hegel says, in hypnosis. But Hegel presents birth first, in the section preceding the one on hypnosis. The pathology of animal magnetism can no doubt serve as the privileged revelation of the *state* of the affected soul, because only this pathology is accessible to experience, and because it thus presents the form of passivity in an already identifiable subject: it is still true, however, that the essential determination of this pathology comes from elsewhere, an elsewhere without which, accordingly, the experience of hypnosis could not receive its "speculative consideration."

Hypnosis is only the visible form of the invisible state of gestation, in which the truth of the soul is deposited as *feeling*.

This truth—and, consequently, the truth of affection, according to which the awakening of the soul (and not of consciousness) takes place within its slumber—will therefore have to have been known already for hypnosis to be comprehensible. Hegel had already described the child in the mother's womb—the state of passivity. He possessed this knowledge, properly called *immemorial.*

He possessed it as if he had received it from one of those hypnotic "clairvoyances"[17] that are "immediate knowledge" without "the mediation of the understanding," "a life of feeling which sees and knows inwardly." Nevertheless, he refuses to grant these clairvoyances the power to attain "universal validity," although he does not deny their access to certain truths. He simultaneously subordinates and grants a proper power to the affective ("irrational") soul, giving it the Platonic name *manteia,* power of vision, of divination. Knowledge about the child in the mother's womb is mantic, and Hegel is a soothsayer and a seer,[18] but he cannot recognize it any more than Plato could. It is not just that philosophy, here, resists a knowledge proper to affectivity. It is that this knowledge *is not* to be recognized as knowledge. It is not knowledge that, either in certainty or in verification, appropriates its own scientificity for itself. Hegel may seem here like a seer: but only by not recognizing it does he "recognize" (in spite of himself, necessarily) an impartation of knowledge that knowledge does not resorb, a truth of affection that true knowledge can neither know to be true nor declare false, and that withdraws from knowledge within knowledge's own matrix.

Perhaps it is not a question of Hegel's visions or vaticinations but simply, if this can be simple, of his love for his mother, or for his wife or his children. Nothing autobiographical or "personal"; rather, affected being, in spite of everything, also at work in the "encyclopedia of the philosophical sciences"—and, for example, a being whose affection would have to "know" something, in the "encyclopedia" and yet beyond its compass, about the origin of the very subject of the "encyclopedia."

Indeed, "this kernel of this feeling being . . . contains not only the natural disposition, the temperament, etcetera, in themselves unconscious, but also maintains through habit all further bonds, as well as relationships, fates, and principles." Hegel in his mother's womb is still the same one, the very one, who became a philosophizing subject. The opening of the *Encyclopedia* shows that, as far as beginnings go, philosophy either "has no beginning, in the same way as the other sciences have"—philosophy being "a circle which closes with itself"—or it only has a beginning "in relation to a person who proposes to commence the study" of philosophy.[19] This will and this decision of a subject, "external, as it were," to philosophy, from which the subject must be separated at first, as from its object, cannot themselves proceed from anything but the subject's soul. Philosophy is a question of feeling. When philosophical science comes to the moment of determining the subject itself according to the affection from which its philosophical feeling originates—for example, this "youthful experience of the new age which . . . greeted with rapture the dawn of the intellectual renaissance," as written in the first Preface, in 1817—it is both prescribed and precluded that this science should become identical with the soul's affection. It is necessary and impossible for the consciousness of knowledge to be hypnotized, for the philosophizing subject to know itself as having its self in another—in its mother or, as we shall see, in woman. And the subject has never wanted anything else, to the extent that it has decided to philosophize, than this knowledge of self outside self. The decision in favor of philosophy concerns a "separate" object only in that this separation has to do with the subject itself.

In one sense, in this object and as object, in philosophy as such, the subject will always have been born, have died, and have reawakened. As for this birth of itself in the affection of another, the subject will always have appropriated it and left it behind as such in the oblivion of the immemorial. But in another sense, which makes no sense and produces no meaning, the subject is born right here—hypnotized, visionary, or diseased. At least this is how it is on the verge of representing itself. But it does not. In its affected soul, it contemplates a gestation, a birth, an alteration still not at all diseased but not appropriable by thought, which nevertheless names, describes, and appropriates it. What it contemplates in this way it calls the "*magical* relationship" between mother and child.

The *Encyclopedia* devotes no special development to magic. What could most resemble it—astrology and, in general, the correlations of human life with "cosmic, sidereal, and telluric life"— has been put aside as corresponding only to the state of a few peoples still unadvanced in culture and in the freedom of spirit.[20] The "*magical* relationship" (Hegel's emphasis) between child and mother is without example and remains without concept. This "magic" is not an object of science (whereas hypnosis, for which "magic" nevertheless provides the principle, is forced to become something of the sort). It is a "magic" that intervenes in philosophical knowledge, notwithstanding that knowledge. No philosophy of magic presides here, nor does any magic of philosophy sneak in. The word "magic" merely names a knowledge of affection prior to any knowledge, and a being-affected of the subject of knowledge itself. Hegel does not name magic philosophically (conceptually), any more than he does the "*Genius*" discussed in the same paragraph.

He names them, if you will, poetically. But this poetry is not an exaltation or an overload of the philosophical will to knowledge. It does not claim to substitute feeling and divination for discourse, in order to penetrate the soul's stupor. Discreet, effaced, barely inscribed in the straight line of scientific discourse, this poetry signals only the default, or rather the suspension, of discourse, that is, *at the same time* the imminence of the speculative and the intimate proximity of affection. In this sense, section 405 of the *Encyclopedia* is a poem—but it is not a fiction.

Identity and Trembling

The immemorial truth of the child in the mother is not, however, completely lacking in experiential knowledge. A trace of it subsists when Hegel, still only in the middle of the "Remark" of section 405, mentions "the surprising accounts of determinations fixed in the child as a result of violent disturbances of mood, injuries, etcetera experienced by the mother."

Thus is convoked the long tradition of considering "splotches," "birthmarks," or other singularities as products of emotions felt by the pregnant mother. Malebranche, for example, had already exploited this tradition for the analysis of the passivity of "feminine" or "effeminate" spirits.

But Hegel does not stop there. This tradition bears, for him, only the most superficial and, while "surprising," the most limited witness to the general communication from mother to child, which in fact even constitutes, as we shall see, more than a communication. This communication does not concern only accidental marks. It is communication of the *self* of the child itself.

The child in the mother is, in reality, the soul's first moment, or spirit in the stage of its obscurity. The child certainly exists as a "monadic individual," but by that expression nothing more is meant than a discrete numerical identity. The child is "one" in relation to the mother, who differs from it. But it is only a formal or abstract identity. The child has its difference entirely outside itself, and therefore does not have it as a moment proper.

Its identity has not *passed* through the differentiation of self. The child has not been born, it has not awakened. Thus it is "not yet as it is itself . . . and it is therefore *passive*."

Passivity is not the state of an individuality constituted as identity. Passivity is an individuality without identity, which is not the same as itself and cannot relate itself to itself. One can hardly say that the child is a passive individuality: rather, it is individualized passivity, numerically detached as a distinct unity. But this unity "is," so to speak, only its detachment, only its being-detached; it is not yet even the same as itself, or if it is, it is so without entering into any relation with itself. Passive being is as much being without difference as it is being completely different from itself, being disconnected in its being from its very being.

Its passivity is not therefore a property—it cannot even properly be called a *state* or a *form*. It is the "property" of the absence of property, but in terms of an absence that is not a lack, for it is very much a matter of the individuality of a *soul*, and of a soul that has *feeling*, consequently, in an "interior individuality." But the "property" of this interiority is *not* to be in its own interior, and thus to be exterior to itself. Its *self* "is a subject which differs from it," but in such a way that this difference is not internal to the subject. This difference *in* the subject is not the difference *of* the subject, and so it poses or imposes *outside* the subject what is "properly" the subject's "interior." The subject does not *have* this difference; even less has it *passed* through this difference: it *is* this difference—in such a way, however, that the subject is not thus *its own, proper* difference but is, rather, different from that of which it is properly the subject. These two formulations are certainly not far, however, from being confused with each other. Nevertheless, they are absolutely distinct. The child has no power over its difference; it cannot differentiate itself *by itself* or *from itself.*

To the same degree that this child, as "monad," is simply posited, or thrown into numerical difference, it is, as *self,* also posited or given outside its monad. Its numerical difference—its individuation—is in fact the very thing that puts it outside itself. In this double difference, it is indifferent. Passivity is the indifference of the different. The formula, here again, could be confused with that of fully realized identity. But the latter posits its difference, and the sublation of this difference, as *identity itself.* Passive being posits neither its difference nor its indifference as itself. What it *is* is not *its own.* What it is in its difference can be given it only from elsewhere—and, in truth, it can hardly be said that *this difference* is *given to it.* It is given—and, being given, it is what *makes it,* from somewhere else. The speculative subject will never have been able to know such a somewhere else—and does not know it in this instance, either, but it sees (with what vision?) its knowledge of itself and of its origin affected by this somewhere else.

This is why the "subject which differs" from the monad "can also be another individual." This simple *possibility* reserves the other possibility, by which the subject could be the same as the monad, outside itself in itself. But this last eventuality will not be articulated. It figures, very allusively, only as a rapid concession to what the truth of the Subject would require: that the child have in itself power over its difference and over its identity. In fact, however, the soul cannot, itself, overcome its own stupor; that is to say, its actually different difference—what, in difference, does not allow itself to be brought back to identity, *what differs* within difference—requires "another individual."

In the affective soul, difference *takes place*. It is not already past or passed over. Here, difference comes to pass. It *happens*, which is to say that it has not yet happened. Not that we are present at the present of the process itself: to be presented, it must already be past. One is never present at the "happening." There is no present here, only presence of difference—that is, its being-given—or passivity, and what happens to it.

Passivity "is" in fact only that: the fact that something happens to it, from somewhere else, from the other. The fact that some difference happens to it. Passivity is not the property of being passive—of, for example, letting such or such a mark be given or imprinted. Passivity does nothing, not even in the mode of "doing" that would be letting something be done. More "passive" than what is called passivity, the soul is itself only in that it is affected from outside. Its "passivity" is given to it with the affection. Its passivity does not come first, like a property of soft wax. The soul *is* affected, it is in that it is affected—by its identity.

In the "Remark," the "other individual" will be determined, as the mother for the child, at the level of "immediate existence." But in the body of the section, nothing has yet specified this relationship—or this alterity. The mother and the child will provide the immediate paradigm—the "matrix"—of a general alterity, constitutive of the soul in general. The other individual can be the other of the human community. He or she can be the other of love. What the affective soul brings into play is neither properly nor exclusively maternity (and paternity, which would be its correlate, is not to be found here); through maternity, a sociality and an erotics, archioriginary and indissociable—and more "maternal" than maternity, more archaic than any gestation or any genesis—are brought into play.

The "substance" of the monad "is merely a dependent predicate." As such, "it excludes all resistance." The soul is the offered substance. To the gift of identity corresponds the offering of substance without identity. Thus there is, strictly speaking, neither giver nor receiver—and there is no appropriation, either. There is gift, abandonment without resistance—to something like possession, but "possession" here means mutual abandonment.

The monad is "trembled through" (*durch-zittert*) by the *self* of the other individual. It is penetrated (as the French translation renders *durch*), but it is not penetration as such that counts. It cannot be known whether this penetration had a beginning, or whether it was decided upon. Passivity is not confronted by an activity. But the *self* of the other is already within the "same" that is not itself. It trembles through the "same," shudders through it so that all at once the "same" gives way and finds itself determined. The other *transits*, or *entrances*, the "same" and makes it come to pass.

If one seeks to interpret this as a sexual scene—which it "obviously" is—it will be impossible to assign roles. It is no more a question of masculinity or femininity than of maternity. The trembling of the soul is not indifferent to the difference between the sexes. It *is* this difference, or an even more archaic but still sexual difference—or it is the difference of love, insofar as this difference imparts the soul, neither man nor woman, but either one in the other, and makes the soul tremble: transits the soul, entrances it.

The trembling of the "same" is its identification. The soul trembles to be the soul itself—and to be it through the other. That its determination occurs in trembling means that this determination is not imprinted on it by an alien force, but that it takes place only as the perturbance of substance by the other—which is its self. The soul trembles because its subject is other to it, and because its identity takes place only in the alteration of its substance. The trembling, the *trance*, is also a vibration—almost a rhythm of the soul, a palpitation. This rhythm is nothing but the rhythm of its sleep, the beating of sensation in sleep and in the imminence of the passage to awakening. In this rhythm, identity is determined not only in passivity, but *as* passivity; again, passivity takes place only in this trembling, in this vibrant interval whose substance is affected, and which is its affection.

The soul is not *passed over*—nor made *past*—by trembling. It trembles continually—it passes, its identity passes. What passes is the finite. The identity of the soul is finite identity, the finitude of difference that comes to it as actual difference, from another that is infinitely other. The finitude of the soul stems from this constitutive alterity of its *self*—whose vocation as subject requires an infinite completion and closure. Beyond birth, the subject will complete itself infinitely, it will be the sublation of its infinite determinations. It will be what originarily divides itself, *sich ur-teilt*, engendering from itself its difference and its identity.

But this originary self-division will have been preceded by a more deeply buried origin—which perhaps, never having passed, never ceases to occur. Here, the *Urteilen* is exterior to the soul. It is the soul's own only by being the other's. This is what takes place in the mother's womb: beyond the "the surprising . . . determinations that establish themselves in the child," it is the whole psychic *originary-impartation* "of substance, in which the female nature, like monocotyledons in the vegetable world, can break in two." In this relationship, the difference between the sexes redistributes no roles. Rather, "the female nature" reveals itself as the difference of difference, as what, in difference, differs: it breaks in two; its nature is to split in this way.

Now, this nature is not the constitution of a subject dividing itself from itself. The analogy to the vegetable world indicates that "female nature" is not in the register of subjectivity. The parts of the plant do not yet have "an essential existence as members."[21] Feminine splitting is not a self-differentiation in the fully organic sense. Splitting is inscribed in this nature as an essential fragility, which also forms its most characteristic possibility. The "mother"— or the *woman*—of this paradigm is not the fertile mother, nor is she the nurturing mother. She is not the origin dividing itself by itself. Woman is not judgment, but rather gift (and forgiveness).

The maternal figure, or the Great Mother, is absent from this maternal womb, which is also not the womb of a virgin engendering by herself. This mother is in no way phallic—although she does seem to occupy the position of the Subject *him*self. But at this very spot there is only a disarmed mother, a breaking that does not even mean that the child's soul *comes from* the mother, but only that this soul, as soul, is feminine, whatever the sex of its subject.

The trembling of the soul corresponds to the splitting of female nature. In truth, they are the same thing, and the child "does not have its determinations *communicated* to it"; rather, they have been "*received-and-conceived* in it at its origin [*ursprünglich in sich empfangen hat*]." This sameness forms something like the inverted reply of a subject originating itself. But the origin "is" splitting's trembling—not the differentiation of self, but the self different from itself. This difference is still not that of the other caught in the specular process of recognition and desire for the same. Rather, the soul differs from itself with a trembling—nothing more than a shuddering and a pulsation, which makes it swoon and offers its identity in this collapse. Trembling differentiates, defers, identity: that is how identity is given. Such is the "*magical* relationship."

Genius

"The mother," Hegel writes, "is the child's *genius*." The mythological figure of the Latin *Genius* designates "the selfhood and totality of spirit insofar as it exists for itself," outside an individual "which is only posited externally as an individual." The Genius is the "compact condition" or the "intensive form of individuality." It is the same thing as what is also called "the *heart*" or the "*disposition*" (*Gemüt*, which in this sense also means "soul" or "heart"). The Genius is the heart of identity, insofar as the affective soul is really the kernel of all the determinations and all the dispositions of the subject. The philosophizing subject itself also proceeds from its heart or its Genius.

The Genius represents this identity outside the individual, as another individual, because this identity is precisely this other identity—trembling or shuddering, nonindividual—whose more than originarily female nature is really nothing but nature itself, or the "property" of trembling, of shuddering, of splitting, of feeling, of being affected. Passivity is not individual: one can be active alone, but one can be passive only in company. Passivity is what trembles and draws away from the individual, drawing the individual away from himself, adding the space of a pulsation. Indeed, it is the *heart* as the rhythm of an impartation.

The subject, here, is born. There is no present of its birth—and no representation of it, either. But birth is the modality of the presence of the heart, that is, of impartation. The Genius is not the individual, because it imparts him: it makes him tremble, and it imparts him from and with the other. This is not an immediate and total community—as if there were a single Genius of humanity— for the Genius *is* the difference of the individual, without being the individual himself. Birth takes place in a community of impartation—that of the mother's womb, that of love, that of being-together-among-many.

Impartation itself signifies birth (*partum*). To be born—not to have one's birth behind one, but incessantly to be born, in trembling—is to be imparted. It is not the *having been*, and it is exactly what the subject will never be able to have behind it, as a past or as the present of its past. But the subject never ceases being born, or trembling. This is how difference comes to identity: it *occurs* to identity. Identity itself does not let itself be identified, and it gives identity. Identity is given by the difference that is not *its own*.

Identity as difference *proper* is given by difference without property. It is not that the proper does not come to pass; it does so only by ceaselessly originating from the improper—whose destination, in return, is only this coming to pass, this birth that never ends. Identity that is born thus comes to pass; it never ceases occurring to its identity. But it cannot be indifferent. Its provenance makes it different, and singular: it is the child (when does the man cease to be one?), it is man originating in woman, it is woman in turn awakening, it is the stranger, it is the friend, it is you and I. Identity *for itself* is indifferent, but a singular and different identity is always given, always occurs.

Announcing the passage to hypnosis, Hegel's Genius is already shared with Freud's:

Sporadic examples and traces of this *magical* relationship are found elsewhere in the sphere of conscious, self-possessed life—for example, between friends, particularly between women friends suffering from delicate nerves (this relationship can develop to the point of producing magnetic phenomena), between husband and wife, among family members, etcetera.

Freud must have known better than anyone else that the subject never ceases being born, and that hysteric, hypnotic, or affective communication in general does not "communicate" anything from one subject to another, but imparts them all with another and the same birth, another and the same presence, another and the same identification. The site of the impartation, which is also the site imparted, he called "unconscious." As in Hegel, this is still only the negative and the expectation of a consciousness. (Like Hegel, Freud was unable or unwilling to know anything about what his soul knew . . .). "The unconscious," however, awaits nothing, no more than do the soul, the Genius, the heart. Not that it is self-sufficient, like a Narcissus. Narcissus satisfies himself in the dreams of the slumbering soul. But sleep is run through by a trembling that owes nothing to this "tableau of mere images." Trembling is not an image; it is the rhythm of the affected soul, and the impartation of the unconscious—that is, the "unconscious" as our portion, our part. That means our community, our destiny, our Genius. That means we are imparted by the genius of "female nature." But this Genius is not *a* Genius. "Consciousness" is knowing that there is no knowledge of this genius, not because it would be out of reach, the object of a worship beyond reason, but because this "nature" is never a *nature*. It is nothing given or already given; it is not past and passed over. It "is" the gift, which cannot be given; the offering, which cannot itself be offered.

Not being a nature, it is also not something that could be divided or shared. Such an impartation would be the portioning out of an infinite identity, of the Subject itself, in concrete singularities, distributed and articulated at the heart of a totality. But "female nature" is the *finitude* of identity, the originary-impartation, the

Urteil of *nothing* that could be given out for portioning: an impartation of the unimpartable. The unimpartable is as much the individual as it is birth, sleep, death, the unconscious. The "originary" impartation does not portion them out and, strictly speaking, does not divide them: it makes them tremble with the trembling of *finite* identity. "Female nature" is finitude, which *is* not, but which forms the *concrete* immateriality of the imparted soul.

Finite identity is not that of the separate individual. On the contrary, it is trembling separation itself, the alteration of monadic substance and closure—impartation and affection. Only the infinite identity of the Subject could ensure an actual individuality. In the realm of finite identity, by contrast, one is never born alone, although one is not born collectively. One never sleeps alone. And one never dies alone. But solitude does still exist: it is the infinite consciousness of finite identity.

TRANSLATED BY BRIAN HOLMES

§ Abandoned Being

The whole West is in abandonment.[1]
—Bossuet, *Histoire*

We do not know it, we cannot really know it, but abandoned being has already begun to constitute an inevitable condition for our thought, perhaps its only condition. From now on, the ontology that summons us will be an ontology in which abandonment remains the sole predicament of being, in which it even remains—in the scholastic sense of the word—the transcendental. If being has not ceased to speak itself in multiple ways—*pollakōs legetai*—abandonment adds nothing to the proliferation of this *pollakōs*. It sums up the proliferation, assembles it, but by exhausting it, carrying it to the extreme poverty of abandonment. Being speaks itself as abandoned by all categories, all transcendentals.

Unum, verum, bonum—all this is abandoned. Which amounts to saying, saying to us, that being *has* ceased to speak itself in multiple ways, although this cessation does not constitute an end or decide a destiny. The cessation pursues a destiny.

Being's speech, or the speech of being, is not appended to being itself. Being is not, has never been—if it has ever been—anything but the *pollakōs legomenon*, the spoken-in-multiple-ways (the *spoken*, or, in Heidegger's reading of the Greek, in the Greek of philosophy or thought, the *gathered*, and what is let lie, the *open*.)[2] If from now on being *is* not, if it has begun to be only its own abandonment, it is because this speaking in multiple ways is abandoned, is in abandonment, and it is abandon (which is also to say

36

openness). It so happens that "abandon" can evoke "abundance." There is always a *pollakōs*, an abundance, in abandon: it opens on a profusion of possibilities, just as one abandons oneself in excess, for there is no other modality of abandon.

~

That abandoned being, for us—and by us, perhaps—should correspond to the exhaustion of transcendentals therefore means a cessation or suspension of the discourses, categorizations, challenges, and invocations whose proliferation constituted the being of being. Abandoned being immobilizes the *dialectic* whose name means "the one that abandons nothing, ever, the one that endlessly joins, resumes, recovers." It obstructs or forsakes the very *position*, the initial position, of being, that empty position whose truth of nothingness, immediately turned back on and against being, mediates the becoming, the inexhaustible advent of being, its resurrection and the parousia of its absolute unity, truth, and goodness, arousing and pouring back into it the foam of its own infinity.

But this also means that abandoned being finds itself returned at last, left, to the *pollakōs* that it was, and of which it is not possible to say "the *pollakōs itself*," for the *pollakōs* has no other identity than its default of identity, its lack of being, wherein being resided, *being* the *pollakōs legomenon*.

At the end of the dialectic, at that end which the dialectic never abandons and which, consequently, it carries forward from its beginning—in the *It is* of Parmenides—being no longer speaks itself in multiple ways. It speaks itself in the one, true, and good way of the absolute that assembles it or that it assembles. Being speaks itself, absolutely, as of the absolute and absolutely says to itself the absolute: *it is*. This *it* is not neuter, although it is neither masculine nor feminine. *It* is the self-categorization of being transcending transcendentals, abolishing, sublating, or confounding the *pollakōs* in the conquest of the self-positing and self-termination of being.

At one time in history, this was uttered as *I am*. But the *it* of being, the it that being *is* when it is (and does not speak itself in any way) is the true *I*. No doubt the *I* gives *it* structure and substance.

But the *I* still *speaks* itself, it does nothing else and is made of nothing else. *I* requires a mouth that opens, it requires me to have dragged myself, hurled myself, outside me beforehand, to have abandoned myself. The voice is already an abandonment.

It requires nothing that being has not already, always, arranged in its silent being. The *esti gar einai* of Parmenides means that the infinitive of being—or its substantive, the infinity of its substance—conjugates itself only to itself, in the third person of *it is*. Three readings, three declamations, or three dictions are made together there:

> *It is* indeed being.
> It is indeed *being*.
> It is *indeed* being.

But no one takes the floor there, no one declares anything, no one addresses anyone. There is nobody, no dialogue—and it is not even a monologue. *It is* has the tremendous adherence to itself, mute and immobile, of a stone sphinx in the desert, in our desert. The sphinx calls itself God, Nature, History, Subject, Illusion, Existence, Phenomenon, Poiesis, Praxis—but it is always a single mass of stones, fugitive versions of the unique *it is* that no one utters. For no one can utter it: Plato knew this already.

~

Abandoned being is abandoned to the *pollakōs*. At the same time, *pollakōs legetai* is completed, resorbed, comprised in the Logos and as the Logos that it is, and the same *pollokōs legetai*, which as such is abandoned, gathers up being. For being is exactly what the dialectic abandoned and doomed to nothingness with its first negating step [*son premier pas*]. Or rather, the dialectic abandoned being in the transition to nothingness. Abandonment is not nothingness. Being is what remains before nothingness and before the power of the negative. Being is what remains at the inception of the dialectic, what all the force of the dialectic is not able to draw out, put in motion, alienate in its propulsive identity. Being remains abandoned. From that point on, the *pollakōs* also remains in abandonment. Its multiple manner no longer conforms to the unity, whether infinite or asymptotic, of a Logos. Until that point, *pollakōs legetai* remained under the surveillance of a *monōs legetai*: that being should speak itself in multiple ways is something that is determined and valued on the basis of what a unique and univocal *logos* offers. Plurivocal being let itself be ruled, or had itself ruled, by this univocality. Thus it is not abandoned to simple pluri-vocality, which in turn is abandoned. What is left is an irremedia-ble scattering, a dissemination of ontological specks. As a result, this scattering itself is not left—at least not as the remainder of a subtraction, or as the remains of a fragmentation, which leave something to keep hold of. It is not left as an ontological proba-bility, in which the characteristic possibility of a calculation would be preserved. To be abandoned is to be left with nothing to keep hold of and no calculation. Being knows no more safekeeping, not even in a dissolution or a tearing apart, not even in an eclipse or an oblivion.

The oblivion of being must be understood in two ways. If it is the oblivion of *being*, thought invincibly *keeps* the form and the nature of an immense reminiscence. The being of being comes forth, resplendent, from oblivion and once more dictates, silently, its own *it is*. The oblivion of being, then, is oblivious of being's abandonment.

On the other hand, oblivion may also understand, in its very oblivion and, in sum, *as oblivion*, that what is forgotten is not being but its abandonment, and that abandonment does not constitute the being of being but rather its condition—not in the sense of a "condition of possibility" but in the sense of a "miserable condi-tion," whose very misery provokes oblivion. Oblivion then under-stands itself to be inscribed, prescribed, promised in abandonment. Indeed, abandonment pledges to oblivion, and this oblivion safe-guards no reserve of recoverable, curable memory. (The tension of this double comprehension, which in no way is a conflict of inter-pretations around a "thought" that would be "the thought of the oblivion of being," makes up *all* our thinking, determines all the ontology that summons us and that also summons, whatever opinions they hold, those who merely smile at "ontology," that is, "philosophy."

Of the fact that being was abandoned, that *it is* abandoned and abandons itself, there is no memory. There is no history of this abandonment, no knowledge or narrative of how, where, when, and by whom it was abandoned. This is not impossible to know: very simply, it *is* not. It did not take place. Being *is* not its abandonment, and it abandons *itself* only by being neither author nor subject of abandonment. But there is abandoned being, and *there is* does not mean *it is*. Nor does *there is* mean *es gibt*: neither one can be translated, neither by the other or otherwise. In languages, too, as between languages, the very being of abandonment is abandoned.

~

But haven't we known for a long time that this was so?

Weren't we born in abandonment, Greek and tragic (that of Oedipus), Jewish and exiled (that of Moses), both of them defined or fated by abandonment, to the point where we do not know where either figure begins or ends, or to what degree the one is Jewish and the other Greek? They are abandoned *at birth*: that is, from the beginning, in their beginnings, and doomed indefinitely to be born. To be born means precisely never to cease being born, never to have done with never fully attaining to being, to its status, to its stance or to its standing, and to its autonomy. Birth abandons Oedipus and Moses up to the hour of their death. The third figure, Christ, interminable in his turn, mediates them again at the moment of his death (as though there were a dialectic of abandonment, as inevitable as it is unbearable). He cries out—the recitation of a psalm:

> *Eli, Eli, lama sabacthani!*
> *Thee mou, Thee mou, ina ti me enkatelipès;*
> *Deus meus, Deus meus, ut quid dereliquisti me?*

Dereliquisti me: you have given me up to dereliction, where there is nothing left to me of you, you who let me be left. You have not left me to some task, to some station, to some suffering, to some expectation. You have left me to abandonment.

What "the God of love" means is that love alone abandons. What is not love can reject, desert, forget, dismiss, discharge, but love alone can abandon, and it is by the possibility of abandonment that one knows the possibility, inverted or lost, of love. And it is also in this way that one knows the justice beyond justice of love, which the images and words of "Christian love" have falsified for us (from the time of the Gospels, no doubt, up to the Romanticism that is the Christianity of our time).

Nevertheless, there is not a nature of love, and no one has managed to pervert it for us. Christianity is no more a perversion than metaphysics is a lapse of memory. Abandoned being can be neither safeguarded nor betrayed. We must have done with our evaluations of history, with our evaluating, self-evaluating history. Hegel understood that history is necessity. But we, Hegel and ourselves, have not understood what necessity is. Nietzsche understood: *amor fati*.[3] But we have not understood, nor perhaps did Nietzsche understand, what *amor* is.

There is this, at least, which Nietzsche wrote, even if he did not understand it: *Ecce Homo*. Behold man, the one who cries: *ut quid dereliquisti me?* Behold abandoned man, the abandonment of man. Behold man, the abandoned being. The destiny of *amor* is bound up with this abandonment.

The time of abandonment is the time not of man but of a voice that declares: *Ecce homo.* Whose voice, designating whom? This question, these two questions that are the same question, is in abandonment. Perhaps it must be abandoned. The time of abandonment is not a time full of questions, this time that is uplifted, distended with expectation, marshalling the future under the direction of the question, promising and finally projecting into that future the rectitude of the response. It is not the artificial time of anticipation, but it is time, the only time—the time that never suspends its flight.

The time of abandonment is the time, the wavering, of the instantly abandoned instant; time abandons itself, and that is its definition. And in time we are abandoned to time, just as time abandons us. Thus our time—our epoch—is more than ever the time of time, the time of the temporal ontology of abandonment, and of the end of History in the sense of History's desperately holding on to time, resisting it and sublating it. This History is abandoned by history. What is abandoned, what abandons itself, *is* only in the transition, the tilt, the teetering—"between the ungraspable and the grasp"[4]—and in the skip of a beat, of a heartbeat; and even the transition, the defection, the swoon, *is* not. One cannot even say *the* transition, *the* flow, *the* flux, *the* duration, much less *the* heartbeat or *the* skipping of a beat. Time's duration, which constitutes time, has no other fixity than its incessant vanishing. Time does not fly, but a flight constitutes time. Time's system is not the skipped beat; rather, time skips, and skips itself: suspension, pulsation, continuity broken off and started up again on its very disjunction, thus the same (the same time) and never the same (*never* the same time). Which does not mean: abandonment *always*, for there is no permanence of abandoned being.

Such an absence of permanence, the impossibility of fixing abandonment and settling into it, is what renews and revives it. Its figures pop up everywhere, a sickening whirl, Oedipus, Moses, Jesus, but also Roland, Robinson, Olympio, Phèdre, Tristram, Jean-Jacques, la Traviata, Josef K., and Hyperion, and the proletariat, and the sovereign.

But these are not the figures of an essence. This is the *pollakōs* in which an interminable abandon of the essence of being interminably exhausts itself. The structure of all our mythography is the myth of abandonment, while the origin of our whole science of myth is that myth has abandoned us. Thus, moreover, this very science, by definition, does not know what it is talking about. We have no idea, no memory, no presentiment of a world that does not abandon us, a world that holds man in its bosom. A statement of Brecht's has the importance of a paradigm for our whole history, for the whole West:

If it is said that the theater came forth from the realm of ritual, what is meant is that it became theater when it left that realm.[5]

Being came to pass by means of an abandonment: we can say no more. There is no going back; being conveys nothing more ancient than its abandonment. Of a myth or a rite prior to being, there is nothing to know and nothing to regain. These are words to qualify, or rather to camouflage—quite poorly—the abandonment through which being reaches us, and through which we reach being.

All our Ideas, on the contrary, rest on a belief in the virtue of the question "Why is there something, and not nothing?" An antecedence of being could be the answer. But now we know that this question already answers itself in secret: "Since there is something, and not everything, it is because this thing is in abandonment, it is because everything is abandoned." And it is not permitted us to ask by whom.

Thus the thinker says, in our time, that abandoned being, being-thrown-to-the-world in dereliction, constitutes a positive possibility of being-in-the-world.

But this positivity posits nothing and is not itself posited. Attempting to think about it would mean renouncing thinking, and it could mean that this renunciation might *be* nothing, that it might make no claim to abdicate the positivity of the concept or of poetry (thinking positioning, in general), in order to give itself up, for example, to a praxis swollen with this renunciation's own immanence. It would be necessary to renounce without renouncing, not to determine dereliction in any way at all or invest it with any desire or provide it any model. Such self-deprivation magnetizes the mystical will of Ignatius Loyola, and haunts the philosophical will of Heidegger. But that is still not what summons us now: all our spiritual exercises must be rid of the will, must disengage from "exercise" and "spirit." We would finally have to let ourselves be abandoned. At the end of words, that is what "thinking" would mean.

$\sim$

Let ourselves be abandoned to what, if not to what abandonment abandons to? The origin of "abandonment" is a putting at *bandon. Bandon (bandum, band, bannen)* is an order, a prescription, a decree, a permission, and the power that holds these freely at its disposal. To *abandon* is to remit, entrust, or turn over to such a sovereign power, and to remit, entrust, or turn over to its *ban*, that is, to its proclaiming, to its convening, and to its sentencing.

One always abandons to a law. The destitution of abandoned being is measured by the limitless severity of the law to which it finds itself exposed. Abandonment does not constitute a subpoena to present oneself before this or that court of the law. It is a compulsion to appear absolutely under the law, under the law as such and in its totality. In the same way—it is the same thing—to be *banished* does not amount to coming under a provision of the law, but rather to coming under the entirety of the law. Turned over to the absolute of the law, the banished one is thereby abandoned completely outside its jurisdiction. The law of abandonment requires that the law be applied through its withdrawal. The law of abandonment is the other of the law, which constitutes the law. Abandoned being finds itself deserted to the degree that it finds itself remitted, entrusted, or thrown to this law that constitutes the law, this other and same, to this other side of all law that borders and upholds a legal universe: an absolute, solemn order, which prescribes nothing but abandonment. Being is not entrusted to a cause, to a motor, to a principle; it is not left to its own substance, or even to its own subsistence. It is—in abandonment.

Abandonment respects the law; it cannot do otherwise. That does not mean that there is any question of a forced respect, one consequently deprived of the characteristic value of respect. That "it cannot do otherwise" means it cannot be otherwise, it is not otherwise. Abandonment is abandonment to respect of the law, to respect of the wholeness of the law's other side. Prior to all other determinations, and as the origin of all other determinations (fear and trembling, submission, veneration, imitation, compliance), respect is a gaze, a regard (*respectus*). It is not an optical regard, and still less a speculative regard, which would stare at the law. It is a regard that does not raise its eyes, and perhaps does not even open them. It is also, and in the first place, a look back (*re-spicere*): turned toward the *before* of abandonment, where there is nothing to see, which is not to be seen. It is not a regard for the invisible, it is not an ideal or ideational regard. It is the *consideration* of abandonment. By respecting the law, abandonment respects itself, so to speak (and the law respects it). It turns back—not to perceive itself, but to receive itself.

One would like to think that it is a question of a *gift* (the German word is *die Hingebung*: the gift to . . .). But *mettre à* [to put at] *bandon* is not *donner à* [to give to] *ban*, and the latter syntagm, which certain scholars have looked for, has not been verified. Being is not given with abandonment, if the gift supposes a reserve and the provision of riches, an initial accumulation as well as the generosity of a donor. The law gives nothing; it orders. Being is not given—or a gift is not given to it—unless a gift, well short of what we imagine and what we practice in its name, is or should be always abandoned. One thinks one hears, one would like to hear, *donner* [to give] in *abandonner*, but the opposite is true. ("Don't give with one hand and withhold with the other," says the law; but it is the giving itself as such that must not be withheld.)

One abandons to a law, which is to say, always to a voice. *Bannan, bannen*, in ancient and middle High German (to order or prohibit, under threat of penalty), are grafted onto a "root" (*bhâ) of speech, of declaration. *Fari* and *phanai* are part of the "family," and so, as a result, is *phone*. Abandoned being is returned or left to *phone*, and to *fatum*, which in turn derives from *phone. Amor fati* addresses the law and its voice.

Ontology is thus a phonology. But here the voice is no longer an acoustic medium or the articulation of a discourse. The voice *constitutes* the law, to the extent that it orders; and, to that extent, the law *is* the voice. What this voice utters, however, perhaps can no longer be described as the command of an action to be carried out or as the injunction of a provision to be observed. Perhaps this order says, in some strange way, *ecce homo*. It is not a prescriptive, but a constative, as a linguist would say. Nevertheless, here the constative would be heard as a prescription.

Behold (or "see here," *voici*) is an imperative. If it is true that it orders (but up to what point is it true? up to the boundary, so fragile, of the ellipsis or suspension of a *you*; what is needed for this ellipsis, the tone of voice it engages, its fragility—all this remains to be thought), then what it orders cannot be described, for the *here* of "see here" is not shown. The law of abandonment is that this *here* not be designated at all, not here, not there, not anywhere. *Ecce homo* orders what we once called the *ecceity* of man: its presence, for itself, in this or that "here," independent of its attributes, of its very essence. Ecceity is being that is stripped of everything that is not its being-here—or its being-there.

～

Being is thus abandoned to the being-there of man, as to an order. This is a categorical imperative, not only in that it suffers no restriction and submits to no condition, not only in that it constitutes the absolute law of being, but also in that the categorical imperative, in keeping with the category of the categorical as established by the table of judgments, cannot contain anything but the inherence of a predicate in a subject (by contrast with the hypothetical and with the disjunctive). Categorical judgment says that this is that. The categorical imperative says that man is here. But it gives the order to *see* him *here*, for the inherence of the predicate in the subject, in this case, is only the inherence of ecceity, of being-there, of presence. Nothing is thereby judged, asserted, or negated *on the subject* of man, nothing is predicated about his being, which instead is abandoned. That is the reason why the imperative supplements an impossible categorical judgment: man (whose being, in its abandonment, remains unqualifiable)—behold him here. But *here*, let us repeat, is not shown. Nothing is shown but showing itself in its singular generality: *idou ho anthrōpos*, behold here the man. As soon as this phrase, with which Pilate abandons Jesus, no longer belongs to Pilate—and indeed it no longer does—it becomes an order, and its "here" is no longer assigned. Man is only ordered as being-there, or to be there—that is, *here*.

(*Here*: most strictly, there, where it is written, before you. Here is written here, here is never more than an inscription. *Here lies* its abandoned letter.)

～

Man is the being of abandoned being and as such is constituted or rather instituted only by the reception of the order to see man here, there where he is abandoned. The order to *see* is still an eidetic, or theoretical, order. But what it gives the order to see, the *there* of man, offers no Idea, gives nothing to be seen.

A place gives itself to be seen, configures itself. But *here* or *there* (it is the same, and the other), although it imparts places, although it broaches space and outlines its schemas, itself remains invisible. *Here* opens a spacing, clears an area upon which being is thrown, abandoned. Ecceity opens an *areality*. But the areality of the area (of being) is not its design, not its configuration. It is its tracing, beginning from the here. The here has no place: at every moment it is here and there, here and now, for here *is* now. *Hic est nunc.* Here is not made of the space that it opens or cuts, here is the time of this incision. *Ecce homo* means: behold the time of man, behold his abandonment.

Ontology will be, from now on, an anthropology that has no other "object" but the dereliction of being—and thus, once again, its *pollakōs*, for there are cruel abandons and gracious abandonments, some sweet, some pitiless, some voluptuous, frenetic, happy, or disastrous, some serene. Abandonment's only law, like that of love, is to be without return and without recourse.

TRANSLATED BY BRIAN HOLMES

§ *Dei Paralysis Progressiva*

In January 1889, in Turin, Nietzsche does not disappear. He becomes paralyzed. "*Paralysis progressiva*": that is the diagnosis of the psychiatrist Doctor Wille when Overbeck brings Nietzsche back to Basel. Nietzsche is paralyzed for eleven years of fixed existence—one third of the thirty-three years that will have passed between his first written publication and his death. This paralysis is not primarily a cessation, an annulment or a destruction. It is above all a presentation. It presents him whom it strikes, immobile, in the posture and figure in which he is overcome, and it progressively accomplishes this presentation, to the point of offering, definitively immutable, a death mask and the eternity over which it closes (but his face had already become "like a mask" when he appeared at the clinic of Jena, as Peter Gast wrote).

The posture and figure in which Nietzsche is paralyzed are the posture and figure of God. He who announced and proclaimed the death of God—with no resurrection—died *in persona Dei*: God outliving himself, but paralyzed.

Or else: God did not die in the Nietzschean statement, in Nietzsche's text (who, in a text, ever died a death not fictitious?). God died by the death of Nietzsche. And for eleven years, progressive paralysis identified God and he who could write nothing, say nothing anymore. God resuscitated one last time: paralyzed, mad, alienated, so congealed in the anticipated posture of death—preceding death itself, death not ceasing to precede itself—that he could never resuscitate again. For death, now, was to him no longer the absolute accident which the spirit knows how to confront and pass over with no less absolute a power. Rather, death had become the very being of God.

In 1889 God is no longer simply dead, as he was or could have seemed to be in *The Gay Science*. That is to say, the quality or state of death are no longer simply attributed to his being, which would bear them and perhaps ultimately even transmit to them in return something of his divinity. Rather, death is *in* his being. (Nietzsche had noted one day: " 'Being'—we have no idea of it apart from the idea of 'living.'—How can anything dead 'be'?")[1]

In other words: the cry "God is dead" no longer allows itself to be accompanied, in 1889, by that muffled and limiting echo, "At bottom, only the moral God has passed away." For this echo accused the expression "God is dead" of being a metaphor, and authorized the thought of another life of God or of another living God, beyond morality. At present, however, God is truly dead, his being is abolished. And that is why there is no longer any voice to announce this predication "God is dead," for there is no longer any subject to whom a predicate can be attributed. ("Who should be the subject of which we predicate that it is dead, here and now?")[2] Rather, there is God "himself," who does not say his own death (no one can). On the contrary, he proffers his own identity, with a mad, gaping, and progressively paralyzed voice—for this identity no longer is. No longer does one hear a sentence saying something (that God is dead), one hears someone no longer able to say himself, for he no longer is, and he disappears in his choked voice.

When the madman cried out, "God is dead!" one heard someone's voice, with his tone and accent. It was the voice of Nietzsche, author of *The Gay Science*—and, all told, it was also the poetic and embellished voice of Prince Vogelfrei. But here one no longer hears the voice of anyone. It is not an anonymous voice. It is still the voice of "Nietzsche," but it pronounces nothing anymore but the effacement and dispersion of this name, it pronounces nothing but the drift and delirium of its own provenance and emission. It no longer speaks, it vainly shapes articulations (sounds, names) that might procure for it the point from which a word can be spoken. It is too late, it has lost the power of speech, even the possibility of experiencing it as unattainable. No longer, by speaking, can it expose itself to the test of language and the word, nor, as a consequence, to that of silence. It unravels a language beyond or behind language itself, where names are infinitely interchanged, no longer naming anything or anyone, where the play of meaning is at once dissolved at the limits of the arbitrary and seized in a blocked necessity. It is the voice of God, insofar as "God is dead" now means: the Unnameable names itself, it assumes all names, it paralyzes language and history, and it presents itself in this way, a living mouth articulating death. (Before ceasing completely to speak, in the years 1892–93, Nietzsche used to repeat phrases such as "I am dead because I am stupid," or else, without syntax, "in short, dead.")

God is dead, but this time it is not news anymore. It is the presentation of the deceased, and this is why, instead of showing us churches as tombs closed over the absence of God, as the madman did, the scene in Turin shows us someone who "attended his own funeral twice": God presents himself dead, and his death makes him present with an absolute presence, incommensurable with all past modes of his presence, of his representation or absence. This presence cannot be endured: the absence of God caused anxiety, but the presence of God dead, and of his voice, paralyzes. Nietzsche is the name and body of this presence. In contrast to Christ or as his pendant, he is the incarnation of the dead, not the live, God. In addition he is not the son but the Father:

> What is disagreeable and offends my modesty is that at bottom I am every name in history. With the children I have put into the world too, I consider with some mistrust whether it is not the case that all who come *into* the "kingdom of God" also come *out* of God.[3]

In Turin God the Father is incarnated directly, without mediation—and without a Mediator for any sort of health—that is to say, without a Mediator by which to pass through death and resuscitate from the tomb. No longer is there any tomb. It is in the middle of the street, in full gesticulation, in the middle of the written page to Gast or to Burckhardt that God presents himself dead. He is incarnated dead, or as death itself, presenting and preceding itself in paralysis. God present as death is God present as *nothing*, or as that immobile suspension in the "nothing" that strictly speaking cannot even be called "death" since it has no identity. Rather, it takes away all identity. In the becoming-dead of God the identity of God is taken away. It loses itself in the loss of identity of him who has become God, assuming all divine names with all names of history. Nietzsche paralyzed presents God dead: he does not represent him, for the authentic reality of God dead is not to be found in another place, from which it might delegate or figure itself as "Nietzsche." Instead, God dead *is* there, for Nietzsche's paralysis—which is the precession of his death—presents this: that there is no God, or that all there is of "God" is but in death and as death. Nietzsche presents nothing other than that which is presented by all human death—simply this, that it is death, and the "God" is immersed in it even before having been. (God is immersed in it because *God* is death conceived as unnameable, death conceived under a name and as the presence of this name—death presented, the end of named and presented presence.)

With Nietzsche and in Turin, there occurs that moment in history where death precedes itself to show what it "is." Until that moment, "God" had always signified, as long as there had been a "god," that death *is not*; and God had always been that which infinitely overtakes death, withdrawing its prey from it in advance, conceding to it no more than the simulacrum of its mortal operation. That is why, once this significance is abolished, once this *meaning* [*sens*] that had asserted itself for centuries (or for millennia) comes to touch its own limit and to close, a moment arrives, in Turin, where it is death that overtakes itself and that shows itself for what it is: paralysis and death.

No longer "death is not," but rather "the being of death is nonbeing, and such is also the being of God." Thus God no longer precedes death, and does not suppress it or sublate it into himself.

Rather, it is death that precedes itself in him. Thus God sees himself dead and presents himself dead. (Jean Paul, whom Nietzsche had read, had already written the *Discourse of Christ Dead, That There Is No God.*) God presents himself as a paralyzed creator of a caricature of creation: "son dio, ho fatto questa caricatura." And the caricature is that of God. God declares himself his own caricature, for he is not. When Nietzsche slaps passersby on the back in Turin and tells them "ho fatto questa caricatura," it is himself that he shows, and thus he says: "I am God, I made this caricature, this man with the large moustache who walks around in his student's coat, forty-four years old, for there is no God, for I do not exist." Yet still, if he is every name in history, it means that through all these names he is the name of their provenance and of their transcendent recollection, the name of God, while at the same time he is *no more* than the names *of history*, for the name of God is not the name of a being, and Nietzsche is paralyzed in announcing himself through the impossible name.

In Turin that moment of history comes to pass where it is shown that the name of God is no longer the name beyond all names, that it is no longer the extreme nomination of the Unnameable (for the name of God was never anything but the name of an impossible Name), but that it is rather the emptiness of all nomination, an absence of name furrowed behind all names, or else, the paralysis and death of all names. As God, and as God "the successor of the dead God," in his words to Overbeck, Nietzsche presents the haggard, stray, and frozen countenance not of him who has an impossible name (who would at least reserve in himself the secret of his nomination) but of him who has no name, of him who is no name, and who has no way of being called, for he does not exist. "God" has become something other than a name or the name of a name: it has become the cry of him who sees himself not being.

He is one who has entered into death, and who, in a certain way, recognizes and rediscovers himself there. (In his last letters, Nietzsche identifies himself both with dead people and with murderers. He camps on both banks of death, and it is in this being-between-two that he is God.) He is thus very close to the Hegelian Spirit, which "endures death and in death maintains its being."[4] Nietz-sche's paralyzed spirit is the twin brother of this Spirit, or its caricature, or even, and here this is the same thing, its truth.

In fact, the spirit that "in death maintains its being," and, in consequence, resurges from this death to affirm itself in its plenitude, is spirit as *Self.* The Self—or subjectivity—is the deter-mination of being (or life, what Hegel calls "the living substance") as self-production and self-positing. In the ontology of Self, the relation-to-self (the phenomenological face of which is self-consciousness) is not subordinate to the positing of a "self-itself" (as an external and empirical consideration of self-consciousness might make it seem). On the contrary, the relation-to-self is ante-cedent and generative. The Self *comes from* "relating to oneself." It is the constitutive movement of the ego, and it is already that of Montaigne's "I." Now, in order for the relation-to-self to take place, in order for it to articulate itself, what is necessary is the moment of the outside-oneself, of the negation of self through which a self-relation can be produced (both in the sense of establishing a relation and of restoring a property). Death is this moment, in itself void, whose nullity allows the Self to be mediated.

The Self would not be able to be immediate, for what is immedi-ate is not produced, has not become, has not been actualized—which, for Hegel, and in truth for all philosophy, comes down to not being effective. Death, consequently, is the moment and the movement of the effective production of Self. The same is the case in the death of God and even in the mortal paralysis of his caricature. With this difference, however, that now what is pro-duced is the opposite of a production: it is nothing more than the reproduction of the productive instance. The paralyzed Self does not present the Subject resurrected from death. Instead, it presents death as the truth of this subject. It presents death itself stopped in its tracks (in what metaphysics would represent as a move, a pas-sage), death paralyzed; and it presents this death as the true subjec-tivity of the subject. That is what God now means in the sentence "I am God," and it is also the meaning of the irony or sarcasm with which it charges the sentence, that is, the consciousness of mad-

ness. A mad consciousness of conscious madness constitutes the
self-consciousness of the subject that is achieved paralyzed.

For one should not mistake this sentence. One might be tempted
to see the announcement of a theophany in it. A god would be
coming to show himself, and would thus be declaring his coming.
Nietzsche, up until Turin no doubt, had awaited nothing else (cf.
his famous exclamation, "How many new gods are still possible!").
In Turin, he was the first person in our history to know that this
epiphany would never take place. But whether it could or could
not—and whether it ever did or did not—take place, what is in any
case certain is that it cannot be accompanied by such a sentence. By
definition, a divine epiphany does not have to be declared or re-
flected in an enunciation of itself. In such an epiphany, an unpro-
duced immediacy is revealed immediately. (A careful reading of
theophanic texts could show it: when the god declares himself, and
says "I am God," he has *already* been recognized at the bottom of
the heart or soul; his divinity has already presented itself, for otherwise his enunciation would not be understood.) "I am God" is the
statement of someone who sees his divinity abolished.

On the other hand, it is the statement of a subject who affirms
himself to be anterior to his own production. He affirms that he has
presided over the operation of the self-relation, which would therefore not be anterior to him. In effect, it is nothing but the logic of
the self-relation taken to its most rigorous extreme. At this extreme
it turns out that the Subject is identical to the null moment
required by its production, that necessary and impossible moment
of self-production where no "itself" is available, or ever will be—
that moment of pure and simple death. "I am God" means "I am
dead." This new statement does not mean that the *I* has lost its
living quality; it means that the *I* never had this quality, and that it
never will have it. It means that the self-constitution of the self-
relation is identical to death, or that it does not occur except as a
death which does not occur unexpectedly to something living, but
is only death preceding itself infinitely. For only death is really
capable of such preceding. And yet at the same time it reveals that
this precession—the ontological self-precession constitutive of the

Subject—is not and cannot be anything but a paralysis. The Self is an ontological paralysis, the truth of which could be articulated in this way: *only death is self-productive, but thus produces nothing.*

This truth was already at work when Descartes understood that the *ego sum* also belongs to madness. It was the tenebrous truth of the blind clarity from which the *cogito* issues. It was perhaps on account of this truth that Hegel once thought he was going mad. It was through it that God, less than a century later, entered into the *paralysis progressiva* of Nietzsche.

What Nietzsche would have become aware of in Turin, by a sort of final implosion of Cartesian clarity, or by a last convulsion of the "life that preserves itself in death itself," is that "one can die of immortality," as he himself had written. In other words: the Subject is nothing but death, that is, nothing but *his* death. But this does not involve a death of the Subject. It involves this: that, in the absolute constitution of the self-relation, subjectivity does not attain or present anything but its own absence. Yet this absence is so much *its own* that it is not an absence at all. That is to say, it is not the default of the presence of something or someone who might have been there before; it is the vanishing of a presence in the very process of its presentation. The subject, says Hegel, is "being . . . that does not have mediation outside it, but is this mediation itself."[5] Now, death is mediation. In death and as death, the subject actualizes and presents itself: immobilized before having begun to budge; paralyzed; its glance fixed, and fixed on nothing that is presented to it but the unreality of its presence ("Death," says Hegel again, "as we may call that unreality").[6] The subject attends its own burial—and attends it twice, for in truth this blocked epiphany repeats itself unendingly and vacuously.

"I am God" is the utterance of such knowledge, and the word "God" operates the de-nomination of the Subject: it has no name, it traverses history blowing all names, leading all the children of God, along with itself, back to the vacancy of the heavens. Paralysis freezes on Nietzsche's face the absent traits of him no longer inscribed by anything anywhere, who leaves no trace (the last letters are only a way of covering over, and then of effacing, the traces of the person named Nietzsche), and who, instead of being taken away by death, takes away from death, beforehand, its power of reaching him, for he is already no longer. Death itself, eleven years later, will be insignificant. It will not come to cut the course of Nietzsche's life. It will only confirm what God is: the absolute and void self-knowledge of the complete night in which the Subject produces itself, that is to say, paralyzes itself.

It is impossible to imagine the cold horror that must have been, for eleven years, the confrontation between the Self and the efface-ment of all inscription.

Yet is it not possible to imagine a strange gaiety, and even a shimmering joy, not *in* this night but next to it, as an infinitesimal gleam in the corner of Nietzsche's eye? This is the gaiety that animates most of the Turinese letters—for example, in the last one to Burckhardt, after he has designated himself God the Creator: "I salute the Immortals. M. Daudet belongs to the *quarante*." And this is the joy of the note to Peter Gast:

Turin, January 4, 1889

To my maëstro Pietro.
    Sing me a new song: the world is transfigured and all the heavens are full of joy.

The Crucified[7]

Whence comes this joy, sung with the words and cheerfulness of the psalmist? What reason have the heavens for rejoicing? Precisely because God has abandoned them to fix himself in the thick darkness of the Subject. The heavens with no Self, with no Su-preme Being, are the heavens delivered from the necessity of sub-jectivity, that is to say, from the self-production and self-positing of being. Otherwise put—and this is why the *world* is transfigured—they are heavens opened onto their new truth. No longer the abode of the world's support, they are the free spacing in which the world is cast without reason, as if by the game of a child. This child is still a god—*pais paizōn*—the child-god of Heraclitus, "Zeus the big child of the worlds," as Nietzsche called him.

But the child-god is not God, not even a small god. He is the play of the world, whose being is not the subject. And this game is no game: it is the mittance of the world in the space of a freedom that disengages it from the paralyzing compulsion of the Self, but engages it at the same time in an obligation: that of "singing a new song." Nietzsche does not sing this song, he tells others to sing it. He says it laughing beside his madness, laughing at it and at God paralyzed—a silent laughter turned towards the rejoicing heavens.

To him the heavens are no longer the heaven one reaches after passing through death. Here, too, death shrinks into insignificance, now no longer because it precedes itself in paralysis, but because the life which will attain it, which is always already in the process of attaining it, does not, in it, touch on the moment of its mediation. This life need not mediate itself so as to appropriate its substance in the form of a subject. It simply exposes itself to its end, just as it has been exposed to the space of the play of the world. Its end is a part of this game; in its space it inscribes the trace of a name—here, that of Friedrich Nietzsche—in the same way that each time, with each name of history, a singular trace, a finitude whose limit puts into play each time anew the whole spacing of the world, inscribes itself. Each name, each time that its subject is progressively paralyzed, discloses again, instantaneously, the whole space of the world; or else it discloses, that is, inscribes, a new spacing. The spacing of a bountiful community, whose *history* does not consist in accomplishing an *end*, but in letting new names, and new songs, arise unendingly.

As Nietzsche wished to read it, against the Christian reading (and perhaps against all possible readings of this text), in the Gospels, "death is not a bridge, not a passage," for "the Kingdom of God" is not something that one has to wait for; it has no yesterday and no day after tomorrow. It does not arrive in a "thousand years"—it is the experience of a heart; it exists everywhere, it exists nowhere. . . . Death therefore is indeed *the end*, and in this sense Nietzsche's jubilation pronounces nothing but his paralysis. But for this paralysis the end is endless: it fixes the subject's regard on the eternity of its nothingness. While Nietzsche's "heart" is filled with the cheer of this kingdom delivered from God, where all beings, like children, are simply borne into the world.

TRANSLATED BY THOMAS HARRISON

§ Hyperion's Joy

The image of man has eyes, whereas the moon has
light.
　　　　　　　—Hölderlin, "In Lovely Blueness . . ."[1]

Bellarmin to Selenion

It has been a long time now, it is true, since Hölderlin stopped
writing to me. Since then, so many and such great disturbances
have afflicted the land of his exile that I can certainly imagine a
few letters may have been lost. At least one or two would not have
failed to reach me, however: he needed only to say the word and
some army survivor, or a refugee driven out by poverty or banishment, would carry out this task for him. How many of them have
we not seen suddenly appear amidst us! As for the news of his
death, it is difficult to imagine that I would not have heard it from
one of the countless travelers who nowadays make the pilgrimage
to that country henceforth restored to peace (or at least, as with so
many others, to the painful simulacrum of peace). So he is alive,
believe me. But he no longer lives for us, he no longer lives to tell us
about himself, as I had asked him to do, nor to reminisce about
times gone by. He lives—this is how I imagine him—for a present
or for a future of which we know nothing, and about which
perhaps he would be incapable of communicating anything to us.
Does he thus leave us the task of understanding his silence by
ourselves? Is there in his silence some design for us to reflect upon,
some precious enigma that we should decipher? Even this, I could
not say. "Oh you who live in this age with me!" he wrote to me

one day, "seek not counsel of your doctors nor of your priests when your hearts wither away!"[2] I would add henceforth, for you and for us all: and do not question him who has fled us either. In his night, in the abyss of mourning, the power to speak is lost as well.

Whatever I myself may have wished, and whatever you may have been able to suggest or ask of me, when all is said and done, it seems to me absolutely impossible to write a philosophical study on Hölderlin. Or to be more exact, I suspect that this enterprise is destined to have very narrow limits—even if it is true that such a study may still be written, and even if it is no less true that the thing has been done several times, and done well. I will not cite anyone, for fear of insulting both your knowledge in this field and your modesty. It is true that you asked me to examine in particular the discreet but close ties formed between Kant and Hölderlin—ties which were not brought about by any proximity of the persons or their works, nor really, to be exact, by any continuity of doctrine— but these ties can be discerned as the secret correspondence of two minds, or are perhaps themselves nothing other than the commu- nity of thought in the incommensurability of two minds whose sources and natures differ as much as Prussia from Swabia, or all of Germany from Greece (at least as much as both Kant and Hölder- lin—though in different ways—believed they did).

In truth, if one were to undertake such a study, it is not of a community of thought that one should speak. Hölderlin was part of just such a community at Tübingen, or at Jena with Sinclair, or again in Frankfurt, with Hegel. With Kant, one should speak of a *sameness* of thought. The same thought is at work in both of them, on the near and far sides of speculative idealism: a same thought, shared or divided in its sameness, between the eighteenth and the nineteenth centuries, between the end of the Enlightenment and the beginning of a modernity that does not recognize itself as "modernity" (whether this concept be a Romantic, positivist, pro- gressive, or Mallarméan one), but rather as "the cold night of men,"[3] toward which Hyperion turns back one last time, and toward which, perhaps, he never stops turning back.

Selenion to Bellarmin

. . . What would Kant have thought of *Hyperion*, if he had read it? What did he think of it, if he did read it? We will never know. Heinse, Hölderlin's friend and the person to whom "Bread and Wine" was dedicated, later thought that he knew something about this. In 1797, shortly after the publication of the first volume, he writes: "There are passages here with a warmth and a penetration that would captivate old Kant himself and would draw him away from his pure appearance of all things." He writes this to Sömmering (so that Sömmering would repeat it to Hölderlin)—to the Dr. Sömmering whose work *On the Organ of the Soul* Kant had commentated the previous year, and who is the Gontard's doctor, Diotima's doctor. A series of strange compositions thus take shape for us: Kant, Hyperion, medicine, Suzette, and the soul. (Hölderlin was no doubt to recall the organ of the soul when speaking of the organ of the spirit in his essay "On the Workings of the Poetic Spirit.") They are neither allegories nor scenes that one could re-enact or imagine. They are constellations, interlacings torn from history, devoid of form and genre. All that one can say is that not only Hölderlin's thought, but his heart, has an affinity to Kant's in many ways. Several years earlier, Wilhelmina, who bore him a child, asked Hölderlin to tell her about the *Critique of Judgment*. (His notes on this book, as you wrote to me, have been lost.) Early in '94, she had brought him "Kant's last published text." That might have been "On the proverb . . . ," or perhaps "On the Influence of the Moon on the Weather. . . ."

Bellarmin to Selenion

I had not yet finished my reply to you. What I am afraid of, as perhaps you have already guessed, has nothing to do with what some might invoke as the untouchability of the poet, with the fear of massacring the song with the concept. I am afraid that philosophy may still be incapable of facing the cold night of men.

Or else, which amounts to the same thing, that it can hardly understand this:

> Little knowledge, but much joy
> Is granted to mortals.[4]

Selenion to Bellarmin

. . . He named him, as you very well know, "the Moses of our nation" . . .

Bellarmin to Selenion

Your insistence will have won me over. Judge for yourself how well-founded my reticence is, once you have seen me try to overcome it.

The sameness of Kant and Hölderlin is not their own in the manner of an absolute exclusivity that would immediately distinguish them in all respects from all the others. I can only make you see this sameness by going to look for it at the heart of the community of the entire era, before taking into account its divisions and internal oppositions. The era is very much Kant's (that is, as far as what was epoch-making at the time is concerned): the era of the requirement of an unconditional *unity*. Kant's *Critique* divided everything up—the empirical and the ideal, the theoretical and the practical—but at the same time it also *required*, with an even greater force, a new production of unity. After Kant, the One is no longer something simple or given, but the object or focus of the ultimate requirement:

> That is why experience too, considered objectively, i.e., in the way experience as such is possible (ideally), must constitute a system of possible empirical cognitions, and it must do so in terms of both universal and particular laws: for the unity of nature requires such a system, in terms of a principle of the thorough connection of everything contained in that sum total of all appearances.[5]

Fichte, Schelling, Schlegel, Hegel, and Novalis all share the same preoccupation: the preoccupation with the One. That is to say, a preoccupation with both the One and the Whole (*hen kai panta* was at Tübingen a sort of motto that Hegel and Hölderlin had in common) and with the internal difference of the One that must make up plurality—*hen diapheron heautōi* ("the one differentiated in itself"), "the great saying of Heraclitus" that Hyperion repeats.[6] What came to all of them, via Kant, what commanded or destined them, was the necessity by which thought (philosophy, politics, art) could no longer think in terms of the distinction and the complementarity of the particular and the universal (as Kant, despite everything, still thought), but rather must think in terms of totality, and consequently in terms of unity. In terms of unity, and consequently—since unity is conquered in the multiple process of the whole (and cannot be available by itself, apart, like the universal)—in terms of the requirement, and therefore the tension, the suspense, even the tearing apart of unity (as Kant already thought). Hyperion speaks for them all: "To be one with all—this is the life divine, this is man's heaven."[7]

They all have the same preoccupation with being-one—with one-Being and with being-One—with the passage through the difference of the One and with reconciliation, with the unique reconciliation. " 'Like lovers' quarrels are the dissonances of the world. Reconciliation is there, even in the midst of strife, and all things that are parted find one another again.' "[8]

These are Hyperion's words, they are the words of them all. They do not bear witness, as is often said, to an "optimism" on Hölderlin's part in 1799. They bear witness to a very large and very constricting necessity of thought. This necessity has nothing to do with belief or confidence in unity, with its institution or restitution. Rather, the necessity, in its very affirmation, responds to the fact that unity *is not given*. Reconciliation is "in the midst of" strife, but it is not given; it is neither posited nor available anywhere, it is neither transcendent nor immanent. This is what the loss of Greece signifies, for it merely borrows the appearance of nostalgia. And nostalgia is (almost) nothing here: it expresses the awareness of an unknown destiny—of the unknown aspect of every destiny—to which nothing is given except infinite striving [*unendliches Streben*] toward the One, that is, once again, the non-disposition, non-possession of the One, but unity as a task, as a path, a process, a departure and a dispatch [*envoi*]—to us, my friend, and for us.

Hölderlin belongs to this community brought together in the dwelling place of reconciliation, in the thought of union and reunion. This is not merely an idea dating from his earliest period. Much later, he would write for Zimmer:

> The lines of life are various; they diverge and cease
> Like footpaths and the mountains' utmost ends.
> What here we are, elsewhere a God amends
> With harmonies, eternal recompense and peace.[9]

Hölderlin's difference—the difference of this *one* who differs within the identity of his time, within the identifiable of our time—does not stem from this preoccupation with the One. Conversely, neither does it stem—whatever those whose pathos shamelessly solicits him may think about it—from an idea of irremediable dissonance, of being torn apart, of pure devastation or wandering. "These fragments to which all human creation is reduced," of which Diotima speaks to Hyperion, do not constitute a disenchantment so much as they constitute (as for Novalis) a magical enchantment. But although the thought of the One entails, for Hölderlin as for the others, the representation and the desire (the representation, therefore the desire) of the figure of the One, of its stature and nature (Nature with a capital "N," Greece, the Gods), with Hölderlin this thought nevertheless forms, before all else and on the deepest level, an idea of the non-advent of the One.

Non-advent does not mean rupture, or incompletion. It is every bit as distinct from a "tragic vision" in the current sense of that expression as it is from the projection of the One into the bad infinity of an interminable task—and yet it is just as separate from the good infinity of the dialectic actualization of that task. The non-advent of the One does not mean that the One, in not coming about [*n'advenant pas*], would not be able to be the One that it

must be, and would abandon itself to the distress of a pure disloca-
tion, or to the exhausting and rather laughable flight of an asymptotic course (although these motifs are *also* present in Hölderlin's
writings). But the One as such does not come about. It is the One
that it is in its non-advent. It does not *compose* the unity of its
being-one and its non-advent; it lets them posit themselves, together and separately, in a sort of cadence:

> There is a forgetting of all existence, a hush of our being, in which
> we feel as if we had found all.
> There is a hush, a forgetting of all existence, in which we feel as if we
> had lost all, a night of our soul, in which no glimmer of any star nor
> even the fox fire from a rotting log gives us light.[10]

Thus Hölderlin is, at this point, as close as possible, the *same* as
Kant—across their extreme difference.

. . . .
>   . . . Forever
> This remains: that all day always concatenated whole is
> The World. Often, though, it seems
> A great man cannot fit
> A great thing. Every day the two stand, though, as if on the
>   brink of an abyss, one
> Next to the other. . . .[11]

. . . .

Their difference could be expressed in this way: Kant uses beauty
to think the One; beauty is thus nothing to him, it merely undoes—but irreversibly—the possibility of a *concept* of the One (and
this is certainly the stumbling block of the third *Critique*, which is,
however, in the end unanimously avoided or emptied in different
ways by the Fichtes, Hegels, Schlegels, and even by Schelling).
Hölderlin thinks beauty starting out from the One: this does not
mean for a moment that he would oppose the poet's One to the
philosopher's *one*, which does not come about, according to the
well-known (too well-known) schema and dialectic. On the con-

trary: Hölderlin's difference is that he is the poet "who had the audacity to become a thinker," as D. Janicaud has written in *Hölderlin et la philosophie d'après Hyperion*. But this means that he thinks beauty *starting out from the One that has no concept*—from the One that is not a Subject, that is neither Idea nor Substance— starting out from the one that, as one, does not exist. What needed to be understood, in reading the third *Critique*, is that the One *as One* does not exist, that it essentially does not come about (whereas others sought in the *Critique*, by forcing the text to fit their commentaries, the rule or the outline of a production of the One, or, quite simply, of *one* production):

> But the mind listens to the voice of reason within itself, which demands totality for all given magnitudes, even for those that we can never apprehend in their entirety but do (in presentation of sense) judge as given in their entirety. Hence reason demands comprehension in *one* intuition, and one *presentation* of all the members of a progressively increasing numerical series, and it exempts from this demand not even the infinite (space and past time). Rather, reason makes us unavoidably think of the infinite (in common reason's judgment) as *given in its entirety* (in its totality).
>
> The infinite, however, is absolutely large (not merely large by comparison). Compared with it everything else (of the same kinds of magnitudes) is small. But—and this is most important—to be able even to think the infinite as *a whole* indicates a mental faculty that surpasses any standard of sense. For thinking the infinite as a whole while using a standard of sense would require a comprehension yielding as a unity a standard that would have a determinate relation to the infinite, one that could be stated in numbers; and this is impossible. If the human mind is nonetheless *to be able even to think* the given infinite without contradiction, it must have within itself a faculty that is supersensible.[12]

What needed to be read in the text was that a "faculty that is supersensible," in other words a faculty that is *absolutely* great—*a sense* of the One—can no longer itself be one faculty: neither one, nor a faculty. And it would only come about as an excess, over and above any advent. The entire *Critique* is at pains to give a discursive account of such an excess, and of its necessity. But here we have Hyperion:

> "What is it for which man so immeasurably longs?" I often asked myself; "what is eternity doing in his breast? Eternity? Where is it? who has ever seen it? Man wants more than he is capable of! that seems to be the truth of it! Oh, you have experienced it often enough! And as it is, so it must be. This it is which bestows the sweet, rapturous sense of power: that our powers do not flow forth as they will—this it is, and nothing else, which creates our fair dreams of immortality and all the enticing, all the colossal phantoms that ravish men a thousand times over; this it is which creates his Elysium and his gods for man: that the line of his life does not run straight, that he does not speed to his goal like an arrow, that a power outside of him stops him in his flight."[13]

Continuation

Being "stopped in his flight," as you know very well, is not the effect of an obstacle or a hindrance. Nor is it something that can be converted, sublated, or transfigured. But the broken trajectory brings about what does not come about—it is not an arrow, there is no contact with a target, it is interrupted and begins again: "the sublime lies not so much in the magnitude of the number as in the fact that, the further we progress, the larger are the unities we reach."[14]

But in the end, this progress—and no end to history, no perfection of art properly fulfills the concept of *progress* in Kant—merely moves toward its own excess. Even its excess is not the infinite overabundance of the One, because the One, the incommensurable, does not exist. "Reaching larger unities" does not amount to infinitely increasing the sum total which the One would add up to. Infinity is not "situated" even at this extremity: it is simply the dissolution of all unity. But neither does the One operate by virtue of the stratagem of a pure loss where all would, at the same time, be won. In this negative route, as in the positive route, the ultimate and absolute richness could, as such, only befall a subject, that is, *one* subject. But the *one* of the subject—the subject in the subject, which is closer to the center than any substantiality or any property, even if it were the property of a "transcendental I" (unity's last, but empty and vacillating, recourse in Kant: "For in what we entitle 'soul,' everything is in continual flux and there is nothing abiding except [if we must so express ourselves] the 'I,' which is simple solely because its representation has no content, and therefore no manifold, and for this reason seems to represent, or [to use a more correct term] denote a simple object")[15]—the one of the subject is what has been endlessly undone or forbidden since Kant. Or else it has been limited: "A power outside of him stops him in his flight." Sublime excess is the excess of the One over and above it*self,* sameness itself as a limit, a finiteness and deposing of identity—a deposing with no repose.

"May this unique thing outlive myself in me . . . *so soll dies Einzige doch mich selber überleben in mir . . .,*"[16] this cry of Hyperion (is it a cry? is it even audible?) both preserves and does not preserve unity. It neither loses nor wins it. *Überleben,* to outlive or live on: we still understand this word in terms of maintaining a life beyond the limit, as a perpetuation, a conservation. But it could easily be . . . the *same* thing, barely, almost: to live outside of life, to live without life, thus with death, and yet without death. "Living on goes beyond both living and dying, supplementing each with a sudden surge and a certain reprieve, deciding [*arrêtant*] life *and* death, ending them in a decisive *arrêt,* the *arrêt* that puts an end to something and the *arrêt* that condemns with a sentence [*sentence*], a statement, a spoken word or a word that goes on speaking."[17]

Why has Hölderlin, as they say, "outlived himself" for so long— and his "poetry" along with him? And why does he thus live on— not down to us (like so many other "immortal authors"), but for us? Why, perhaps, is he already outliving *us*?

Here it concerns a kind of brimming over that casts literary and philosophical evaluations into insignificance, that condemns any celebration of Hölderlin (this along with the others). He only lives on *for us* at this price.

What does it mean, therefore, to *brim over*? And in what way, at what point, how does Hölderlin brim over? Brimming over (living on) does not take the logic of limits beyond the limits themselves. It means undoing the limit on the limit itself, by keeping it, by retracing it with the gesture that erases it (and what erasure does not necessarily retrace what it erases?). It means including the inside within the outside, the outside within the inside, but without expansion or transgression of one or the other—without an illegitimate extension beyond the limits of possible experience. *Possible experience* for Kant—the single circumscription without any ultimate unity of the phenomenon, of the appearance of all appearing—is the experience of the limit within the exigency of the One, the exigency of the One within the limit of experience.

Continuation

"Even in a limited existence, man can know an infinite life, and the limited representation of divinity, stemming for him from this existence, can itself also be infinite."[18]

Even in a limited existence, man can know an infinite life: this is living on, this is exceeding. Infinite life neither *succeeds* nor brims over *life. Non coerceri maximo, contineri minimo, divinum est* ["Not to be confined by the greatest, yet to be contained within the smallest, is divine"].[19] This thought is not only the most constant and the most insistent in Hölderlin, it is his thought itself, the thought of finitude. It is not, as for Descartes or Hegel, a thought of finiteness that always relates (man's) finite being to an infinity that founds man and toward which he is drawn. But Hölderlin's thought thinks being-finite as the paradoxical, untenable circumscription of the infinite: the *maximum* is in the *minimum*; there is no outside. The infinite brims over inwards: this is the entire Kantian problematic of the "supersensible power" of the infinite, which means that the thought of finitude *is* the thought of the *sublime*. This thought is not a "sublime" thought, but simply, and patiently, the thought of the unqualifiable unity of the One, of its incommensurable greatness:

. . . There are Gods here too, and they reign;
Great is their measure, yet still man too readily measures with his
    span.[20]

The Kantian thought of finitude and the Hölderlinian thought
of the One are man's thought through and through. It thinks (it
does not conceive of) man starting out from the one, and the one as
man's share or part. This is not a circle: it is a conflagration. Man is
the catastrophe of the One, the One is his being mortally torn apart
and his life lived on.

. . . .

We are a sign, without meaning
Without pain, and we have almost
Lost our language in foreignness.
For when there is an argument about humankind
In heaven, and when the moons powerfully
Follow their courses, the sea also
Speaks and the streams must
Seek their path. But doubtless
Is one. Every day he
Can alter how things are. He hardly needs
A law. Then the leaf rustles and near the glaciers
The oak trees sway. For the heavenly ones are not capable of
Everything. Mortals reach
The brink of the abyss before them. Thus the echo turns
With them. Long is time, but there occurs
What is true.[21]

. . . .

The presentation of the tragic is founded particularly on the fact that
the monstrous, as the god, pairs itself with the human and the power
of nature and man's innermost depths limitlessly become one in anger,
grasps itself so that the limitless becoming-One purifies itself by a
limitless separation.[22]

. . . .

What is true inevitably occurs in the limitless separation of man.
There is no other place for what is true. And no other unity for

man. "Nothing can grow like man, nothing so utterly wither away. Time and again he compares his woe with the darkness of the abyss, his bliss with the ether, and how little does that tell of either!"[23]

My friend, not only have we not finished thinking this thought, but we have not begun. This certainly does not mean that Hölderlin would have thought it and that, contrary to the law of time, we are lagging behind him. I will tell you again: let us not expect anything from him. Kant had not thought the things Hölderlin found in reading him; Hölderlin had not thought what Heidegger deciphered in his work. Nonetheless each one did think the thought of the other. Perhaps this thought has neither end nor beginning. But what do we call thinking? . . .

Yes, let us try to say that this thought—the only one perhaps that this period of history has to think—can no more be begun than finished in our thought. It began for us, but somewhere else, without us, with this period of history but not as its fruit, nor its reason, nor its genius.

This thought itself, the most precise and the most incisive, is not *one* thought, with its order, its sequence and the *telos* of its concept. It begins where it ends, it ends at the point where, as a thought, it begins. The most painful aspect of our epoch is that currently we still believe that philosophy could be the construction of a thought about the world, the dared graph of a trajectory of definitions, evaluations, interpretations, and prescriptions, with which one could measure, calculate, provoke or animate a meaning [*sens*]. But the *one* of meaning in meaning does not come about. It is not that there is no meaning. But the non-advent of the one of meaning is the only thing that counts in meaning. May this unique thing outlive meaning in meaning! "Hölderlin" is for us the name of this living on, which is why he does and does not efface himself, for us, differently from all the others. Whence the excess of forgetting and celebration.

Is enough attention paid to the fact that Hyperion is a survivor in the present of the novel, a survivor of war, of love, and of philosophy? The story of his life is made up of all of his letters, but his life has not yet ended. It has not brought him to any ending, except itself—his life is unended, and yet complete, deposited on its limit, on a Greek hillside. He lives it over again; he outlives it. He is himself beyond himself, he is nothing but this life—this limited existence—infinitely so. He is thus both at home with himself, and elsewhere, with and without Diotima, incessantly confronted by an end that ends nothing:

> Like an immense shipwreck, when the gales have been hushed and the sailors have fled and the corpse of the shattered fleet lies on the sandbank unrecognizable, so before us lay Athens, and the forsaken pillars stood before us like the bare tree trunks of a wood that at evening was still green and, the same night, went up in flames.
>
> "Here," said Diotima, "one learns to accept one's own fate in silence, be it good or bad."
>
> "Here," I continued, "one learns to accept all things in silence."[24]

It is perhaps thus that "the demand for unity and eternity in every moment"[25] is paradoxically accomplished.

Continuation

The point is that eternity and unity can in truth only exist in the moment, in the passage of the moment that the moment itself is. (In this respect, the passage is almost like the Hegelian *Moment*; the latter, however, as the "moment" of force of a lever, unfailingly elevates everything whose truth only passes by.) That time should be the form of inner meaning—the amorphous form and empty substance of the subject—is Kant's transcendental condition (that is to say, precisely, not transcendental, and not immanent either: thinking the transcendental condition means thinking the limit of thought) to which Hölderlin submits his entire thinking about the One.

> At the outermost limit of suffering there persists nothing but the conditions of time or of space.
>
> In this, man forgets himself, because he is entirely within the moment; the god forgets himself, because he is nothing but time; and

both are unfaithful, time because in such a moment it swerves categorically and in it beginning and end absolutely cannot rhyme; man because in this moment he must follow the categorical turn, and by in what follows absolutely cannot be equal to what was in the beginning.[26]

The *categorical* turning of time is nothing other than time "itself," its imperious succession and separation. The imperative (with the idea of rigor, of decisiveness) is of course connoted by the term "categorical" (and doubtless, as you will see further on, more than connoted). But the *categorical* in Kant refers back first of all (and for the imperative itself) to the concept of *categorical judgment*, which is none other than the simple attribution of a predicate to a subject. It affirms the pure position of an inherence, the property of a substance. Thus: "Time . . . has nothing abiding."[27] The concept of this time that "turns," deviates or turns away (and man with it), is stated in the title of the essay "Das Werden im Vergehen," *the becoming in passing away.*

> The declining fatherland, nature and men: insofar as they stand in a particular reciprocal relation, insofar as they constitute a *particular* world that has become ideal and a connection of things, and insofar as they dissolve, whereby out of this relation and out of the remaining generative powers and the remaining forces of nature—which are the other, real principle—a new world, a new, yet particular reciprocal relation forms itself, just as that decline emerged from a pure, though particular world. For the world of all worlds, the all in all, which always *is*, only *presents* itself in all time—whether in the decline or in the moment or, more genetically, in the becoming of the moment and at the beginning of time and a world.[28]

Hyperion *is* (when he writes, but he is only there, only at the moment that is the moment of the novel) at all times of his life, and at all times he is simply his becoming in his passing, the blossoming or declining—blossoming *hence* declining—of his particular existence (and as you have just read, there is no total existence). Thus, perpetuating his blossoming in his decline, he is nothing but reminiscence—the story that is constituted by his letters:

Thus dissolution as necessity, from the viewpoint of ideal memory, becomes as such the ideal object of a newly unfolded life, a look back at the path that had to be traversed from the beginning of the dissolution up to where out of this new life a memory occurs of what was dissolved, and out of that, as explanation and unification of the gap and the contrast that occur between what is new and the past, the memory of the dissolution can follow. This ideal dissolution is fearless. The beginning- and endpoint are already posited, found, secured; therefore this dissolution is also more certain, more irresistible, bolder; and thus it presents itself as what it actually is, as a reproductive act whereby life runs through all of its points and, to acquire the sum total, lingers over none, dissolves itself in each, to produce itself in the next.[29]

As you can read for yourself: this is how the sum total is acquired. But did you read carefully? The sum total *is* dissolution.

Thus in its memory dissolution becomes, because both its ends are firmly fixed, entirely the certain, inexorable, bold act that it actually is.

Every period in its dissolution and production is endlessly interwoven with the total feeling of dissolution and production, and everything in pain and joy, in strife and peace, in movement and repose, in form and formlessness endlessly penetrates, touches, and ignites, and thus a divine fire, instead of an earthly one, takes effect.[30]

The divine is always the dissonance of unity and of separation. The divine *is* thus the dissonance of the divine and the human. This is the categorical turn of the divine in Hölderlin. It includes the Kantian idea of the sublime, which is the idea of presenting the impossibility of the One's presentation. But Hölderlin does not content himself with including it. The divine is no longer subjectivity's judgment of its own insufficiency; it is this insufficiency (and this excess). In a sense, then, it presents this insufficiency: but in another sense, it entails a withdrawal of presence from the very heart of what Kant named "negative presentation" (and in this sense, Hölderlin attaches less importance than Kant to the sublime possibilities of nature or art; Hölderlin believes less in poetry . . .). Divine (poetic) existence consists of remembering this dissolution, because every particularity dissolves, and only exists by virtue of this passing—which is not a past (the being-present in and of the past), but the passing itself, with no other truth than its passing. ("Time, which is the only form of our inner intuition, has nothing lasting about it, and consequently only allows us to know the change of determinations, and not the object to be determined.")[31] Thus the One fails divinely to come about, but passes and becomes as it passes, remembering itself but exceeding itself anew, coming to pass and brimming over in remembrance itself.

It is almost as if "Das Werden im Vergehen" appears at the end of the *Phenomenology of Spirit*—it is perhaps even, to all intents and purposes, precisely this end of Absolute Knowledge, in which the Spirit brims over in the foam of its infinity (but then this quasi-identity has two sides, if not a double edge: for Hegel asserts this brimming over of infinity by the sharp turn that his discourse takes in the final quotation of two lines from Schiller).

(. . . Why would Hegel not have quoted his friend? These lines, for example, from "To the Ether":

> . . . and out of your eternal fullness
> Streams the soul-giving air through all the reeds of life.[32]

—or these, from *Empedocles*:

> And recalling his origins, he seeks
> Life, living beauty, and opens up
> Out of pleasure in the presence of the Pure.[33]

Yes, why would Hegel not . . . ?)

Here the difference between them cannot, perhaps, be appreciated. Both Hegel *and* Hölderlin oppose Kant's time with a recapturing of time by time itself, the remembrance that restores becoming to being, the perishable to the divine. Both of them thus inaugurate the modern age, which for us is still dedicated to their memory. There is no difference between them: except that for Hegel it is history; Hölderlin is the poet that enacts remembrance, recollection, and resurrection. This difference is in its turn of no significance for the form or perhaps the nature of this remembrance, of no significance for the reappropriation of the past. One should not take at face value the incompleteness of Hölderlin's essays, their moments of awkwardness and their singular complications, which occasionally confound a mind that, unlike Hegel's, did not invent the absolute mastery of the speculative, but that *wants* the speculative no less: wanting, here, is more of a commitment than succeeding is. (As you see, here I am skirting, fringing Lacoue-Labarthe's "Caesura of the Speculative.") And Hegel's success is perhaps less, or a different kind, of a commitment to mastery than is believed—at least in the *Phenomenology.* Hölderlin, along with Hegel and before him, brings idealism to a close; he organizes it around this "harmoniously opposed ONE," a formula that is, in a sense, the emblem of "Das Werden im Vergehen."

But the difference between history and the poet is not insignificant for the *subject* of remembrance, and therefore of unification. History, the becoming of Spirit that moves from the self to its recollection, is time itself becoming one: here the structure and the process are those of the subject. The same cannot be said of the poet: he is not time itself; he does not give it its substance. The poet is Hyperion (the Father of the Sun, or the Sun itself; Hyperion does not stop at the zenith, nor at the nadir; he is the Sun's course, its rising and setting—Hyperion whose name begins and ends with the same letters as Hölderlin, as Joseph Claverie pointed out in *La Jeunesse de Hölderlin jusqu'au roman de Hypérion,* a book whose author died in the First World War without having completed it . . .).

He is also, then, what one might otherwise term a "subject": an individual, someone, a singularity. A posthumous fragment contains the following: "The *apriority* of the singular over the whole." "Poet" denotes the apriority of someone, of a someone. But some *one* is not *One.* Even the poem entitled "The Only One" speaks of the oneness of Christ only within the multiplicity of Divine Beings. The term "poet" denotes the apriority of the singular [*l'individuel*] that is not *one,* but is the necessary (narrow, restricting, anguishing) *passage* of the nonadvent of the One.

> Whether it's early or late, always a measure exists,
> Common to all, though his own to each one is also allotted,
> Each of us makes for the place, reaches the place that he can.[34]

This *a priori*, whose content owes nothing to Kant, preserves the general essence of apriority, that is, of the transcendental: within it the limit of thought is thought through, and a limit is set to the constitution of the whole. The constitution of the *whole*, if it exists, depends on the condition of possibility of the singular, thus of non-totality. *Hen kai pan* is a disjunctive conjunction. It is not so much that the individual is a part (Hölderlin raises doubts on that point too) as that he is resolutely not-one. Non-unity is the condition of identity:

> The Ego is only possible through the separation of the Ego from the Ego. How can I say "I!" without self-consciousness? But how is self-consciousness possible? Through this: that I oppose myself to myself, separate myself from myself, yet despite that separation recognize myself as the same in what has been opposed. But to what extent the same? I can, I must pose the question in this way; for in another respect it is opposed to itself. Thus identity is not the union of the object and the subject, which would happen absolutely; thus identity is not = to absolute Being.[35]

But it is on this condition that there can also be the particular *whole* of beauty in works of art. Or rather: the condition of individuality is realized as beauty; put another way, beauty's singular totality is the condition of individuality, itself the condition of the whole. Beauty makes itself "known" through its passage, through its *passing* within the poem (the poem *is not* beauty, but beauty passes through it). The work is not for Hölderlin an *opus*, or the infinite of Romantic *Dichtung*, but the place and *time* of a passing, which is not the passage *of* beauty, but beauty itself in its irreconcilable sameness.

> When [the poet] has finally understood how the conflict between spiritual content and ideal form on the one hand, and between material change and identical progression on the other hand is reconciled at resting points and culminating moments, and that, insofar as

they cannot be reconciled in these moments, they also become in these moments, and precisely for this reason, perceptible and felt, when the poet has understood this, then. . . .[36]

Then we have an example of what Benjamin has described: "In the true work of art, pleasure is able to make itself elusive, to live in the moment, to vanish and renew itself" (*The Origin of German Tragic Drama*).

Or to put it yet another way: one can ask oneself whether, after Hölderlin, lasting beauty still deserves its name. Beauty turns into the passage of beauty. "The poet" *is* the—categorical—singularity of this turning. It is thus that Hölderlin thinks beauty starting out from the One without a concept—starting out from Kant. He thinks the very disappearance of the One, whose presence Kant, despite everything, still wanted to preserve.

Continuation

When Hyperion writes, he has certainly passed through the circles of experience in the classical—and Romantic—manner of the heroes of his time, and in the manner of the Hegelian Spirit. But he does not elevate himself to finish above this life, and neither does he leave it behind. He relieves and outlives it. He is what he has been: neither a hero nor, to tell the truth, a demigod, but a *man*, an *individual* close to the divine (close to love, to Greece, to beauty, and to philosophy), losing this proximity as it comes about. This explains, no doubt, why this novel, unlike all of its models or contemporaries, has aged so little or so well, as they say. *Hyperion* always tells us something about our intellectual adventures, our wars, our loves, our resolutions, and our returns to Greece. Do not mistake this for the subjectivity of a "literary judgment." *Hyperion's* form is in all respects that of *allegory* in the sense that Benjamin identified: writing about a world of broken fragments, all referring to each other without forming an organic whole, the amorphous form of the "incompleteness and brokenness of the sensible, beautiful *physis*" and the metamorphosis of the "ancient Gods into their dead thingness" (*Origin of German Tragic Drama*). Hyperion is not an "allegorical character" but an allegory, a non-unified (artificial, even, for that very reason, deceitful) writing. He is *the writing of the disaster* as Blanchot understands it, and even as Blanchot writes it: in its very composition that book is almost another *Hyperion*.

Hyperion shares everyone's error, uncertainty, and fault—the *brilliant poverty* of human culture of which Kant speaks. Like all of us, he does not do what he would like to; he wants what he cannot do; he does not do what he says. He leaves Diotima for a war of liberation that turns into banditry:

> And many a Greek in Morea will hereafter narrate our heroic deeds to his children's children as a tale of robbers.
>
> Bands of madmen are bursting in on every side; rapacity rages like the plague in Morea, and he who does not also take the sword is hunted down and slain, and withal the maniacs say they are fighting for our freedom.[37]

However:

> But let not pity, now or ever, lead you astray. Believe me, there is one joy left for us everywhere. True grief inspires. He who steps on his misery stands higher. And it is glorious that only in suffering do we truly feel freedom of soul. Freedom! if any understand the word—it is a deep word, Diotima.[38]

. . . .

Here there is, properly speaking, no reconciliation. There is only, forever, what remains in mourning. What remains is a joy. This joy is freedom. But this word is only understood by the poet—(and) by Diotima. That amounts to exactly the opposite of what people believe: not that the poet alone (being privileged by the gods, or inspired) understands freedom, but that the person who understands it will be named poet (or Diotima). What, then, does it mean to understand freedom? It entails affirming simply this: "The law of freedom *commands*, however, without any consideration for nature's help. Whether or not nature supports the exercise of the law, the law commands. Rather, it presupposes a resistance in nature; otherwise it would not *command*."[39]

Understanding freedom is not conceiving (and it is ultimately with Kant that freedom as something inconceivable, the inconceivable *as* freedom, originates)—it is not conceiving, but receiving: welcoming and upholding an order. This is where the categorical turning of time, of man, and of beauty becomes imperative. Hölderlin, despite everything, despite his thirst for poetry as a beautiful form—as an advent of the One in beauty, as a reconciled philosophy—attempted to think "the poet" (this name matters little; it henceforth means its opposite: this *poète* does not *produce*—after Hölderlin, poetry is only the disappearance of a production; it is, or must be, the shadow or parody of itself) as the one who upholds the law, and not as the one who causes the One to open up. That he who upholds the law should have a relationship to beauty was something Kant did not think—he glimpsed it perhaps, but he nonetheless subordinated beauty to morality. Hölderlin does not subordinate—*if taken to the limit . . .*, but then he is nothing but limit—either of the two. By thinking them *together* (and perhaps by no longer thinking either beauty or morality as such), he thinks the unity that cannot go to *make* the One. The difference between Hölderlin and Kant is equivalent here to the difference between Hölderlin and Hegel. It is thus in us, for us, the difference between us and *all* our past, the difference between us and ourselves.

The One does not come about, because the law commands. Command implies a gap, a distance, and a hardness. It excludes the fusion between whoever obeys and whoever commands—however desirable that may be. And what commands is not a "who," not *one*, but—the law (of freedom). No one gives the order, someone receives it, it is the order to be *one*; but this one does not *come about* in whoever is only defined, in his limited existence, by the fact that he receives this order: *factum rationis*, Kant would say.

Hölderlin thinks the poet as the one who receives the order and upholds it:

> Him, the most High, should I name then? A god does not love
> what's unseemly,
> Him to embrace and to hold our joy is too small.

Silence often behooves us: deficient in names that are holy,
　　Hearts may beat high, while the lips hesitate, wary of
　　　speech?
Yet a lyre to each hour lends the right mode, the right music,
　　And, it may be, delights heavenly ones who draw near.
This make ready, and almost nothing remains of the care that
　　Darkened our festive day, troubled the promise of joy.
Whether he likes it or not, and often, a singer must harbour
　　Cares like these in his soul, even if others do not.

The poets, and those no less who
Are spiritual, must be worldly.

　　And hence it is that without danger now
The sons of Earth drink heavenly fire.
Yet, fellow poets, us it behooves to stand
Bare-headed. . . .[40]

For us, Hölderlin should not be anything that we can take as our
authority, or model, or oracle (and his difference from all of our
past is also his difference from Heidegger's Hölderlin, who is,
moreover, the greatest of Hölderlins—but Hölderlin is not "great").
He is the one who communicates only this to us: "*us it behooves to
stand / Bare-headed. . . .*"

We do not possess what thus behooves us, and this causes us to
suffer. However, we should repeat what comes back to us: "*Little
knowledge, but much joy / Is granted to mortals.*"

With the memory and the stigmata of his misfortunes, in a
homeland that has become a place of exile, Hyperion finds joy. But
joy is not something that can be found and gathered up. Joy is in
the mourning for joy.

"I now live on Ajax's island, dear Salamis.

"I love all of this Greece. It wears the colors of my heart. Wherever
you look, a joy lies buried.

"And yet there is so much that is delightful, so much that is great,
about one."

"I play with Fate and the Three Sisters, the holy Parcae. Full of
divine youth, my whole being rejoices over itself, over all things."[41]

What remains in mourning is not something that is conserved, reserved, or sublated. Mourning, here, is not a lament that is completed, but a dissolution that is repeated—with so much grace and greatness. What Hyperion's joy *is*, is not inexpressible: it seeks neither to be expressed nor thought. It remains silent, without stealing away, without stealing or holding back anything else. This joy is the *a priori* of the very apriority of the singular over the whole. It *is* infinite life in a limited existence: but it *is* nothing, it does not come about, and it brims over itself. Hyperion's joy essentially *passes*, it passes because it *comes to pass*, it is only insofar as it comes to pass—without coming about.

Hölderlin to Bellarmin

> And a desire endlessly yearns for that
> Which is unbound. There is much to
> Hold on to. One *must* be faithful.

> Let me now fall silent. To say more would be excessive.
> We will doubtless meet again.[42]

. . . .
. . . .

(Hölderlin, alone, writing)

"It is through joy that you will try hard to understand the pure in general, men and all living beings; it is thanks to this joy that you will grasp all that is essential and characteristic, all of the successive chains: repeat to yourself in their conjunction all of the parts that make up this chain, until living perception bursts forth once again more objectively than thought, through joy, before the need arises; intelligence, which proceeds only from necessity, is always biased.

Still, at other times, looking out to sea, I think I am seeing my life over again, its ebb and flow, its happiness and mourning, and I think I hear."[43]

TRANSLATED BY CHRISTINE LAENNEC
AND MICHAEL SYROTINSKI

§ The Decision of Existence

I

We propose here a partial study of "decision" in *Being and Time*. More precisely, we propose to study an aspect of the ensemble or series formed by "disclosedness" (*Erschlossenheit*), "decisiveness" (*Entschlossenheit*), and "decision" (*Entscheidung*).[1] We propose no more than the study of a single aspect, for it is out of the question, in this context, to envisage an exhaustive commentary on the system of these three terms in the totality of the book (which itself no doubt obeys this "system" throughout). This aspect will be provisionally defined, at the threshold of our study, as *the mundanity of decision*. By this we mean to say that decision is not open to, or decided by anything other than, the world of existence itself, to which the existent is thrown, given up, and exposed. Decision decides neither in favor of nor by virtue of any "authenticity" whereby the world of existence would be surmounted or transfigured in any way whatsoever. The decision is made (it grasps itself, is grasped by itself, surprises itself) right in ontical experience, and it opens to ontical experience. In fact, there is no other experience, and only in illusion could our decision claim to decide for and within another "world" (and yet even illusion is part of experience . . .). Ontical experience takes place *right at the "they,"*[2] and nowhere else. Moreover, there is no "elsewhere": that is the "meaning [*Sinn*] of Being," and that is exactly what is represented by the major existential characteristic of decision, or by the decided character of existence, or again by the fact that existence is, as such, the *decision of existence*.

We understand (*we*: this time, "you"; beforehand, "I"; each time yours, each time mine—*jemein*—and each time ours, for we can *understand* only in common, and *we* are also, paradoxically, each time singularity, community, and the experience of these, as well as the misrecognition of that experience, misrecognition and misunderstanding *as* experience—so that *we* are each time implicated in the "*they*," an implication that could be called "*jeman*")—we understand, then, the stakes of a precise and determined interpretation, of an interpretation clearly decided in favor of the mundanity of decision.[3] It renders unacceptable any interpretation privileging a decision that would be taken in favor of (and on the basis of) something beyond experience, call it what you will—"Being," "history," "destiny," "ideal," "spiritual mission," etcetera.[4]

A decision in favor of an understanding elaborated in keeping with the mundanity of decision is taken in the current of Heidegger's text, and just in that very text. If decision, for this very reason, must at one point or another also understand that text against itself (which, in the end, will amount to the slightest of differences, but this difference will be decisive), it is because the text, like all those that open thought to itself, must in turn be reopened and redecided by what comes to it from far outside itself, from far ahead, in thought and in experience—from the "advance" of experience and of existence, which always precedes thought and which, in truth, decides its course and brings it to its decision.

I I

Let us establish the horizon of the analysis that is to follow. For this, a few initial considerations are necessary: these are, indeed, the principles of the existential analytic (even if they are not made explicit as such). That is, they engage the philosophical decision from which the analytic proceeds.

This philosophical decision is not a decision taken with respect to a plurality of possible philosophical attitudes (at least it cannot be reduced to that, no more than any veritable philosophy can be). Rather, it is philosophy's decision to be what it is. That is, not the "true," the "only," the "authentic" philosophy, but the philosophizing that decides to philosophize (or to think—here, we will not make any distinction between the two). Philosophizing decides to think, not when it grasps a specific "philosophical problem," although it may be a remarkable problem, one authorized by the noblest of traditions, but rather when it grasps the fact that existence unfolds in the midst of an understanding of Being, and the fact that, while understanding Being in a "*vague, average*" manner,[5] existence finds itself, in a wholly exceptional and precise way, in an *essential* (that is, *existentiell*) relation to its own understanding. This is the relation of "philosophy," or of "thought." Thought is a decision in favor of the understanding-of-Being that existence *is*, or rather in favor of the understanding-of-Being according to which existence reaches its decision—which, *above all*, is *not* to say that philosophy is decisive *for* the understanding of Being! It is exactly the opposite. The understanding-of-Being that reaches its decision to be what it is (or not to be what it is) is decisive for the "philosophical" gesture (which philosophy, as actually practiced, may well forget or betray). The philosophical gesture does not open onto the well-insulated domain of "theoretical" investigation; rather, it is itself a gesture of the existent as such. Heidegger writes, "The roots of the existential analytic . . . are ultimately *existentiell*, that is, *ontical*. Only if the inquiry of philosophical research is itself seized upon in an existentiell manner, as a possibility of the Being of each existing Dasein, does it become at all possible to disclose the existentiality of existence."[6] *Thought in its decision is not the thought that undertakes to found Being (or to found itself in Being). This thought is only the decision that risks and affirms existence on its own absence of ground.* But, quite clearly, this decision itself is not a decision taken by "thought" about (or in favor of) existence. Here, it is existence that reaches its own decision, as thought.[7]

Given this qualification (which, in short, engages the contract of a philosophical decision of *reading*, as will soon be seen more clearly), we will ask: Does the essence of decision reside in the fact that it cuts through to something, or in the fact that it is itself cut, exposed, opened—on its very incision, so to speak? We will no doubt have to respond with both hypotheses. Unquestionably, decision cuts through. In the *existentiell* decision, a knot of already present possibilities is severed. But what, under the rubric of "decision," is envisaged as an *existentiale* is not *another* decision (which would cut through higher possibilities, at another level of sublation). Indeed, "one would completely misunderstand the phenomenon of decisiveness if one should want to suppose that this consists simply in taking up possibilities which have been proposed and recommended, and seizing hold of them. *Decision is precisely the disclosive projection and determination of what is factually possible at the time.*"[8] In the *existentiale* of decision, it is a question of what "possibilizes" the possibilities, of what, each time, makes them possible for an existence (and makes them the possibilities of an existence). Therefore, it is a question of what makes the existent exist as a function of possibility: as the entity that in its Being has its very Being at issue *as* possibility, and consequently has its Being as the (in)decidability of existence. Existence is the decision to exist (and/or not to exist), and thus to decide (and/or not to decide). But "to be or not to be" are not previously present possibilities. Existence alone, insofar as it is itself thrown to the indecidability of "to be or not to be," decides their status as possibilities. But if this is so, it is only because existence itself has no essence (which would be, for it, a previously given possibility/necessity), or because existence is itself its own essence.

"The essence of this entity [Dasein] lies in its 'to-be' (*Zu-Sein*). Its Being-what-it-is (*essentia*) must, so far as we can speak about it at all, be conceived in terms of its Being (*existentia*). . . . *The 'essence' of Dasein lies in its existence*. Accordingly the characteristics which can be exhibited in this entity are not 'properties' present-at-hand . . . ; they are each time possible ways for it to be."[9]

The "essence," here, is in the "possibility," what is "each time possible" for Dasein. The existent *has* nothing, it *is* everything that

it "has" (its "characteristics"). It *is*—that is, it *exists.* "To exist," in
this transitive sense, would mean to bring forth, to let come forth
in advance of the self, the very possibility of being (the self). To
bring forth Being, and to let Being come forth as its own Being.
But Being is not a property. The single property of the existent's
Being is found, on the contrary, in its advent to existence, and
consequently in its "advance" on existence or, if you like, in its
"Being-offered" to existence, by reason of which it is unappropriable. If the existent appropriates something—that is, if it exists this
thing—what it exists is never anything but the advance and the
offering of Being. This, more strictly, is not an advance or an
offering *of* Being, since the latter is not "something" (it is only the
fact *that there is* something in general). By existing, the existent
makes the advance and the offering, as such, its own. It becomes
itself advance and offering of existence.

This is what "possibility" means. The relation to the "possible" is
nothing other than the relation of existence to itself—which, let us
note in passing, is what constitutes the unsubjectivable mode of the
Being of a singular "subject": a relation to the "self" wherein the
"self" is the "possible." But the relation to the possible is that of
(in)decision. (In)decision is therefore the ownmost mode of the
existent's Being (its mode of being "advanced" and "offered"). In
(in)decision, the existent proves to be passible to the decision by
which and *as* which it can exist, or rather by which and as which its
existence can make *sense.*[10] The existential possibility of sense is
inscribed in the passibility to decision. Existence as such is "essentially" and incessantly passible to a decision, its decision.

Thus decision, in this sense (in a sense that no meaning of the
word "decision" will suffice to open, or to decide), is what most
escapes existence, or it is that to which and in which existence is
most properly thrown—*and* what offers existence its most proxi-
mate, its ownmost or most intimate, advent: *Ereignis.*

We should say: *Ereignis is,* or *makes,* decision, and decision is, or
makes, *Ereignis.*

But exactly what that means cannot simply be presented as a
theme or a thesis produced by thought. Here we must embark on

"a path that leads ahead . . . and lets itself be shown what it is brought to."[11] The thought of decision must consist in a decision of thought that lets itself be shown the decided-/deciding-Being of existence. Now, thought will not *let* itself be shown anything of the sort if it does not render itself passible to the decision of existence— that is, if it does not let itself, in its ownness, be offered (to) an experience that it does not make its own. The thought of decision is thought *at the limit* of the decision that already has brought it, *existentielly*, into play as thought. The thought of decision can have nothing to do with any "decisionism" that might descend from on high to cut through to specific possibilities and objectives of existence. On the contrary, "decision" is, for this thought, the undecidable "object" par excellence. Thought lets itself be thrown before this "object" with all the force of decision itself. In this way, thought *is nothing but the exercise of the appropriation of decision, which lets itself be shown that the decision of this appropriation always precedes it, and does not belong to it.* Nowhere else do we grasp with equal intensity the degree to which "thought" is neither "abstract" nor "gratuitous," and the degree to which it is *finite*—that is, the degree to which it is the infinitely open inscription of the finite-Being of existence.

I I I

Each term of the verbal sequence "*Erschlossenheit–Entschlossenheit–Entscheidung*" overlaps the preceding one, so to speak, composing a thematic consecutiveness (even, and why not, a system, and perhaps *the* system of *Being and Time*[12]). This overlapping sequence corresponds to nothing other than the growing concentration and determination of the same instance: it is the "disclosedness" that, as "decisiveness" (or "decidedness," in the two senses of the word "decided"), provides the occasion for, and effects itself as, "decision." (*Entscheidung* could also be translated literally as "cutting separation," and therefore as "opening separation.") In other words, decision and disclosedness are linked from the start in an essential way, and their link is formed in the term *Entschlossen-*

heit (which as *Ent-schlossenheit* means "openedness"). In other words, then, the activity, the mastery, and the authority implied by decision are in intimate composition with the passivity and the abandonment of disclosedness, of the opening up.

We will be ceaselessly preoccupied with this intimate composition. But we must come to an understanding here. The passivity of decision cannot be identical to just any passivity—but it also cannot be a dialectical coupling of activity and passivity. The *act* of decision has, precisely, the highly singular property of an action that is not an action "on" the given world or an action outside the world; rather, it is the action of thrown Being right in the world. What kind of passivity is in action here, and how does it determine decision's own action?

We will broach the answer by reading one of the first passages where "decision" takes center stage in *Being and Time*. This passage also concerns reading, decision in reading, as well as, no doubt, the decision or decisions that bear on the reading in which we find ourselves engaged: the reading of the book *Being and Time* itself— that is, the reading of the assertions [*énoncés*] that explicate the existential analytic.

This passage speaks of reading, considered as an extension of the reception of ordinary speech in the manner of the "they"—that is, as an extension of the type of discourse we have become used to translating in French as *bavardage* (*das Gerede* or, in English, "idle talk": a familiar, too familiar, motif of the analytic of the "they"). We know the context in which *Gerede* is introduced: it appears as the first, indeed as the primordial, ontical form of "understanding" (we could call it "*on-tique*"[13]). The latter, always inseparable from "state-of-mind" [*Befindlichkeit*; also the state of being affected] constitutes the Being-open of Dasein insofar as it is thrown to the world. First of all, in its Being or as its Being, Dasein is thrown in or to "the disclosedness of Being-in-the-world."[14] This disclosedness is not the disclosedness *of* something or of someone (of some subject) that previously had been closed off. On the contrary, Dasein (and this is one of the reasons for giving it this singular name, or rather this "title") has its Being—the Being of existence,

which makes up its essence—in Being-open. The open is determined as affective-comprehensive ("Affection always has its understanding. . . . Understanding always has its mood."[15] We will
recall this inmixing when we see the reappearance of decision's
"basic moods.")

"Understanding" determined as "clarification"[16] has been ap-
prehended previously in speech, which is "*equiprimordial with
affection and understanding.*"[17] At this stage, Heidegger finds it
necessary to recall that the existential analytic has "Dasein's everydayness" as its "phenomenal horizon."[18] Consequently, "the disclosedness of Being-in-the-world" must be grasped according to
the precise mode of "the disclosedness of the 'they.' "[19] (An amphi-
bology is concealed in this expression "the disclosedness of the
'they.' " Dasein is opened to the "they," to which it is thrown as to
its everyday world; this means, in the way we ordinarily understand
it, to a world of mediocre and "inauthentic" banality from which
Dasein should *decide* to extract itself. But the expression can also
signify—and *must* signify, according to the deepest logic of analysis—that the "they" carries disclosedness along with it, gives disclosedness, and even that it is, before everything else, the site of
disclosedness. Before everything else: But what else would there be?
What other world? Isn't the *everyday* the place, and the taking-
place, of the *each time* according to which existence appropriates its
singularity?)

"Idle talk" offers the first form of the everydayness of Dasein.
Das Gerede: this is *Rede*, speech, as a globality of communication
in which we talk "with one another" but still do not "participate"
in "the primary relationship-of-Being toward the entity talked
about."[20] This "communication" does not "communicate" ("die
Mitteilung 'teilt' nicht") the understanding-affection of the entity's
Being, from which it nevertheless proceeds or, better yet, of which
it is the "thrown" or "open" site. Instead, this "communication"
chains speech to itself, drags speech over itself, is the "re-saying"
(*Nach-rede*) of speech.[21] The theme of *Gerede* therefore indicates
much less a critique of chatter than the necessity of understanding
this: in the prattle or, if you will, the parlor of speech, in the

originary re-saying of speech, understanding as the disclosedness of
Being to existence both gives and withdraws itself, opens itself up
and closes itself off, already.

It is difficult, at the very least, to avoid saying that something is
"lost" in this. This is the difficulty with all our discourse, where the
negative is stamped with a sign of diminution, of shortfall or
decline. But we know that the analytic will vigorously oppose the
interpretation of *verfallen* everydayness ("quotidienneté échéante,"
as Martineau renders it) in terms of decline or deterioration. What
is lost in this must therefore be understood as the "loss" in the
"they" by which the disclosedness of Dasein *is truly opened*—just as
by sinking deeper, by losing ourselves in the reading of the philosophical text, not by rising above it, we will have some chance of
opening ourselves to what it "says," although that "saying" is also a
blotting out.

This may very well be what is at issue when Heidegger extends—
in a way that is rather unexpected (and seemingly unnecessary, at
first glance: that is, for the "average understanding" of the "they,"
that is, "we," the readers of the text)—*Gerede* to a *Geschreibe*
["scribbling"],[22] the globality of speech to a globality of writing:[23]

> And indeed this idle talk is not confined to vocal gossip, but even
> spreads to what we write, where it takes the form of "scribbling" [*das
> Geschreibe*]. In this latter case the gossip is not based so much upon
> hearsay. It feeds upon superficial reading [*dem Angelesenen*].[24] The
> average understanding of the reader will *never be able* to decide what
> has been drawn from primordial [*ursprünglich*] sources with a struggle
> and how much is just gossip. The average understanding, moreover,
> will not want any such distinction, and does not need it, because, of
> course, it understands everything.[25]

What follows names only *Gerede* and pursues on its account the
clarification of the "average understanding" as a "closing-off" (*Ver-
schliessen*) of the primordial understanding, as an obstruction, a
repression, or an immobilization of the "primary and primordial
relationships" with the world and with the existent's Being. What,
then, was the use of the supplementary and apparently superfluous

example of writing and reading? It seems to have introduced—but only fleetingly, and without any return to it in this context—the theme of *decision*. Access to originary understanding (and to the originary affective mood), access to Being as to what is most properly at play in existence, depends on a decision, which would make a distinction and which would cut through average understanding to understanding proper. Now average understanding, from the outset, closes off all possibility of acceding to such a distinction, as well as all possibility of even envisaging access to it, because it "understands everything." The closing-off is proportional to the opening up, and each takes place just at the other. The "average understanding" of the "*they*" is by itself the closing-off of access *to its own difference*, to the difference in understanding between the understanding of speech and the understanding of what is spoken of. This difference can therefore also be articulated as the difference between understanding Being (and feeling Being), on the one hand, and understanding and feeling an entity, on the other. The understanding of an entity is not understood as the understanding of Being; that is, it is not understood as what it actually is, as its own difference. But is this understanding's inability to accede to itself (and the affect's corresponding inability) not, perhaps, the final lot of an understanding that, as the grasp of (and by) Being, is the grasp of no entity, of *nothing* that is—but only of *Being*-delivered-over to entities, which is existence? Or would appropriation, here, not be identical to the unappropriation of a "difference proper"? The whole question is here—or, rather, the whole *decision* is here.

(In another way, this difference also articulates itself as the difference between the ontical hearing of discourse and the "hearing the voice of the friend whom every Dasein carries with it," which characterizes "hearing" as "the primary and proper way in which Dasein is open for its ownmost potentiality-for-Being."[26] Here, we will not question the identity of this "friend." We will only point out that the distinction to be made, and decided on, is also the difference between the ontical self of the existent (along with the "selves" of others) and the "friend" that the existent carries with it. Neither the same nor the other, the "friend" perhaps names only this difference itself.)

But, again, why writing and reading? Reading, as we have seen, "feeds" on a "harvest," a reaping or a vintage. Reading exemplifies, discreetly (with a discretion whose motives we will grasp better in a moment), the "hearing" of understanding as absorption of what one would, speaking in another style, call the bread and wine of the spirit. Reading exemplifies a communion in communication, a "sharing," a *teilen* that goes as far as consummation.[27] Reading and writing exemplify—still with the same discretion—the most "authentic"[28] essence of sharing-communication as the communion of (to) Being. Thus, in reading, it should be a question of a relationship with "what has been drawn from primordial sources [from the origin] with a struggle." In reading-writing, we see for an instant (at each instant) the half-opening of the possibility-necessity of an access to the originary, and a sharing of this access. In the re-saying of *Rede*, just in speech and the "they-say," we see a half-opening of the sharing of that *of which* we speak, of that *whence* we speak, and of the one *who* speaks (listens).

This is seen *halfway*: Dasein's disclosedness, to that to which it is by its essence open, profiles or evokes itself here. Consequently, the *decision* capable of differentiating the originary, of making the difference in disclosedness itself, also profiles and evokes itself here. It is to the originary that disclosedness is opened (the source opens to the source); by way of the originary and as it, the openness of disclosedness takes place. The originary: the Being of existence open to the world. *Decision* profiles or evokes itself as the making-the-difference of disclosedness in its very self.

IV

It now becomes clear that the example or case of *Geschreibe* is even more determined than we first made it out to be. It is a question, finally, of nothing other than the reading-writing of philosophy, or of thought—and, even more precisely, of the reading-writing of the philosophy or the thought that attempts to think and share the relation of existence to the disclosedness that makes up the essence of existence. The phrase "the average understanding of the reader will *never be able* to decide" offers us an exemplary ambiguity: it is a question both of the reader in general of all writing in general and of the reader (but how could this not be *the same* reader?) of *Being and Time*, of the reader who reads this sentence, at this very moment, right here, each time that we (you, me) read *Being and Time*.

They read—that is, *we* read—without knowing, at first, that we read that; but enough discreet marks have been laid down for *us* to finally "understand" that we cannot decide what it is, in this text, that touches the origin, not even when the "originary" (or "Being," or "disclosedness") is named, thematized, or thought by the assertions of this text—not even then, and perhaps above all not then. The thought of decision at the origin (philosophy, the "science of first principles") says that decision does not belong to the writing-reading of its *own* text. In other words, the discourse set down here has no privilege and is not more appropriate to ownness [see below, section V] than any other (im)proper discourse would be.[29] Even as it thinks through decision, this discourse thinks that it neither appropriates decision nor renders decision more appropriate—and it thinks, moreover, that this is the way it "thinks decision" (understands/is affected by decision), or that it *reaches its decision to decide* (lets "them" reach their decision to decide).

The discourse of the existential analytic is caught up, throughout, in *Gerede*. By simply hearing this discourse, by simply reading it (as *we* do here, for example), we cannot be certain of any access to the originary, or to the "authentic." Here too, here as everywhere else, or—who knows?—here more than anywhere else, we can always content ourselves with speaking about something (about Being or existing) and hearing what is thus re-said, the they-say. We can hear "them" speak about the disclosedness of existence, without in the least being actually opened to (by) this discourse.

This is a classic philosophical gesture. It is customary for the discourse of philosophy to warn its reader that what is to be understood is not within the reach of the ordinary way of understanding the philosophical text. Descartes demands that we accompany the real movement of his meditation rather than judge its discourse alone. Hegel warns us that repeated readings will be necessary to surmount the exteriority of his propositions, and to sublate this exteriority into the pure interiority of thought. Heidegger, in a sense, does nothing else, and a little farther on he indicates—discreetly, once again—what a hearing capable of the "originary" should be turned toward. This hearing would no longer be the hearing of the "reader" as such, turned toward *Geschreibe* as such: to the "curiosity" discussed after "idle talk," Heidegger opposes the bearing and the stance of a "leisure of tarrying observantly," in which is produced the "wonderstruck contemplation of entities—*thaumazein*."[30] In the whole of its tradition, there could be no better way to designate philosophy. There could be no better way to recall, in one and the same movement, the task of a repetitive, reanimating, and liberating "destruction" of that tradition, which is the historial task correlated with the task of the existential analytic. Therefore, there would be no better way to indicate that it is a question of opening or of reopening, in philosophy itself and in the exercise of its communication, the very opening to what is originally at issue in philosophy, which is the experience of Being as the Being of entities. It is a question of reopening the philosophical decision in philosophy itself, of reopening philosophy as decision. And this infinitely exceeds all philosophical demonstration.

Nevertheless, and according to the very logic of such a (re)opening of philosophy to its own open-and-decided-Being (which is also to say, to its own historical *existence*), Heidegger's gesture does not simply reproduce these traditional gestures, even though they remain its models, for in them Heidegger's gesture also confronts the decision that makes them exemplary. It reproduces them to the extent that it makes us understand that what matters is a hearing of which all *Gerede-Geschreibe* is incapable. To this extent, Heidegger simply reproduces philosophy, and with it the idea and the ideal of a pure meaning—absolute, reserved, and floating outside the limits of discourse. But Heidegger also does *not* reproduce these gestures, to the extent that he actually says nothing of the sort, or at least does not say it "in truth."

What is indeed said by the ensemble of the text on *Gerede* is that the situation of *Gerede* (and its exemplification in *Geschreibe*) is itself, in its ownness, the situation of disclosedness—insofar as it is a situation wherein decision is impossible. After having insisted on the "closing off" that is the lot of the "average understanding," section 35 goes so far as to place in this state of closedness the very possibility of disclosedness—that is, the ownmost possibility of existence. The understanding of *Gerede* is "uprooted."[31] But this uprooting is "existential"; that is, it belongs to the constitution-of-Being of existence. ("This uprooting is constant," the text notes.) It is even necessary to say that the uprooting belongs in an essential or archi-essential way to the Being of existence, if the latter must indeed be defined by the property, or archiproperty, of *not having* any essence. *To be* its own essence: such is indeed, as must always be recalled, the property of existence. Being-the-essence is itself without essence (or, rather, its essence is in its decision).

Thus Heidegger can write, "To be uprooted in this manner is a possibility-of-Being only for an entity whose disclosedness is constituted by discourse as characterized by understanding and state-of-mind. . . . Far from amounting to a 'not-Being' of Dasein, this uprooting is rather Dasein's most everyday and most stubborn 'Reality.' "[32] It is therefore in this "reality," it is *as this reality*, that Dasein is properly open. It is as *Gerede-Geschreibe* that *Rede* belongs to existence, and exposes in existence the possibilities of Being-affected and of understanding. No doubt Dasein is "uprooted" in existence, it is cut from its origin, from its origin of Being and from the *Being* of its origin. But this is the way it *is*, insofar as it is in the world. "It holds itself in suspension [*er hält sich in einer Schwebe*]." This suspension *is* the condition and the constitution-of-Being of the existent as such.

In suspension, by definition, decision escapes; it does not take place; it can never take place. To the extent that the uprooting is constant, undecidability is the rule. But absolute precision is necessary here. The nature of this suspension has yet to be understood in a specific way. In no way, contrary to appearances, does it consist in a floating. *Gerede-Geschreibe*, and its hearing-reading, do not float in the mediocre more-or-less of what one takes to be the lax vulgarity of the "they." That would be impossible, because *Rede* in general does not float above existence and the world, nor does it give rise to approximations and nebulosities of sense: "Assertion is not a free-floating kind of behaviour [*kein freischwebendes Verhalten*] which, in its own right, might be capable of disclosing entities in general in a primary way: on the contrary it always maintains itself on the basis of Being-in-the-world."[33]

What was said about assertion goes for the whole sequence that runs from state-of-mind–understanding to the everyday "they speak, they write"—and to the everyday writing and reading of the everyday philosophical text: in all of this, nothing glides above the world, above reality or existence. *All of this, on the contrary, takes place only through Being-in-the-world, all of this takes place only through the taking-place of existence thrown to the world.* (It is easy to prove this: nothing is more constant in *Being and Time*, and nothing better captures its predominant *tone*, than a stubbornly, emphatically drawn contrast between all that could "float" in an "ideal" mode and the throw that, by throwing, suspends Being to the decision of existence.)

Dasein's "suspension" in the everydayness of "average understanding" is therefore not a mediocre floating in average indecision, in vague, more or less myopic glimpses of the "meaning" of existence (and of the world, and of others, and of thought). But the "tenacity" proper to this "suspension" is not a simple firmness opposed, by dualism or dialectic, to floating. *Suspension is suspended, and firmly maintains itself, just in the average ontical floating.* And that is where it decides / reaches its decision.[34] The type of average understanding that "understands everything" can also be the sharpest, most accurate, most perspicacious intelligence. We think, we write, we read philosophy the way *they* think, write, and read. But what we cannot decide in this way is *the originary undecidability of Being-thrown-to-the-world* (to the "*they*"), in which, by which, and as which the Being of existence takes place. To decide its course—to decide on the originary—would be to open its opening, so to speak, or open it to its own opening. But thus mastered and appropriated, that opening up, that disclosedness, would no longer exactly be the opening that it *is*.

What is to be decided is disclosedness's difference from itself, by reason of which (a reason with neither fundament nor reason) *disclosedness cannot be made one's own* and thus is what it is, in its ownness: to exist. Therefore, "to decide" means not to cut through to this or that "truth," to this or that "meaning" of existence—but to expose oneself to the undecidability of meaning that existence *is*. This can take place only *just at* "uprooted" everydayness, and *just at* "the impossibility of deciding."

Right at this everyday Being, there is no ground to stand on. Heidegger goes on to write, "Idle talk discloses to Dasein a Being towards its world, towards Others, and towards itself—a Being in which these are understood, but in a mode of groundless floating."[35] Thus *Gerede* that maintains itself, as *Rede*, in the "basic state" of "Being-in-the-world" immediately dissolves this "basis" in a "floating." But this dissolution—which is nothing other than the fact of *thrown Being*—is not the degradation or the loss of an initial, solid, consistent state. No substantiality is volatilized in the floating. That the ground should be withdrawn from existence is what makes the existent's Being, and what makes the existent be. Or again, the "suspension" is itself the "ground" and the "basis."

In these conditions, how can we distinguish between the basis and the suspension, and how can we decide to discover or to rediscover—and to make our *own*—the ground, the root of existence, its originary Being? Will it suffice to say, as has been said, that we must decide in favor of the impossibility of making the distinction? In one sense, we cannot get beyond this result. But in another sense, the same result seems to offer nothing more than a dazed resignation to the daze of the "they." Heidegger's text never stops wavering between these two directions. The text also floats, is in suspension, does not cease to suspend itself: it is the finite thought of the finite access to the originary Being of existence.

What this thought brings into play is decision: that is, as we see more clearly now, the decision that would distinguish between the decision of disclosedness—disclosedness itself as decision, reaching its decision (to be) open—and decision that closes off. The latter, decision that cuts through—in short, decision proper (according to the sense of the words in the most obvious and persistent *Rede*)— belongs in reality to the reign of the "they." Under this reign, basically, we think that openness "can guarantee to Dasein that all the possibilities of its Being will be secure, genuine, and full. Through the self-certainty and decidedness of the 'they,' it gets spread abroad increasingly that there is no need of understanding proper or of the state-of-mind that goes with it. The supposition of the 'they' that one is leading and sustaining a full and genuine 'life,' brings Dasein a *tranquillity*, for which everything is 'in the best of order' and all doors are open."[36]

Self-assured, reassuring decided-Being, which gives itself or be- lieves it can give itself the guarantee of authenticity,[37] belongs to the reign of closedness. This decidedness is in truth the same one that "will *never be able* to decide" its own relation to what, for it, is properly originary. The essence of veritable "decision," of decision that does justice to the difference of the origin, must therefore be sought elsewhere than in the assurance that cuts through. To be what it is, to exist, Dasein does not have to be a "decider." But it has to decide, and reach its decision in favor of its own existence. Therefore, we will have to distinguish between the two decisions— rather, we will have to decide in favor of what, in decision, properly decides.

V

It is, of course, *just in* all the assured decisions, and all the floating indecisions of the "they," that the *decision of existence*— which is neither "decision" nor "indecision"—comes into play.

That it cannot be a question of two decisions with distinct essences, but that the decision of existence cannot be the *existentiell* decision, becomes clear from everything that has gone before. We are not to leave behind the "they" in order to attain another, more "authentic," register of existence. On the contrary, bringing into play the Being of existence takes place right in existence. *There is no existentiale that is not at once, and as such, caught in the* existentiell. (And this major thesis of the analytic is simultaneously the thesis in which the status of thought as existential thought comes into play: the latter, as well as thought in general, thinks only while being at once and as such caught up in the *existentiell* possibilities of its writing, its reading, and its [mis]understanding.) For this reason, Dasein's thrownness and "fallenness" do not constitute the decline of a superior form of existence into an inferior form. "Dasein *can* fall only *because* Being-in-the-world understandingly with a state-of-mind is an issue for it. On the other hand, existence *in its owness* is not something which floats above falling everydayness; existentially, it is only a modified grasp in which such everydayness is seized upon."[38]

This last sentence is *decisive* for the understanding of the analytic in its largest dimensions. This sentence plays out decision on the decision. Indeed, it asserts that the *owness* of existence—its own truth, its own sense—*does not distinguish itself in any way* from what could be called *existentiell* existence except insofar as the former is a "modified grasp" of the latter. The essence of the decision in favor of the originary—and the originary essence of decision—can consist only in this "modification" of the grasp. But, reciprocally, this "modification" (change of mode: from the *Modus* of the "floating" to the *Modus* of the "decision," but without any change of the "ground," that is, "suspension"), this modification, about which the text teaches us nothing else, can be determined only as the stakes, even the act, of decision.

Here, before continuing, it is necessary to introduce an issue of translation that will intrude from now on, one that the available translations already present, which concerns the word "authentic." This word has long been current, not only as the equivalent of Heidegger's "*eigentlich*" but also in the they-say of the general, diffuse commentary on the thought of *Being and Time*. In the decisive sentence that we have just quoted, we have translated *eigentlich* by "in its owness,"[39] and we will maintain this translation in what follows. The stakes here are considerable. The category of the "authentic" essentially implies the idea of a purity of origin or provenance, of a native excellence, in relation to which one can represent or bring about an "inauthentic" falsification or degradation.[40] But we have just seen that an opposition of this type is specifically excluded by the existential analytic. To speak of "authenticity," above all in a sentence like the one we are examining here, is therefore inconsistent. German has its own word, which Heidegger uses, for the idea of "authenticity": *echt, Echtheit,* whose potential to be used critically or ironically we saw above. *Eigentlich,* by contrast, speaks nothing but "ownness," what belongs to someone or something as the person's or thing's own, what can be said of something in its own right. Moreover, the reader of German cannot help grasping the continuity, in Heidegger's text, among the words *eigentlich, Eigentlichkeit,* and the other words that so frequently appear: *eigen, eigenste, eignen,* own, ownmost, to appropriate or make one's own. Finally, we cannot neglect the quasi-magnetic pull that must be exercised on every reading of this text by the importance that the *Ereignis / Enteignis* (the appropriating/depropriating event) takes on in Heidegger's later work (we will come back to that event). "Ownness" and "authenticity," no doubt, are not without a certain relation. But, as it happens, thought about the decision of existence proposes, precisely, to make an essential distinction between the two, in spite of this relation. Therefore, translation must not decide on an "authenticity" of meaning by repressing *echt* with *véritable* (Martineau) or promoting *ownness* to *authenticity.* Heidegger himself says that he employs *Eigentlichkeit* and *Uneigentlichkeit* "terminologically," that is, as technical terms, taken "in their strict sense."[41] What more is there to say, if not this: that decision-modification must not look to some "authenticity" floating in the air, but rather to the very *ownness* of the ownlessness in which and as which existence exists, each time and constantly.

Having said all that—and since this is not a question of scrutinizing some "authenticity" in favor of which one might decide, but rather of thinking the ownness of a decision in which existence reaches *its* decision—we will now go directly to where the decision is decided: the analysis of *Entschlossenheit*, with respect to which *Entscheidung* is, in sum, the properly active punctuation.

Section 60 posits that "Decisiveness [*Entschlossenheit*] is a distinctive mode of Dasein's disclosedness [*Erschlossenheit*]."⁴² Being-opened, in this "distinctive mode," does not resolve itself into any thing other than what it is, or according to any thing other than what it is. It decides itself open, it opens itself up to the decision of this opening. The opening up offers decision, but decision itself makes the opening up. In other words, the existent does nothing but make its ownmost Being its own: it appropriates existence itself as disclosedness. *Entschlossenheit* is nothing but a making-its-own in the opening up, as opening up: the *Zueignung*, which forms the ownmost possibility of the ownness of existence as such, the *Zueignung*, or the *Ereignis*. The *Beiträge* will say that "the essence of Being deploys itself and presents itself [*west*] in the appropriation of the decision [*in der Ereignung der Entscheidung*]," and that "the advent of the appropriation [*das Ereignis der Er-eignung*] encloses within it the de-cision."⁴³

In decisiveness, there is no decision to be made, or not to be made, by a subject of existence of any sort whatsoever, or by a subject-existent who would emerge to cut through the possibilities offered in the exteriority of the world, in a way that would be consistent or inconsistent with respect to its own Being. (It would be necessary, if we wished to speak of a "subject," to say that decision itself is the "subject.") But what is in play here is solely existence's own mode of being. This mode of being is not something that could be objectified, in one way or another, for the subject and for its decision (as if, knowing that we are humans and what it means to be human, we could resolve to be properly human). Rather, this mode of being—existence—is the mode in which Being itself *is*—that is, in this case, is open to the fact that it is, in its Being, the disclosedness of Being. Consequently, "decision" is nothing but the existing by which existence relates itself to itself, in its ownness.

The "decision" therefore has the configuration, if we can put it

this way, of an *ego sum, ego existo*. Existence attains itself there as
such, in its Being detached from all possible ground except that of
its own de-cision, which itself is its detachment.[44] The difference,
however, stems from the fact that existence does not proceed from a
suspension of all judgment, at the end of which *ego*, what suspends,
finally makes itself count and makes itself indubitably known.
Existence *is* itself *suspension*, which is not a suspension of judgment
but rather an originary state of suspense of Being, and of suspense
as Being—that is, the absence of fundament, foundation, reason, or
ground "on" which the existent could "maintain" itself. This is not
an auto-opening but rather an onto-opening. Or the auto- is here
in the mode of the onto-, which itself *exists* in the mode of the
"*they.*"

Such a "maintenance" of self is, finally, without tenacity, without
consistency, and without assurance. That is what is indicated by the
suspension of disclosedness, and by Being as the possibility of
Being. But this "maintenance" without stance, stability, or installa-
tion is not, for all that, a "floating." The existent's Being is not an
undetermined or ill-determined Being. It is not a feeble, languid,
vaporous Being. If it is indeed abandoned to existence, if its
existence *is* this abandonment, it is at the same time strictly and
absolutely determined by this abandonment and in this abandonment. This is why its opening—which certainly is errance, thrown-
Being, discarded-, precipitated-, or deserted-Being—is nevertheless
the very site wherein it *maintains itself,* maintaining and grasping
itself, in this archi-originary place or taking-place, *as the open
difference of its sameness of Being.* And that is why such a maintenance of difference, which does not master the latter in order to
close it off, but which maintains itself in the openness of difference
itself, has the firmness and consistency of a "resolution." Decisive-
ness/decidedness indicates nothing but the singular mode of this
unbolstered firmness. And this unbolstered firmness is not an
attribute of the existent subject; on the contrary, it is *the very
consistency of its existence.* Thus "decision" and "decided-Being" are
neither attributes nor actions of the existent subject; they are that
in which, from the first, existence makes itself into existence, opens

to its own Being, or *appropriates the unappropriable event of its advent to Being, from a groundlessness of existence.* Existing has nothing more its own than this infinite ownability of unownable Being-in-its-ownness. That is the truth of "finitude" (and that is the sole "object" of the existential analytic).

The truth of finitude: what is to be made our own (to be decided) is nothing but Being-thrown-to-the-world, and therefore to the world of the "they." But there is neither impoverishment nor derision in this. Disclosedness does not have to disclose itself or resign itself to the mediocre insignificance, or all-significance, of a world of banality. The very idea of banality, the idea of mediocrity, and the idea of the "average" (as in the "average understanding") are already (whatever Heidegger, on his part, might attempt to do to neutralize the disdainful character of these terms, unsuccessfully bridling his own disdain for the banality of the world . . .) meanings superimposed on the world of everyday experience.[45] The opening opens itself to the "*they*," or decides in favor of the "they," to the full extent that the "they" *is* abandonment to the ownlessness of Being, which existence must make its own. The "they" is, in the first instance, nothing but this opening because it is itself, as such, as thrown "they," the ontico-ontological undecidability in which, and *by reason* of which, existence must reach its decision as existence. It is because it is without essence that existence is delivered over to[46] ontico-ontological undecidability. The latter means that Being—through the existent—is wholly in play in the world of entities. But it does not mean that, on this account, we can no longer make any distinction between Being and entities. On the contrary, ontico-ontological undecidability means that precisely *what we must do* (in the strongest and most "praxical" sense of the word *do*) is to make the distinction between Being and entities. But the difference between the two is existence. It is existence that we must make, or exist—that is, decide, since existence has no essence decided for it and outside it, in some ideally floating ontological region. *Undecidable existence convokes itself to the decision of existence.*

But to *make* this difference is not to evaluate it, to appreciate it, to measure it. That is precisely what is impossible, because of undecidability, which is the same as saying that this difference, itself, *is* not,[47] as is easily and necessarily deduced. It *is* not, but it "is made," or it "acts," and its making and its acting have the essence of decisiveness. This is what makes the difference according to which *Being withdraws from/within entities* (and withdraws all their foundations, in the *Nichtigkeit* of its freedom) *to the exact degree that it exists*, and to the degree, therefore, that it exists according to the mode and the world of the thrown-"they" of existence. Thus *undecidability itself makes the decision.*

V I

Thus, "decisiveness, by its ontological essence, is always the decisiveness of some factual Dasein at a particular time."[48] What is the *factuality* proper to Dasein? The phrase that immediately follows indicates it very simply, by returning to the central assertion of the entire analytic: "The 'essence' of Dasein lies in its existence." The factuality proper to Dasein is that of existence. This means two things simultaneously:

1. The essence of this entity does not "float" in some domain of essences, which would be separate from the world and from the Being-in-common of existents in the world.

2. Because it does not "float" in this way—and, so to speak, "so that" it should not float in this way—existence takes place in the disclosedness of decision. In sum, its factuality *is made* in decision.

Thus, as was stated a bit earlier in Heidegger's text:

Decisiveness, as proper *Being-one's-own-Self*, does not detach Dasein from its world, nor does it isolate it so that it becomes a free-floating "I." And how should it, when decisiveness, as proper disclosedness, is, *properly*, nothing else than *Being-in-the-world*?[49]

Entschlossenheit is the ownness of disclosedness, which is nothing but the very property of Being-in-the-world. What is the property of this Being delivered over to the world and to "Being-among-one-another," or to "Being-in-company," if not the property of being, insofar as this means to *be* delivered over to this common/mundane existence, that is, to the "they," in an essential "indetermination"—or, more exactly, to be determined-destined according to this indetermination? ("The *existentiell indetermination* of decisiveness never makes itself definite except in a decision [*Entschluss*]; yet it has, all the same, its *existential determinateness.*")[50] That is existence: Being determined according to indetermination, in such a way that, to be what it is, it must decide/reach its decision. In deciding/reaching its decision, it opens its own possibilities—but it opens them, and opens itself, only by way of its ownmost possibility, which is precisely its decision. In it, the opening reaches its decision as opening, existence reaches its decision by existing, and Being comes into its own.

In other words, the opening receives itself as such when it decides/reaches its decision. Its decision is the activity of its passivity, or it is the act of its passibility to sense (to Being). Its passivity is its offering to itself (to *the Self*) as opening. Section 62 states: "By 'decisiveness' we mean 'letting oneself be called forth to one's ownmost *Being*-responsible.'"[51] To what is the existent responsible? To existence, insofar as it is not attributed to Being as an essence, but addressed to it as a call—a ("friendly") call that emanates from its own difference, or from the indetermination of Being according to which it exists.

But in this way, once again, the existent must respond *to* (that is, decide) and answer *for* nothing but what constitutes its factual Being. It answers to (for) the thrown-Being that it is. It answers to (for) the mundane thrown-community of existences. Only insofar as it is, *there*, thrown to the uncanniness (to the *Unheimlichkeit*) of the absence of essence must it answer for this uncanniness, as for its very ownness.

That is why whatever or whoever sends out the call cannot be interpreted as an objectifiable (or subjectifiable) "power"[52] exterior to Dasein. Which means, first of all, that the call or the caller is not more *powerful* than the response, or that the responsible respondent himself is *powerful* only in the cutting of his decision. Not that it is necessary to reverse everything, and speak of weakness. The passivity that is in play here is not a weakness (any more than it is a "floating"). It is *the self-reception of the opening as such, which in this way firmly decides/reaches its decision to hold (itself) to the opening that it is and (from) where it calls (itself).*

This means, correlatively, that the interpretation of the call as exterior would be "a way for Dasein to escape by slinking away from that thin wall by which the 'they' is separated, as it were, from the uncanniness of its Being"[53]—a singular topology, or uncanny anatomy, to describe the uncanny relation between being-"they" and the Being of the "they." To answer the call and to answer for the Being of the opening, it is therefore fitting to remain *just at* a wall, a wall whose presence indicates the incommensurability of the "they" with its uncanniness of Being, but whose thinness indicates the (quasi-osmotic) communicability of the one with the other. By not pulling away from the wall (or from difference), by remaining stuck to it, to its thinness, Dasein occupies its space— the space of its nil and impenetrable thickness. On this limit, everything makes the difference, and nothing determines it. That is why the call emanates from here. Ontico-ontological non-distinction calls on itself to make the distinction between its Being and the entity that it is. Which means: it calls on itself to exist, it calls itself to the decision of existence. The latter decides, just at the "they," to make the difference of the "they" (to "modify the grasp").

The decision of existence does not aim at an "empty ideal of existence" but rather "*calls us forth into the Situation.*"[54] The *situation* is the existent's Being-*there*, right in the world and the community. Right in the situation, decisiveness does not "stem from 'idealistic' exactions soaring above existence and its possibilities; it springs from a sober understanding of what are factually the basic possibilities for Dasein."[55] Not the intoxication, the enthusiasm of floating ideals, but the simple fact of existence. The latter, however, is not the given to which one submits oneself; it is the fact of the yet-to-be-made, of the need-to-make (something with) one's possibilities (and here we also have to deal with a specific function of "ideals," a function that must be negotiated). To decide: to decide to exist, to render oneself possible to non-essence.

Here are rediscovered, at the heart of decisive and opened "understanding," the affects or "basic moods"[56] in their intimate composition with understanding (indeed, in the manner whereby they *compose* understanding). "Along with the sober anxiety which brings us face to face with our individualized potentiality-for-Being, there goes an unshakeable [*gerüstete*] joy in this possibility."[57] Decisiveness is what opens to anxiety *and* to joy, or in anxiety to joy, or to the accord of anxiety and joy. This accord is not a mixture or dosage of "positive" and "negative." It designates joy liberated in an existence that exists only in its existing—that is, in the free "nullity" of its foundation of Being. To be and not to be are the same for the existent. But by deciding—just in "their" world, right in the world of "their" thrown Being—to *be* according to this very with-it-ness, *they* make the difference. We make the infinite difference of the finite exposition to the absence of essence. We make the difference of *Being itself.* And it is the essence of Being that thus reveals itself as "decision," that is, as the own-making event of the disclosedness to fundamental ownlessness.

Where does this event take place? To answer this question, and to answer *for* what it brings into play, it is necessary to return to the impossibility of deciding on the sole basis of reading a text of thought. Nothing takes place, nothing is decided / reaches its decision merely through the understanding of a text (an understanding that is itself open, impossible to complete). Rather, it is necessary to understand that decision, its anxiety, and its joy take *place* "outside" the "text"—in existence. (But this also means that decision takes place in what the text, through its writing, ceaselessly *exscribes* as its ownmost possibility. The *exscription* of a text is the *existence* of its inscription, its existence in the world and in the community: and it is in existence, and only therein, that the text decides / reaches its decision—which also means in the *existentiellity* of the text itself, in the anxiety and the joy of its work of thought, its play of writing, its offer of reading.)

Just as little as existence is necessarily and directly impaired by an ontologically inadequate way of understanding the conscience [it is a question of the *Gewissen*, of the responsible conscience], so little does an existentially appropriate Interpretation of the conscience guarantee that one has understood the call in an *existentiell* manner. It is no less possible to be serious when one experiences the conscience in the ordinary way than not to be serious when one's understanding of it is more primordial.[58]

Thought neither dictates nor guarantees what we have to decide or that we actually decide it. This is its archi-ethics, and its ownmost responsibility. At most, thought elucidates the fact that *we* decide and that we reach *our* decision, in the anxiety and the joy of existing on vanished ground. But for such an elucidation, thought must, each time, in this text or the next, bring its own decision of existence into *action*. This is its responsibility as thought, a responsibility that is not simply thought about or left floating in thought. It engages and exposes itself in the mode of existing that is thinking and writing. But this mode can decide nothing for the other modes of existing. Rather, it must recognize just how fully the decision of existence belongs to itself and comes about only from itself, the event of an own-making that is each time singular and each time singularly modalized.

Thought abandons itself to its own opening and thus reaches its decision, when it does justice to this singularity that exceeds it, exceeding it even in itself, even in its own existence and decision of thought. It is also in this way that it does justice to the community of existents. This means that thought has no decision of practical, ethical, or political action to dictate. If it claims to do so, it forgets the very essence of the decision, and it forgets the essence of its own thinking decision. This does not mean that thought turns away from action and is hostile or indifferent toward it. On the contrary, it means that thought carries itself in advance of action's ownmost possibility. It does not think action in the sense in which it would subsume action under "theoretical" or "ideal" rules; rather, it thinks, *as its own limit and as its own difference* (and as that which makes it think, in its ownness), the essential, active decision of existence. Its necessity is also called freedom, and to itself it sounds freedom's most demanding call. But freedom is not what disposes of given possibilities. It is the disclosedness by which the groundless Being of existence exposes itself, in the anxiety and the joy of being without ground, of being in the world.

TRANSLATED BY BRIAN HOLMES

§ The Jurisdiction of
the Hegelian Monarch

I begin with a preliminary remark: Hegel should not be considered here in his singularity, or as *one example* of a political philosopher among others. In the question that I lift from him, I address myself in fact to a limit point of political philosophy in general and of philosophical politics, a limit point to which Hegel, for reasons that are not unrelated to his *final* position in philosophy (final in all senses of the word), gives special relief and sharpness. I do not mean simply that Hegel brings this limit point to light insofar as he represents a closing-off—and an opening-up—of philosophy. I mean also, and more precisely, that this same point appears, although differently, in the *Statesman* of Plato, for example, in the Sovereign of Hobbes or of Rousseau, and that it reappears with its problems in the "sovereignty" of Bataille. The analysis I shall propose should engage with all the analyses thus programmed.

The general form of the question posed on this point is the following: How do things stand with respect to the minimal articulation between the juridical and the political that is the articulation of the *actualization* of the law [*droit*]—not of its execution or of its application as a practical or material process, but of the *decision* that makes the law effective? This decision is itself an act of law. But it is not in the order of the generality of the law; it inheres in the order of the particularity of its employment [*mise en oeuvre*]. (I adopt here the terms of the *Social Contract*, III, 1.) This employment, however, is nothing other than that of the social institution as such, if this requires necessarily and originally something like a right [*droit*]—"right" understood here not as an instrument of regulation but as that by which the social institution recognizes itself or "symbolizes" itself reflexively (that is to say, institutes itself).

The political articulates with the juridical at this point as the latter's *operative implication*. But since the law is such only if it declares and decides itself actually as the actual law of such and such a collectivity, the juridical articulates itself equally well at this point to the political, as to its own *instituting condition*: a double articulation which, one could show, is that of the *sovereign* and of the *prince* in Rousseau. It is in general the articulation of the judgment that decides as to the law, of the judgment that pronounces legitimacy as such (and whose problematic, as we shall have to point out, perhaps goes beyond the habitual framework of the so-called "decisionist" problematic). This judgment is the particular judgment of the generality of a law [*droit*], and the general judgment of the particularity of a law (and by virtue of this, in Kantian terms, the perhaps unrealizable synthesis of a determining judgment and a reflective judgment).

Since the term "jurisdiction" contains the motif of the declaration that decides and, in its modern sense, the motif of the actual power of the law (of the law or of the power of judgment in one district or another), I shall call this articulation *political jurisdiction*.

And so I come to the jurisdiction of the Hegelian monarch.

I will not dwell on the general scheme, which is well known and up to a point established, that characterizes Hegel's *Philosophy of Right* as the thought of the totalitarian State itself, in that it is the thought of the social totality as an organism or as the organic character of the life of the Subject, which is the mind of the people, which in its turn is the fulfillment, according to history, of the "self-consciousness of the world mind."[1] It is in this way that "the State is the actuality of the ethical Idea" (§257), and that one might say (although overlooking, it must be admitted, some difficulties that remain on a closer examination) that the State is the final truth of

the total system of subjectivity. (One could in any case appeal to
the end of the remark at §552 of the *Encyclopedia*: philosophy exists
in the end only as the State, as the State that develops the truth of
the Protestant religion.)

But in pronouncing that truth is the State, one has not yet said
anything. It is still necessary to determine the content of this truth,
that is to say, of the State as such. Hegel determines this, in the
most radical fashion, in opposition to the State conceived as the
administration of relations between individuals, that is to say, to
civil society:

> If the State is confused with civil society, and if its specific end is laid
> down as the security and protection of property and personal freedom,
> then the *interests of the individuals as such* become the ultimate end of
> their association, and it follows that membership in the State is
> something optional. But the State's relation to the individual is quite
> different from this. Since the State is mind objectified, it is only as one
> of its members that the individual himself has objectivity, genuine
> individuality, and an ethical life. Union as such is the true content and
> aim, and the individual's destiny is the living of a universal life.
> (*Philosophy of Right*, §258)

A number of other texts confirm the importance of this opposition,
in particular the marginal notes in the sections on property.

That *union as such*—"die Vereinigung als solche"—should be the
veritable content of the State means that the State actualizes relation, it does not police or regulate it. The actualization of relation is
true subjectivity, thus subjectivity is the truth of the State. That is,
the truth of subjectivity is not individuality—with its needs, its
interests, and its rights—but the relation between individualities as
relation to Spirit and relation of Spirit to the self.

In a sense, and all other differences aside, nothing else determines the *zōon politikon*, man's political "animality" or "natural-
ness" for Aristotle: the commerce of ethical discourse, which aims
at the city's "living well," a living together according to the good
independently of needs and interests. *Union as such* denotes the
excess of the specific nature of the *zōon politikon*, its excess with

respect to the social organization of relations that benefit the partners, and finally the actualization of relation itself as absolutely in excess of any regulation of relations. As opposed to or as absolutely diverging from a policing of society, "union as such" defines politics as the (immanent?—we shall see to what degree) transcendence of the collective life.

We should keep clearly before us this fundamental determination, which is here, surely, that of the total State—that is, of subjectivity as an organism that transcends social organization but that is nonetheless, and simultaneously, in its nature as actualization of relation and in its description as transcendence, the locus of an inevitable question (Can we simply not take into account something like a requirement to actualize relation? Isn't that, on the contrary, an ultimate and crucial question, not only "as man's last question," but, "taking it farther still, the last question of being," to twist only slightly one of Bataille's phrases?[2]) and the locus of a singular complication in Hegelian theory itself.

This complication is that of the theory of the monarch. This is true, in the first place, for a reason as formally simple as it is apodictic: if the State is truth, the truth of this truth is the monarch. Indeed, the monarch is, to quote only a few phrases, "the summit and the base of everything" (§278), the "absolutely decisive moment of the whole" (§279), and "the existence of sovereignty as the personality of the whole, within the reality that conforms to its concept" (§279). The monarch is the truth (the reality) of the truth of the State; he is, therefore, the truth of the "true end," that is, of "union as such." Or again, the oneness and uniqueness of the monarch—the concept of which is determined above all by the *monos*—make the truth of union, the *ein* of the *Vereinigung*, and thus the *actual* fulfillment of relation, and the immanence of its transcendence.

We cannot therefore examine the Hegelian State without examining the monarch, that is, without standing aside, for the moment, from the question commentators consider of greater importance, that of the State as government, the State as apparatus, the State as its functionaries, in short, the State as machine, or rather, the State as organism, in the sense of a collective organism. This gesture of reading is further supported by certain items in the commentaries, in Fleischmann, for example, or E. Weil, as well as by B. Bourgeois's study.[3] This gesture requires, furthermore, that for a moment we isolate and neglect the part of "ideological sliding" out of the speculative as such that the theory of the monarch certainly, but on one plane only, requires. (The phrase "clumsy ideological sliding" is Adorno's, from the third of his *Etudes sur Hegel*;[4] as it happens, the phrase in context accompanies an odd sliding on Adorno's own part, which cuts off his quotations from Hegel's text at the very moment of Hegel's speculative deduction of the monarch—while the excised quotation is used in Hegel's favor in the first of the *Etudes*.) In this respect, it is enough to keep to E. Weil's principle (but more faithfully than he does himself): "the Hegelian thesis [of the monarch] deserves to be judged on the plane that it claims as its own, that of reason."[5]

Finally, the last condition if we are to answer correctly to the internal necessities of the system: not so much to seek in the Hegelian monarchy a form of constitution, even were it the best (this would still be "monarchy in its narrow sense," as §273 has it, and here the analysis I propose differs in principle from that of Bourgeois, although the two converge), as to seek the truth of all constitutions, the truth of the *political* as such. (A precise examination of Hegel's early thinking on politics would support this: the first inklings of the theory of the monarch are at least visible as of 1802.)

The Monarch the Whole of the State

The necessity of the monarch follows from the very necessity, the most absolute and compelling there is, of subjectivity, or of Spirit. Section 278 puts it as follows: "in its truth, subjectivity exists only as *subject*, and personality only as *person*." Spirit's logic is the actualization of the abstraction of subjectivity in and as the concreteness of the existence of the subject. The subject exists as *an* empirical subject, as *that* person. The State cannot exist save through and in such an existence. We recognize in this necessity *the* absolute necessity of the system and of the process of Spirit in general, the necessity for the concept to be actualized, according, for example, to this phrase from the end of the *Phenomenology*: "the concept is the necessity for and the rising of existence, which has substance for its essential nature and subsists on its own account."[6] It is to this absolute and ontological constraint, which simultaneously involves the logic of the concept, the manifestation of spirit, and what one might call, in many senses, the physics or the physiology of the Idea, that the very singular position and complication of the monarch correspond.

This monarch is thus really neither the substance, nor the finality, nor the foundation of the State; nor is he either its right or its power. But he is *all that at once insofar as he is absolutely—but only— the "at once" of all that.* He is the co-presence of the elements of the State and of the moments of its Idea (institutions, powers, and persons), as this organic co-presence itself, that is to say, as an actual presence, the *Da-sein* of the political, of the essence of the political *existing* in and as this *zōon.* Thus he is in no fashion a concentration of powers (he is not an absolute monarch), still less a personal power (he is not a despot). Distinct from the people (insofar as it is a true people according to its spirit) as well as from the legislative and governmental powers, he is—and is only—the synthesis of the State, that is to say, its organicity existing *for itself,* selected out of itself, autonomized (that is to say, autonomizing itself) and existing as such. The monarch, at that rate, is less the supreme individual *in* the State than the superior individual *of* the State, or the State itself as individuality—and this individuality, as such, is not so much superior (in the sense of a hierarchy of powers, of functions, or of rights) to the other individualities as it is superior even to anything that, in the State, creates a hierarchical superiority and subordinate relations. Hegel can write in §284: "only the councils or the individuals composing them are made answerable. The personal majesty of the monarch, as the final *subjectivity* of decision, is above all answerability for acts of government."

This "above answerability" of power designates a superiority so *absolute*—so *separate*—that it is really of another nature from the superiority of command or of administration. According to a logic which is perhaps still that of sovereignty (now the monarch is the existence of sovereignty; cf. §278), the "supremacy" (this word is a doublet of "sovereignty") of the monarch is beyond the system of supremacy, or of superiority in general. If the monarch is the "summit" (§273), it is not as the top of an edifice, as the last stone of a pyramid, but as the perfection of the edifice realized for itself (he would be then not the placing of the last stone of the pyramid, but the form or the nature of that stone, which is itself a pyramid, and the only pyramid in the whole pyramid . . .). If, as §279 puts it, "sovereignty exists only as subjectivity"—that is to say, as a "self-determination with no foundation" and an "ultimate element of decision"—and if "subjectivity exists only as subject," then the sovereign is beyond sovereignty itself, not through some new superiority but through the incarnation of that very sovereignty.

The monarch is thus the whole of the State—its "all at once"—as something *extra*, that is to say, as some*one* whose personal unity accomplishes that of the State. (Everything thus refers to the axiom that unity in general is personal, and that the person is unitary.) The monarch is a man *in addition*, who is not to be numbered with other individuals but who on the contrary causes their *union* to exist as a *unity*. The monarch *is* the fulfillment of relationship—as a relationship to itself.

The problematic that emerges in him is thus less a political problematic than the problematic of the existence of the political as such, the problematic of the individuation of the *zōon politikon* as such. Section 279 makes this clear: "a society, a community, a family, as concrete as it can be, does not have a personality except as an abstract moment"; on the contrary, "the personality of the State is real only if it is a single person." The existence of the *zōon* is the existence of *a zōon* (and this determination would not be, in the end, unfamiliar to Aristotle; what belongs only to Hegel or to the modern age is the assignation of the *zōē* as subjective life).

And this necessity—that of existence in general, that of the existentiality of existence, which means that, precisely, there is no existence "in general"—recovers or redoubles the necessity of the concept, which is to effect the passage to existence, to conceive itself as existence and to engender itself as an existent, that is to say, necessarily as *a certain* existent, as the "this" of a "natural existence," says §280. This necessity is nothing other than the one established by the ontological proof, as the same section says, the necessity of the "passage from the absolute concept to being." And since, at least according to one side of the systematic consideration of the relationship between the State and religion, "ethical life is the divine Spirit insofar as it resides in the consciousness of self, in the consciousness of a people or of the individuals who compose it" (*Encyclopedia*, §552), it is possible to say that the existence of the monarch stems from the ontological proof both according to a montage "in series" and according to a montage "in parallel" (both being essentially authorized by the expression of §280: "the *same* passage from the concept to being"—*dasselbe Umschlagen*: it is not a passage but rather a conversion, a metamorphosis and a precipitation).

Thus the monarch executes the *Umschlagen* of the State within existence, the conversion of *union as such* into the unity of a real person. Now it might well be that the problematic of the *Umschlagen* in existence, of the concrete execution, is nothing other, in a determination as old as philosophy, than the very problematic of the political. As the Platonic science of the *kairos* (*Statesman* 305 c-d), or, in Aristotle, as the architectonic science of *praxis*, or again, with Rousseau, as the discourse that is a political *act* (*Social Contract*, Introduction), the philosophy of the political always allies itself principally with a logic of actualization, of *Verwirklichung*. The concept of the political is at least *also* that of the concrete actualization of its essence—and perhaps, if the content of this essence, as the true Good or the ethical Idea, is itself nothing political, perhaps then the concept of the political is just that of actualization (and thus, of the actualization of the philosophical). It is this also, for example, that the eighth of the *Theses on Feuerbach* says or evokes in its way: "Social life is essentially *practical*." The problem of the political in this sense is not determined from the political as a point of departure, but from the problem, or rather the metaphysical requisite, of *existence*. The essence of the political consists in this sense of the existence of the *logos* or of the substance of humanity—in the existence of *union as such*. If political philosophy is the problem of a science, it is always a question of the problem of a science of actualization and of the actualization of this science. A science of the transcendence of the concept in its existence (see also §§27, 28, 29, and Remark to §337 of the *Philosophy of Right*).

The Monarch in No Way Symbolic

The monarch, as *this* real person, is thus the truth of the union because he is its existence. Now the union must be envisaged in two ways:

1. As to its content, the union should be the fulfillment of the relation that is essential to the person in general ("the particular person finds himself essentially in relation with another particularity," §182). Now the *person* (and we remember that the monarch, even more than a subject, is a *person*) is not simply the subject, it is "the singularity that knows itself as an absolutely free will" (*Encyclopedia*, §448), and that as such is essentially in relation to the "being of other persons" and to their recognition (ibid., §490, 491). Thus the person is still and finally the singularity of the subject according to the *people*, or rather the division into singularities of the efficacy of a people (which, in this way, is not "divided" but rather actualized), for the people is "the substance that knows itself free" (ibid., §514). For all these reasons, the fulfillment of the relation of persons is nothing other than the actualization, in the particularity and in the relation essential to it, of right in itself and in general, if right is defined as "the *Dasein* of free will [*vouloir libre*]," through which, as Hegel clarifies it, "right must be taken not just as juridical right, but as englobing the presence [*Dasein*] of *all* the determinations of freedom" (ibid., §486). Now the totality

of these determinations is found in the relation of free will [*volonté libre*] to free will, or in the people as such.

The monarch, being the existence of the union as such of the people, is the very presence, the *Dasein*, of right—or more exactly, he is the presentation in existence of the actual presence of free will and of its recognition. He does not *operate* this presence, which in the relation between persons and in the mind of the people is already efficacious, but *he presents it*. To fulfill the relation (of freedoms, of freedom) does not mean to perfect it, to completely finish it, but to incarnate the perfection that it is in itself. The monarch is, to make it redundant, the present existence of right. Or: his existence is not, by itself, any property or quality of right, but only—and absolutely—in sum its *ecceity*. This ecceity—or existence as pure position, as *da*-sein—is no specific right, but the being-there, here, in person, of right, or, again, its *Darstellung*.

Now the proper determination of right is precisely, as the *Dasein* of free will, not simply "the unity of rational will and of singular will," but the actual (and active) *positing* of this unity: "the *law* [*das Gesetz*] is [the content of this truth] *posited* [*gesetzt*] for the consciousness of intelligence with determination as a power having validity" (ibid., §485). *Right is by its essence an actual positing* (just as it is "the empirical existence . . . of freedom conscious of itself," *Philosophy of Right*, §30). The actuality of right is, in sum, the right of right, its *sensible declaration* to the intelligence, and the *exercise* of its legitimate power. Right is right decided and posited. Position (*die Setzung*) is *juris-diction*.

The actuality of union is thus position, ecceity as *Gesetz(t)-sein* of the jurisdiction of freedom. The monarch does not incarnate union to furnish it in some fashion with flesh and a visage. He incarnates it because union as such is right and right as such is the *Da*-sein of "right" as a general form of freedom—the latter constituting legitimacy in itself. (We should of course dwell at some other time on the nature of this freedom.)

Thus, and with respect to the content of union or of the State, the existence of the monarch is justified not only by the ontological proof applied or pursued as far as the Spirit of the people, but also by the ontological determination that requires of right as right its factuality, the ecceity of its jurisdiction.

We thus touch for the first time on a singularity that is perhaps the most determining singularity of the existence of the monarch: it is that his incarnation is in no way a representation, a figuration, a symbolization. It is hard to understand how E. Weil, for example, can write on several occasions that the monarch "represents" the universal, or sovereignty, etc. Precisely, the monarch is what he is— that is to say, *exists*—only because a necessity, unique but polymorphic, requires that the representation both of the people and of the right should be, in the principle of the State, gone beyond and transcended in actual presence. In no way does the Hegelian monarch have a symbolic role. At the same time, he has no power (with one exception, an important one, as we shall see), and especially not any absolute power—but he *is* (and does not symbolize) the absolute *position* of power, the might of the people and of right with no other content than its actuality—and this content makes the essence of right, for "concrete right is the absolute *necessity* of spirit" (marginal note to §28), or again, according to another note in the same section, and in a formula of a dizzying radicality: "ethicality [*ethicité*] has a right—existence." The monarch, then, does not symbolize, in the most general sense of the term. On the contrary, he opens perhaps the question of a *symbolization*, caught between a Greek meaning and, let us say, a Lacanian meaning of the term, which would be the symbolization of the people and of right (or of one in the other)—a question in which this acceptance, enigmatic for the moment, of symbolization would designate nothing other than the actuality *of relation as such*.

Let us conclude on this first aspect—that of the content of union, and hence of the content of the person of the monarch: between a simple, immediate presence and a representation, the monarch poses the question of an absolute (that is to say, of a putting aside, an individuation) of co-presence as such, or of reciprocal presence, or of relation—a question that is nothing other, in fact, than the question of the *subject*, if the subject is not first of all the subject of representation, as the support of the idea or of the image (that is to say, of the second representation), but is first of all the suject of a presentation to itself that necessarily passes through the presentation of a self to a self—through relation as such.

The question of relation lies at the heart of the second aspect under which union should be considered.

2. Union *as such* should in effect be envisaged via its "form," or via its "modality."

In other words, in order to understand the existential unity of the monarch as it fulfills relation, we would need to understand relation itself. The Being—or modality—of relation as such should be questionable *before* its absorption, its reabsorption, its solution, or its relief in the monarch's subjectivity. That alone would permit us to discern the being or the specific modality of this subjectivity, which is *a* subjectivity as the existence of an individual subject, but whose substance must precisely not be the substance of this individual, but rather the contents of relation itself. (At the same time, an interrogation of relation would necessarily be an interrogation of the essence of right—and of freedom.)

Now we must observe that, in many ways, the question of relation poses a limit-question, indicated everywhere but never examined in itself by Hegel—at least never without *presupposing* the resolution of relation in an archi-teleological unity. This resolution therefore constitutes the presupposed condition of the monarch. However, the determination of the monarch is precisely what makes this presupposition come forth and renders it problematic. Such is the double hypothesis to guide us in our work, and it also marks the ultimate edge of incertitude, of vacillation, even of transgression, of philosophical thought about the political in general.

(A remark is in order before we envisage the question of relation: to the extent that the *Philosophy of Right* places itself in the System, I leave aside, for this question, the text of the *Phenomenology* on the struggle of self-consciousnesses, and on the dialectic of master and slave. For many reasons either known or to be explored, the

Phenomenology does not *fit* into the System as such. It is no accident if, at the same time, the *Phenomenology*'s text on relation presupposes the resolution of this question less or otherwise than the System does. And if in addition—or at the same time—the political is not the element of the completion of the *Phenomenology of Spirit*. We may come back to this question. For the time being, the logic ordered by—or for—the State should guide us.)

I shall envisage three successive modes of access to the question of relation:

1. Taking things, as far as possible, in terms nearest to those of the *Phenomenology*, the first elements that could bring relation to our attention would be—though in the *Encyclopedia*—the element of the struggle of consciousnesses for and in the process of recognition that constitutes them as such. I will recall in a word how this recognition, in order to be that of freedom—of my existence as freedom—implies the risk of death, but how, because the death of the other suppresses recognition at the same time, life manifests a requirement just as essential as freedom, and the struggle ends in the relation between master and slave. This *relation* is immediately, and in conformity with what produced it, itself a *community*, which is that "of need and of the concern to satisfy it" (*Encyclopedia*, §431–34).

One might suppose that this would be an entry into the first level of social institution. In a sense this is not untrue—but then we see that we would not be entering it except according to a mode of relation: (a) resolved in favor of a single subjectivity; (b) whose community, as a community of need, is not that of freedom.

We will not derive the State from this—moreover, we know that the State is of a different essence from civil society. (By contrast, it is not possible to consider the master-slave community as a civil society, if it belongs properly only to the modern world, as the addition to §182 puts it; the master-slave community is neither a State nor a civil society, it has not yet or not really any jurisdiction.) Even more, as a principle of spiritual substance and subsistence of society as such, the State "must precede civil society as an independent reality" (ibid.). The relation of freedoms must precede the community of need. We would therefore be entitled to seek, even in place of *relation* not yet stabilized in domination and need, that is, in *struggle* itself, the principle of the State. As we know, the *Philosophy of Right* indicates nothing of the kind: the struggle for recognition, or relation as struggle, is even absent from it. The dialectic of master and slave only concerns, says §57, the stage of consciousness, not that of the objective spirit. Thus the relation of domination is only *natural* (ibid.), which is to say, essentially nonpolitical. This very relation, which puts at stake the recognition and the affirmation of freedom, sees itself "repressed," if I may so put it, into the status of the natural and "unreal" "point of view," outside of which or beyond which right is "already" present from the start (ibid.). This "already" condenses the difficulty: of itself it forbids our knowing how one *accedes* to right—except as indicated in a marginal note to the same section (§57): "The idea of freedom is genuinely actual only as the State."

But the reason for putting aside the struggle is clearly indicated in the System (in the sections of the *Encyclopedia* to which I have referred) in the very place that we should concentrate upon: in the place of struggle. The Remark to §433 says:

> The struggle for recognition and the submission to a master is the *phenomenon* within which the living-in-common of men was born, as a beginning of *States*. *Violence*, which, in this phenomenon, is a foundation, is not for all that a foundation of *right*, although it constitutes the *necessary* and *justified* moment in the passage that goes from the *state* of consciousness drowned in desire and in singularity to the state of universal self-consciousness. It is the exterior or *phenomenal beginning* of States, not their *substantial principle*.

Struggle is thus separated from the principle of the State and of right for, as violence, it is only the unleashing of desire plunged in its singularity, which therefore does not know itself as freedom in relation to a freedom. However, this violence is a phenomenon of principle, a necessary and justified one. But nothing is said about this justification, nothing is said of the strange right of this rightless state that leads to right. Nothing is said about the jurisdiction of violence where right would "begin" externally, and as if by the opposite of right. Nothing is said either about the link, here, of the phenomenon to the principle, nor about the process of passage from closed singularity to universal consciousness. But this is because, in a completely general fashion, exteriority as such could never furnish a principle for the State. (Thus, for example, the *Encyclopedia*, §544: "To represent to oneself the institution of the State as a pure Constitution conceived through the understanding, that is to say, as the mechanism of an equilibrium between forces internally external to one another, goes against the fundamental idea of what a State is.")

In violence, exteriority must thus be a "phenomenon" of an interiority of principle *between* consciousnesses, of a presupposed subjectivity in common. The question of relation as struggle is thus "skipped over" as "phenomenal." Which amounts to saying that there is in some way no real "phenomenology of the State."

But this is the moment to recall that it is precisely in *war* that the State-subject, with its monarch and by its monarch, will nevertheless realize itself completely. The struggle of States will be the actualization of the universal interiority of the World Spirit. Everything happens as if the "leap" beyond relation as such were to produce a final resurgence of relation—and this time in the personal authority of the monarch (who carries in his person the right to war, the only right he really holds), in his authority exercising itself as violence. (What, in this presupposition of a principle without exteriority and without violence, as well as in the resurgence of war as a truth of the State, is overlooked in the matter of *death*, which is what is at stake in the struggle? Death *avoided* in the beginning, and *glorified* at the end? [Cf. *Philosophy of Right*, §324–28.] This is a question that will have to be taken up elsewhere.)

2. Now we can seek the true "substantial principle" of the State—thus, of relation. This principle is *the people*: "The *substance* which knows itself *free*, and in which the absolute *duty-to-be* is no less *being*, has actuality as the spirit of a *people*" (*Encyclopedia*, §514).

The people is thus the true element of ethical life and its reality.

As an addition to §156 of the *Philosophy of Right* makes clear, we cannot take the individual as a starting point, for that would be "a point of view devoid of spirit, which leads only to a collection." The ethical Idea thus has its reality according to relation. But it is quite difficult—or impossible—to find what relation as people or according to the people is. If in fact it is a question of the ethical substance of the people, we find it *already* posited and disposed of as a custom—as the *Sitte* where *Sittlichkeit* appears (§151); in the same way, we shall find each people positing the constitution corresponding to "the nature and the degree of culture of the self-consciousness of this people" (§274). As for the question of the formation of the people itself, we will find only this, in §181:

> The extension of the family, as its passage into another principle, is, in existence, sometimes the peaceful extension of the family into a people—into a *nation*, which has as a result a natural common origin, sometimes the combination of familial collectivities that have been dispersed, a combination that can be either the effect of the domination of a master, or a voluntary union brought about through the link of needs and of mutual help in satisfying them.

The three possibilities indicated never correspond to the substantial principle of right: either nature, or domination, or need (besides and in addition, the first and "peaceful" possibility contravenes, for its part, the necessity of "phenomenal" violence in the "beginning" of States). In other words, the question of the origin of sociality as sociality of right is carefully avoided or bypassed.

In the "First Philosophy of Spirit" of Jena, Hegel presented the explicit development of the passage from the family to the spirit of a people: the singular totality of the family, as singular, is only an ideal totality, and as such is suppressed; it exists only as a possible totality, not for itself, and so it is "always ready for death and has renounced itself."[7] The suppression of singularities, on the contrary, fulfills the act of becoming oneself in another, where universal consciousness emerges, the absolute ethical substance or spirit of a people. Now, on the one hand, in the text itself, the suppression of familial singularity is indiscernible from the suppression of individual singularity in the struggle for recognition, and there is a perpetual hesitation between a presupposition and an engendering of relation (unless—a more interesting hypothesis—it is understood that the struggle for recognition takes place in the bosom of the family, which would nonetheless leave in place a model in some ways "Oedipal," one that would confront as many problems as Freud's). On the other hand, the people, appearing as the universality of ethicality, does not permit the universal *singularity* of the spirit of *a* people to be determined—which is nevertheless essential to the concept we are examining.

It is true that at the same epoch, in the *System of Ethical Life*, the ethical Idea, which had already for its "concept" "the absolute being-one of individualities,"[8] had for "intuition" "an absolute people." Individuality then appeared as the exterior multiplicity of the concept, subsuming intuition as interior. In these conditions, the first moment of ethical life was determined "according to relation," in Hegel's own terms. But *relation* only designated a state of "imperfect unification," whose perfection—a unity made up of intuition and of the concept, to be understood thus as beyond a subsumption of intuition still dispersed in the individualities in relation—was supposed to be democracy, "the exhibition of the absolute reality of ethical life in everyone."[9]

We see then that our difficulty was already present, in the presupposition of the people as intuition, that is to say, in the presupposition (and in the intention) of a *presentation* of relation as *union*. But we also see that, in passing from democracy to monarchy, Hegel did not only swerve, or regress, politically: he *also* sharpened the point of the most difficult question. By designating the concrete existence of the monarch as the person *of* the people, Hegel finally inscribes intuition in the element of intuition, of sensible presentation. The monarch *is* or *makes* the "exhibition" that democracy was supposed to be. But also he makes more visible, if I dare put it thus, the mystery of the incarnation of relation.

3. We must now turn toward an element or toward a moment never yet mentioned, but to which the narrow—if obscure—imbrication of the family in the people was to lead. (That imbrication

can lead to a confusion or an even more obscure indecision, when we read in §156: "the ethical substance . . . is the actual spirit of a family and a people": this "and" has no recognizable status.) This element is love. The relation of which struggle is the phenomenon has love as its substantial content. Section 535 of the *Encyclopedia* says it clearly:

> The State is, *conscious of itself,* the ethical substance—the union of the principle of the family and that of civil society; the same unity that is in the family as the sentiment of love is the essence of the State, which at the same time, thanks to the second principle of the knowing and self-active will, receives the *form* of a *known* universality.

(I pass over the questions that the whole apparatus here indicated might raise—for example, the absence of the people. Each presentation of the State's principle seems to displace, deflect, or give the lie to the preceding one.)

Love is thus the true element—the essence—of the State, thus of union. And it is so, as many texts confirm, insofar as it actualizes the existence of the self by another—insofar as it actualizes relation. It should be shown how the texts of the young Hegel about love furnish the true description of relation, and furnish it in terms that imply or that program a political problematic. I shall content myself here with a brief passage from *The Spirit of Christianity*: "There is no true union, no love properly so called, except between living beings of equal power, who are thus entirely living for one another." But love is also, in the same text, set over against abstract universality:

> The love of men, conceived as having to extend to all those of whom one knows nothing, with whom one has no relation at all, this universal love is an insipid invention. . . . The love of one's neighbor is the love of men with whom everyone enters into relation. A being that is thought cannot be a being that is loved.[10]

Thus the monarch could perfectly well be, once again as a present, tangible existence, the true and unique possibility of union, the locus of political love. To be sure, the love of the king will not be evoked, for in a general manner love as such remains in the order of the immediacy of feeling, and, as the addition to §158 puts it: "In the State, feeling disappears, there we are conscious of unity as law; there the content must be rational and known to us."

(In the same way, a marginal note to §157 makes clear the opposition of the State to the family: "Emergence from natural unity—unity is only purified in the being-for-itself of two beings": the relation of two beings does have the essence of love, but in being-for-itself, in the autonomous person, the being-by-the-other of love is "purified" [*Einigkeit reinigt sich*]; there is thus some impurity in love.)

Nonetheless, it remains that the "known" rationality of the State is the *Aufhebung* of the immediate truth of union, and thus of love. And if this *Aufhebung* is not, or is scarcely, designated as such (whereas the principled positing of love is without ambiguity), it is perhaps also for a reason at the opposite limit from the one Hegel explicitly proposes: not the natural immediacy of the feeling of love, but the elusive excess of mediation that is operative in love. In fact, the text of the addition to §158 continues—recapturing in sum the tone of the early writings:

> The first moment in love is that I do not wish to be a self-subsistent and independent person and that if I were, then I would feel defective and incomplete. The second moment is that I find myself in another person, that I count for something in the other, while the other in turn comes to count for something in me. Love, therefore, is the most tremendous contradiction; the understanding cannot resolve it since there is nothing more stubborn than this point of self-consciousness that is negated and that nevertheless I ought to possess as affirmative. Love is at once the propounding and the resolving of this contradiction. As a resolving of it, love is unity of an ethical type.

"The most tremendous contradiction" (to say nothing of the fact that all contradictions are tremendous for the understanding, and that there is thus here an excess of the general tremendousness of mediation) is mediation itself as the real mediation of real persons. Now it is just this mediation that the monarch actualizes as a person and in his person. That is why, as §279 and §281 stress, the monarch is not, any more than love, accessible to understanding. What is accessible only to speculative reason, in the monarch, is "immediacy without foundation, being concentrated in itself beyond which one cannot go" (§281). But this concentration *is* that of union—in the same way, moreover, as the concentration in himself of a person in general really happens only by means of his existence through the other. In the monarch, this very otherness is concentrated, unified, and presented. The monarch is the objective truth of love, if the State is in general the objective truth of union.

Nevertheless, love, which is the *Aufhebung* of the exteriority of individuals, should itself be *aufgehoben* in the State. What must thus be *sublated* is not the sublation that love brings about, but rather what in love makes the moment opposed to the autonomous personality, thus the moment of the abandonment of the self to the other: not the *Aufhebung*, but the *Aufgebung*. How far can an *Aufhebung* of the *Aufgebung*, how far can a sublation of the gift of self be thought as an assumption of love, and from what point does it not constitute on the contrary a "pure and simple" negation of love, or a *renunciation* of love (which would be in some way an appendage to the renunciation of death, or to the avoidance of death of which we have spoken)? This is a question whose close investigation must be reserved for another occasion. But it contains the principle of the conclusion that we should draw from it here.

The "substantial" truth of love for the State is posited, all things considered, only if twice juggled: once because love has no place in the State, and again because love is the "tremendous contradiction." To which it is worth adding a third "trick": that of relating the substance of love to the phenomenon of struggle, for if both pertain to the determination of the people, their relation and its process should be presented as such—something for which Hegel does not furnish the slightest indication.

In raising this last difficulty, I am simply bringing together the pieces of the general difficulty we have traversed: the people—which is finally a people only if it is a State (§349), and which is a finished State only if it "has" (or "is"?) a monarch—has the reality of a double relation, of struggle and of love, which finds itself twice put aside from the *proper* formation of the State, inasmuch as its two terms find themselves distanced from each other, and inasmuch as each remains subjected to a modality of nonunderstanding (either because it is *only* a "phenomenon," or because it is the "tremendous contradiction"), or as each is in some way referred back to the extreme limit of the conditions of the functioning and apprehension of the dialectic itself.

The Monarch a "Tremendous Contradiction"

The search for relation as such thus leads to a triple impasse. But this search also proves that relation is at work everywhere, and that the truth of the monarch cannot be anything other than the truth of relation. It is so, however, as the simultaneous resurgence of everything concerning relation that has remained unresolved—as well as being the final exhibition of everything concerning relation that had always been supposed to be resolved already.

The impasse thus consists in the presupposition of the solution or of the resolution of relation: but this presupposition brings out all the more, against an emptiness, the *question* of relation. The monarch comes to fill this emptiness with his whole actual presence, with his body. But this body, which *must not* be symbolic, also finally remains elusive.

It is certainly not a matter of reproaching Hegel with an insufficiency in his interrogation of the *origin* of relation or of the ultimate and essential *being* of relation. The very form of such a question has every likelihood of being falsified in advance, if relation itself is not substantiated—being only *relation*, not the autonomy of its terms or its subjects—and if relation is perhaps necessarily without being and without origin. But just this would have to be "recognized." Hegel, because he masks the question or the impossibility of the question, shows the impasse of the philosophical solution of relation, and opens up at the same time the necessity of thinking relation without origin and without realization in a substantial unity.

Which amounts to saying that the monarch resolves the triple difficulty, but in fact conceals it, and thus rechannels and exacerbates it until it arrives at his own singularity.

The singularity of the monarch is in fact the strangest that can be imagined. He also, he perhaps above all, is a "tremendous contradiction."

A contradiction of position, first of all. The presupposition of the union of persons being that of right, as soon as right is presupposed (accomplished by the people), the juris-diction of the monarch is only its *formal* manifestation or presentation: and in fact, not only is the monarch's own personality insignificant ("it is a mistake to require of a monarch objective qualities, he has only to say 'yes' and put the dots on the *i*'s"—addition to §280), but his power is only formal: "[We cannot] say that the monarch may act capriciously. As a matter of fact, he is bound by the concrete decisions of his counselors, and if the constitution is stable he has often no more to do than to sign his name. But this name is important. It is the summit beyond which it is impossible to go" (addition to §279).

The juris-*diction* of the monarch, on this account, is only the naming of right, of union as right. "But this name is the summit," not because it would sanction right—it does not have the power for this—but because it fulfills it, completes it as actual individual existence. The name of the monarch is the real *Setzung* of the *Gesetz*. But by this account it is indeed right, the juridical sanction of right.

The scales immediately tip from the side of pure formality toward substantial actuality. The dots on the *i*'s, the signature, the name, and the mouth of the monarch who says "I will" (§279) constitute and are the *decision* that, even if it adds nothing to the content of the people's right, transforms the saying of the law and of the councils into the doing of a subjectivity.

(But the decision itself is infinitely undecidable: it adds nothing, and it adds itself. The text of §279 is formidably ambiguous: "This last reabsorbs all particularity into its single self, cuts short the weighing of pros and cons between which it lets itself oscillate perpetually now this way and now that, and by saying '*I will*' makes its *decision* and so inaugurates all activity and actuality." This "I will," as many additions make clear, is the "abstract and empty I will":[11] the monarch gives it only the concreteness of his mouth. But this mouth *is* by this fact concrete will.)

This transformation of abstract will into concrete will is a performative [*performation*]. The monarch is the subject of the enunciation, while the people—the spirit of the people—is the subject of the statement [*énoncé*]. But the statement is not actual—that is to say, it is not *stated*—except in the enunciation. This very simple, but obviously very formidable, general constraint rules the position of the monarch. We must recognize in it the homologous (and perhaps homogeneous) constraint that the theoreticians of "decisionism" stress in the law [*droit*]: the necessity for the juridical act in general always to contain an ultimate residue that established, prepared, written, or deliberated law does not contain and that is the performative of this law, the decision that law should make right, that it is effectively *gesetzt*. The constraint of enunciation, as a general constraint of the *existence* of discourse, is precisely the constraint of juris-*diction* (this constraint of diction being, as we know, inscribed not only in Roman law, but in the Roman concept of law as such). And this constraint (which, moreover, is perhaps not just an isolated case, that of juridical discourse, but which on the contrary makes jurisdiction in general the constraint of every discourse, of the whole order of discourse) always requires the existential positing of a *judex*, of an unique individual who says the right, and who is unique not because he takes this power to himself (he must be legitimated: the monarch is legitimated by the Constitution), nor because people have decided to give it to him (for then this decision, taken by others, would be the real decision, the paradoxical decision of giving up one's power to decide), for it is not, properly speaking, a question of a "power." But the *judex* is unique because *only a single individual can speak*. The monarch is the individual that he is because juris-*diction* is individual, that is, because *juris-diction is indivisible*. In this sense the monarch is the hypostasis of the indivisible unity of the modern State as the

French Republic "one and indivisible" had (self-)proclaimed it. The monarch *makes* the voice of the people, because the voice as such is unique, indivisible, incomparable, and because for that very reason it should be distinguished, given special status, personified in the strongest sense of the word.

So much for the position of the monarch—and now for his being.

Insofar as he actualizes the solution of relation, the dis-solution in the "union as such" of something whose unity will always have been presupposed, the monarch simply actualizes the logic of subjectivity. It is this logic that, in principle, hides or prohibits the question of relation. There is no "real" problem of relation once relation—even thought of as the actualization of a self in another— takes it origin in the movement of a *self* that goes to *its* exterior in order to *appropriate itself.* And it is this logic that intervenes in the truly *initial* movement of the *Philosophy of Right* as the process of the formation of the State.

The origin that we could not find in struggle, in love, or in the people we now find in another instance of relation, namely, the *contract.*

The contract is the birthplace of right insofar as it is the exchange of property according to the rule of a reappropriation, even a superappropriation of the property thus alienated:

> By distinguishing himself from himself, a person relates himself to *another person*, and it is only as owners that these two persons really exist [*Dasein*] for each other. Their implicit identity is realized through the transference of property from one to the other in conformity with a common will and the maintenance of the rights of both. This is *contract.* (§40)

(In a certain fashion, contract thus has the same "form" as struggle and as love, the form of passage into or through the other. Nevertheless, here it is something other than the person who "passes": it is his property—through which, however, he is as a person. Reciprocally, if the contract is not an element in struggle or in love, it is because in both there is an *Aufgebung* of the self, to which the notions of "common will" and "the maintenance of rights" are no longer pertinent.)

We have here the beginning of the relation of right—and yet we can also perfectly well affirm that the principle of the State cannot be here. For the development of the contract is carried out in civil society. Now the State precedes and exceeds this, and the monarch is this excess. The right of the State is lacking in its most clearly attested origin. After all, the principle of contract is opposed by itself to the essence of monarchy itself, as Hegel had remarked in 1802 in his *The Scientific Ways of Treating Law*:

> The form of such an inferior relation as the contractual one has forced its way into the absolute majesty of the ethical totality. In the case of the monarchy, for example, the absolute universality of the center and the oneness of the individual therein is understood, now according to a contract of full authorization as a relation between a supreme civil servant to the abstraction of the State, now according to the relation of an ordinary contract as a matter between two specific parties each of whom needs the other, and so as a relation of quid pro quo—and by relations of this kind that are wholly in the sphere of the finite, the Idea and the absolute majesty of the ethical totality are destroyed.[12]

(However, it is not clear that the primitive contract of the *Philosophy of Right* proceeds from need. Rather, it proceeds from a superior necessity, that of the constitution of identity, but Hegel does not establish a superior category of contract.)

If, in spite of this, the contract furnishes the origin of right (even if it will be once more refused, against Rousseau, as a principle of the State, in §258, in favor of the monarchy), it is because the contract brings property into play. In and through property the singular person is constituted, that is, in relation to himself. The moment preceding the contract is this one: "Possession [*Besitz*], which is property-ownership [*Eigentum*]. Freedom is here the freedom of the abstract will in general, or, *eo ipso*, the freedom of a single person related only to himself" (§40).

Thus a person enters into relation with another only in differentiating himself from himself, and is only differentiated from himself in property, by which he relates to something as *his own*. (Which passes through taking-possession, whose analysis should be developed, particularly to show how Hegel avoids looking at it straight on as a violence of appropriation that is nevertheless legible between the lines, and how in a similar way taking-possession is treated under the prior consideration of a recognized right of the original owner [see §50], whereas at this stage the right is still to be born. The gap that we constantly find appears here as the absence of articulation between taking-possession and the struggle for domination.)

So it is not exactly property that founds personality, but it is property-of-self that founds every appropriation, by which this property objectivizes itself. The person's personality consists in the possibility of relating to oneself before relating to anything else (and, by this intermediary, to anyone else). Before property and the contract, there is thus the person's differentiation of self:

> Personality begins not with the subject's mere general consciousness of himself as an ego concretely determined in some way or other, but rather with his consciousness of himself as a completely abstract ego in which every concrete restriction and value is negated and without validity. In personality, therefore, knowledge is knowledge of oneself as an object, but an object raised by thinking to the level of simple infinity and so an object purely self-identical. (§35)

The sentence that immediately follows assigns this moment or this process identically to individuals and to peoples: "Individuals and nations have no personality until they have achieved this pure thought." (This thought which, however, as the addition to this section shows, is also the thought of an "unbearable contradiction" in the order of nature: for the person is "the highest" of man as well as "the lowest" of his singular and as such despicable contingency. The person is thus what "bears" the contradiction of the person. It is doubtless also what the monarch bears more than anyone. But there again, the contradiction, unbearable or tremendous, has already resolved itself in the identity of the principle.)

The differentiation of self is the productive differentiation of the

Self as such—and *here* at least it takes place, in its principle, *by itself.* And it is *this* personality, the personality *proper* to the Self, that "essentially involves the capacity for rights," as §36 puts it. *Here,* in the beginning, right is only the relation to self. And the people is a self as much as the individual is. The secret of the people is the secret of the Self. That is why the origin and the nature of the people remained undiscovered—and why once discovered they are indistinguishable from those of the person. The relation *to the other,* difference as actual exteriority and the passage *into* the other, will never in the long run be anything but derived and subordinate—and this subordination (however foreign to the profound logic of self-consciousness in the *Phenomenology*) permits the *Aufgebung* of the self in the other to be contained or overlooked.

By this account, the monarch fulfills the *Self* of union, he fulfills it *as self*—and this accomplishment also swings over into the absolute nonproperty of the monarch, pure material punctuality of a subject who is only the subject of his signature (and who thus, doubtless, knows himself as an object, not even being as yet a proprietor of anything at all: the pen with which he signs belongs to the State), a subject exchangeable with any other (except that his birth must determine him in the natural lineage of a family, as a hereditary monarch, and that furthermore, "just because everyone is capable of being the king, it must be arranged that it is not everyone, but a single one . . . because in the State there is only one [sic: *da im Staate nur einer ist*]."[13] But this fulfillment also fulfills the absolute property of the State. On the one hand there is this superior property in which mine must disappear: "Abandonment [*Aufgeben*] of the person—not to have any private property—but something (or: some property) better," says a note to §46, thus indicating that the *Aufgebung* is only recognized insofar as it gives way to a "better" reappropriation. On the other hand—and as the summit of this reappropriation—there is the person of the monarch, in his singularity, as the holder of the real and ultimate *power* of decision. It is in fact the monarch *as an individual* who *decides* the relation of the State-individual to other State-individuals, that is to say, war and peace (cf. §320–29). In this case, his "I will" is not the form but the total substance of juris-diction. Not only does his mouth open, but he himself—and not the councils or the assemblies—decides. The logic of existence, the logic of performance, and the logic of union finally arrive at their synthesis in a logic of punctual and indivisible decision. (And it is doubtless on this point that a critical analysis of "decisionism" should be concentrated, and on the presupposition of indivisibility it contains: an ontological, semiological, performative, and existential indivisibility. Is the *voice* in general, and the voice of *sovereign* jurisdiction in particular, definitively indivisible, atomic? Would it not be already divided when it enunciates [itself]? The Hegelian monarch allows the necessity of these questions to stand out better perhaps than decisionist theories do, and precisely by what his being keeps as undecided or uncertain. But war puts an end to this indecision. . . .)

The Monarch Separate from the Totality

In the very center of this realization of the State-Subject is lodged, however, as the ontological necessity of this realization, the singularity of the monarch, that is to say, his detachment, his separation, his *Absonderung*. It is as *this* individual that he has value. Everything happens as if the monarch realized himself in the order of sensible certainty, of the *this* that is the richest and the poorest certitude at the beginning of the *Phenomenology*. Also, the position of the monarch, as a position, escapes the deduction that necessitates it. As the *Phenomenology* puts it:

> When philosophy is requested, by way of putting it to a crucial test—a test which it could not possibly sustain—to "deduce," to "construe," "to find a priori," or however it is put, a so-called *this thing* or *this particular man*, it is reasonable that the person making this demand should say *what* "this thing," or *what* "this I," he means: but to say this is quite impossible.[14]

The *Philosophy of Right* (which recalls, in presenting the monarch, the "immanent development" of "philosophical science," §279) faces this "crucial test" without facing it: this monarch, so called (X,

Y, or Z), is the spirit of a people who can produce him, by its
Constitution and by the legitimizing of a reigning family; the spirit
of the people as such should be "deduced (or any way one wants to
put it)": we have seen what this was a question of. And if, in the
end, "the Germanic peoples" are designated (§358, with "the Jewish
people" in counterpoint as "the people of suffering" from the loss of
the former world), nothing yet designates the actuality of the true
Constitution (to say nothing of the "barbarism" of these Germanic
peoples, as §359 evokes it). But such is the fundamental constraint
of logic put into play in the people and in the monarch.

The logic of the ontological proof in general deduces the necessity of an actuality whose *existence* can only emerge at a distance
from the deduction, in the contingency of its position. And it is
this *Umschlagen* in existence that produces at once both the *majesty*
of the monarch (for, says §281, he unites the ungrounded nature of
the will, absolute subjectivity, to the ungrounded nature of con-
tingent existence) and the fact that, as the same section says:
"the majesty of the monarch is a topic for thoughtful treatment
by philosophy alone, since every method of inquiry other than
the speculative method of the infinite Idea, which is purely self-
grounded, annuls the nature of majesty altogether."

On one side, only the self-groundedness of speculation can think
the ungroundedness of majesty. On the other side, this thought,
which thus excludes all comprehension by the understanding, is
itself a contemplation (*betrachten*), which is perhaps in its turn, by
reason of its "nature" (What is "contemplation"?), or of its object
(the ungroundedness of the existent), or for both reasons together,
less a process of appropriation than the indication of an infinite—
and infinitely distant—relation between philosophy and the monarch. In this sense, philosophy at once masters the monarch *and*
recognizes only in his majesty the unbridgeable distance from
existence to the concept. That is to say, in this case, the unbridgeable distance from union as such to the concept of its subjectivity,
the distance from the actual people to the concept of the organism—or the distance from the relation to Self in general. What
philosophy can only contemplate here, insofar as it contemplates

the singular *separation* of the monarch, is separation itself as the institution of relation. Philosophy contemplates the relation, separation—and if I may so put it, thus itself avows its separation from the separation that makes relation, this separation that it has not been able to assume in love, or in struggle, or in the people.

Thus the subject who is the monarch is so only at the price of negation or rather of the bursting or dispersion of subjectivity in himself. Inasmuch as he is neither an absolute monarch (even with respect to war, he should not by right be that) nor a simple symbol, the monarch—or rather the *majesty* that he is—confirms himself as being necessarily the opposite of a subjectivity. Not a dialectical opposite through which subjectivity might sublate itself (this sublation is impossible, for sublation is always, precisely, the subject), but what might be called a distancing in itself of subjectivity, a splitting in which, finally, something like relation might—just barely—come to light.

On the one hand, in fact, this monarch can only be delivered over to the universalizing logic of the *this*: "When I say *myself*, *this singular* self, I say in general *all the selves*; each of them is just what I say: me, this singular me."[15] The monarch, as we saw, only says "me," or rather "I" (in German, it is always *Ich*), only signs, affixes his name. And the singularity of the proper name is never, as we know (as Derrida knows), singular enough not to be iterable. As an absolute singularity, the monarch fits also into absolute iterability, or better, he *is* exactly, juridically and exactly iterable and interchangeable. Which means that his jurisdiction is absolutely "democratic" in a nonconstitutional sense of the term.

On the other hand, this same positing of the singular-State is to be understood above all as the totalization in the Subject of subjects and of their union. By this account, whether monarch, Party, or *Anführer* (the term is in §280), it is all the same: the essence of the totalitarian State is in subjectivity, and in the organicity that makes up its structure and its process. The monarch is the organ or the superorgan of organicity itself, of the "*Grund* determining itself" of §278, which is thus finally (dialectically) the *Grund* of *Grundlosigkeit* itself.

But this very determination nevertheless contradicts the actual separation of the ecceity of the monarch. And this contradiction, which Hegel wants to resolve but cannot, opens in law the possibility of a *dis-organization* of totalitarian politics. Between the totality of subjectivity and the individuality of the monarch, there is as much dialectical linkage as absolute rupture. For individuality, to say it now in terms more Bataillean (that is to say, hyper-Hegelian) than Hegelian, is necessarily in the separation, thus in the noncompletion of relation (also in love) and of subjectivity. Strictly speaking, we should say that in the organic totalization of the Hegelian State the monarch is *lacking*: either he is not an individual, or else he is one, and then he is excepted from the totality, he exceeds it or he remains withdrawn from it. It is thus that we can solicit the opposed meanings involuntarily placed by Marx on the [French] expression *La Souveraineté Personne* [either "personified sovereignty" or "the sovereignty of nobody"] with which he characterizes the monarch in his commentary—as just as it is erroneous—of these paragraphs of Hegel.

The closure of individuality brings about, as such, the incompleteness of relation. The monarch records this incompleteness just as much as he actualizes union. Or rather—and beyond what Hegel thinks—he actualizes union by not completing relation, by inscribing it in the space of separation, which is that of relation itself.

For the incompleteness of relation *is* relation itself. This does not mean that according to another and more subtle dialectic the monarch fulfills, completes, relation. It means that in spite of the dialectic the Hegelian monarch inscribes something—which is not a political solution, but which forms the limit, the inevitable stumbling-block, of the solution of the Political according to subjectivity. Relation resists, insists, and inscribes itself as separation.

Separation is visible or legible everywhere upon the monarch: as ecceity, he has value only through his body, his immediate natural being; as jurisdiction, he is only the singular difference of the mouth that pronounces or of the hand that signs. In all these respects, his individuality is insignificant: what signifies is only his separation. But separation does not *signify*, it distances, and in this sense it inscribes.

What it inscribes is the *finitude* of relation. Relation is in finitude because it is incompleteness. (Thus it *is* not.) And the thought of finitude is doubtless necessarily, beyond what in Heidegger seems to subject it to a "unity" (even a nonsubjective one), a thought of relation. Now finitude in general (or finiteness, if Hegel never thinks of finitude as such) is also, for Hegel, the inevitable element of jurisdiction as such. He says so in §529 of the *Encyclopedia*, about the decision of justice:

> That 3 years, 10 thalers, etc., or only 2½ years, 2¾, 2⅘ etc. to infinity, should be what is lawful, cannot in any sense be decided from the concept, and yet it is of the greatest importance that a decision should be taken. Thus, of itself, what is positive intervenes in the law as the contingent and arbitrary, but only to *put a term to the process of decision*, from the point of view of external considerations. This is how it happens and how it has always happened of itself in every legislation; it is only necessary to have a determined consciousness in this respect against spurious goals and chatter, as if in *all* respects the law can and must be determined by reason or juridical understanding, on purely rational and intelligent grounds. It is an empty exercise in *perfection* to demand and expect anything of this kind in the domain of the finite.

Juris-diction is not the application of an already substantially present reason, it is entrance into the determinate relation of that through which finite individuals place themselves first of all in relation: right—the copresence of freedoms, but in finitude and separation. To be sure, one can also find quickly enough, along this path, something arbitrary about the monarch. But the Hegelian monarch must, as we have understood, henceforth give us to think something other than a monarch—and especially this, that what I have called "political jurisdiction" requires, from the very center of and by the avowal of the philosophical thought of the political, an essential *withdrawal* of the Political as subject and as organicity. A withdrawal which responds to relation, which brings relation back everywhere in "union"—which "desocializes," one might try to say, organic sociality, and which "depoliticizes" the political subject. The question of the monarch becomes the following: how to think political jurisdiction so that it consists neither in submission to the Subject, nor in a simple symbolism (a flag is enough), but in the circumscription of a "place" of the "symbolization" of relation itself, if a "symbolization" is not a subjective fusion, but exactly the establishment of a relation, and the trace of its separation.

This question would be that of the "voice" of a "people," insofar as a people would not be *a subject*, and as its voice would pass through a place, a mouth, apart—and separated from itself. There doubtless remains to be invented an affirmation of separation which is an affirmation of relation—and which is what the State denies, refuses, or represses. Such a task, I make clear in closing, does not present itself for me—as will have been understood—under the rubric of "society against the State," which always runs the risks of reducing these questions to the topic of "civil society" and of ignoring the exigency encountered here. The affirmation of relation would have to be a *political* affirmation, in a sense that remains for us to discover.

TRANSLATED BY MARY ANN AND PETER CAWS

§ Finite History

This paper sketches only the outline of a possible approach to thinking history today. It does not develop, or even present, the whole system of topics and arguments that should be involved in such a project (in particular, a discussion of the problem of history in Heidegger, Benjamin, Arendt, Adorno, Foucault, Paturca, or Ricoeur). For this reason, I will indicate some of those topics or arguments only through brief remarks, explicitly indicated as "parentheses."

For the same reason, I want to give first, as a kind of epigraph, the thesis or hypothesis itself toward which I shall attempt to move: history—if we can remove this word from its metaphysical, and therefore historical, determination—does not belong primarily to time, nor to succession, nor to causality, but to community, or to being-in-common.

This is so because community itself is something historical. Which means that it is not a substance, nor a subject; it is not a common being, which could be the goal or culmination of a progressive process. It is rather a being-in-common that only *happens*, or that is happening, an event, more than a "*being.*" I shall attempt to present this happening of being itself, the noninfinity of its own existence, as *finite history.*

It is therefore the question of what happens when we risk saying "we are inaugurating history," instead of simply saying "this has been history"—in other words, when we treat historicity as performance rather than as narrative and knowledge.

We shall begin with the following premise: what today *is past*, what *our time* recognizes as *being past*, is no longer nature (which can be claimed to have already, long ago, become part of history); it is history itself.

Our time is no longer the time of history, and therefore, history itself appears to have become part of history. Our time is the time, or a time (this difference between articles by itself implies a radical difference in the thinking of history) of the *suspense* or *suspension* of history—in the sense both of a certain rhythm and of uneasy expectation. History is suspended, without movement, and we can anticipate only with uncertainty or with anxiety what will happen if it moves forward again (if it is still possible to imagine something like a "forward movement"), or if it does not move at all. All this, of course, is well known, but, as Hegel says, "What is well known is not known at all." Let us summarize, then, even if it is only to repeat, what constitutes the contemporary suspension of history.

First of all, history is suspended, or even finished, as *sense*, as the directional and teleological path that it has been considered to be since the beginning of modern historical thinking. History no longer *has* a goal or a purpose, and therefore, history no longer *is* determined by the individual (the general or the generic individual) or the autonomous person that Marx frequently criticized in the speculative, post-Hegelian way of thinking.[1] This consequently means that history can no longer be presented as—to use Lyotard's term—a "grand narrative," the narrative of some grand, collective destiny of mankind (of Humanity, of Liberty, etc.), a narrative that was grand because it was great, and that was great because its ultimate destination was considered good. Our time is the time, or a time, when this history at least has been suspended: total war, genocide, the challenge of nuclear powers, implacable technology, hunger, and absolute misery, all these are, at the least, evident signs of self-destroying mankind, of self-annihilating history, without any possibility of the dialectic work of the negative.

§ *Parenthesis one:* Perhaps one of the best literary presentations of this is found in Elsa Morante's *History: A Novel*,[2] a book that has a "double conclusion." The first is a "fictive" conclusion: "With that Monday in June 1947, the poor history of Iduzza Ramundo was ended" (p. 548). The second, after one last reminder of the most important "real" world events since 1947, says: "and history continues" (p. 555). This could also mean that historicity and narrativity have the same "history," and that, at the end of history, we reach—or we already have reached—the end of narrative. Unlike Lyotard, I would claim this of any narrative, big or small. The History that "continues," our time as it occurs as a time, continues beyond history and the novel. In this case, the literary mode, or the mode of discursivity accorded to this "historicity," would be quite different. As we shall see later on, it could be a certain mode of declaration, of announcement or of promise.

§ *Parenthesis two:* It is not without interest to remark that this narrative of history, from its beginning or almost from it, has also been curiously involved in a dramatic, tragic, and even desperate consideration of the same universal stream of events whose narration it was supposed to be. Hegel, even Hegel, spoke about history as "a picture of most fearful aspect [that] excites emotions of the profoundest and most hopeless sadness, counterbalanced by no consolatory result. We endure in beholding it a mental torture."[3] From its own beginning, history as narrative is and must be a theodicy within thought, but it remains at the same time paralyzed in its feelings by the evil in itself.

Therefore, our time no longer believes in history as being the "ruse of reason," the ruse by which reason would make the rose of ultimate, rational truth bloom. Also, our time is no longer a time able to feel and represent itself as a time *making* history, as a time producing the greatness of History as such. Our time is conscious of itself as a nonhistorical time. But it is also a time without nature. Therefore, it remains only the time of historicism or of historization, which means that all knowledge (except technological knowledge, which has no need of its own history), is unable to open itself to any future (even if rediscovering from time to time the idea of "utopia"), and unable to determine any historical present. It projects all its objects (and even the object "history" as such) under the unique, vague or indefinite law of a "historical determination," a kind of para-Hegelianism or para-Marxism. The "historical determination" indicates only *that* everything is historically determined but not *how* "determination" works, for "determination" is precisely understood as historical causality, and history is understood as a complex, interacting, even unstable network of causalities.

The secret of history is thus causality, and the secret of causality is history. History therefore becomes a causality of causalities, which means the unending production of *effects*—but never the *effectivity* of a beginning. But it is precisely the question of beginning, of inaugurating or entering history, that should constitute the core of the thinking of history. Historicism in general is the way of thinking that *presupposes* that history has always already begun, and that therefore it always merely continues. Historicism presupposes history, instead of taking it as what shall be thought. And this is true of every kind of historicism, monological or polylogical, simple or complex, teleological or nonteleological. As Adorno writes: "When history is transposed into the *existentiale* of historicality, the salt of the historical will lose its savor."[4] According to the historizing way of thinking, one could say that everything is historical, but also that nothing is "historic." I refer, of course, to the representation and use of history by our time. I do not want to criticize the outstanding historical work done by historians *and* the considerable reworking of historical knowledge that has been accomplished with the help of sociology, anthropology, biology, or the physical sciences. Neither do I want to erase the unerasable truth that everything—including "nature"—becomes and has become historical, always inscribed in change and becoming, always carrying the many marks of this inscription. This, moreover, is also the condition of the thinking of history itself and implies that a history of the many historical ways of thinking history could never itself be historicist. It should achieve a quite different status in terms of its own "historicity." But, as Nietzsche already knew, the more history becomes a broad and rich knowledge, the less we know what "history" means, even if historical knowledge is also an excellent critical and political tool in the fight against ideological representations and their power. It does not, however, at the same time allow for the possibility of a radical questioning of the representation—and/or the presentation—of history as such. Therefore, this word runs the risk either of silently keeping a kind of para- or post-Hegelian meaning or of slowly returning to the Greek meaning of *historia*: the collection of data.

If historicity—assuming that we can retain this word, which is here necessary and impossible at the same time—if the historicity of truth is at least one of the most important indicators of our time, then it should mean, first of all, that the truth of this "historicity" cannot be given or measured by any history or historical thinking. The "historicity" of truth cannot be simply a qualification of truth (as it is often understood): it has to be a transformation of its concept or thinking—and therefore it implies a transformation of the concept or thinking of "historicity" itself, as far as this "historicity" remains caught in a pre-historic thinking of truth.

§ *Parenthesis three:* Understanding everything in terms of "historical determination," which is quite different from thinking the historicity of truth, was not, at least after 1844, the method of Marx himself, of the Marx who with Engels wrote that "*History* does *nothing*," meaning by *history* what has become "the history of the *abstract* spirit of mankind, thus a spirit *beyond* a real man,"[5] or what he called in his "Response to Mikhailovski" "an all-purpose historico-philosophical theory whose supreme virtue is to be suprahistorical."

§ *Parenthesis four:* At the same time—in our time—we have become conscious that historical reality cannot be separated from the "literary artefact" (Hayden White's term) in or through which

it is read. But it is as if we were acknowledging that history is our
modern form of myth, and that, at the same time, a certain
"historical reality" remained, behind textuality and subjectivity, as
the real, infinite or indefinite development of time. It is as if we
were suspended between both: either something happens that we
cannot grasp in our representation, or nothing happens but the
production of historico-fictitious narratives.

Now, philosophically understood, history, behind its watered-
down historicist form, is the ontological constitution of the subject
itself. The proper mode of subjectivity—its essence and its structure—is for the subject to become itself by inscribing *in its "becoming" the law of the self itself,* and inscribing in the self the law and
the impulse of the process of becoming. The subject becomes what
it is (its own essence) by representing itself to itself (as you know,
the original and proper meaning of "representation" is not a "second presentation," but "a presentation to the self"), by becoming
visible to itself in its true form, in its true *eidos* or *idea.* The end of
history means, therefore, that history no longer represents or reveals the *Idea* of the self, or *the Idea* itself. But because metaphysical
history, by developing the visibility of the Idea (and the ideality of
the visible world) not only develops "content," but also develops
itself as the "form" and the "formation" of all its contents (in fact,
the true form is the form of the continuous formation of any
"content"), we shall conclude that history now no longer presents
or represents any history, any *idea of history.* (There is thus no
longer any History of the Idea, any Idea of History.) For example,
this, I believe, is what Lyotard means when he says that there is no
place for a "philosophy of history" within the form of "critical
thinking" he claims as his own.[6] But this is precisely what philosophy now should think. I mean that it should think of history as that
which would be *per essentiam* without an Idea (which means,
finally, *per essentiam sine essentia*), unable to be made visible, unable
to be idealized or theorized, even in historicist terms. This does not
mean, however, that historicity is something that is not offered to

thinking; the historicity of history could in fact today be what provokes thinking to think "beyond the Idea."

We shall come back to this later, but let us remember that the Idea of history—History itself as an idea, and the Idea History should reveal or produce—is nothing but the Idea of humanity, or Humanity as an Idea, as the completed, presented shape of Humanity. However—and that is what our time, at least, knows—the accomplishment of any kind of presented essence (which is the "Idea") necessarily puts an end to history *as* the movement, the becoming, and the production of the Idea. Accomplished Humanity is no longer historical (just as accomplished History is perhaps no longer human). This is why Derrida wrote: "History has always been conceived as the movement of a summation of history." (Or: "The very concept of history has lived only upon the possibility of meaning, upon the past, present, or promised presence of meaning and truth"—where "presence" here corresponds to "summation," or resorption into a single figure.[7] Resorbed history is presented history; the presence of subjectivity to itself, the presence of time as the essence of time, which is the *present* itself (the past, the present, and the future made present), time as the subject.

This is the most intimate as well as the ultimate contradiction of history. Not the dialectical contradiction within a historical process, but the contradiction, beyond or behind dialectics (or at its heart), between moving history and resorbed history, between subjectivity as process toward itself and subjectivity as presence to itself, between history as becoming and happening and history as sense, direction, and Idea. (This is true even for history thought as an indefinite or perpetual process: for subjectivity, in this case, presents itself to itself *as* the process itself, or, what amounts to the same thing, as the subject always already present *to* its own becoming.) This is the "double bind" of history—which is easy to find in every philosophical theory of history.

Insofar as history has already resorbed itself as an Idea (and even as its own Idea), we are, if one can say this, outside history. But insofar as this resorption *happened* as such in our recent past (or has been happening since the beginning of philosophy), and insofar as we already have a "historical" relationship with it, we are perhaps exposed to another kind of "history," to another meaning of it or perhaps to another history of history. (Once again, it was Marx who wrote: "World history has not always existed; history as world history is a result"—and those sentences are preceded by some notes: "*This conception appears as a necessary development.* But, there is the legitimation of chance [of freedom among other things]."[8] Between both possibilities, to be outside history or to enter another history (for which the name "history" no longer perhaps applies) is the "suspense" specific to our time.

But what does "our time" mean? "Our time" means precisely, first of all, a certain suspension of time, of time conceived as always flowing. A pure flow of time could not be "ours." The appropriation that the "our" indicates (we will have later to ask about this very special kind of appropriation) is something like an immobilization—or, better, it indicates that some aspect of time, without stopping time, or without stopping to be time, that some aspect of temporality, *as temporality*, becomes something like a certain *space*, a certain field, which could be for us the domain, in a very strange, uncanny fashion, of property. It is not that we dominate this time— our time—(indeed, how little we do!). But it is much more that time presents itself to us as this spatiality or "spacing" [*espacement*] of a certain suspension—which is nothing else than the *epoch*, which, of course, means "suspension" in Greek.

What is the proper operation of space? "Space 'spaces'"—"der Raum raumt," as Heidegger writes.[9] What is spaced in and by the epoch? Not some spatial points, which are already spaced, but the points of temporality itself, which are nothing but the always becoming and disappearing *presents* of time. This spacing (which is, as such, a temporal operation: space and time are here inextricable, and they are no longer able to be thought according to any of their traditional philosophical models)—this spacing spaces time itself, spacing it from its continuous present. This means that something *happens*: to happen is neither to flow nor to be present. A happening happens between present and present, between the flow and itself. In the continuous flow, or in the pure present (which is finally the same thing, if we remember what Kant claimed in the first *Critique* and elsewhere: namely, that in time everything passes but time itself), nothing can happen. This is why historicity itself is resorbed in history conceived as time, as succession and causality within time. Nothing can *take place*, because there is no place (no "spacing") between the presents of time, nor between time and itself. There is no place "*from* time *to* time" (but one could also say: there is no *time*). Happening consists in bringing forth a certain spacing of time, where something takes place, in *inaugurating* time itself. Today, the resorption of history takes place as our historical event, as the way we *eventually* are in history.

But how does it take place? By being *ours*. The possibility of saying "*our* time" and the possibility of this making sense (if it does) is given by a reciprocity between "our" and "time." This does not imply a collective property, as if first *we* exist, and then we possess a certain time. On the contrary, time gives us, by its spacing, the possibility of being *we*, or at least the possibility of saying "we" and "our." In order to say "we," we have to be in a certain common space of time—even if by our "we," "we" mean to include all mankind. According to such a statement, the common space of time is some several million years (but it is not by chance that such a statement is rarely made; a million-year-old community is not easy to conceive). According to this other statement, "our time is no longer the time of history," the common space of time is from thirty to fifty years. But it is, of course, not a matter of chronological time. It can exist—or it can happen—for only one day; that is, "our time" can be the history of one single day. This is finite history—and there is perhaps no other kind. It is a matter of the space of time, of spacing time and/or of spaced time, which gives to "us" the possibility of saying "we"—that is, the possibility of being *in common*, and of presenting or representing ourselves as a community—a community that shares or that partakes of the same space of time, for community itself is this space.

The determination of history as something *common*, or its determination as the time of community—the time in which something happens to the community, or the time in which the community itself happens—is nothing new. From the beginning of historical time, that is, from the beginning of history, history belonged to community, and community to history. The story of a single person, or of a single family, becomes historical only insofar as it belongs to a community. That means also that history belongs to politics, if politics means (as it does throughout *our* entire *history*) building, managing, and representing being-in-common as such (and not only as the social transaction of individual or particular needs and forces). The "communitarian" aspect of history or even, I would say, the "communist" aspect of history (which is perhaps not just one "aspect" among others) is the only permanent thing we can find in *our history*, as the history of history. And we can and must recognize it even in the age of the end of history, for this age is *our time.*

Because we partake in the end of history, and because this issue leads us to exchange opinions about it or dispute it, we are in this way given to ourselves, by time, in a certain kind of community— which is, at least for us, perhaps not exactly a sign of history, but at least a certain opening, without either definite signs or ideas, onto some "history," as well as onto "us."

How can we think of history in a new fashion, or perhaps, how can we think of something "beyond history," if "history" has only its philosophical-historical meaning? How can we do this in terms of community?

§ *Parenthesis five:* The fact that "history," perhaps like many other concepts within our discourse, has no other meaning than its philosophical-historical one, implies two different things. It means first that the meaning or the several meanings of "history" are established and enclosed within a certain epoch of history—or within *history itself as an epoch.* This epoch is precisely the epoch of the establishment and enclosure of *meaning* as such, or of *significa-tion* as such, that is, of the presented ideality and of the idealized or "eidetic" presence of the "signified" of a "signifier." Insofar as "history" means the signification or the significability of human time (of man as temporal and of temporality as human), with or without some final, "eternal" signification, it is in this sense (in the semiological-philosophical sense of *sense*) definitely closed. But this also means, in a second sense, that the meaning of "history," or that "history" as meaning—as the process of meaning itself—*has happened*, and that it has happened not only within our history, but as our history—which means also that Western thought (or Western community), as the thought that thinks of itself as historical, has happened, and that, by definition, "history" is no longer relevant for this "happening" as such. However, this does not mean that sense has nothing to do with happening. On the contrary, sense, understood if possible as being different from signification, as the element within which something like signification or nonsignification is possible, sense as our existential/transcendental condition— which means, the condition where existence is itself the transcendental, and therefore the condition in which we are not simply and immediately what we are—sense in this "sense" is not the meaning of any happening, nor of any historical process; sense is not the signification of what happens, but it is only that something happens. This is the sense within which we exist, even if we think of ourselves as non-sense, even if we transform history into absurdity (as we regularly do throughout our entire history). Sense is perhaps itself the happening, or what always happens through the happening, behind and/or beyond the resorption of history in its signification.

Let us now come to community. We shall proceed with a brief analysis of this concept, in order then to come back to history. Since this can only be a brief detour, I am forced to summarize what I have developed elsewhere on this topic.

What is community? Community is not a gathering of individuals, posterior to the elaboration of individuality, for individuality as such can be given only *within* such a gathering. This can be thought in different ways: in Hegel, for example, self-consciousness becomes what it is only if the subject is recognized as a self by another self. The subject desires that recognition, and because of this desire, it is already not identical to itself, not the subject that it is. In other words, it is a question of what is stable in the meaning of "I"—that is, for an "I" to have its own meaning, it, like any other signification, must be capable of being repeated outside of the presence of the thing signified. This can only happen either by means of the "I" of another individual or by means of the "you" with which the person addresses me. In each case, "I" am not before this commutation and communication of the "I." Community and communication are constitutive of individuality, rather than the reverse, and individuality is perhaps, in the final analysis, only a *boundary* of community. But community is no longer the essence of all individuals, an essence that is given prior to them. For community does not consist of anything other than the communication of separate "beings," which exist as such only through communication.

Community therefore is neither an abstract or immaterial relationship, nor a common substance. It is not a common *being*; it is to be *in* common, or to be *with* each other, or to be together. And "together" means something that is neither inside nor outside one's being. "Together" is an ontological modality different from any substantial constitution, as well as from any kind of relation (logical, mechanical, sensitive, intellectual, mystical, etc.). "Together" (and the possibility of saying "we") takes place where the inside, as an inside, becomes an outside; that is, where, without building any common "inside," it is given as an external interiority. "Together" means: not being by oneself and having one's own essence neither in oneself nor in another self. It is a way of not having any essence at all. This is *existence*: not having any essence, but having being, as existence, as one's only essence (and thus this essence is no longer an essence). This is the principal notion on which Heidegger's *Dasein* is founded—if it can be called a foundation. To exist does not mean simply "to be." On the contrary: to exist means *not* to be in the immediate presence or in the immanency of a "being-thing." To exist is not to be immanent, or not to be present to oneself, and not to be sent forth *by* oneself. To exist, therefore, is to hold one's "selfness" as an "otherness," and in such a way that no essence, no subject, no place can present *this otherness in itself*—either as the proper selfness of an other, or an "Other," or a common being (life or substance). The otherness of existence happens only as "togetherness." As Marx wrote: "It seems to be correct to begin with . . . society, which is the foundation and the subject of the entire social act of production. However, on closer examination this proves false. Society is an abstraction."[10] Community is the community of *others*, which does not mean that several individuals possess some common nature in spite of their differences, but rather that they partake only of their otherness. Otherness, at each moment, is the otherness of each "myself," which is "myself" only as an other. Otherness is not a common substance, but it is on the contrary the nonsubstantiality of each "self" and of its relationship *with* the others. All the selves are related through their otherness, which means that they are not "related"; in any case, not in any determinable sense of relationship. They are together, but togetherness is otherness.

To be together, or to be *in* common, therefore, is the proper mode of being of existence as such, which is the mode where being as such is put into play, where being as such is risked or exposed. I am "I" (I exist) only if I can say "we." (And this is also true of the Cartesian *ego*, whose certitude is for Descartes himself a common one, the most common of certitudes, but which we each time partake in only as an other.) This means that I exist only as (un)related to the existence of others, to other existences, and to the otherness of existence. The otherness of existence consists in its nonpresence to itself, which comes from its birth and death. We are *others*—each one for the other and each for him/herself—through birth and death, which expose our finitude.[11] *Finitude* does not mean that we are noninfinite—like small, insignificant beings within a grand, universal, and continuous being—but it means that we are *infinitely* finite, infinitely exposed to our existence as a nonessence, infinitely exposed to the otherness of our own "being" (or that being is in us exposed to its own otherness). We begin and we end without beginning and ending: without having a beginning and an end that is *ours*, but having (or being) them only as others', and through others. My beginning and my end are precisely what I cannot have as mine, and what no one can have as his/her own.

What results is that *we happen*—if to happen is to take place, as other, in time, as otherness (and what is time, if not the radical otherness of each moment of time?). We are not a "being" but a "happening" (or rather, being is in us exposed to happening). This happening as the "essential" otherness of existence is given to us as *we*, which is nothing but the otherness of existence (more than the existence of otherness). The "we" is nothing but finitude as a subject, if subjectivity could ever be finite (rather, it is, as such, infinite). And this is the reason that the "we" is a strange subject: who is speaking when I say "we"? We are not—the "we" is not—but we happen, and the "we" happens, and each individual happening happens only through this community of happening, which is our community. Community is finite community, that is, the community of otherness, of happening. And this is history. As Heidegger writes: "History [*Geschichte*] has its essential importance neither in what is past, nor in the 'today' and its 'connection' with what is past, but in the proper happening [*Geschehen*] of existence."[12]

Community, therefore, is not historical as if it were a permanently changing subject within (or below, as the *sub*ject was once defined) a permanently flowing time (or having this time as its subject or as its subjectivity, which is the metaphysical ground of any historicism—and which could be said, to some extent, to be the case even for Heidegger). But history is community, that is, the happening of a certain space of time—as a certain spacing of time, which is the spacing of a "we." This spacing gives space to community and spaces it, which means that it exposes it to it(self). And this is the explanation for this very simple and obvious fact: for why history was never thought as the compilation of individual stories but always as the proper and singular mode of common existence, which is itself the proper mode of existence.[13]

One could even say that the "minimum meaning" of the word "history," or its *nucleus semanticus*, is not history as the succession of events, but as their common dimension. It is "the common" as such, as it happens, which means precisely that "the" common is not given as a substance or a subject, not even as the subject-time, nor present as a subject, but that it happens, it is given as "historic."

In this sense, history is finite. This means exactly the opposite of finished history. Finished history is, from its beginning, the presentation of being through (or as) the process of time: the "resorption of history." It is history maintaining its end and presenting it, from its beginning (either as a catastrophe or as an apotheosis, either as an infinite accumulation or as a sudden transfiguration). Finite history is the happening of the time of existence, or of existence as time, spacing time, spacing the presence and the present of time. It does not have its essence in itself, nor anywhere else (for there is no "anywhere else"). It is then "essentially" exposed, *infinitely exposed to its own finite happening as such.*

Finite history is the occurrence of existence, in common, for it is the "togetherness of otherness." This also means that it is the occurrence of the freedom and decision to exist.

§ *Parenthesis six:* I cannot develop here the implications of the phrase "the freedom and decision to exist." It should not be interpreted in the sense of subjective freedom, which implies either a free subject with regard to history—in fact, a subject freed from historical limitations—or history itself as a subject, as Hegel envisioned it (to a certain extent), or perhaps in a more naive form, as Spengler or Toynbee conceived of it. Freedom shall be understood precisely as the proper character of the happening and exposure of existence. Not simply a way of being "free" of causality or destiny, but a way of being *destined* to deal with them, to be exposed to these factors (which, in themselves, do not constitute history). Freedom would mean: to have history, in its happening, as one's destiny. It does not imply any sort of "metahistorical" causality or necessity. It means that only freedom can originally open us—or open "being" as such—to something like "causality" or "destiny," or "necessity" or "decision." It means that we are entirely historical beings (and not being whose history would be either an accident or a determined process). This again means that history is the proper exposition of existence, which we are destined (this is "freedom") to think and/or to manage as causality and/or chance, as process and/or happening, as necessity and/or liberty, as fugacity and/or eternity, as unity and/or multiplicity, etc.[14]

Finite history is the presentation or the becoming present of existence insofar as existence itself is finite, and therefore common—which means, once again, that it does not have an essence, but that it *is*, in its "essence," happening (or, better, the happening of the possibility of something happening or not happening). Community does not mean a common happening, but happening itself, history (the *Geschehen* of the *Geschichte* of the community). Community is the "we" happening as the togetherness of otherness. As a singular being, I have a singular history (I exist) only insofar as I am exposed to and as I am within community, even if I do not have any special or important role to play with respect to community. "I" within "we" and "we" as "we" *are* historical because we belong, in our essence, to this happening that is *the finitude of Being itself.* The fact that Being itself is finite means that it is neither substance nor subject, but its being (or its *sense*) consists only in being *offered in* existence and *to* existence. Being is the offer of existence—and it is of the specific character of the offer to happen (to be offered). This is what one could call our "historical communism": what happens as, or to, the *we*.

Finite history, then, does not consist of the accomplishment or representation of the subject. It is neither mind nor man, neither liberty nor necessity, neither one Idea nor another, not even the Idea of otherness, which would be the Idea of time and the Idea of History itself. Otherness has no Idea, but it only happens—as togetherness.

§ *Parenthesis seven:* This could be the starting point for a rereading of Hegel's philosophy of history, or of Hegel's philosophy as history. Because if history is the history of mind, or of reason, as it is in Hegel's *Philosophy of History*, this means that reason itself is immanent to historical existence and that it realizes itself in this existence and through it. Now, this could also imply that reason is nothing but historical existence, that reason becomes reason inasmuch as it is the "happening" of historical existence. (In this way, dialectics "can be seen," as Suzanne Gearhart writes, "to work against itself."[15]) In this sense, reason would not be so much the essence or the subject of history, as history would be the only existence of reason. Therefore, the rationality of this reason would have to be understood in a quite different way than the ordinary "Hegelian" way. This rereading of Hegel would be a rereading of the philosophical discourse of history in general. Its principle or its schema would be that philosophical history, as the processing of the identity of the mind (or of man, mankind, etc.), as the identification of identity as such, has always been at the same time the infinite difference or differentiation of identity.

Finite history: it should be clear by now that finitude and history are the same, and that the term "finite history" is a tautology, that is, it is as long as "history" is considered apart from its self-resorption. Finite history, or history as history, history in its historicity (assuming that the word "history" is still appropriate), is not the presentation of any accomplishment, or any essence—not even of its own process or flow. It is the presentation of the nonessence of existence. (Which is itself, as the concept and discourse of "existence," an element of a philosophy that puts itself into question, a historical event, the happening of History revealing itself as an epoch.)

Finite history is the presentation of existence as it is, *qua* existence and *qua* community, never present to itself. When we enunciate in a historical context any "they," such as "they, the Greeks," or "they, the Founding Fathers," or "they, the members of the Russian Soviets in 1917," when we enunciate this "they," which is, properly speaking, to write history, we say in their place the "we" that simultaneously belongs to "them" and does not belong to "them," because it is their historical or historic community, which appears only through history, through *our* making of history. When the Greeks themselves said "the Greeks," something of "the Greeks" was already lost and a new spacing of time was already opening the "Greek" community to its own future. Historical existence is always existence outside presence. The "they" the historian writes shows that the "we" it implies is not and was never, as such, present. The "we" comes always from the future. So does our "our," when we think of ourselves as the community occupying the space of time of the end of History.

History, in its happening, is what we are never able to be present to, and *this* is our existence and our "we." Our "we" is constituted by this nonpresence, which is not a presence at all, but which is the happening as such. To write history—which is always the way history is made (even when we think and speak of *making* history in the "present," of being at a historic opening, we speak of *"writing"* history)—is not to re-present some past or present presence. It is to trace the otherness of existence within its own present and presence. And this is why history is essentially *writing*, if writing is the tracing of difference through the difference of the trace. As Werner Hamacher writes, to write history is "a 'farewell' to the presence of the historical event"; in German, "Was geschieht ist Abschied" (what happens is farewell, and/or separation, which is the literal meaning of *abschied*).[16] To be present in history and to history (to make judgments, decisions, choices in terms of a future) is never to be present to oneself as historic. It is to be "spaced"—or to be written—by the spacing of time itself, by the spacing that opens the possibility of history and of community. This always comes from the future; but this "future" no longer is a future present, coming to us through its representation. "Future" means the spacing of time, the difference which is not *in* time, but which is the difference *of* time—the space by means of which time *differs* itself, and which is the space of community in its existence.

If time is understood as permanent succession and flow (and there is no other understanding of time as such), history does not belong to time, or history requires a quite different thinking of time—a thinking of its spacing (*espacement*). (For the same reason, history does not belong to causality, either as a unity or multiplicity of causal series—even if causality is not given, but only represented as an Idea.[17]) For the permanency of the permanently changing times (time as substance, according to Kant) is presence present to

itself—even if it never gives a presentation of itself. History, however, is a "coming-into-presence," it is the coming ("from the
future") *as coming*, as happening, which means: as not present.
This is not the permanency of a becoming. History becomes
nothing—for history is not becoming, but coming. It does not
belong to the present of time, to the times of presence (as the
present-past, the present, the present-future). Nor does it belong to
memory. Memory is the (re)presentation of the past. It is the *living*
past. History begins where memory ends. It begins where *representation* ends. The historian's work—which is never a work of memory—is a work of representation in many senses, but it is representation with respect to something that is not representable, and that
is history itself. History is nonrepresentable, not in the sense that it
would be some presence hidden behind the representations, but
because it is the *coming* into presence, as the happening. What is to
come? What is the peculiar constitution of "to come," beyond
presence and absence?—that would be the question of a more
precise approach to history than this one.

As Hannah Arendt emphasizes in her essay "The Concept of
History,"[18] only the modern thinking of history gives us the understanding of time as a temporal succession in the first place. One can
add that the concept of causality is implicated in this way of
thinking. Causality does not allow for happening as such—it does
not allow for happening *as it happens*, but only as one event
succeeding another. It ignores happening as it comes. Temporality
and causality do not have to do with happening. They only have to
do with change, which is still the change of particular substances or
subjects, and they never become the happening (the birth or death)
of the substance or subject in itself (that is what Kant says about
causality). This means that temporality and causality belong to a
nature, and history in this sense is a natural process, or it is (it was)
nature as a process, the process of mankind as a growing nature
(even if "nature" was thought to be the process itself).

The time of succession is the self-succession of time. It is, to
speak in Kantian terms, the succession of phenomena, and the
phenomenon of succession, but it is not the happening of phe-

nomenalization as such. It is not the birth or the death of something. It is not the *taking place* of something, the spacing that
allows its singular emergence or disappearance.

This spacing of time itself is nothing else than otherness, heterogeneity emerging in time. What does "emerging in time" mean? It
means that something that is not time, neither a presence, nor a
succession of presences, nor the substance of the process, occurs in
time, but not in a temporal fashion—which means not emerging
"out of" time back "into" time, not self-succeeding, but emerging
out of nothing—or going into nothing (birth or death). This nothing—which is always "future"—is *nothing*: it is not another, negative substance beside the self-succeeding one. This nothing means
that nothing *takes place* in the happening, for there is no place to
take; but there is the spacing of a *place* as such, the nothingness
spacing time, opening up in it an otherness, the heterogeneity of
existence.

§ *Parenthesis eight:* In a sense that we should carefully distinguish from its ordinary meanings, this nothing, or this emerging of
nothing as the *opening* of time, is eternity. Eternity shall not be
understood here as being *outside* of time, nor as coming *after* time
(as another future time). Eternity is existence emerging in time.
This is history, which is therefore our finite eternity. Eternity is
finite, because it does not have its essence in itself. Eternity is
nothing other than exposure to the time of existence, as well as the
exposure of this time. This topic should also involve a rereading of
Hegel (especially his *Encyclopedia*, §258), as well as Benjamin's
"Theses on the Philosophy of History."[19]

Whatever happens—or rather, *that* something happens—does
not come from the homogeneity of a temporal process or from the
homogeneous production of this process out of an origin. Happening means, on the contrary, that the origin is not and was never
present. This is the same as to say, with Heidegger, that Being *is*
not: this also means that *we* do not succeed ourselves in the pure
continuity of a substantial process, neither individually nor collec-

tively, but that *we* appear as *we*, in the heterogeneity of community, which is history, because we do not share any "commonness" and thus we are not a common being. We do not have and we are not our own origin. History in this sense means *the heterogeneity of the origin*, of Being, and of "ourselves."

Such a heterogeneity, however, is nothing but the heterogeneity of time itself; for succession would never be succession if it was not a heterogeneity between the first and the second time—between the different "presents" of time. Between the presents, there is no longer time, there is no longer the permanent substance and presence of time. To *emerge*, as happening does, or to emerge in time, means that time itself emerges out of itself, emerges out of its self. It is the timelessness of time—which is, in a certain sense, the same as a "timefullness"—it is also the "event," time full of its own heterogeneity, and therefore, spaced. Existence, as the ontological condition of finite being, is time outside itself, the opening of a space of time in time, which is also the space of the "we," the space of community, which is open and "founded" by nothing other than this spacing of time.

"Foundation" can be seen as a model for the "historic" event. Then, what is foundation besides the spacing of time and heterogeneity? Foundation does not, as such, come after anything else. Foundation has, by definition, no foundation. Foundation is nothing but the tracing of a limit that spaces time, that opens up a new time, or that opens up a time within time. Each time, what is opened up is a *world*, if "world" does not mean universe or cosmos, but the proper place of existence as such, the place in which one is "given to the world" or where one "comes into the world." A world is neither space nor time; it is the way we exist together. It is *our* world, the world of *us*, not as a belonging, but as the appropriation of existence insofar as it is finite, insofar as it is its own essence, which is to *exist*, to come into a world and to open up this world at the same time. But this time is not the time of an origin, nor the origin of time: it is the spacing of time, the opening up of the possibility of saying "we" and enunciating and announcing by this "we" the historicity of existence. History is not a narrative or a statement, but the announcement of a "we" (history is writing in this sense).

§ *Parenthesis nine:* In this sense, any foundation of an institution—or, if one prefers, any institution, as such, in its own instituting happening—is a kind of spacing, an opening up of the spaced time of history, notwithstanding the closed and enclosing space it can produce at the same time.

§ *Parenthesis ten:* Obviously, this is nothing other than an attempt to comment on or develop (even if it does not directly engage Heidegger's theory of history) the *Ereignis* of Heidegger—that is, Being itself as the happening that appropriates existence to itself, and therefore to its finitude in the sense of nonappropriated existence or nonessentiality. The logic of *Ereignis* is what Derrida expressed as the logic of "differance," which is the logic of what in itself differs from itself. I would add that this is the logic of existence and (as) community, not as they exist or are "given," but as they are offered. We are offered to ourselves, and this is our way to *be and not to be*—to exist (and not to be present or to be) only in the presence of the offering. The presence of the offering is its coming, or its future. To be offered, or to receive the offer of the future, is to be historical.

I am very aware that those three concepts (*Ereignis,* differance, offering) cannot be taken precisely as "concepts" and that using them one cannot build another "new theory" of "history," of "community" or of "existence." For they are themselves only offered at the boundaries of an epoch and at the limits of a discourse that are *ours* and are no longer *ours* at the same time (the time of the end of "History"). Therefore, they only *offer* us the chance to proceed from them—from their meanings and from their absence of meaning—*to* another space of time and of discourse. Through these fragile "signals" (rather than "signs"), it is history that is offering itself to us. It is the chance, which we have to take, to have another history come, to have another utterance of the "we," another enunciation of a future. This is not a theory, for it does not belong to a discourse about (or above) history and community. But this is—these words, concepts, or signals are—the way history offers itself, as happening, to a way of thinking that can no longer be the thinking of "History." To offer is to present or to propose—not to impose the present, like a gift. In the offer, the gift is not given. To offer implies the future of a gift, and/or the not-yet-given gift of a future. With respect to the offer, we have something to *do*, which is: to accept it or not. We have to decide, without knowing *what* is offered, because it is not given (it is not a concept, it is not a theory). The historicity of the truth lies in the fact that it offers itself to our decision and is never given.

Time opened up as a world (and this means that "historic" time is always the time of the changing of the world, which is to say, in a certain sense, of a *revolution*), time opened up and spaced as the "we" of a world, for a world or to a world, is the time of history. The time or the timing of nothing—or, at the same time, the time of a filling, of a fulfilling. "Historic" time is always a *full* time, a time filled by its own *espacement*. Benjamin writes: "History is the object of a construction whose place is not homogeneous, empty time, but time filled by the 'now' [*Jetztzeit*]."[20] Yet, what is "now," and what does it mean to be filled by "the now"? "Now" does not mean the present, nor does it represent the present. "Now" presents the present, or makes it *emerge*. The present, as we know, throughout our entire tradition, is not presentable. The present of the "now," which is the present of happening, is never present. But "now" (and not "the now," not a substantive, but "now" as a performed word, as the utterance that can be ours, performing the "we" as well as the "now") presents this lack of presence, which is also the coming of "we" and of history. A time full of "now" is a time full of openness and heterogeneity. "Now" says "our time"; and "our time" says: "We, filling the space of time with existence." This is not an accomplishment; this is happening. Happening accomplishes— happening. History accomplishes—history. This is to be destined or exposed to history, that is, exposure to existence is a way of being without accomplishment, without accomplished presence. And this is, for *us, today,* the way of Being as such. As Henri Birault writes: "Being in its entirety is destined to history."[21] That is, all of being *is* nothing but this destination or exposition, the finite exposition of existence to existence—of our existence, which is the possibility and the chance to say "we, now."

"We, now" does not mean that we are present in a given historical situation. We are no longer able to understand ourselves as a determined step within a determined process (although we cannot represent ourselves except as the result of the whole epoch of history, as a process of determination). But we have to partake in a space of time just as we have to partake of a community. To partake of community is to partake of existence, which is not to share any common substance, but to be exposed together to ourselves as to heterogeneity, to the happening of ourselves. This also means that we have to partake of history as a finitude. This is not to receive what we are from any essence or origin but to decide to be *historic.* "History" is not always and automatically historic. It has to be taken as an offer and to be decided. We no longer receive our sense from history—history no longer gives or enunciates sense. But we have to decide to enunciate our "we," our community, in order to enter history.

We have to decide to—and decide how to—be in common, to allow our existence to exist. This is not only at each moment a political decision; it is a decision about politics, about if and how we allow our otherness to exist, to inscribe itself as community and history. We have to decide to make—to write—history, which is to expose ourselves to the nonpresence of our present, and to its *coming* (as a "future" which does not succeed the present, but which is the coming of *our* present). Finite history is this infinite decision *toward* history—if we can still use the word "history," as I have tried to do, at least for today. In time, today is already yesterday. But every "today" is also the offer of the chance to "space time" and to decide how it will no longer just be time, but our time.

§ The Heart of Things

This immobile heart does not even beat. It is the heart of things. The one we speak of when we say "to get to the heart of things." The heart of all things: the same heart for all things, for every thing, a unique way of not beating—which has nothing to do with a death. For all things, for every thing: an absolutely singular, local restraint, fugitive and tenacious. A position, a disposition, an exposition against which thought comes up short, off which it ricochets: that there is something there, and still something else, the thing itself, at the heart of this thing.

But thought in turn is a thing. "One could have the idea that it is something simple, thought, a rawness presumably without identity, radically hesitant, which flings itself, loses control, and recovers itself in phrases."[1] Before it can recover itself in the phrase, in its "before" (irrecoverable like every "before"), the heart of thought does not beat, either, this immobile heart at the heart of an extreme and bewildering, ceaselessly bewildered, disconcerted mobility gripped by the innumerable heart of all things.

Things, thinking: *Dinge, Denken.* In this assonance, Hegel wanted to hear a predisposition of language, attuning the disposition of things to the exposition of their truth. (Still elsewhere, another assonance: *Sage, Sache,* saying and the thing about which one says something.) Listening this way, Hegel took words as the things they also are. At the heart of words, a truth-telling throbbing of the heart of things. The presence of a veracious god flush with the thing-word, guarantor of the consistency of all things in the thing-thought. The real is rational. Nevertheless, Hegel remained unaware that this throbbing, this reason, is immobile in truth. *Immobile in truth:* there, the thing restrains the word from speaking at the very moment it speaks, and the two do not surrender to the expressive mimesis that Hegel wanted to see in them. There is certainly a thing at the heart of the word, but that implies no kind of "meta-speech" but rather a non-speech of the words themselves, which is always immobile in them, even in speech.

(Why is our thought always so subservient to the domination of a "meta-speech"? Words, for us, must always say more, and do more. We think of things, on the contrary, as "simply" things. But precisely this "simplicity" must be the issue.)

Dinge/Denken—Sage/Sache: syncopation, not syntax; dissemia or dyssemia, not hypersemia. At the heart of things, where this heart is identically the heart of words and the heart of thought—a black hole from which nothing escapes, no light, a hole of absolute gravity—truth absolutely halts all movement of the concept and, with its gravity, impedes all momentum, all succession of sentences, all motion, all impulse of intelligence. At the heart of thing-words, as at the heart of all things, there is no language.

The more terms and operations that thought mobilizes, the more it draws away from the heart of things, and from its own heart. Conversely, the more thought lets itself be taken in by the powerful restraint of things, by the inertia of the buried heart of their presence, their pressure, and their appearance, the more it *ponders*, that is, the more it *weighs* on this heart of truth, and the more it lets this heart weigh on it.

But the two movements are not mutually exclusive, and it is yet another illusion to oppose the chatter of intelligence to grave meditation on things themselves. "To think," in the sense of setting the activity of discourse into motion, is to lead discourse itself toward the moment of this gravity, toward this "black hole" that it designates as its most characteristic limit, and toward which, finally, it cannot help precipitating itself in one way or another (stupidly or clairvoyantly, arrogantly or confidently).

That is why philosophy has always known (accepting it or not, which is another matter) that it could not be anything other than a "return to the things themselves," and that it must not cease coming back, and bringing itself back, to this return. Ever since Plato's anamnesis, it has been a question of nothing else: the truth, the gravity of the *on*, of the thing insofar as it *is*, beyond all *toiouton* (this or thatness). And that, very clearly, is why anamnesis must memorialize the immemorial, the immemorable.

At the heart of thought, there is *some thing* that defies all appropriation by thought (for example, its appropriation as "concept," or as "idea," as "philosophy" or as "meditation," or even as "thought"). This thing is nothing other than the immanent immobility of the fact *that there are* things. ("There are more things in heaven and earth, Horatio, than are dreamt of in your philosophy.") There are things, and their "there are" makes space for still another thing, which is thought, the supplementary memorial of the immemorial thing.

Thus for thought all things are there, and there is also thought itself, the taking (its) place of this "there is." This might seem to constitute two orders of things, and yet that is not the case. How could the taking-place of all things not also, and identically, be the thing itself? In this point (in this hole), which is the initial and ultimate point of thought, thought cannot be anything other than the thing in its presence. Which, strictly understood, would mean thought without reflexivity, without intentionality, without "*adequatio rei et intellectus.*" For the *there is* (some thing) is the point where thing becomes thought and thought becomes thing.

The thing *in itself*, the selfsame thing—thinghood as pure essense (Hegel)—stems from this point of distinct indistinction, from this heart-thing: nothing beats *there*, because it is the *there*. Every thing *is there* (every "being-there" is being-thing), but the *there*, by definition, is not there. That is why, here at the heart of things, one must not seek the living beat of a universal animation.

This is not death, either, but rather the immobile, impassive gravity of the "there is" of things. *There*, the "there" offers being and/or offers *itself, there*, to being. It offers itself to be being: it is the place of the taking-place, the statement of the place insofar as it is the simple place of the statement "there is." A statement that remains unarticulated (no one speaks there), an articulation that remains without statement (nothing is said there but the *there*). Not immediate, this immediacy—and yet without mediation. A punctual, naked, impassive conflagration of being. An imploding explosion of being-there. An apotropaic and apophantic place: "there is" *and* there is not "there is," for "there is" implies "there it is," but *it* is there without there being yet any *presence* there at all.

Things, in their determination as this or that, come from there, they *are from there*, because the thing itself, the thinghood of the thing, does not cease being *there* and coming *there*. Present since before all presence. Irrecoverable *before* of the present itself, inscribed/exscribed in it. A coming into presence that has not taken place, that will not take place, that only comes, and forever comes before taking place. Being *before*, without *taking*: the coming of presence, into presence. Thing.

Thought leaps: it leaps into things, trying to get there with the same leap as the "before," to recover the irrecoverable. It touches the thing itself, but this thing is also thought itself. The necessary leap is useless, the useless leap is necessary—and the thing of thought proves just as irrecoverable, just as immemorial. Faced with itself or with anything else, thought discovers the inappropriable property of the thing.

Nothing can be thought—in truth, one would not think at all—without the pondering or the weighing of this unthinkable thinghood of thought. Unthinkable, and yet thought, the very existence of thought, and its essence. One can think nothing without thinking this inappropriable property of the thing, and without thinking it as the heart of thought itself.

"To think the thing" or "to think things": to what else could thought be devoted? But if thing and thought turn out to be the same thing, the same immemorial heart, the same "before" that cannot be taken hold of, how could thought still think *itself, there,* and consequently (or differently), how could it think the thing? It is in the thought of the thing that thought finds its true gravity, it is there that it recognizes itself, and there that it collapses under its own weight. Thought finds itself at the heart of things. But this heart is immobile, and thought, although it finds itself there and attunes itself to that immobility, can still think itself only as mobility or mobilization. *There,* the heart of things creates an obstacle; *there,* it remains unmoved.

A heart of stone, so to speak. But instead of being without affect, the stone of this heart would be an extreme concentration, withheld in itself *and* as such exposed, a concentration of all motion, tender or violent, joyous or anguished, tender and violent, joyous and anguished. This heart of stone, far more originarily than any ambivalence, would be the indetermination of affect insofar as this indetermination is affect itself. It would be this passivity, or rather this possibility,[2] that is concentrated within itself only to the extent that, simultaneously and identically, it is completely exposed outside itself, before and ahead of itself. Impassive possibility, which does not display a presence but shows only *that there is* there, coming before all presence and from before all present, *some thing* that, as such, is passible to presence.[3]

The heart of the stone consists in exposing the stone to the elements: pebble on the road, in a torrent, underground, in the fusion of magma. "Pure essence"—or "simple existence"—involves a mineralogy and a meteorology of being. "The thing," "some thing," "all things," name being as a position of existence unto itself, exposed just at itself, the element that uses it and wears it away (agglomerates, fissurings, shatterings, cleavages, fusions, opacifications, vitrifications, granulations, crumblings, crystallizations, buryings, rustings, washings, traces, calcinations, etc.). As the wind erodes a stone, so is existence just at itself and a thing just at that selfsame thing, and so thought thinks.

That is how a thing takes place. That is how something comes to pass. The event itself, the coming into presence of the thing, participates in this elementary essence. It is lodged there, it is caught or comprehended in its compaction and in its porosity. The event is the taking-place of the being-there of the heart of things. It is the surprise of an appropriation without movement. It opens up, but it is also the always already open. *There* is a measure of space, of spacing, that gives time its origin, *before* time. Movements, histories, processes, all times of succession, of loss, of discovery, of return, of recovery, of anticipation—all this time essentially depends on the space opened up at the heart of things, on this spacing that *is* the heart of things.

That is why this heart does not beat—not "yet." Instead, there is "at first" the disclosedness, the exposed stone. Time will repeat this opening, from stone to stone, at the same pace or impasse of time, the same *pas de temps*, that moves an immobility forward. With each pace, time is opened so that something can *come to pass*. Time exposes the impassive passibility of the "there is." Arranged only along the spacing of the *there*, a thing is passible to something that can "occur to it," that can "come to pass" or "take place" for it. And, first of all, its own "there is" occurs to it. "There is something" occurs to every thing—and to no thing, giving way to all things, without preceding. *The world of things is without precedent.*

But as soon as there is something, this thing that has come, and its coming, are passible *to sense*. "Something comes to pass": that is, something is offered to the possibility of making sense, or of being caught by sense. Rather, something is already sense, is already in the element of sense, because it comes to pass. In this sense, "sense" precedes, exceeds, and exposes all "significations." It renders them all possible and consumes them all. Before/after all possible significations (that there is a world for this or for that, for a certain end or for no end . . .), "there is" gives the meaning of that whose meaning is not to be given. The world is passible to this in every thing and in all things. Such is *the sense of things*, the sense of existence at the heart of things.

Acknowledging that "there is something and not nothing" does not amount to convoking a pathos of wonder before Being. It refers first of all, more soberly, to the necessity of this acknowledgment itself. That there might be *something* is surprising, and in the acknowledgment (even more when it is given the form of a question: "Why is there something, and not nothing?"), the possibility that there is something *or* nothing makes no sense if there does not exist, first of all, something. Kant posited that there cannot, without contradiction, be a possible without any real. He concluded that something necessarily exists.

That there is some thing is necessary. *Some thing is*, necessarily. With itself, this necessary being posits (as its essence, as the essence that the existent is for itself) the passibility of sense: it comes to pass that some thing, in existing, is immediately passible to its own existence, as "sense." Impassively, of necessity. But the necessity *of* this necessity (the necessity of the necessary being) is that it is passible to sense. Such a necessity cannot be traced to a determination deduced from some possible, before any real. (All the problems of the philosophies of divine creation revolve around this point.) This necessity—this passibility—is that of the always already given reality of the real: the thing, always antecedent, but without precedent.

As a result, this necessity might well have to be identified otherwise than as a function of the necessity of a deduction, or of a production. As "freedom," for example—this, no doubt, is how Spinozan substance necessarily exists and is necessarily free (and alone in being so). It is necessarily freely that there is something. *This* necessity is the possibility of freedom, which we are not free to accept or refuse. It is not ours: it belongs to existence.

(The thought of such a freedom is no doubt the most difficult thought, for thought must grasp itself there, it must touch itself there as the *thing* of this freedom . . . Here again, in a Spinozan mode, is thought as the attribute of this unique substance, which it co-expresses with this other attribute, extension . . . Perhaps Spinoza is the only one to manifestly offer a thought-thing. Or to offer himself to it.)

Of the thing as any thing, as anything whatever: in "there is some thing," "some" is doubly redundant, as much with regard to "there is" as to "thing." This is the redundance of indetermination. "The thing" means "any thing at all." "A thing" is anything whatever. It is necessary that there be some thing, but not that there be a *particular* thing. Nevertheless, the undetermined-being of the thing is not a privation, nor is it a poverty. The "whatever" of the thing constitutes its most characteristic affirmation, with the compaction, the concretion, wherein the thing "reifies" itself, properly speaking. We can define it: a thing is a concretion, any one whatever, of being.

This takes nothing away from the differences between things. The "whatever" is not the "banal"—and it is only against the background of "whatever" that differences can arise. (In any case, the "whatever" implies that there are necessarily many things; otherwise, "whatever" would be abolished, all by itself. One should always say, "There are some things, and not nothing.")

But insofar as it is posited, exposed, insofar as it is the thing itself, every thing is whatever. The whatever of "there is," or the anonymity of being, is being itself in the withdrawal through which it is the being of the thing, or rather the being-a-thing, its "coming to pass," its coming into presence, its free exposition with no foundation and no end. Or it is the existence of the thing insofar as it is absolutely founded (and thus finished, finite, or final) in the being-whatever of the thing, in the being-the-whatever that is being. That *some* thing exists (or some things)—that is free necessity. *It is necessary that there be no necessity to whatever existence.* "Whatever" is the indeterminateness of being in what is posited and exposed within the strict, determined concretion of a singular thing, and the indeterminateness of its singular existence.

To think this: to leave behind all our determining, identifying, destining thoughts. That is, to leave behind what "thinking" usually means. But, first of all, to think this, that there is something to think, and to think the *some* of this thing at the heart of thought. This would be completely the opposite of "whatever" thought. This would be the thought—itself undetermined, included as it is in all thought—of what determines us to think: neither concept nor project, but rather thought brought up short against the heart of things. Our history today is concentrated, suspended, at the point where this exigency piles up.

"Some" is anonymous, and speaks of anonymity: here, it is not a question of names. Nor, therefore, is it a question of the negativity or the negation of divine names in a negative theology. Rather, it is a matter of *pro-nomination*. (*There* functions as an adverbial pronoun.) This is a matter from *before* all names—or again, a supplementation and replacement of names. Certainly there are proper names, and there are deictics. Certainly each thing can be shown in the concretion of its singularity: "this stone" or "the Kaaba."[4] But finally, what is shown in denomination is the fact *that* the thing is showable (and that it is therefore never ineffable or unpresentable)—whereas what is shown in the thing, *this* that it is, the matter of the reference, shows itself only as the external limit of deixis. "This stone" is the stone that my statement designates *and* before which my statement disappears. Or, instead of inscribing this stone in a lexicon, my statement comes to *exscribe itself* in this stone. At the heart of things, there is no language.

(The thought of things should situate itself upstream from any consideration of "the thing and the name." Already, in this name of "thing," every activity and therefore every question of denomination is shown to be in the process of dissolution.)

In another way, taking a negative theology beyond itself, we could say that the failure of divine names must be understood as follows: it expresses nothing other than the generalized failure of names in the face of things (including those things that names also are). This would not drive us back to the ineffable. This would lead us to the *exscription* of sense as the essence of language and of all inscription.

"Exscription"[5] means that the thing's name, by inscribing itself, inscribes its property as name *outside* itself, in an outside that it alone displays but where, displaying it, it displays the characteristic self-exteriority that constitutes its property as name. There is no thing without a name, but there is no name that, by naming and through naming, does not exscribe itself "in" the thing, or "as" it, while remaining this *other* of the thing that displays it only from afar.

Eventually, we will have to examine the pervasive tendency to distinguish, in language usage, between a banal, informative usage, governed by the signified alone (Mallarmé's "small change"), and a grander, supposedly poetic usage, wherein language would be its own end. In truth, language always ends outside itself. In all usage and from all usage of language arises what is absent to all language, a monstrosity that language alone can demonstrate, but by exscribing itself therein. No thinking about "writing" has had anything at stake but this: the stake of the *thing*. The thing that is named, the thing that is thought, is not the thing named and thought. But the two do not maintain the relationships of simple exteriority and of the sign's reflection of a referent. They are exscribed in each other as *the same thing*, for here it is a question of the sameness of the thing. The thing itself takes place in the infinitely different unity of a "there is" that *is* what it enounces, but only as a denounced and exscribed statement. (This could still be the question of a generalized performativity of language: every statement would be performative but, in return, every thing would be exscription of a statement. Exscription would be the performative [*performation*] of the performative [*performatif*] itself . . .)

The same goes for this thing that is thought. Thought exscribes itself. It corresponds to *itself* (as it must, to be what it is) only in this outside of itself to which it alone remits (or rather, emits, and throws, and abandons). That is certainly also what calls for the statement that "to think is always . . . to do something other than thinking—a something other that is not something other: it is to distract oneself, without, however, renouncing thought."[6] This "distraction" in "something other," which is precisely the same thing as the thing of thought, would be where thought thinks, because it excribes itself there, or because it performs itself there as thing. To think this . . .

That *this* thing exists, and that it is *some* thing, is the content of an absolute knowledge *that precedes thought in thought itself.* It is the experience of the necessity of existence, as experience of freedom. The coming of the world, to the world and in the world. The world as the taking-place of all comings, and of their abandonments. *Some thing* affirms a coming into presence, some thing affirms itself as coming into presence, coming without coming from anywhere, only coming *there*, indeterminate in its determination, unfettered by any attachment to or foundation in a substance or a negation of substance. The experience in question here is not the one that takes place in the circumscription of a "possible experience." Its reality precedes all possibility. It is the impossible and real, the *impossibly real* experience of some thing.

Philosophy never does enough justice to the *some* of the thing, and so it never does enough justice to the thing itself. (But it is no doubt impossible to *do justice* here, and philosophy, in spite of everything, goes to the limit . . .) This is not at all because philosophy restricts itself to concepts and abstractions, for the concept and the abstraction are also things, just as philosophy, for its part, is a thing. They are things in the fray, the exchange, the friction, the flash, and the wearing away of all things among themselves. But philosophy makes the thing its thing, whereas the *some* of something does not let itself be appropriated.

(What, since Heidegger, has been called the "end of philosophy" is nothing but the moment of depropriation at the heart of philosophy, or the moment, thematized and thought for itself, of the exscription of philosophy in the thing of thought.)

It is instead the *some* of the thing that could be appropriative. There is some thing, some thing comes to pass: by this we will always already have been appropriated. Existence is first of all appropriate to and appropriated by abandonment to the "there is/ there comes to pass." As soon as philosophy wants to appropriate this appropriation for itself, it reverses this movement, and it finally claims to make itself into the thing of thought. It is here that we rediscover Hegel's *Dinge/Denken*, in its properly speculative grasp— that is, in the reappropriation of the exscription on whose edges it maintains itself.

Now, it is another and similar treatment of words, another and similar denomination, that opens the thought of the thing for

Heidegger: "If we think of the thing as thing, we spare and protect
the thing's presence in the region from which it presences. Thing-
ing [*Dingen*] is the nearing of the world."[7] The possibility of such a
thought "takes up residence in a co-responding which, appealed to
in the world's being by the world's being, answers within itself to
that appeal." How could one not recognize another figure of the
same appropriation, and, consequently, how could one not recognize that the thought of the end of philosophy has not yet thought
enough about this end?

From Hegel to Heidegger, a *weighing* of thought on itself is
ceaselessly specified, ceaselessly aggravated, and it offers to let the
thing itself weigh with all its weight as thing. That is not only
important, it is the most important thing in the tradition as
handed down to us, and we all have to deal with it. Nevertheless,
when Heidegger himself designates the thing, it is always a matter
of correspondence, by sound or by sense, by sound as sense, by
sense as sonorous thing, it is always a matter of an appropriate,
well-attuned response. But what if the heart of things does not even
beat, if the *whatever* heart of things does not even address a call, or
any question? What if this heart only *exscribes* all our questions, all
our demands?

(There seems, though, to be a strange *idiom* of things. An idiom
in that it is a language reserved for the thing in general—but, since
the thing in general does not *exist*, an absolutely singular idiom of
each thing. *"There is" is said in as many idioms as there are things.*
Absolutely private languages, idiotic, non-significant, as all true
idioms must be. Not saying anything, but each time in a unique
code and style, they are inimitable yet indefinitely substitutable
among themselves, for they are whatever . . . Saying nothing,
saying the "nothing"—the "no" of the thing, the *rien* of *res*—but
saying it "somehow, anyhow": "Everything suspends itself at the
point where a dissimilar comes forth, and from there, something,
but something black."[8])

As a result, all appropriation must still be depropriated, even the
most "open" and "welcoming" appropriation. The *some* of the
thing, of every thing, must be what thought does not approach,

what it cannot allow to approach, but what first makes thought submit to this: that thought itself is nothing but some thought, any thought. Anything at all, among so many anythings at all.

(And here, the *that* of the thing, the "that" that it is. This time, "there is" equals "that is." It is the neuter of the thing, but neuter does not mean "neither one nor the other." It means one *or* the other, any one at all, but always one. One and one and one. Never *one*, therefore, as in "there is a thing [and there is only one]." Not one. Any one at all, indefinitely. To exist: to be in the middle of all that. And all that is an indefiniteness of centers: "To live, for a thing, is to be in the center."[9])

This thing touches, strokes, destroys, sets in motion other things, which in turn press on it, free it, make it, and undo it. The thing-thought does the same, and it is made, made and remade, in the same manner. But all philosophy *ends*, in one way or another, by attributing (and while attributing) to the thing the thought that it elaborates about the thing. For Paracelsus, the text of knowledge and of wisdom is the text of the book inscribed in all things, and the knowledge of man is a penetration into the immanent knowledge of things. There is in all philosophy, always, too much of Paracelsus. There is always too much magic, too much alchemy, there are always too many "correspondences," there is always too much mysticism or gnosis even in philosophies based principally on reason— and are there really any others? Reason cannot stop demanding, demanding without respite, the appropriation of the thing by some sense that is or should be its own (including the "simple" sense of being). In the same way, it occasionally demands that this sense even conform to the sound that says it—and here we have all of poetry recruited by philosophy and placed in turn at the service of this: that the thing should be appropriable. As matter and/or spirit, as appearance and/or reality, as presence and/or absence, as individuality and/or generality, as mystery and/or the code of mystery, etcetera.

But we must not oppose irrationality to reason! Irrationality remains definitively ignorant of things. It passes by the matter at hand, and so nothing comes to pass. It is more appropriative than reason itself, for it is so by annihilation. The "irrational," and any other form of "sur"-rationality, is always a sorry mess of thought. It is *in* and *from* reason that things must come to exercise their weighing upon reason. Then reason knows, at its limit, that "gravity is the sign of the presence of the world, and of a presence that not only *surrounds* the thing, like an environment, but is in each thing. . . . The world is in each thing, in the form of its weight."[10]

In reason, it is not reason that should interest us, but rather what weighs on it, whose weight demands that it be what it is, "reason." But as *logos*, or as *ratio*, or as "pure Reason," or as "speculative Reason," reason always has to be *the reason of the thing*, the reason of everything, and so in each thing it has to be, if we can put it this way, the thing of being-thing itself. For it is not a question of the thing's *cause* (although both *chose* [French for *thing*] and *cause* derive from the same *causa*), and it is not a question of a *raison causante* [a founding and explaining reason]. It is a question of the being-thing as such, of the being-some-thing, and of the being-this-thing-here (of *Jediesheit*, as Heidegger says[11]), or of an "ecceity" (formed from *ecce*, behold), or of the *haecceitas* of Duns Scotus, of the singular actualization *qua substantia fit haec* (by which the substance is made into this). Reason: it is a question of what makes a thing a thing. It is a question of the heart of things. Before and after the cause, the thing has its being-some and its being-this *just at itself*, just in its singular coming to its presence *here*.

The *thing* exists only as the withdrawal of its *cause*. The cause is withdrawn from the being-here of the thing, from its *there*-here [*y*-ci] where in each instance there is some thing.

The heart of things: here lies the thing in its very reason, reason in its very thing. But it is not a question of death or of a tomb. Here there is only the exscription of an existence.

Ontology, interred here (but neither dead nor alive). An ontology of the thing's self-coincidence, stealing its existence away from any cause, by essence or by principle.[12] An ontology of the existence that is its own essence. Here, being assigns logos, not the other way around. It is the non-dependence of the thing, in itself—in its "some"—in submission to nothing except its own arrival, advent, and abode in its *here*. Now, "here" in no way pre-exists the thing. "Here" ("behold," *ecce*) names and exscribes the *here* by which the thing exists—and existence *lies here*, thrown to the world. In this laying out, existence lays bare a reason that is nothing other than the singular freedom of this *here lies*.

Things always come into presence in layers. As soon as we address ourselves to a thing, to this one here, to this other one here, as soon as we undertake to think it or to think *thereon*, we are dealing with a geology. It is a disposition of slabs, of strata pressed and folded one upon the other. The world is the cut of their multiple contiguities. But it is also the topography of their distinctions, of the total discretion of their "heres." No thing-here is the same as another thing-here; such is Leibniz's principle. If this thing here does not distinguish itself from that thing there, it is because the latter's *there* coincides with the former's *here*.

The thing co-incides: it falls with itself on itself, in itself. It falls on its *here*, coming *there*, but only its fall and its coming make the *here*. This is both fall and surprise. The fall, here, is identical to the pure and simple position of being, and the surprise is identical to its exposition.

The thing falls: but it falls from so high—from all the height of the world, we would have to say—that nothing any longer indicates the opposition of a "high" and a "low." The thing does not fall from any celestial arch: this is a disaster with no astral substance from which things might separate. Neither night nor day. The thing falls *from the limit*, from the extremity of all things. "Wouldn't the disaster be . . . the affirmation—of the singularity of the extreme?"[13] Or again: the thing confounds itself with its fall, and with its *clinamen*. And, in the end, the very fall confounds itself with the *here lies* of the world.

Represented according to its co-incidence, however, the thing reveals that its identity is not simple immediacy. Just as its position *is* exposition, so is its identity the difference of here/lies, and of the thing/itself, and of the coming *into* presence. But the non-immediate, here, is not mediation. The proper register of the thing is the register of *immanence without immediacy*.

In immediacy, there would be no *here*; there would be only an indistinct "over there" and, strictly speaking, *there* would not be. No longer would ontology be buried, subterranean: it would be nil. Mediation, on the other hand, is the becoming-other of the thing, which is capable of qualifying it and thus of positing it: for example, it becomes an *object* for a consciousness, or a *subject* of this consciousness.[14] This is a phenomenology. To speak of the thing's immanence without immediacy would be to try to say that the thing remains in itself (*in-manere*) but that in this manner of remaining, in this manner of lying, there is nothing that weighs or that posits, but there is a pause in weight: not the effect of a gravity, but gravity itself—and position is suspended there, bringing about its ex-position. The beating heart of an immobility, the unbeating heart of co-incidence.

To think this is to come instantly up against the thing of thought, against this thing that it is, this pineal gland, this hard point, material/immaterial, the material of immateriality, this pointed-ness that drills into thought and uses it up, that cannot help going so far as to threaten it—and that lets it know, finally, that it *is not* the thought of the thing, never immanent enough, never lying-here enough . . . And yet it is always thought, which is never general, but always this thought here . . .

To be in each instance this thought *here* founds thought's certainty and discourages it from thinking, exasperates and abandons it.

How much must thought be mistreated, and how much must one let oneself be mistreated by it, for something of the thing merely to rise to the surface of thought? There can be no half-measures. One can only press on.

The heart of things: where thought knocks against itself, where it knocks. Hard thought: that does not mean "difficult." On the contrary, it is always too simple.

The *here lies* of the thing, and of its thought, if it is indeed an inscription—that is, an exscription—is therefore not engraved on a tomb. It is not a question of death, or of the sepulcher, or of funerary stelae. If it were, the thing would be only its own monument, that is, to the monument of the Proper, and thought would be only its keeping and conservation. The world would be its own mausoleum. Thought must always take care not, first of all, to have enshrouded things. It must resist this enshrouding and hold to the laying out of things.

The thing belongs to finitude, or rather finitude is the mode in which the thing is appropriated as thing. If we insist on putting it in these terms, it therefore also belongs to death. But not to death elevated to the status of a thing and of a monument to things. The heart of things, in its suspension—and this is also the heart of dead things—indicates, in finitude, something other than the monumentality of death, and something other than existence posed on death's parvis. Rather, it indicates an extreme reserve, an extreme discretion of and toward death: the opposite of a denial—a recognition, if you will—but one that, there in death, does not claim to recognize *itself*. There is no *there* for death.

A thought of the thing would seek instead to formulate something like this: "the thing" means, in all things, in all existences, what does not accede to itself, or does not accede to a Self, but still coincides, being the thing "in itself." There would be no "self," and no "subject," to which *this*, and this *here*, would not already be presupposed, but in such a way that this is not yet another "subjectum." This is being-thrown, without supporters or support. The *being-there* of the thing is the presupposition that one cannot even call "presupposed." In this respect, the thing's being-there is finite, incapable of attachment to an infinite concatenation of being. By it, being is finite. And being therefore never finishes being so, as long as there is some thing—and there are necessarily some things . . .

That, the thing "there," surely does not then belong to Life, to this life, conceived as the life of the Universe, as the life of Spirit, or as the life of History (or as the life of the Living). But it does not belong to Death, either—for death is without property. "Life" and "death" represent, respectively, the absolute antecedence of self-appropriation and this appropriation's absolute failure to pass itself on. But at the heart of things, existence, withdrawn even in its visibility, appropriates itself in a completely different manner, in the discretion of the "there is/there occurs something" and the "there is not/there no longer occurs anything." Finitude does not signify, first of all, mortality (monumentality): it signifies first of all that the appropriation, and the property, of every thing, or that the being-thing-in-itself of every thing, takes place as "there is," and takes place only in this way (in which "there is no longer" is included, since "there is" is emphatically not a prop for being or for essence). *Here is exposed the finite, and the infinite exposure of the finite.*

For this reason, too, let's not speak too hastily of the "wonder of being." This "wonder" is a mere trifle: only the thing, almost nothing. (As we know only too well, the French word for "nothing"—*rien*—comes from *res*, the Latin word for "thing.") But almost nothing suffices to make a world—which also means that a world is no big thing, that this world *here* is no big thing (and, of course, *there isn't* any other: Descartes, Spinoza, Leibniz, Kant, Hegel, Nietzsche, Husserl, Heidegger, and we ourselves have never stopped thinking *that*). But "no big thing" doesn't mean nothing; it is still some things, and we are *there*. If, resigned or cynical, we say "no big thing," it is because we are still measuring things by the monumental, and trying to grasp each thing as a sublime inscription on the Mausoleum of the World.

With Sartre, "things" began to nauseate us—and Sartre was the last to try erecting a monument (a "historic" totalization, but one integrating an errancy and a singularity of existence), which is also to say that he was the first to *touch* the breakup of the monument (he exhausted himself in this, and was no doubt touched to the quick by it, to death). But long ago things had already become problematic or suspect to us: "objects," "merchandise," "reifications."[15] And art is no longer exactly—no longer simply as "art"—an opening to their strangeness. It could be that what is called the world "of technology" proposes to us nothing other than the challenge of things. It would be neither simply nor initially a question of technical things themselves (systems, materials), but rather of this: "technology" no longer pertains to the order or to the aim of the monument. When technology is colossal, that is not in order to raise itself to the status of monument; in technology the "colossal" is inseparable from diversification, from variation, from fleetingness.

To the exact degree that we lack a thought of things, the distaste and the fear that we have projected onto "things" (objects) flows back onto us (subjects) and makes us take our existences for things (toys), with which there is not even anyone left to play.

At bottom, the West has not stopped seeking to give a supplement of soul to a world of things (even if the expression is shopworn, and just because it is: a stillborn expression, worn out ever since its birth). That is why, even though we are already there, we are not yet in the world, in things, in some thing.

"Some thing" is whatever. The "whatever" of each thing would be, approximately, in Husserlian terms, the non-presentified, non-evaluated thing, the thing that is not the correlate of an intention: "a transcendence of the world," but insofar as the world remains in its immanence. But this would not be worn-out banality, nor would it be the insignificance of what ends up on the trash heap. This would precede all usage and all wear, and it would have the *common* characteristic of the "banal." It is common to all things to be, and in this way, being is their "whatever." But it is common to each one to be some thing, this particular thing here. There is no "common" thing that is not singular. A multiplicity of singular things is therefore, as has already been said, a principle.[16]

The banality of the "whatever" thus reveals the community of things. There is not only a community of subjects, there is also one of things, in which subjects are also found. Community does not mean possessing a common being, in the sense of all things' being constituted of the same banal substance. It means: to be *in* common, to remain within this "in" (*therein* . . .), in this "between" of the continuous-discontinuity, of the singular-discretion according to which, in every instance, there is "coincidence."

What marks the community of things? As *whatever* sort of things, they are interchangeable with one another. In this register, the world is not primarily the defined order of an ensemble of determinatenesses, an order that posits and exploits their differences and their relations (it is not, in short, a *cosmos*, and it is not a world structured like a language). The world is primarily made of the permutability, of the interchangeability, of all things. One could say, as if in a non-psychic, non-subjective, non-destinal version of metempsychosis: *some* thing is free to be a stone, a tree, a ball, Pierre, a nail, salt, Jacques, a number, a trace, a lioness, a marguerite. These determinations are interchangeable—not in the sense in which they would be equivalent: we are not talking about "value" here. We are talking about non-presentified things, whose being-in-common does not make up a common being but, on the contrary, offers the possibility of the greatest ontological differences. But this must be understood in the sense that neither anything in the world nor the world itself—an unsummable totality, unassumable by the "there is"—obeys any other necessity than "there is." And this necessity of existence is radically removed from the existence of any necessity.

That is why it must be called "freedom," even if the freedom of the stone [*pierre*] can in no way coincide with that of Pierre. The "whatever" of things resides in the freedom of the necessity of existence. "There is" is "free" because in it all necessity of *cause* (principle, production, reason, finality) withdraws into a necessity of thing.[17]

In a logic of the cause, all the properties of the thing caused are attributed to the thing that causes, even the power of effectuation itself. In principle, cause and effect are indiscernible in this thing. The world is indiscernible from the monument erected to its beginning and its end. (Whether one presents the monument as a "determining" or "dogmatic" force or says that it is a matter of a merely "regulatory" thought, this changes nothing.)

In a logic of the thing, the only question at stake is the appearance/disappearance of the thing in itself. It is only a question of its coming into presence and/or of its departure—coming from nowhere, going nowhere, because *there* isn't anywhere else. It is, if we wish to speak a language of this kind, a question of the effectivity of the effect, which renders it incommensurable to any cause, and by which alone the thing, instead of being indiscernible from the cause, coincides only with itself. In this respect, it is strictly not interchangeable. Nothing takes the place of this thing *here* (especially not a monument). It is the very incidence, or the accident, or the occasion of the coincidence: its fall, its flight, its case, its *clinamen*, its *kairos*, its *Ereignis*.

The existence of the thing co-incides insofar as, in this incidence, it *spaces*, opens a *continuum* (which does not exist) through the discrete quantity of a *there*, which is its very quality as thing. The spacing of time (which forms time itself), the spacing of space (which forms space), the spacing of the "subject" (which forms the subject), etcetera. Being is the "spaciousness" of such a spacing. Not spatiality, but spaciosity. Not geometry, but presence, the coming into presence of the immobile heart of things. *Hen panta*, the One-All, does not designate the "one and the same thing" of all things but, on the contrary, the "being the spacing of all things" of the One, which is not a thing. To think this, the hardest thought, the exscription of thought: that we are *there*.

Ding, *thing* (and, analogously, *Sache* and *chose*): they first signified the tribunal, the place where rights were regulated, the assembly of free men. What case is debated in the thing? And who is *chosé*[18] ("accused," in Old French)? In every instance, it is a case of thought brought before the thing itself. Philosophy has never ceased to be this tribunal—or to be accused there. Thought is accused of not measuring up to the thing, to the level of the thing, and thus to *sense*—while the law of freedom requires thought initially (and finally) to coincide with this *some thing* that it also is, and which is precisely the occurrence of whatever case as such, the incidentality of being, the thing in itself.

Nevertheless, let's not grant too much to these etymologies. The thing resembles nothing, does not resemble anything. The heart of things resembles nothing, because it does not resemble anything. It does not resemble anything known, but that doesn't mean that it never stops coming into presence, and putting us in its presence, the presence of this concretion of being, always unique and always "whatever." To think this: to let oneself be led toward concrete thinking.

TRANSLATED BY BRIAN HOLMES
AND RODNEY TRUMBLE

§ Corpus

A *corpus* is not a discourse: however, what we need here is a corpus.

We need a *corpus*, a *cata*log, the recitation of an empirical logos that, without transcendental reason, would be a gleaned list, random in its order or in its degree of completion, a corpus of the body's *entries*: dictionary entries, entries into language, body registers, registers of bodies. We need a passive recording, as by a seismograph with its impalpable and precise styluses, a seismograph of bodies, of senses, and again of the entries of these bodies: access, orifices, pores of all types of skin, and "the portals of your body" (Apollinaire). We need to recite, to blazon, body after body, place after place, entry by entry.[1]

All this would be possible only if we had access to bodies, only if they were not impenetrable, as physics defines them. Bodies impenetrable to language, and languages impenetrable to bodies, bodies themselves, like this word "body," which already withholds itself and incorporates its own entry.

Two bodies cannot occupy the same space simultaneously. Not you and me at the same time in the space where I speak, in the place where you listen.

A discourse must indicate its source, its point of utterance, its condition of possibility, and its shifter [*embrayeur*]. But I will never be able to speak from where you listen, nor will you be able to listen from where I speak—nor will I ever be able to listen from where I speak. Bodies are impenetrable: only their impenetrability is penetrable. Words brought back to the mouth, or to the ink and the page: there is nothing here to discourse about, nothing to communicate. A community of bodies.

We need a *corpus*: a simple nomenclature of bodies, of the places of the body, of its entry ways, a recitation enunciated from nowhere, and not even enunciated, but announced, recorded, and repeated, as if one said: foot, belly, mouth, nail, wound, beating, sperm, breast, tattoo, eating, nerve, touching, knee, fatigue. . . .

Of course, failure is given at the outset, and intentionally so.

And a double failure is given: a failure to produce a discourse on the body, also the failure not to produce discourse on it. A double bind, a psychosis. I have finished talking about the body, and I have not yet begun. I will never stop talking about it, and this body from which I speak will never be able to speak, neither about itself nor about me. It will never experience speech's *jouissance*, and speech will never enjoy it.

This program is known from the start: it is the only program of a discourse, of a dialogue, of a colloquium devoted to the "body." When one puts the body on the program, on whatever program, one has already set it aside. Who can tell, here and now, which body addresses which other body? But should we talk about address? And in which sense? Does one require *adresse*, skillfulness, *tact*—that is to say, the right touch—in order to consider bodies as the addressees they must inevitably be? How does one touch? An entire rhetoric resides in this question. But what would happen if we understood the question non-metaphorically? *Comment toucher?* And as the question or program of a rhetoric, of an art of speech, is it only metaphorical? What does a word touch, if not a body? But there you have it: How can one get hold of the body? I am already speechless.

～

Of course, the point is not to suggest that the body is ineffable. The idea of the ineffable always serves the cause of a higher, more secret, more silent, and more sublime word: a treasury of sense to which only those united with God have access. But "God is dead" means: God no longer has a body. The dead, rotten body is this thing that no longer has any name in any language, as we learn from Tertullian and Bossuet; and the unnamed God has vanished together with this unnameable thing. It might very well be that with this body, all bodies have been lost, that any notion, any truth, any representation of bodies has been lost. But there remain the bodies themselves, and a discourse divided by them. One should not stop speaking about what cannot be said, one should not stop touching its speech and its tongue, pressing it against them. From this body to body contact with language one must expect a birth, the exposition of a body, which a tongue outside of itself will exscribe, will name by touching and by falling silent.

In truth, the body of God was the body of man himself: the body God had made for himself *ex limon terrae*, with a "putty" symbolizing the whole of his creation. "In oculis est ignis; in lingua, qua vocem format, aer; in manibus, quarum proprie tactus est, terra; in membris genitalibus, acqua." (In the eyes there is fire; in the tongue, which shapes speech, air; in the hands, to which touching belongs, earth; and water in the genitalia.)[2] As an image of God, the body of man was a resemblance to and a manifestation of the creative power *in persona*, the radiance of its beauty, the temple and the song of its glory.

With the death of God, we have lost this glorious body, this sublime body: this real symbol of his sovereign majesty, this microcosm of his immense work, and finally this visibility of the invisible, this *mimesis* of the inimitable.[3]

However, in order to think such a *mimesis*—and to elaborate the whole dogmatics of Incarnation—, one had to dispense with the *body*, with the very idea of body. The body was born in Plato's cave, or rather it was conceived and shaped in the form of the cave: as a prison or tomb of the soul,[4] and the body first was thought *from the inside*, as buried darkness into which light only penetrates in the form of reflections, and reality only in the form of shadows. This body is seen from the inside, as in the common but anguishing fantasy of seeing the mother's body from the inside, as in the fantasy of inhabiting one's own belly, without father or mother, before any father and mother, before all sex and all reproduction, and of getting hold of oneself there, as a nocturnal eye open to a world of chains and simulacra. This body is first an interiority dedicated to images, and to the knowledge of images; it is the "inside" of representation, and at the same time the representation of that "inside."

From the body-cave to the glorious body, signs have become inverted, just as they have been turned around and displaced over and over again, in hylemorphism, in the sinner-body, in the body-machine or in the "body proper" of phenomenology. But the philosophico-theological *corpus* of bodies is still supported by the spine of *mimesis*, of representation, and of the sign. At times the body is the "inside" in which the image is formed and projected (sensation, perception, memory, conscience): in this case, the "inside" appears to itself as a foreign body, as an object to be examined from the outside, as a dissected eye, or as the hallucinated body of the pineal gland. At other times, the body is the signifying "outside" ("zero degree" of orientation and of the aim, origin and receiver of relations, the unconscious): in this case, the "outside" appears to itself as a thick interiority, a filled cave, a property prior to any appropriation. As such, the body is the articulation, or better yet, the *organ* or *organon* of the sign: it is, for our entire tradition, that *in which* sense is given and *out of which* sense emerges. But as such, regardless of the perspective used—dualism of body and soul, monism of the flesh, symbolic deciphering of bodies—, the body remains the organon, the instrument or the incarnation, the mechanism or the work of a *sense* that never stops rushing into it, presenting itself to itself, making itself known as such and wanting to tell itself there. The body, *sense*—in this double sense of the word that fascinated Hegel.[5]

In this way, and in this posture, the body never ceases to contradict itself. It is the place of contradiction *par excellence*. Either it is by the body and through it that signification occurs, and then signification falls within its boundaries and is worth only what a shadow is worth in the cave, or it is from the body and on it that signification takes shape and is deposited, and signification never stops reaching toward this proper locus where it should endlessly curl up into itself. There is finally no difference between this opaque darkness and the darkness of the shadows. The body remains the dark reserve of sense, and the dark sign of this reserve. But in this way, the body is absolutely trapped by the sign and by sense. If it is the sign, it is the sense; (How then does one reckon the economy of a soul?); if it is sense, then it is the indecipherable sense of its own sign (And doesn't one still have a soul or a spirit?). The late Merleau-Ponty enjoyed citing Valéry's phrase "the body *of* the spirit."[6]

～

Literature as much as, if not more than, philosophy exposes this problematic. In a sense, one is tempted to say that if there has never been any body in philosophy—other than the signifier and the signified—in literature, on the contrary, there is nothing but bodies. In yet another sense, one could say that literature and philosophy have never stopped wanting to relate to and/or oppose one another as body to soul or spirit. But actually, literature (I mean here the philosophical determination of literature from which the word "literature" itself can never really be disengaged, though it comes down to the same thing if I say "Literature" according to our "literary" [or "theoretical" or "critical"] understanding of the matter)—literature therefore offers us one of three things: either fiction, which is by definition bodiless, with its author, whose body is absent (in fact, we are imprisoned in his cave, where he gives us the spectacle of bodies); or bodies covered with signs, bodies that are only treasuries of signs (the bodies of Balzac, Zola or Proust—sometimes, if not often, those signs are in the first place carnal signs); or else writing itself abandonned or erect like a signifying body—such as for Roland Barthes "the beating (enjoying) body" of the writer,[7] the body signifying to the point of non-significance.

In this way, we do not leave the horizon of the sign, of sense and of *mimesis*. Literature mimes the body, or makes the body mime a signification (social, psychological, historical, heroic, etc.), or mimes itself as body. In this way, in all these ways at once, sense always comes back to the book as such, that is, to literature itself, but the book is never there: it has never abolished itself in its pure presence, it has not absorbed the sign into sense, nor sense into the sign. The body of the book, which should be the body of bodies, is there without being there. Literature, and with it, once again, the relationship between literature and philosophy, is a long sequel to the mystery of the Incarnation, a long explication of it, a long implication within it.[8]

In its turn, politics represents the same thing, the same endless explication of the mystery. Either one has to designate the community, the city as a body, or else the social, civil body, given as such, must engender its own sense of community and of city. As a body of forces, as a body of love, as a sovereign body, it is both sense and the sign of its own sense—but as soon as it's the one, it loses the other.

~

Sign of itself and *being-itself of the sign*: such is the double formula of the body in all its states, in all its possibilities. All our semiotics and all our mimologies are contained within these extremities, in the *materia signata* that the body according to St. Thomas Aquinas is.[9] (One should also say, in the most emphatic senses of the word, the *symbol* of itself and the *being-itself* of the symbol. Or else, one should say that in the body and as body, the sign demands the reality of the symbol: that is, the material reunion and co-presence of sense with the senses, the *body of sense* and the *sense of the body*.)

If the signifier "body" denotes nothing other than this circular resorption, would this mean that it renders its signification equal to the totality of sense, and turns it, in the process, into a vanishing signification? Of course, and it is precisely for this reason that "the body" has not ceased being stretched, exasperated, ripped to shreds between the unnamable and the unnamable. Paradoxically, the flesh of Merleau-Ponty—this "texture which comes back to itself and matches itself,"[10] where the world and my body are woven together as sense itself, of which Merleau-Ponty writes: "what we call the flesh, this internally shaped mass, has no name in any philosophy"[11]—offers a response to the decomposed corpse of Tertullian.

Body is the total signifier, for everything has a body, or everything is a body (this distinction loses its importance here), and *body* is the last signifier, the limit of the signifier, if what it says or would like to say—what it would have liked to have said—is nothing other than the interlacing, the mixing of bodies with bodies, mixing everywhere, and everywhere manifesting this other absence of name, named "God," everywhere producing and reproducing and everywhere absorbing the sense of sense and of all the senses, infinitely mixing the impenetrable with the impenetrable.

~

It is here and nowhere else that *spirit* arises as infinite concentration into the self. If soul is the form of the body, spirit is the sublation or the sublimation (or perhaps the repression?) of any form of bodies in the revealed essence of the sense of the body—of the body of sense.[12] The *spirit* of Christianity is incorporated here in full. *Hoc est enim corpus meum . . .*

But here there arises yet another way of exhausting the body and the sense of the body. It is the deported, massacred, tortured bodies, exterminated by the millions, piled up in charnel houses. Here too, the body loses its form and its sense—and sense has lost all body. These bodies are not even signs any longer, nor are they at the origin of any sign. These bodies are no longer bodies: spiritualized into smoke, as an exact reversal of, and response to those who evaporate into spirit. Similar, even though different, are the bodies of misery, the bodies of starvation, battered bodies, prostituted bodies, mangled bodies, infected bodies, as well as bloated bodies, bodies that are too well nourished, too "body-built," too erotic, too orgasmic. All those are only signs of themselves; they are the being-itself of the sign where nothing offers any sign to anything.

Such are the sacrificed bodies, but sacrificed to nothing. Or rather, they are not even sacrificed. "Sacrifice" is a word that says too much, or not enough, to designate what we have done and

what we do to bodies, and with bodies. "Sacrifice" designates a
body's passage to a limit where it becomes the body of a community, the spirit of a communion of which it is the effectiveness, the
material symbol, the absolute relationship to itself of sense pervad-
ing blood, of blood making sense. But sacrifice is no more.[13] The
blood that is spilled, is spilled atrociously, and only atrociously.
There was a spirituality of Christ's wounds. But since then, a
wound is just a wound—and the body is nothing but a wound,
even when it protects itself and oils itself, dresses itself as if to
render itself inaccessible to any lesion.

The body is but a wound. None of our wounds, in a sense, is
new, regardless of the economic, military, police, psychological
techniques that inflict them. But from now on, the wound is just a
sign of itself, signifying nothing other than this suffering, a forbidden body, deprived of its body. It is not simply a misfortune or a
malediction, for these things still offer a sign (those tragic signs that
have become indecipherable); and it is not simply illness (as if we
knew what we suffer from and where health is), but it is pain [*le
mal*], a wound open onto itself, a sign resorbed into itself, until
finally it is neither sign, nor itself. "Eye without an eyelid, exhausted with seeing and with being seen": this is what Marcel
Henaff says of our Western body when he reaches the end of a
project first outlined by the Marquis de Sade.[14] Or in the words of
Elaine Scarry: "the world, the I, the voice are lost in the intensity
of the suffering of torture"; "dissolution of the world, de-creation
of the created world."[15] We must understand this "created" world
as a world of bodies, a world in which bodies come to presence.
That is, a world in which bodies are the bodies they are.

But what is this *being*? What do we know of the being-being of
the body, and of the being-body of being? Perhaps nothing yet.
Philosophy is certainly not the one to tell us.

In the meantime, there are five billion human bodies. Soon,
there will be eight billion. Not to say anything of the other bodies.
Humanity is becoming *tangible*, and also tangible in its inhu-
manity. What is the space opened between eight billion bodies?
What is the space in which they touch or draw apart, without any

of them or their totality being resorbed into a pure and nil sign of itself? Sixteen billion eyes, eighty billion fingers: to see what, to touch what? Since we know that it is all for nothing, for no other purpose than to exist, and to be *those bodies*, what will we be able to do to celebrate their number?

To the extent that the body is a wound, the sign is also nothing but a wound. Are we still capable, are we already capable of confronting the wound of the sign, this flaying where sense gets lost? Sense is lost in this pure sense that is also the wound. The wound closes the body. It multiplies its sense, and sense gets lost in it.

Everything is possible. Bodies resist. The community of bodies resists. The grace of a body offering itself is always possible. The pain of a body suffering is always available. Bodies call again for their creation. Not the kind of creation that blows into them the spiritual life of the sign. But birth, the separation and sharing of bodies [*le partage des corps*].

No longer bodies that make sense, but sense that engenders and shares bodies. No longer the semiological, symptomatological, mythological, or phenomenological pillage of bodies, but thought and writing given, given over to bodies. The writing of a *corpus* as a separation and sharing of bodies, sharing their being-body, shared out by it, and thus divided from itself and from its sense, exscribed all along its own inscription. This is indeed what writing is: the body of a sense that will never tell the signification of bodies, nor ever reduce the body to its sign.

To write the sign of oneself that does not offer a sign, that is not a sign. This is: *writing*, finally to stop discoursing. To cut into discourse. Corpus, anatomy. One must not consider the anatomy of dissection, the dialectical dismembering of organs and functions, but rather the anatomy of configurations, of shapes—one should call them states of the body, ways of being in the world, demeanors, respirations, gaits, pelts, curlings, masses. Bodies are first to be touched. Bodies are first masses, masses offered without anything to articulate, without anything to discourse about, without anything to add to them.

Discharges of writing, rather than surfaces to be covered by writings. Discharges, abandonments, retreats. No "written bodies," no writing on the body, nor any of this graphosomatology into which the mystery of the Incarnation and of the body as pure sign of itself is sometimes converted, "modern style." For indeed, the body is not a locus of writing. No doubt one writes, but it is absolutely not where one writes, nor is it what one writes—it is always what writing exscribes. In all writing, a body is traced, is the tracing and the trace—is the letter, yet never the letter, a literality or rather a lettericity that is no longer legible. A body is what cannot be read in a writing.

(Or one has to understand reading as something other than decipherment. Rather, as touching, as being touched. Writing, reading: matters of tact.)

I repeat: we ask for the body of a sense that would not give signification of the body, and that would not reduce it to being its sign. I repeat and I ask again, asking first of myself, a tact of writing, a tact of reading that I know discourse is unable to provide. The body insists, resists, weighs on the demand: for it is after all the body that requests, demands this anatomical and catalogical writing, the kind of writing that would enable it not to signify (not to turn into either a signifier, a signified, or self-signification). The contrary, or more than the contrary, of an incarnation. In incarnation, the spirit *becomes flesh*. But here we are talking about a body that no spirit *has become*. Not a body produced by the self-production or reproduction of the spirit, but a body given, always already given, abandoned, and withdrawn from all the plays of signs. A body touched, touching, and the tract of this tact.

~

Corpus of tact: to touch lightly, to brush against, to squeeze, to penetrate, to hold tight, to polish, to scratch, to rub, to stroke, to palpitate, to handle, to knead, to hug, to embrace, to strike, to pinch, to bite, to suck, to hold, to let go, to lick, to carry, to weigh . . .

A body always weighs; it lets itself weigh, be weighed. A body does not have a weight, it is a weight. It weighs, it presses against other bodies, onto other bodies. All bodies weigh against one another: celestial bodies and callous bodies, vitreous bodies, and all others. This is not a matter of mechanics or gravity. Bodies weigh lightly. Their weight is the rising of their mass to their surface. Endlessly, the mass rises to the surface, and peels off as a surface [*s'enleve en surface*]. Mass is density, the consistency concentrated in itself: but this concentration in itself is not that of spirit, for here the "self" is the surface whereby mass is exposed. Massive substance is supported only by a spreading, not by interiority or by a foundation. So, as Freud remarks, "Psyche is spread out"—adding "she knows nothing about it."

This non-knowledge is the very body of Psyche, or rather, it is the body that Psyche herself *is*. This non-knowledge is not negative knowledge or the negation of knowledge; it is simply the absence of knowledge, the absence of the very relation of knowledge, whatever its content. Using a certain vocabulary, one could say: knowledge wants an object [*de l'objet*], but with bodies there is only subject [*du sujet*]; with bodies, there are only subjects. But one might say that in the absence of an object there is no subject either, no transcendental ground, and that what remains is precisely the body, bodies. *The "body" is grounds for not having any object* (grounds for not being a subject, subjected to not being subject, as one says "subject to bouts of fever"). The substance that only touches on other substances. A touch, a tact, as "subject" before any subject. Uninscribable, exscribing everything, starting with itself.

The body does not know; but it is not ignorant either. Quite simply, it is elsewhere. It is from elsewhere, another place, another regime, another register, which is not even that of an "obscure" knowledge, or a "pre-conceptual" knowledge, or a "global," "immanent," or "immediate" knowledge. The philosophical objection to what philosophy calls "body" *presupposes* the determination of something like an authority of "immediate knowledge"—a contradiction in terms, which inevitably becomes "mediated" (as "sensation," "perception," synaesthesia, and as immense reconstitutions of a presupposed "representation"). But what if one could presuppose nothing of the kind? What if the body was simply there, given, abandoned, without presupposition, simply posited, weighed, weighty?

Body would then first be the experience of *its own weight* (of its matter, its mass, its pulp, its grain, its gaping, its mole, its molecule, its turf, its turgidity, its fiber, its juice, its invagination, its volume, its fall, its meat, its coagulation, its dough, its crystallinity, its twitching, its spasm, its unknotting, its tissue, its dwelling, its disorder, its promiscuity, its smell, its taste, its resonance, its resolution, its reason).

But here the *experience* would be the weighing itself, the weighing that weighs without weighing itself, without being weighed or measured by anything. *Experitur*: it tries, attempts, risks itself, and risks itself right away, all the way to its own limits—it consists in nothing other than these limits, borders and ends, new beginnings of itself, where it touches itself or lets itself be touched, a weighing, a pondering, a fall, a funeral, a lifting, a lip, a lung, an exhalation of breath in which it hardly touches itself, in which it runs the risk of being at its end, of exhausting itself before being itself. An experience of freedom: a body is delivered, born, it is born at its weighing, it is nothing but its weighing, this minute expenditure of a few grams delivered over to quivering on contact with so many common extremities of other foreign bodies, bodies that are so close, so intimate with this body in their own freedom.

There is no experience *of* the body in the same way that there is no experience *of* freedom. But freedom itself is experience, and the body itself is experience. It is insofar as their essential structure (the structure of each of them, and the double structure which folds and unfolds them into one another) resembles precisely the structure of the sign-of-itself and the being-itself of the sign. *The body has the same structure as spirit*, but it has that structure *without presupposing itself as the reason for the structure*. Consequently, it is not self-concentration, but rather the ex-centration of existence. Existence does not presuppose itself and does not presuppose anything: it is posited, imposed, weighed, laid down, exposed.

Thus, the body does not have any way of knowing, and there is no lack here, because the body does not belong to the domain in which "knowledge" or "non-knowledge" are at stake, any more than knowledge itself belongs to the domain of bodies. If one agrees to say, and if it is fitting to say, that thought does not belong to the order of knowledge either, then it might no longer be impossible to say that the body thinks and also, consequently, that thought is itself a body. This comes down to saying only that thought is here taken back to "matter," to its matter—thought *is* itself this renewal that does not come *back*, but that comes, properly speaking, to this existence—posited, suspended, confined in this very block, this network of tissues, bones, minerals and fluids out of which it does not go, because, if it did exit it, it would no longer think.

One must think thought here, one must weigh it as a word not yet uttered, not yet escaped from a mouth, still in the larynx, on the tongue, the teeth that will instantly make it resound, if it is spoken. A word pronounced but not said, posed, as slippery as spittle, itself saliva, a minute flow, an ex-perspiration of the mouth in itself, in its fissure, in its bowels. A swallowed, unspoken word, not choked back, not retracted,[16] but swallowed in the stolen instant of being spoken, swallowed with this bare taste of saliva, barely foaming, barely viscous, a distinct dissolution, impregnation without the immanence of a blandness where what is given is the taste of the swallowed word, washed away before being uttered. This savor is not *savoir*, whatever the etymological link. This voice is not language, and what is more, this voice remains without vocabulary, without vocalization, and without vocalics. It thus resembles the "dialogue of the soul with itself," which is merely another form of the being-itself of the sign, but it engages neither in dialogue nor in monologue. It distances itself from any "logic." It resonates, nonetheless; it is its own echo: that is, a reverberation of the weighing of a body, a reverberation without verb where what is not "in itself" vibrates "for itself." A body is always the imminence of such a voice; it is its trace, the dull, grating noise of a weighing of a thought [*d'une pesée d'une pensée*].

~

One must think the thought of the body thus. A double genitive: the thought that is the body itself, and the thought we think, we seek to think, on the subject of the body. This body here—mine, yours—which attempts to think the body and where the body attempts to be thought, cannot do so rigorously. That is, it cannot give up signifying the body, assigning signs to it—except by allowing itself to be brought back to its own thinking matter, to the very place from which it thoughtlessly springs.

Here is the hard point of this thing "thought," nodule or synapse, acid or enzyme, a gram of cortex. A *gram* of thought: a minimum weight, the weight of a little stone, called a scruple, the weight of an almost-nothing that disconcerts and that forces one to ask why there is not nothing, but rather some things, some bodies. A gram of thought: trace of this pebble [*caillou*], of this calculus [*calcul*, also "stone"], engraving, tiny incision, notch, cut, hard point of a tip, engraver's stylus [*poinçon*], body of the first cut, breached body, body separated [*partage*] by *being this body* that it is and by existing it. The cortex is not an organ, it is this corpus of points, of tips, of traces, engravings, stripes, lines, folds, marks, incisions, schisms, decisions, letters, numbers, figures, writings "engrammed" [*engrammées*] in one another, decoupled one from the other, smooth and striated, even and granular. A corpus of the grains of thought in a body—which is neither a "thinking body" nor a "speaking body"—granite of the cortex, telling the beads of experience.

Of course, there is violence and pain in this thought. It never stops banging into itself, hard, resistant, impenetrable, being destined to think its hardness by means of that hardness itself, impenetrable by dint of essence and of method. To think at the point of the thinking body is to think without knowing anything, without articulating anything, without intuiting anything. It is thinking withdrawn from thinking. It is touching this gram, this series, this range, it is an indefinite corpus of grams. Thought itself touches itself; but it does so without being *itself*, without making its way back to itself. Here (but where is this "here"? It is in no place that can be pinpointed, since it is at the point where place first becomes a place, is occupied by a body, is occupied itself as the body of the place: for if there is no body *there*, there is no place), here, then, it is not a matter of reuniting with untouched matter, nor dissolving into its massive and naive intimacy. There is no "intact matter"; if there were, there would be nothing, not one single thing. But here, at the body, there is the sense of touch, the touch of the thing, which touches "itself" without an "itself" where it can get at itself, and which is touched and moved in this unbound sense of touch, and so separated from itself, shared out of itself [*partage de lui-meme*].

The body enjoys being touched. It enjoys being squeezed, weighed, thought by other bodies, and being what squeezes, weighs, and thinks other bodies. *Body*, because drawn out of the undivided totality that does not *exist*, and a body that *enjoys*, because it is touched in this very withdrawal, through it and thanks to it. Touching one another with their mutual weights, bodies do not become undone, nor do they dissolve into other bodies, nor do they fuse with a spirit—this is what makes them, properly speaking, bodies.

This joy is senseless. It is not even the sign of itself. This very joy is a mass, a volume offered on its surface, and it is a corpus of points, traces, grams, skins, folds, grains. Within this corpus, there is no signifying body, but there is no dissolution either. There is only this other corpus: touching, tasting, feeling, hearing, seeing, being a grain, savor, smell, noise, figure, and color—a random series, as open-ended as it is closed, as infinite as it is finite. This body no longer has any members,[17] if members are the functional parts of a whole. Here, each part is the whole, and there is never any whole. Nothing ever becomes the sum or the system of the corpus. A lip, a finger, a breast, a strand of hair are the temporary and agitated whole of a joy that is each time temporary, agitated, in a hurry to enjoy again and elsewhere. This elsewhere is all over the body, in the corpus of the parts of all the body, in the body of all the parts, and in all other bodies, which each can be a part for another, in an indefinitely ectopic corpus.

Joy does not come back to itself: this is precisely what makes it joy. However, it enjoys nothing but "itself." It rejoices in *itself*.[18] This is how the body rejoices in itself: it enjoys an "ipseity" that consists in not possessing the Self of subjectivity, and in not being the sign of its own sense. *Ipseity* itself, this body itself, this very body, in its very self enjoys, but this enjoying or this joy takes place as the very ex-position of this body. This joy is its birth, its coming into presence, outside of sense, in the place of sense, taking the place of sense, and making a place for sense.

This does not mean that the body comes before sense, as its obscure prehistory or as its pre-ontological attestation. No, it gives sense a place, absolutely. Coming neither before nor after, the sense of the body is given as the place of sense, as its circumscription and its exscription, as its end and its birth, its limit and its outcome, its aim and its obstacle, its being and its abyss. One could say, the *finitude* of sense. But since one often misunderstands this term, since one inevitably turns it into the starting point of a mediation in which the "finite" body must be converted, once again, into the incarnation of an infinite (into the being-self of a Sense or a Non-Sense), it might be better to say that the body is the *absolute* of sense. The ab-solute is what is detached, what is placed or set apart, what is shared out [*partagé*]. This sharing is itself ab-solution. A body allows for a place of absolute, inalienable, unsacrificable sense.

That this absolute place of sense is itself always ectopic changes nothing in the absolute nature of its sense. It is by touching the other that the body is a body, absolutely separated and shared [*partagé*]. The absoluteness [*l'absoluité*] of its sense, and the absoluteness of sense "in general" (if there is any such thing), is not kept "within" it, since it is itself nothing but the being-exposed, the being-touched of this "inside." As body, the absolute is common, it is the community of bodies. "As body": but that is all there is; that is, there is nothing other than this separation and sharing [*ce partage*]. We are not invoking "materialism" against "spiritualism": we are calling on being as absolutely partitioned [*partagé*] from and by sense as such. A single body—if it is possible to isolate such a thing—exposes itself as the sharing [*le partage*] of its separate senses.

Neither signification, nor manifestation, nor incarnation, and not revelation, either. The body exposes—the body; bodies expose each other. A naked body gives no sign and reveals nothing, nothing other than this: that there is nothing to reveal, that everything is there, exposed, the texture of the skin, which says no more than the texture of a voice. The voice again brought back to the mouth, a lip of voice, a skin of thought. Lip, throat, belly, which have nothing to deliver, to liberate, which are themselves liberation.

~

Only the body fulfills the concept of the words "exposition," "being exposed." And since the body is not a concept (since therefore there is no "body"), such a filling in is both nil and infinite, providing always both more and less than what a conceptual logic demands.

Being exposed, exposing: it is the skin, all the various types of skin, here and there open and turned into membranes, mucous, poured out inside of itself, or rather without either an inside or an outside, absolutely, continually passing from one to the other, always coming back to itself without either a locus or a place where it can establish a self, and so always coming back to the world, to other bodies to which it is exposed, in the same gesture that exposes them to itself. Al Lingis calls the skin "an exorbitant, shapeless, mute, inoperative, unexpressive materiality," which "when stroked, deploys a lascivious and exhibitionist nakedness."[19] But the skin is always exhibition, exposition, and the minutest look is a touching that brushes against it, and exposes it once more.

Injury, the wound, closes the body, gives it the function of a sign. But the wounded body is still meant to be touched, it is still offered to the sense of touch, which restores its absoluteness. Thus, the body has been turned into nothing but a wound. We have not simply tried to dominate it through struggle, or hurt it, or even kill it; we have tried to take away its absoluteness from it.

What stands "behind" a face—but also behind a hand, a belly, a buttock, a breast, a knee—the "he" or "she" who hides behind a face stands entirely outside of this face, and this is why, first of all, there is no face. There is, first, skin detaching itself from the world, from other skins, but detaching itself only while remaining attached, attached and exposed, attached by its detachment from the body. Absolute skin. What is a body if not a certain detachment of the skin, of bark, of surface, if not a carrying off and setting aside of a limit that is exposed and exposes itself? The gesture of the limit, the gesture at the limit, is touch—or rather: touching is the thought of the limit. To touch is to be at the limit, touching is *being* at the limit—and this is indeed being itself, absolute being. If there is something rather than nothing, it is because there is this limit made body, these bodies made limit, and exposed by their limits. Absolutely. Thought must touch on this.

Limits of matter (gases, liquids, solids), limits of kingdoms (mineral, vegetable, animal), limits of the sexes, limits of bodies, limits where sense becomes impossible, absolutely exposed, poured out, removed from any mystery, offered as the infinitely folded and unfolded line of all the bodies that make up a world. This world is their exhibition, that is, also their risk. Bodies run the risk of resisting one another in an impenetrable fashion, but they also run the risk of meeting and dissolving into one another. This double risk comes down to the same thing: abolishing the limit, the touch, the absolute, becoming substance, becoming God, becoming the Subject of speculative subjectivity. This is no longer the ab-solute, but saturated totality. But as long as there is *something*, there is also something else, other bodies whose limits expose them to each other's touch, between repulsion and dissolution.

Of course, *there is never* any "touching" as such, nor is there ever any "limit" as such: but this is why there is something, all things, as absolute, separated and shared out [*partagés*] bodies. Consequently, neither substance nor subject, but *corpus*, a catalogue without a logos, which is "logos" itself, bodily entries, entries which would be exposed, touched, one after the other, exposing one another, touching one another, detaching from one another, penetrating one another, withdrawing from one another—entries without any order or system, making neither sign nor sense, but exposing all the entries of sense.

No continuity, no immanence of sense to sense. Sense is body: it is exposed, detached, touched. And not the continuity of transcendance either, between signs and sense, between sign and what is beyond the sign, between sign of self and the self of sign. But a *corpus*, an ectopic topography, serial somatography, local geography. Stains, nails, veins, hairs, spurts, cheeks, sides, bones, wrinkles, creases, hips, throats. The parts of the corpus do not combine into a whole, are not means to it or ends of it. Each part can suddenly take over the whole, can spread out over it, can become it, a whole—that never takes place. There is no whole, no totality of the body—but its absolute separation and sharing out [*partage*]. There is no such thing as *the* body. There is no body.

Instead, there are patient and fervent recitations of numerous corpuses. Ribs, skulls, pelvises, irritations, shells, diamonds, drops, foams, mosses, excavations, fingernail moons, minerals, acids, feathers, thoughts, claws, slates, pollens, sweat, shoulders, domes, suns, anuses, eyelashes, dribbles, liqueurs, slits, blocks, slicing, squeezing, removing, bellowing, smashing, burrowing, spoiling, piling up, sliding, exhaling, leaving, flowing——

TRANSLATED BY CLAUDETTE SARTILIOT

PART TWO

Poetry

§ In Statu Nascendi

Freud, Pleasure, Art, Knowledge

With respect to art and psychoanalysis, it is hardly surprising that the question is no longer "What is psychoanalysis, when it is the psychoanalysis of art?" Instead, it has become "In what sense is psychoanalysis itself an aesthetic?" Which does not mean that an answer is at hand or even that, by asking the question, we have foreseen its entire scope. I would like to contribute here to a *posing*, a *position*, of the question.[1]

I will do so by studying a single notion, fairly well known and even, in a way, familiar to us by now. This is the notion of the *premium of pleasure*, or of *fore-pleasure*, as found in Freud with respect to the work of art, insofar as it is specifically the notion of a *formal seduction* thanks to which the artwork, according to Freud, gives us access to the pleasure of a *content* whose nature is completely different from the artistic form—let us call it an instinctive content.

I do not wish to, and cannot, study anything but the constitution of this notion as it took shape in 1905, in *Jokes and Their Relation to the Unconscious (Der Witz)*, to which must be added, as we shall see, the *Three Essays on the Theory of Sexuality* of the same year.

The purpose here, then, is narrowly circumscribed. But much more is at stake, and it will be useful to sketch out what the stakes are, if only in a preliminary, provisional fashion. The stakes are at least three in number.

1. Once again, quite obviously, it is a question of "form" and "fundament"[2]—a problem perhaps too easily imagined as "solved" or "outdated." If the paired terms "form" and "fundament" have undergone well-known displacements and subversions in literary, aesthetic, semiological, and philosophical theory, they nevertheless remain openly in place in the field marked out as "psychoanalysis and art." Indeed, so long as Freud's ambition to understand art did not return to a questioning of the "premium of pleasure"—of the *Vorlust* (fore-pleasure) that Freud always implicitly determined as a *Formlust*—this ambition blindly retained the principles of an analysis that, by distinguishing form from content, moves from form to content. And it is not at all easy to grasp exactly what the "instinctive" nature of the content might change (by comparison with a content of "ideas," for example) in its nature and position as *content* (we should perhaps even say: if there is a *content* as such, then it is a content of *ideas,* since the content of the idea in general is the idea of content . . .). Thus the status of *psycho*-analysis as an activity that decodes a sense (that decodes the sense of the thing called "psyche," or that decodes a certain "psyche"—for instance, an "unconscious" one—*as* sense) is maintained, by means of the registration and reduction of an array of forms. However subtle the more modern versions of this activity may be, they do not go beyond the extraction of a content *underlying* the forms. Moreover, this also applies to everything considered to be an "application" of psychoanalysis, whether to art or anything else, and to its auto-application, if we may call it that: the decoding of Freud's own text. The rule remains one of an *interpretation* (of content *via* forms) and cannot help remaining so as long as, in one way or another, psychoanalysis interprets itself as interpretation (even interminable). But this is not self-evident, as we will see in Freud's own text—not by interpreting it, but by watching how it works right at the point where it *stumbles* on interpretation.

2. The notion of *Vorlust* takes shape in Freud's book on *Witz.* This book also happens to be the object of a remarkable operation,

which could be called a failure to question. *Der Witz* is revered (Lacan calls it one of the theory's three foundational works), but hardly anything has been drawn or retained from it but this: that jokes betray the unconscious and convey its activity. *Witz* as form, the unconscious as fundament—a meager outcome, in short, for a book of this stature, for a book so dense, so complicated, so unwieldy in its exposition. In this assessment, to give just one example, *Witz* amounts to nothing more than a waking correlate of the dream—and yet this in no way accounts for the difference, surely essential, that makes *Witz* "the most social" of all manifestations of the unconscious and thus *opposes* it to the "completely asocial" dream.[3] Likewise, nothing accounts for the support that the theory of *Vorlust* (on which the social nature of Witz depends) draws from the *Three Essays* (drafted simultaneously with *Der Witz*).

3. Finally, the most general of these stakes: in his treatment of *Witz*, Freud takes up (quite consciously, although he says almost nothing about it) the central motif of an ancient and important branch of aesthetics. Perhaps this is not a question of a simple borrowing, but rather of the recovery and reactivation of a motif that concerns nothing less than the status of aesthetics itself. Thus the following question could be the ultimate horizon of our inquiry: Instead of being a science of the psyche, especially *applicable* to the productions of art, is Freud's work the displaced, disengaged return of aesthetics as it emerged within (and outside) modern philosophy?

What is aesthetics? Only after the fact did it become the theory of art—that is, after the fact of the blow that modern rationalism (as it is conventionally called) dealt itself with the question of *aisthesis*, or sensible knowledge. Aesthetics was first of all (notably in the eighteenth century) the problem of the *cognitio inferior*, of the nondiscursive, subjective, nonconceptual (nonconceiving and nonconceivable) *cognitio* which, it could be said, Carthesian *mathesis* produced by expulsion or exclusion. Obscure to itself, ungraspable, feminine or effeminate, always dependent on a *je ne sais quoi*, *aisthetic* knowledge in its trivial aspect is the *nasus* (the "nose for something"), in its intermediate aspect is *taste*, and in its superior aspect is *genius*. The theoretical fortunes of these three notions—or problems—are well known. And implied in all three, as their common and foremost asset, is *wit*, *esprit*, or *Witz*.

The question of the *cognitio inferior* arises with the realization that the productions of *wit* are not those of *understanding*, and with the corresponding realization that *judgment*—unlike reasoning—is not an "autologic," or self-inherent, faculty, but rather depends on a *je ne sais quoi* that places it very near *taste*: in wit and in judgment, classical reason discovers that it is not entirely accessible to itself.

Thus, what is Kant's *transcendental aesthetic*? The whole question bears on the *aisthesis* that alone gives our judgments a content, but that cannot be reason's aisthesis, because it is not an *intuitus originarius*. The Subject has no other locus, but in this aisthetic locus it neither finds nor constructs itself. This, at the point where understanding encounters its limits, is what makes the Kantian theory of *reflective judgment* necessary, articulated in a theory of the judgment of *taste* and, later on, in a theory of art: aesthetics becomes the supplemental zone of the presentation of the subject.

But what preoccupied Freud when he envisaged the constitution, or the *birth* (certainly quite different), of the subject? He was preoccupied with the birth of *judgment* insofar as it brings about or determines the birth of the ego (compare Freud's article "Negation"), and insofar as that is brought about when reactions to a *taste* are released (in swallowing or spitting out the good or the bad).

Perhaps Freud was preoccupied, in a new context, with something that has tripped up every investigation of the subject—the interpreted and interpreting subject, the analyzed and analyzing subject. Perhaps Freud was preoccupied with this *cognitio inferior*, which in every mode of presentation (various empiricisms, assorted materialisms, sensualisms, pragmatisms, and of course aestheticisms) *both* claims to equal or supplant the *cognitio superior* (or to *mimic* it) *and* is never quite able to attain the standing of a *cognitio*. *Cognitio in statu nascendi*, forever—to get a bit ahead of ourselves. That this *cognitio* can itself never be "known," that it implies a new, unheard-of "science" of "sense" and "sensation" (but without sacrificing anything to romantic ineffability)—here, perhaps, are the highest stakes. Let us call this "science" *aisthetics*. And eventually we will come to wonder whether "psychoanalysis" is not an assumed, provisional, name for an *aisthetics* . . .

The *Vorlust* in *Witz*

Let us approach the birthplace, or matrix, of Freudian aesthetics: the theory of *Vorlust*.

First, elliptically, I will restore its contours. The form of the artwork is said to procure a specific pleasure—an "aesthetic" pleasure, to be precise—whose attraction (the seduction, the *Verlockung* that produces the "premium" of pleasure, *Verlockungsprämie*), by lowering resistances, permits the enjoyment of the unconscious content of the work (which the work simultaneously conceals and conveys). Through this access to the unconscious (or *of* the unconscious to a diurnal, public satisfaction), artists—and, above all, the poet, or *Dichter*—can know at least as much about the unconscious as the analyst does (compare the *Gradiva*, or "The Theme of the Three Caskets"). As for what allows this content to pass through a form, that has to do with the artist's *gift* and with his technique, before which analysis is compelled to stop short, as before a mystery (compare many Freudian texts, especially *An Autobiographical Study*).

This fundamental process of art, and this position of the artist, were probably established or structured by *Der Witz*.

This book does not simply confirm *The Interpretation of Dreams* by extending its range of validity. If, in a way, it does extend this range, it does so by joining to the interpretation (*Deutung*) of the dream the *Deutung* of art, that is, the *Deutung* of something that in many respects presents itself as completely different from the dream, even opposed to it. It is more a question of a new *Deutung* added to the first, as a second and largely independent source of analytic knowledge. (Which did not stop Freud—quite the contrary—from posing, here and quite frequently elsewhere, as the triumphant rival of aesthetic knowledge. The whole introduction to *Der Witz* is saying: "I know more about art than the aestheticians." If knowledge comes to him from the productions of art, it is by means of their treatment by the knowledge of analysis.) It is true that this second source is not exactly *art* as such; nevertheless, in *Witz*, it is very much a question of the artistic process, and this can be verified wherever (beginning with the introduction) the conclusions of the examination are validated for all aesthetic phenomena.

The notion of *Vorlust* arises in response to the question: How can simple play with words (and with meaning) provoke the pleasure, incomparable in its nature and strength, that results from lifting a repression?

It is, Freud announces, a question of a rather complex release mechanism (*Auslösungsverhältnis*: something is liberated, an accumulated charge is let go, forced out with a single rapid movement). This mechanism, then, concerns the relation between the *form* of *Witz* (wordplay) and its *fundament* (the repressed "tendency" whose discharge it permits); the dismantling of this mechanism is what structures the whole of Freudian aesthetics (the whole analysis of the art-form of the unconscious).

The mechanism is dismantled—that is, the "*Vorlust* principle," as Freud calls it, is constructed—in the following way.

Freud first alludes to Fechner's "principle of aesthetic assistance or intensification" (p. 135): the convergence of several determinants of pleasure produces a much greater result than the sum of these determinants. (With this "principle," we are therefore dealing with a schema—comparable to the Fechner-Weber law, according to which sensation increases as the logarithm of excitation—which affects the mathematical allure of an exponential function and the metaphysical allure of a conversion of quantity into quality. In the mathematical model, however, the aesthetic quality—as distinguished from the *aisthesis* of the "determinants of pleasure"—would be an independent variable, whereas in the metaphysical model an aesthetic *quality* arises from an aisthetic *quantity*. This principle is the principle of the aesthetic as trans*formation*—or transsubstantiation . . .—of the aisthetic.)

In the case of *Witz*, Freud continues, we are dealing with an aspiration to pleasure that runs into a (social) inhibition. "Now let us suppose that yet *another* urge makes its appearance, which would release pleasure by the *same process*, though from other sources, and which thus operates *in the same sense* [*gleichsinnig*] as the suppressed urge" (p. 136; my emphasis). With this, we have the possibility of a *Witz* whose spirited play permits the unconscious to overturn the inhibition of a tendency—for instance, an aggressive one (Freud gives the example here of a wittily turned insult).

It is easy to see what Freud adds to Fechner's principle, without saying anything about it and perhaps without seeing anything himself: he adds, between the two aspirations to pleasure, the *identity* of the "mechanism" and the "sense" of each operation (*gleichsinnig*: it is not simply a question of direction, or a parallelism of vectors, but actually a question of *sense*,[4] of the thing's signification). We are forced to understand, or to admit, that our aspiration to the pleasure of insulting someone and our aspiration to the pleasure of the "beautiful form" (of the joke) have "the same sense." Consequently, Freud introduces an identity, or at least an adequation of functioning and of finality (if not of nature), between the pleasure due to access to the repressed and the pleasure due to formal seduction: between a prohibited pleasure and a permitted pleasure. The permitted pleasure, the pleasure of the form, is the one taken in the play with words and with logic. It constitutes, for Freud, the *technique* of *Witz*, its formal technique, which is a tautology: the technique of *Witz is* its form. And the form is what renders "technically" possible the return of a repressed aspiration (erotic, aggressive, cynical, or skeptical).

A first result is worthy of note: if *Witz* is a matrix or a model for the Freudian aesthetic (and, in fact, we rediscover the "principle of assistance" and the notion of *Vorlust* in the article "Creative Writers and Daydreaming," from 1908), it is so in that it puts this technique into operation, and even in that it *is* this technique. Art is brought into play at first, as it is throughout the modern history of the word and of the concept, as *ars*, technique. (The history of the *cognitio inferior* is indissociably that of sensibility and of technique, sensible knowledge and *savoir faire* both distinguishing themselves from rational Knowledge.) It is not initially or directly a question of "beauty," but rather of the *ars* that releases the return of the repressed. "Beauty" merely names the perceptible effect of the process.

(How, in passing, can we fail to note that such an *ars* is inevitably seen as parallel to, or in competition with, the practice of *analysis*? What separates them, except that the analyst *claims* to rely on Knowledge, whereas *ars* is derived from a *gift*, which makes it a secret inaccessible to analysis? But analysis also derives from a gift, a know-how, an aptitude: Freud says so in many of his texts. But we'll leave these problems hanging for now.)

Therefore, Freud's text implies—without, however, envisaging it as such—an adequation that is ultimately substantial, a homology, even a *homoiosis* (a relation of truth), between the form and the fundament of *Witz*. It implies, fundamentally, a community of form and fundament. In order for the *ars* to function, and to "release," there must be *Gleichsinn*. The "form," the "play," and the "beauty" must *already* have to do with the repressed. Consequently, as Reik states in a text from the 1920s,[5] in order for the form to *please*, it must itself "one day" have belonged to the fundament. In its principle or at its origin, the distinction of form from fundament, of the *ars* from the pressure of the repressed, must somehow be dissolved.

Let us say that Freud's text implies something that would be, in short, *the primal scene of art*: an uncannily intimate rapport, a copulation of form and fundament. A scene of seduction, but without the possibility of deciding which one seduces the other— since the two are indistinct. Unless, instead, art itself is the primal scene, both *primary* and already given as a *premium* (in the surplus of the "form").[6]

And this is exactly what Freud's whole analysis of *Witz* forces us to conclude.

Indeed, play with words and with logic—which constitutes the form of *Witz*—is a repetition of the "infantile type of thought" repressed by linguistic and logical education, hardly even visible to the analyst, since it is always "corrected *in statu nascendi*" (p. 170) (and so there is not, for us or for the analyst, any pure "primal" thought; there is only a birth that is already a correction of primitivity). Infantile wordplay is itself linked to infantile *repetition* in general (the *ars* is therefore a repetition of repetition), as well as to "the pleasurable effect of rhythm or rhyme" (p. 125). The repetitive pleasure of rhythm and rhyme: such would be the *status nascendi*, and the "correction," of an "unconscious" pleasure, or of a pleasure of the unconscious. But what is it, in rhythm or rhyme, that pleases, if not—already, again—a pleasure of the unconscious?

(Let us add that wordplay also consists in treating words as things, following the pattern of magical thinking described in *Totem and Taboo*. Art, Freud says there, is the conservation and/or the repetition of magic—that is, an immediate, aisthetic way of treating words and thoughts.)

The form of *Witz*, then, repeats the pleasure of repetition, as the process and profit of an unnameable, unassignable "thought." It repeats this pleasure every time that, in an adult, a thought must shake off the yoke of repressive rationality—and this can be a question of a simple jest or of a new, audacious, and creative thought, as Freud indicates several times (notably in his evocation of *The Interpretation of Dreams*, whose novelty seems to have acted like a *Witz* . . .).

For the moment, here is what we have: one way or another, the formal technique must have something to do with a "thought" content, with the "content" of a thought drawn, as it were, from the very source, from the birth, of thought. And indeed Freud states, but without going on to explore what he thus suggests, that "what we have described as the techniques of *Witz* . . . are *rather the sources* [my emphasis] from which *Witz* provides pleasure,"[7] and that "the technique which is characteristic of jokes . . . consists in their procedure for safeguarding the use of these methods of providing pleasure against the objections raised by criticism" (p. 130). Curiously, then, the "technique" consists in lifting or diverting the inhibition that weighs on that same technique (and therefore not, or not simply, on the repressed) insofar as that technique is a source of pleasure. To free "rhythm and rhyme" would be at least consubstantial with the freeing of a tendency (erotic, aggressive, etc.). As a result, it is impossible to be content with the schema of an extrinsic "technique" in the service of a "content." The economy of the mechanism of *Gleichsinn* requires a *Gleichsinnigkeit* of the *ars* and of the unconscious "tendency."

In this respect, aesthetic pleasure is the pleasure of thought repeating its own birth. Thus, in the strict sense of the term, it repeats its *ingenium*, which properly belongs to it *in statu nascendi*, and it also repeats its *ingeniousness* or its *genius*. Pleasure as premium—none other than *Vorlust*—is the premiere of thought itself.

Up to this point, however, Freud's text has dealt only with "inoffensive" *Witz*, the *Witz* said to be "not yet tendentious" (p. 132)—and our reading will now have to become more nuanced (even though, of course, it has not been reductively simplifying so far).

In "tendentious" *Witz*, we find "other procedures drawing from the same source" (p. 130). Although this formula seems to imply that erotic pleasure, aggressive pleasure, etcetera, have their origin (and thus their nature) in the primal thinking process, let us remain faithful to the schema that Freud follows: *formal Witz* (not tendentious) acts to permit the irruption of a repressed *content* (a tendency).

How does this happen? This is the question of *Gleichsinn*. *Gleichsinn* is possible because in reality *Witz*, even when it is non-tendentious "and thus only serves theoretical intellectual interest," is actually "never non-tendentious," because it pursues an aim: "to promote the thought by augmenting it," thus "guarding it against criticism." As a consequence, then, even when it *appears* inoffensive, *Witz* "goes beyond the production of pleasure." (Here is its specific difference from the *Scherz*, the jest. But it would not take much to show that the pure type of *Scherz* is very difficult to isolate as such. Pure, simple, "innocent" pleasure cannot be found. Either pleasure gives a "plus" to think about, or thinking gives a "premium" to enjoy.) Non-tendentious *Witz* possesses—or incarnates— the tendency opposed to the "inhibiting and restricting power" of "critical judgment." Thus, this "first use of *Witz* . . . points the way to further uses" (pp. 132–33).

Therefore, *Gleichsinn* proceeds from the fact that the logico-verbal play itself proceeds from a tendency: it is tendentious *by nature* (later, Freud would have called it "instinctive"); it is even the primal, fundamental, general tendency to lift critical inhibition. And it is as a tendency that this play can have the "same sense" as an erotic tendency, an aggressive tendency, etcetera. The instrument of all lifting of inhibition is the lifting of logico-linguistic control. This lifting is therefore more than and other than an instrument: it is the matrix of all other liftings of inhibition. It does not "add" a pleasure of form to a fundamental pleasure: rather, all pleasure is inscribed in its pleasure.

Now we understand why *Witz* can "give passage," through its "form" or its "aesthetic," to elements of the repressed. It does not give them passage under cover of the form, but rather because this *form* is *itself* already an irruption of the repressed—and because all other elements of the repressed *are themselves also "thoughts"*—erotic, aggressive, cynical, or skeptical thoughts (this last type of *Witz* is concerned precisely with thought as such . . .)—which defy and "outwit" criticism.

In these two respects, the aesthetic form of *Witz*, that is, a form acceptable to consciousness and to other people—its seductive form, although it is nothing but *Witz* itself—is, in sum, *the presentable side of the content*, and thus it *is* the content to the extent that it can be presented, exposed, exhibited, and insofar as it presents itself. *In statu nascendi.*

Aesthetic form does not function by addition to content (as Fechner's "principle of assistance" could lead us to believe, although in fact this principle does already represent the substitution of a multiplication, or an elevation to the nth power, for an addition). It does not function as the *disguise* of a tendency (although Freud employs this type of image), but rather as the *transformation of the fundament*. The fundament takes form in it, which is to say that in it *the formless forms itself*, in all senses of the expression. This means, consequently, that fundament is always already form, or that by forming itself it is what it is—the fundament of the tendency.

Rather than being a question of transformation, then, this is a question of transfiguration, if indeed it is only as a figure (artistic fabrication) that the "fundament" becomes what it is, a figure in which its formless "figure" is abolished. And consequently it is a question of transsubstantiation, if the substance, here as everywhere ever since Aristotle, is indissociable from its figure. *Witz is* the substance of the tendency—and there can be no question of another substance, anterior to this birth. I will merely recall, in passing, that transsubstantiation, in Christian dogma, is the late figure of the edible being of God, and that this analysis could bring us back to *Totem and Taboo*, that is, to the *status nascendi* of society—and I will add only that as early as the *Traumdeutung* Freud adopted the term chosen by Kraus for the passage from sensation to the dream image. This term is *transsubstantiation*, which perhaps encloses the program of a nascent psychoanalysis— namely, the opposite of a program of translation and interpretation: transsubstantiation, by definition, is irrelevant to the relation between a form and a fundament, between an appearance and a meaning. In it, or by it, the figure *is* the substance. *Witz* is the tendency, in the same way that the bread and the wine are God . . .

Yet another motif seems to confirm these conclusions: the motif of the "non-knowledge" or *je ne sais quoi* linked to laughter in *Witz*. Freud insists on this: one *does not know* what one is laughing about, which is to say that one does not know how to distinguish between the "technique" and the "content." But this failure to know is not just an interference effect achieved through the technique: it is a "fundamental" motif of *Witz*. Freud writes: "This uncertainty of our judgment [when we laugh], which must be assumed to be a fact, may have provided the motive for the formation of *Witz* in the proper sense of the word" (p. 132). This is still a question, then, no matter what "tendency" happens to be engaged, of dissolution of the control of judgment. The repetition of the "infantile type of thought" is the suspension or confusion of critical, controlled judgment and the restoration of the very birth of judgment, whose "form" is the "fundament" of our tendencies.

In this way, Freud says, we always mistake what makes us laugh, overestimating sometimes the form, sometimes the fundament, of *Witz*. For the same reasons, we can laugh at obscene *Witz* even if its technique is "mediocre." In all these characteristics, the function of a "formal" seduction, exterior to content, is constantly erased or blurred.

Aesthetic pleasure does not mask another pleasure; it is a two-faced pleasure all by itself. This is what Freud declares when he stresses the divergence of *Witz* from dream (which is also to say, the divergence of its social function, the same function that, in general, distinguishes the artist from the dreamer or the neurotic):

> For *Witz* does not, like dreams, create compromises; it does not evade the inhibition, but it insists on *maintaining unaltered the play* with words or with nonsense [my emphasis]. It restricts itself, however, to a choice of occasions in which this play or this nonsense can at the same time appear allowable (in jests) or ingenious (in jokes), thanks to the ambiguity of words and the multiplicity of conceptual relations. Nothing distinguishes jokes more clearly from all other psychical structures than this double-sidedness and this duplicity in speech. [p. 172]

This double-sidedness, this transfiguration or transsubstantiation, is what leaves no room for translation and interpretation, by contrast with the "compromise" of the dream. Obscenity (for example) and ingeniousness are given together, at one and the same blow—which is, however, double. In the *Gradiva*, Freud says of the double discourse of Zoe (and therefore of the writer Jensen's text), "It is a triumph of ingenuity and wit [*ein Triumph des Witzes*] to be able to express the delusion and the truth in the same turn of words."[8]

Vorlust, the "premium," is therefore preliminary and exterior to instinctive *Lust* only by means of certain distinctions (form/fundament, technique/content, cognitive tendency/instinctive tendency), which are certainly not empty or null but which are possible *only if*, somewhere, in a place where they are simultaneously annulled and engendered, in the singular adherence of the two faces of *Witz*, their opposing terms function *gleichsinnig*, in and with the same sense—if it is *a sense* . . .

The consequence is double:

1. By itself, *Vorlust* is necessarily, already, an aspect or type of instinctive *Lust*; it is the latter's substance and "selfsame" figure.

2. *Lust*—pleasure—presents itself only as *formed in Vorlust*. It occurs, in short, only as *Formlust*.

In this double manner, pleasure occurs only *in statu nascendi*: the "pure" pleasure of unconscious satisfaction occurs only as always already "corrected" by form, or occurs only in the birth of its aesthetic form. In other words, the only *aisthesis* (that might bring about pleasure) is the aesthetic.

The Sexual Premium

This conclusion, while rigorous, is not without its problems—two, at least:

1. This conclusion is gained *against* the Freudian definition of *Vorlust* (which is merely *Vor-lust*, preliminary pleasure, or *premium* of pleasure, supplementary and, so to speak, free, gratuitous). What might trouble us here has nothing to do with disrespect for Freud's text (after all, only by disordering the already disordered text on the *Witz* were we able to discern what was at stake there). It has to do with the risk of letting another, very simple, text replace it, one that would state that the fundament is the form, and vice-versa. This would be one more version either of "art for art's sake" or of the inverse but symmetrical thesis of an immediate figuration of the primary process. If the "primary" is itself a "premium," if its "form" is also its "substance," then the matter is no doubt more complex—and it does indeed become so, by reason of Freud's own text, whence arises the second problem.

2. Freud's statement of the *Vorlust* principle is accompanied by these words: "I have good reasons to suspect that this principle corresponds with an arrangement that holds good in many widely separated departments of mental life" (p. 137).

This remark evokes an unexpected generality of the *Vorlust* principle. The function of the aesthetic would seem to apply to all other kinds of *aisthesis*. Wouldn't it ultimately provide *the* general principle *of* pleasure? (and thus the principle of the *Lustprinzip*, the principle of the processes at work wherever the *pleasure* principle, or the satisfaction principle, reigns)?

But to understand Freud's remark, we must know what it alludes to.

Freud alludes—in a strangely discreet way—to what, in 1905, he was writing at another desk, at the same time as *Der Witz*: *Three Essays on the Theory of Sexuality*. The *Three Essays* in turn contain a reference—explicit this time—to *Der Witz*. Therefore, we must examine this reciprocal relationship between the two texts.

The question of *Vorlust* comes into *Three Essays* when the workings of adult sexuality must be described. Unlike infantile sexuality, which knows only the localized pleasure of the erotogenic zones, adult sexuality is for Freud, as we know, a process governed by the primacy of a particular zone, an exceptional zone whose satisfaction becomes the *goal* of the entire process. This teleonomy has a double character:

1. It corresponds to the presentation of sexuality as a function of reproduction. (The sexual instinct "becomes, so to say, altruistic," Freud writes;[9] therefore, it becomes social and communicative, like *Witz* and like art.)

2. Sexuality is regulated by its orientation toward a specific pleasure, the pleasure released "by a reflex path" (p. 210) and consisting "entirely" in *discharge* (this pleasure thus resembles that of laughter while still being, as pleasure, homogeneous with if not identical to the emission of the sexual substances necessary to reproduction).

But to reach this pleasure of emission, it is necessary to pass through the pleasurable excitation of the erotogenic zones. This pleasure of excitation is preliminary (discharge is called "*end-pleasure*") and is named *Vorlust*. This *Vorlust*, Freud declares (p. 210), "is the same pleasure . . . already . . . produced, although on a smaller scale, by the infant." It is therefore in the same position as the "technique" of *Witz*. But these analogies, or homologies, do not, as they stand, allow of a simple decoding. It is necessary to take into account the broader economy of exposition in *Three Essays*.

The whole description of the process of arriving at sexual "end-pleasure" unfolds beneath the sign of a question posed by Freud. This question in turn occupies a position comparable to the one bearing on the technique of *Witz*, and yet it is of a completely different nature (or at least it takes on a completely different appearance): it is the question born of the acknowledgment that sexual *Vorlust* is *a tension*. Its character is that of an incomplete satisfaction, and as such it "can give rise to a need for a greater pleasure" (p. 210). How, in pleasure, can one lack something and *tend* toward another pleasure? That, as Freud emphasizes, is precisely the problem.

He returns to this problem—to *the* problem—in the following chapter (after having pursued the description to the point of discharge), and lingers over it all the way to the end of the book, unable (even in succeeding editions and corrections) to find a solution that would be . . . satisfactory.

I will come back to this aporia, which is clearly essential. But first we must pause over the episode that establishes a link with *Der Witz*.

Before reopening the question of tension, at the end of the first analysis of *Vorlust*, Freud concludes with a reference to *Der Witz*:

> I was recently able to throw light on another instance, in a quite different department of mental life, of a slight feeling of pleasure similarly making possible the attainment of a greater resultant pleasure, and thus operating as a "premium of pleasure." In the same connection I was also able to go more deeply into the nature of pleasure. [Here, a note that refers to *Der Witz*; p. 210.]

Freud's reader would be justified in thinking that the explanation of fore-pleasure is to be found in these lines, and in the mutual illumination of the two texts. Very quickly, however, the reader would have to admit that Freud's remarks are hardly illuminating. . . .

If the two types of *Vorlust* do have in common their infantile provenance and their lower intensity, by comparison to that of "end-pleasure," sexual *Vorlust* is still not absolutely presented as a "form" for covering up a prohibited content and rendering it admissible. (Reciprocally, aesthetic *Vorlust* has not been presented as a tension. Freud does say, of course, that the hearer of *Witz* must first be in a "cheerful mood" [p. 127], so as to be disposed to laugh; nevertheless, the problem of excitation—of the painful character of the tension—is not raised.)

Sexual *Vorlust* is not presented as a *Verlockungsprämie* or "seduction premium"—even though Freud does use the expression in his reference to *Der Witz*. It is not presented as an *extra* pleasure (indeed, it seems to be more of a missing pleasure . . .), and yet it is a question here of *seduction*, in the strict sense of the word (*Verlockung*, attraction, enticement, excitation), and not of *Verfuhrung* (the seduction of the "scene of seduction," which calls up the idea of a subornation, even a sexual attack, and not more considerate advances).

The situation is therefore very strange, *unheimlich*, even *funny*, in the two senses of that word: sexual *Vorlust* is referred, for its explanation, to aesthetic *Vorlust*, which is characterized by the sexual metaphor of seduction—but a seduction that in turn finds its principle in aesthetics. Indeed, the first *Vorlust* mentioned in *Three Essays* is the one procured by vision (of the desired person's body), from which arises the "excitation whose cause, when it occurs in a sexual object, we describe as beauty" (p. 209). We therefore seem to find ourselves before a circle, before the vicious circle, the *circulus vitiosus*, of aesthetics and sexual aisthesis.

At the same time, however, the circle offers us the contrast between a process that moves from a permitted pleasure to a prohibited pleasure (in *Witz*) and a process that moves from an unsatisfied satisfaction to a total discharge.

Faced with this situation—where Freud seems to have done everything possible to multiply the enigmas, in order to remain allusive (and perhaps not without his reasons, as we will see)—it is no doubt necessary to risk a hypothesis: let us take up the *Vorlust* of

Three Essays by following the schema of *Der Witz*, since it is on the latter text that Freud seems to place the real burden of the principle's elaboration.

The essential implication of this discussion will be that *Endlust*, and therefore genital sexuality, although it constitutes "normal," admissible, socialized pleasure, nevertheless corresponds to the lifting of an inhibition, so that it must be presented through an admissible aspect—through a "beauty," whose flip side would necessarily be an unbearable ugliness. "Genital" pleasure would therefore bring something else into play (and something more decisive) than what Freud assigns to it with the notion of "discharge" (orgasm, satisfaction, and procreation). It would bring something else into play, and *Vorlust*—partial, preliminary pleasure, the "premium" of pleasure—would constitute the *formation* of this "other thing," in an "infantile" pleasure that would repeat, "re-present" (and stage) this "other thing." The latter could no longer be understood as a physiological discharge, and yet it would still be the total discharge, the extinction of tension that Freud assigns to *Endlust*. But this "*Endlust*," this pure *Lust*, terminal as well as original, would be, as such, unbearable and prohibited—less prohibited by censure than deprived, "by itself," of figure and of substance. Which would mean that this discharge itself, *pleasure* itself, does not occur—not without being, even in orgasm, its own *aesthetic* trans-formation, in a sense of the term that inextricably mixes the aesthetic and the aisthetic.

This would not mean that "*jouissance* is impossible," as Lacan is alleged to have said (although he actually never put it quite that way). Instead, it would mean that *jouissance* is *aesthetic*—a kind of theoretical *Witz* that condenses, in the guise of an aesthete's motto, the principle of the inexistence of a "material" pleasure by itself and, quite simply, the principle of Epicurus (taken up by Kant and later again by Nietzsche): that all pleasure is physical, sensible, aisthetic. But only the condensation of these two "principles" would allow us to say something about *jouissance*: if we like, about the "impossibility" of its "fundament" in the reality of its "form," or about the singular effectivity of a "discharge" that is *at once* [*à même*] its "tension." *Form* and *tension* are the same thing: the thing of *Vorlust*, and the only locus of *Lust*. Pleasure is always a *premium*, it is never *the thing itself* (the thing of the tendency, the instinct, the unconscious, or the primary process).

This would also mean that the "thing itself"—the unconscious, the instinct, and *pleasure* "itself," pleasure in its *principle* and *as* principle, or "the unconscious" as the domain or reign of such a principle—*is* not, has no locus, does not occur. Pleasure as a singular entity occurs neither at the origin, as a principle or a primacy, nor at the end, as a generalized discharge. It occurs only through self-precession— *Vor-lust*, before-pleasure—or through self-addition, as its own *premium*. It is always already transsubstantiated, or always already and always still *in statu nascendi*. This constitutes not a *statute* but only the law of a constitutive trans-formation, or the "complex release mechanism" of what is not a thing or a nature or an event but has only the form (the fundament) of a general "transitivity." Pleasure is *born*, pleasure *comes to pass*, pleasure transits and en-trances. To say that *jouissance* is aesthetic is to say that *jouissance en-trances*.

The Analysis of Analysis

If Freud does not say this, it is precisely because he needs a "thing in itself." He needs, irresistibly, an ultimate stopping point, a genuine primacy and finality of pleasure, and for two reasons that merge into one:

1. He must bring sexuality to its *normal* (or "integrated," as he says in later texts) fulfillment—not for obscurely moralistic motives, but because genital, procreative sexuality furnishes him with a *telos* according to which a positive explanation can be constructed (even, as we have seen, at the cost of unresolved questions).

2. He must have a *telos* (and a referent) of this type in order to anchor psychoanalysis as a "science." Without this reliance on the physiology of discharge and the axiology of procreation (a double "base" whose coherence Freud does not bother to question), his work would necessarily become an aesthetic, not a science. In this

context, an aesthetic means not a knowledge but an art of the unconscious (if the concept of "unconscious," such as it is, can still function here).

Although Freud recoils or flees from such a summons (to which his singularly complex rapport with art bears witness), his texts are not wholly lacking in indications that would allow us to advance the theoretical question opened up by the two works of 1905. I will briefly enumerate these indications, or clues, before pausing at the most important one:

1. In "On Narcissism," the individual's sexuality in its entirety is qualified as a "premium"—in this instance, a premium compensating for the swallowing up of the individual by the species.[10]

2. In *Three Essays*, the discussion of the problem of tension is accompanied from the start by a note that remarks the double sense of the word *Lust* (pleasure/desire). *Lust* thus functions as a *Witz*—and as the *Witz* of pleasure in tension.

3. Another note to *Three Essays*, added in 1915, derives the feeling of beauty from the stimulating sight of the genitals, which themselves are never considered beautiful. Freud makes no comment about the conversion or trans-formation implied by this provenance. There would seem to be a "principle of aesthetic modesty," as it were, inherent in the "pleasure principle."

4. Another note, this one from 1925, refers favorably to Ferenczi's *Thalassa: A Theory of Genitality*, where Ferenczi returns to the problem of *Vorlust* and attempts to undo the teleonomy of genitality, in order to see in it the combination or culmination of the pleasure of the erotogenic zones. The pleasure of intercourse is compared to, among other things, that of *Witz*, and the anxiety present in *coitus interruptus* is interpreted in the framework of a game ("Sexuality also, therefore, only *plays* with danger"[11]) comparable to the games of children, or to those of the actors in a tragedy—comparable, therefore, to an aesthetic game. If Freud does not accept Ferenczi's book unconditionally, and if he fears its "fanciful" character, he does not deny its suggestiveness . . .

But, over and above these clues, it is finally necessary to focus on Freud's last attempt, found in additions to *Three Essays* dating from

1915 and 1920, to solve the problem of sexual tension—even though he offers this "solution" hesitantly, by way of "speculation."

At issue is the chapter "The Libido Theory," which lends the support of this "speculative" concept (libido) to the hypothesis, advanced in the preceding chapter, of a specifically sexual chemistry provoking tension (need combined with pleasure) through a process analogous to that of intoxication. (Let us note that, to explain the anxiety of *birth*, similar recourse is had, in *Introductory Lectures on Psychoanalysis*, to the motif of a "toxic" effect.[12]) Freud presents the following schema: narcissistic libido, "the original state of things, realized in earliest childhood," manifests itself by becoming object-libido. Through the object, it obtains a satisfaction, that is, a "partial and temporary extinction" of the libido. Detached from the object, "it is held in suspense in peculiar conditions of tension and is finally drawn back into the ego," whose narcissistic state "in essentials persists" (pp. 217–18).

Tension, by this account, corresponds to a "suspension" between the object and the ego. Strictly speaking, discharge—in laughter or in orgasm—should be the annulment of such a suspension, the equalization of object satisfaction and narcissistic satisfaction (or the resorption of all objectivity), and the return to the origin. But what Freud indicates here, apparently in spite of himself, is that all discharge, since it requires the object, is "partial and temporary," whereas the double schema of *Vorlust* was constructed on the double model of access to an absolute, definitive discharge—which is also to say on the model of an absolute narcissism as the principle and end (or at least as the normative idea) of all processes. Only an "absolutely narcissistic" individual (like the primal Father that Freud describes in *Group Psychology and the Analysis of the Ego*[13]) could do without art and enjoy a pleasure *without form*. But *there is no such* Narcissus, although Freud never ceases making more or less subtle attempts to erect this figure.

The difficulties of the double exposition of *Vorlust*—its duplicities . . .—are no doubt rooted in the contradiction between this archetype, whose erection (or discharge) haunts Freud's discourse, and the analysis, opened by this same discourse, of an

ineluctable and initial *trans-formation* of the fundament, a trans-
formation of the Narcissus, who attains *himself* (or attains *his*
pleasure) only in the *un-pleasure* of *Vorlust*, in the "form," in the
"erotogenic zone," in the "premium of seduction"—and, we must
remember, in the sociality inherent in *Witz* as well, inseparable
from the "premium." The Narcissus is alone, his pleasure is a
dream. The unconscious (if this is what it must be called) enjoys
the other, takes pleasure from the other, through the other, in the
other, who is not an "Other" with a capital O, but rather the other
who makes himself or herself felt, the other of *aisthesis*, of the
aesthetic.

What Freud touches on, and what he resists, is this *passage* of the
"self" into the "other," of the "fundament" into the "form," of the
"unconscious" into "art." He resists the *aesthetic trance* through
which alone both a "pleasure" and a "subject" can occur. In this
"trance," the "premium" is neither an advance on nor an excess of a
sum of capital or of revenue. Rather, the premium is what *forms the
fundament*, dissolving it *in statu nascendi*: by this dissolution, by
this birth, the identity of the fundament (or of the fund), all
identity, simultaneously disintegrates and is precipitated (in the
chemical sense of the word). Identity is *jouissance*; *jouissance* is
aesthetic.

That is what Freud recognizes and at the same time dismisses.
That is what analysis stumbles on, perhaps to preserve its supposed
identity as science and cure. That is why Freud always comes back
to the "technique" and the "mysterious gift" of the artist as what
exceeds the powers and knowledge of analysis. By so doing, Freud
reassures himself—and psychoanalysis, which *interprets* art while
preserving the sanctity of the poetic "gift," reassures itself. With the
invocation of genius (of the *ingenium*, the nascent or native wit),
Freud does nothing more than repeat—but perhaps not without an
irony directed toward himself as well as toward the artist—the circle
of classical (and romantic) aesthetics. But is is also here that he
broaches the analysis of his analysis—that is, its dissolution. For
Novalis, dissolution was the characteristic force of *Witz*, which he
named, in the alchemical register, *menstruum universale*, "universal

solvant" of contraries and of genres. The dissolution (which could also be translated as "the [ana]lysis") of analysis is not its destruction: it is the transformation of its task into the task, neither aesthetic nor philosophical nor psychoanalytic, of a hitherto unknown *aisthetic*.[14]

A final word, beyond the limits of the present essay: the alchemists' *menstruum* is a neuter noun, but their choice of this word proceeded from the hypothesis of an analogy with women's menses. There is no sexual neutrality in birth, or in pleasure, or perhaps in art—or, above all, in *Witz*.

TRANSLATED BY BRIAN HOLMES

§ Vox Clamans in Deserto

(As the scene opens, a dog barks in the distance, alone in the silence. A cow moos. The dog will bark again once or twice later in the scene. Another animal, perhaps a donkey, may cross the space of representation. This space is bare, well-lit, and sonorous.

Two characters appear. They have very different voices, both masculine, but one is deep and somber, the other light, fragile, somewhat hoarse.)

—I thought I heard a voice, so I came this way. Was it yours?

—I don't know. I may very well have been talking to myself. But there was also a dog barking. Maybe it was his voice you heard?

—I could hardly have confused the two!

—Why not? A dog's barking or the sounds of other animals aren't merely noises. Each animal has a voice, one that we can recognize.

—Do you mean to say that animals have a way of talking?

—No. It's something altogether different. Voice has nothing to do with speech. Obviously there is no speech without voice, but there can be voice without speech. For animals, but for us, too. Because I know you, I could recognize your voice before I could make out what you are saying, as you came toward me.

—Yes, of course—voice is the sonorous aspect of speech, whereas discourse and signification are its spiritual aspects.

—You could almost find that way of looking at things in Saussure, had he really spoken of voice, which is not the case. You could almost find it in his identification of the constitutive elements of speech. But then you notice that it leads him to exclude phonation or vocalization from his study of languages, and even, when you come down to it, from his study of language. He used to say:

(We hear Saussure's voice, delivering his lecture in Geneva.)

Les organes vocaux sont aussi extérieurs à la langue que les appareils électriques qui servent à transcrire l'alphabet Morse sont étrangers à cet alphabet; et la phonation, c'est-à-dire l'exécution des images acoustiques, n'affecte en rien le système lui-même.

The vocal organs are as exterior to speech as the electronic gadgets which transmit the Morse code are foreign to that alphabet; and phonation, which is the performance of acoustical images, has no effect on this system itself.

—And aren't you satisfied with such an analysis?

—I'm not, and what is more, I'm convinced that Saussure himself could not have been completely happy with it. He was too attentive, in spite of everything, to the indissociable unity of what he called "the material substance of words" and what he designated "the system of signs."

—Do you mean to say that the voice is part of language?

—Certainly not. Voice is no more part of language, in the Saussurian sense, than it belongs, properly speaking, to speech. Voice is precisely not to be confused with "phonation" (such an ugly word), since that is nothing more than "performance," as Saussure says. The voice is not mere performance, it is something else, it is anterior to the distinction between an available language and a chosen speech . . .

—Anterior then to all language!

—Strictly speaking, that is doubtless true. But that is exactly what I would like you to understand—and what I am sure Saussure himself was close to understanding—voice, which is something other than phonation, belongs to language *in that* it is anterior to it, even exterior to it in a way. Voice is language's intimate precession, even if a stranger to language itself.

—If you will. But you must tell me then, how a precession can be both intimate and alien?

—You must listen, both to me and to a few others. This man, for example, do you hear him?

(Paul Valéry comes forward. He speaks in a very low voice, almost a murmur. Eventually his words become distinguishable.)

Voix, état élevé, tonique, tendu, fait uniquement d'énergie pure, libre, à haute puissance, ductile . . . l'essentiel ici est le fluide même . . . la voix—évolution d'une énergie libre . . .

Voice, a heightened state, tonic, tensed, consisting of pure energy, free, powerful, plastic . . . essential here is the fluid itself . . . voice—the development of free energy . . .

—I can hear fairly well, but I'm not sure that I understand. And why do you have me listen to this character, rather than explaining it to me yourself?

—Because you have to listen to each voice. No two are the same. Each of us explains it differently, in his own voice. Don't you know that our vocal impressions are the most unique of all, even more impossible to confuse with one another than finger prints, which are, after all, particular to each of us?

(Donning a mask of Roland Barthes, he announces:)

La voix humaine est en effet le lieu privilégié (eidétique) de la différence . . .

The human voice is in fact the privileged (eidetic) locus of difference . . .

—It is not enough to make a speech about voice. One must know on top of that with which voice to pronounce it. Which voice would speak of voice? Here, listen to this one.

(Enter Jean-Jacques Rousseau, who declares:)

L'homme a trois sortes de voix, savoir, la voix parlante ou articulée, la voix chantante ou mélodieuse, et la voix pathétique ou accentuée, qui sert de langage aux passions.

Man has three kinds of voices, namely, the speaking or articulated voice, the singing or melodious voice, and the pathetic or accented voice, which serves as the language for the passions.

—If I understand what he just said and what you were saying before, not only does each person have a particular voice, but also several possible voices. But nonetheless, the voice itself, the vocalization of voice, or its essence as voice, is not to be confused with any of these possible voices. It would be that which neither speaks, nor sings, nor has the tone of passion, even though it is capable of all three roles, just as it can become your voice or mine, this character's or another's. So I must ask you again—how do you define such a thing?

—It is voice itself—and it is not evident that it is a single thing. That is the voice we cannot speak because it is a precession to speech, an infant speech that makes itself understood outside of all speech, even within speech itself: for if it is infinitely more archaic than speech, on the other hand, there is no speech that makes itself understood without voice.

—So that voice, in its archaism, would be at the same time the veritable actuality of speech, which in turn is itself a being in the act of discourse . . .

—It is not voice that is the actuality of speech. That is rather always only a voice, your voice or mine, talking or singing, a different one each time. Voice is always shared, it is in a sense sharing itself. Voice begins where the retrenchment of the singular being begins. Later, with speech, he will recreate his ties to the world and he will give meaning to his own retrenchment. But to begin with, with his voice, he cries out in pure disparity, which has no distinct meaning.

—Each voice cries out in the wilderness, like that of the prophet. And it is in the wilderness of forsaken existence, prey to both lack and absence, that the voice first makes itself heard. Listen to what a woman says, a mother.

(Projected on a screen, the face of Julia Kristeva says these words:)

La voix répond au sein manquant, ou bien se déclenche au fur et à mesure que l'accès du sommeil semble remplir de vides la tension et l'attention de l'éveil. Les cordes vocales se tendent et vibrent pour remplir le vide de la bouche et du tube digestif (réponse à la faim) et les défaillances du système nerveux à l'approche du sommeil . . . la voix prendra la relève du vide. . . . La contraction musculaire, gastrique et sphinctérienne, rejette, parfois en même temps, l'air, la nourriture et les déchets. La voix jaillit de ce rejet de l'air et de matière nutritive ou excrémentielle; les premières émissions sonores, pour être vocales, n'ont pas seulement leur origine dans la glotte, elles sont la marque audible d'un phénomène complexe de contraction musculaire et vagosympatique qui est un rejet impliquant l'ensemble du corps.

The voice responds to the missing breast, or is set off because of the extent to which the coming of sleep seems to fill with voids the tension and attention of waking hours. The vocal cords stretch and vibrate in order to fill the emptiness of the mouth and the digestive tract (in response to hunger) and the breakdowns of the nervous system in the face of sleep . . . the voice will take over from the void. . . . Muscle, gastric, and sphincter contractions, reject, sometimes simultaneously, the air, food, and feces. Voice springs from this rejection of air and of nutritive or excremental matter; in order to be vocal, the first sonorous emissions not only have their origin in the glottis, but are the audible mark of a complex phenomenon of muscular and rhythmic contractions which are a rejection implicating the whole body.

—I wouldn't dispute that. I wouldn't challenge that voice . . .

—Do you think that a voice can ever be challenged? I would like to propose to you, on the contrary, the following hypothesis, that voice, or rather the infinite sharing of voices, constitutes the realm or element of affirmation multiplied ad infinitum; there is no negation there. There is no dialectic of voices, there is dialectic only through and in language.

—But that realm of voices is neither replete, nor unified . . .

—No, it's not. It is made up of the space or disparity between voices. Each one is different, each one is formed by a gap, by an opening, a tube, a larynx, throat, and mouth, traversed by this nothing, by this utterance, by this expulsion of voice. The voice cries in the wilderness because it is itself initially such a wilderness extending through the very center of the body, beyond words.

This, then, is the degree of its affirmation—not the simple counter-part of negation. A wilderness, each time, each voice, a singular wilderness.

—Doubtless you are right. But I wanted to say, without refuting the voice defined as rejection, that we could propose an altogether different way of understanding what rushes out in the cries of infancy. And it would also be another way of understanding the *vox clamans in deserto*. The voice would not be responding to the void, as that person was saying, but it would expose the void, would turn it toward the outside. The voice would be less the rejection than the ejection of an infinite void opening on the heart of the unique being, of that abandoned being. What voice would thus expose, as it offered up the void, would not be a lack. It would be that want of plentitude or of presence which is not a shortcoming, because it most properly constitutes existence itself: it is what opens existence, ever and always beside itself. In voice there would be this: that being is not a subject, but that it is an open existence spanned by ejection, an existence ejected into the world. My voice is above all what projects me into the world. If you will take these words with a certain levity, I would say that there is something in the voice that is irrevocably ecstatic.

—Are you thinking of song?

—How could I not think of it? But I'm not talking about lyric swooning. The one who sings—and the one who listens to sing-ing—are the most surely, the most simply, but also the most vertiginously, outside of themselves. Listen.

(He starts up a tape recorder. We hear the coloratura from the "Queen of the Night," then the scene from Verdi's "Nabucco" in which the king goes mad.)

—Someone singing, during the song, is not a subject.

—Why are you always reiterating that there is no subject in voice? There must be a subject for there to be voice, and moreover, if I've understood you rightly, there must be a subject for each singular voice. I would say that voice is the irrefutable mark of the subject's presence: its imprint, as you put it. And that is how we understand any discussion of a writer's voice: his style, his proper and inimitable mark.

—I concede that each voice has its imprint or its indelible signature. But it seems more crucial to plot in the opening and utterance of voice what is most purely vocal, even before we distinguish the particular imprint of a voice. And that has nothing to do with the subject. For the subject is a being capable both of containing and enduring its own internal contradiction . . .

—I recognize Hegel's voice! . . .

—I thought that you would. But Hegel has more than one voice, like other greats . . .

—A great voice would always be more than one voice? Is that the reason why they so often write dialogues, like Plato, Aristotle, Galileo, Descartes, Heidegger?

—Maybe. But dialogue or no dialogue, there is polyphony at the basis of every voice. Because voice is not a thing, it is the means by which something—someone—takes distance from the self and lets that distance resonate. Voice does not only come out of an opening, it is itself open and opens on itself. Voice gives onto the voice in itself. A voice offers itself simultaneously something like a plurality of vocal ranges, projections . . .

—Excuse me, I'd like to come back to Hegel. You've forgotten him.

—Yes, I had forgotten him. But actually that makes it all the easier to hear one of his other voices. That voice, for example, with which he speaks of voice. Because voice, for Hegel, comes before subject. Voice precedes the subject, which means, of course, that it is intimately linked with the subject—and I will agree with you, that voice frays a path for the subject. But it is not the subject's voice.

—If I follow you, one would have to say, on the contrary, that it *is* the subject's voice—precisely because it is the voice which frays the subject's path—but that voice itself does not have a subject. I still don't know why that should be the case. And we haven't heard Hegel's voice.

—Hegel's first voice is the subject's voice. It declaims, with the imperturbable tone you recognized, that being and truth consist of enduring one's own internal contradiction. The subject is thus the one whose relation to the self entails its own negation, and that is what confers upon one the infinite unity of an inexhaustible self-presence—even in absence, which is to say, in what concerns us, even in silence. With voice, it is not a question of a silence that could signify, or of an absence on the part of the subject that makes itself heard. As I said, it is an affirmation, not a negation. Voice is not a contradiction to be endured, first established and then overcome. Voice exists outside of both contradiction and unity. Now you must hear Hegel's other voice, that other tone with which he speaks of voice. Listen.

(Hegel, talking with Schelling and Hölderlin, who pronounce some of the following sentences, without its being a real conversation. Since they are speaking quietly and walking about, only fragments of their speech are audible.)

Die Stimme fängt mit dem Klang an. . . . Der Klang ist ein *Erzittern*—d.i. durch die momentane ebenso Negation der Theile wie Negation dieser ihrer Negation . . . als ein Oscilliren des Bestehens . . . diese mechanische Seelenhaftigkeit . . .

. . . das Thier hat *Stimme* indem es seine Selbstbewegung als ein freies Erzittern in sich selbst darstellt . . .

. . . die Seele . . . diese Wirklichkeit der Idealität an einem Dasein . . .

. . . das Kind wird von dessen Selbstischkeit durchzittert . . .

. . . zum menschlichen Ausdruck gehört . . . der über das Ganze ausgegossene geistige Ton. . . . Deiser Ton ist eine so leichte, unbestimmte und unsagbare Modifikation . . . ein bestimmtes und ganz unvollkommnes Zeichen für den Geist . . .

—I didn't get much of that. Can you tell me what they were saying?
—I think so. Listen.

(The three speakers remain immobile, and an invisible loudspeaker can be heard:)

Voice begins with sound. Sound is a *state of trembling*, that is to say, an act of oscillation between the consistency of a body and the negation of its cohesion. It is like a dialectical movement that cannot achieve fulfillment, and that would remain a palpitation. . . . In the resonant trembling of an inanimate body there is already soul, a kind of mechanical aptitude for soul. . . . But voice arises first in the animal. . . . It is the animal's mode of trembling freely in himself. . . . His soul resides in this trembling, there is this ideational effectivity which makes up a determined *existence*. . . . The identity of the being—the concrete presence of the Idea itself—always begins in trembling. Thus, the child in the mother's womb, the child not yet autonomous and not yet subject, is subject to a trembling that passes through the originary sharing of the maternal substance. . . . It is not an audible voice, but it must still make a sound in the mother's womb. It is the gabbling vocalization of access to being. . . . The soul is that singular being which trembles when it first appears, whose trembling first makes its manifestation. . . . It is the *singular* subject, which is to say, what is not the infinite unity of subjectivity, but only its singularity. . . . This singular soul gives itself form or figure—that is its work of art . . . the art of trembling. . . . And where man is concerned, this art is the human *physiognomy*: upright, with a hand, a mouth, a voice, a laugh, a sigh, tears . . . and something steeps the whole, a spiritual tone that immediately reveals the body to be the exteriority of a superior nature. That tone is a light, indeterminate, inexpressible modification: it is but the imperfect and indeterminate sign for the universal of the Idea that is herewith presented. That tone is not language. Perhaps it clears the path for language. It is that inexpressible modification, that modulation of the soul trembling, crying, sighing, laughing too. . . . The soul that trembles as it manifests itself, without yet having appropriated its proper spiritual substance.

(The three characters withdraw. One hears the beginning of Schubert's lied "Gretchen am Spinnrade" being very softly sung.)

> Meine Ruhe ist hin, mein Herz ist schwer,
> Ich finde, Ich finde sie nimmer mehr . . .

> Gone is my calm, my heart is torn,
> I will, I will never find her again . . .

—I'm quite taken, I'll admit it. But your Hegel wasn't alone, there were three voices.

—True, but it was he, I assure you, it was he or the voice of an epoch . . .

—As I understand it, this modification of which they spoke, this spiritual modulation which sounds through the entire body, that would be the voice of voice, resonating in a timbre or tone that otherwise trembles in the open throat? This universal tone or timbre—whether in man or animal, in a particular man or a particular animal, the universal tone of a singular vibration—would be the tone of voice, and reciprocally, voice would make the particular trembling of this tone audible. . . . Each would be the voice of the other: a voice which isn't a voice, which is the tone of the soul diffused throughout the body, giving it its existence by means of its resonance, and the voice which is the voice of this existence, uttered by the mouth and throat.

—Yes, I think you could put it that way. So you understand that there is no subject involved here. A voice has a voice outside of itself, it does not hold within it its own contradiction, or rather, it does not sustain such a contradiction: it projects it out in advance of itself. Voice is not present to itself, it is only an exterior manifestation, a trembling that offers itself to the outside, the half-beat of an opening—once again, a wilderness exposed where layers of air vibrate in the heat. The wilderness of the voice in the wilderness, in all its clamor—has no subject, no infinite unity; it always leaves for the outside, without self-presence, without self-consciousness.

—That reminds me of someone who said—I am citing from memory—that man, unlike the animals, has no voice; that he has only language and signification as a way of filling the void of his missing voice, and also as a way of forcing himself toward this absent voice . . .

—That was Giorgio Agamben. He said that voice was the outer limit of signification, not like a simple sound deprived of meaning, but "as a pure indication of the event of language."

(Agamben, on the side of the stage, adds very quickly:)

Et cette voix qui, sans rien signifier, signifie la signification même, coïncide avec la dimension de signification la plus universelle, avec

l'être. . . . Ma la voce, la voce umana non c'è. Non c'è una nostra voce
che noi possiamo sequire alla traccia nel linguaggio, cogliere—per
ricordarla—nel punto in cui dilegua nei nomi, si scrive nelle lettere.

And this voice which, without signifying anything, signifies signification itself, coincides with the most universal dimension of signification, with being. . . . But there is no such thing as a human voice.
There is no voice we can call our own, that we could track down in
language, that we could seize—that we could call back—in that moment in which it succumbs to names or inscribes itself in letters.

—I remember someone else too, who said:

(a child's voice, offstage)

Le sens est abandonné au partage, à la différence des voix. Il n'est pas
un donné antérieur et extérieur à nos voix. Le sens se donne, il
s'abandonne. Il n'y a peut-être pas d'autre sens du sens que cette
générosité.

Signification is left up to the process of exchange, to the disparity
between voices. It is not a given—either anterior or exterior to our
voices. Signification give itself, yields itself up. Signification has perhaps no other significance than that of its generosity.

—The significance of signification is like the voice of voice: only
an opening, the trembling of opening sent forth, in the transmis-
sion of something that is meant to be heard—but nothing else.
Which is to say that it is not meant to come back to one . . .
    —Still, it resonates within itself . . .
    —Yes, but without coming back to the self, without gathering
itself together to be repeated and heard within the self . . .
    —But the voice that hears itself can only do so in silence. You
know that—Derrida has demonstrated it.
    —Of course. And that is why the voice that can't keep quiet, the
voice that is a voice, can't hear itself. It doesn't have within itself the
silence to hear itself proffer a meaning beyond sound. That's
another way of not holding a contradiction within the self. It
doesn't have this silence within itself, it only resonates, outside, in
the wilderness. It cannot hear itself—or not really—but it can make

itself heard. It is always addressed to the other. Here, since you were just quoting him, listen.

(Derrida, speaking into a portable mike held toward him by a young woman.)

Quand la voix tremble . . . elle se fait entendre *parce que* son lieu d'émission n'est pas fixé . . . vibration différentielle pure . . . une jouissance qui serait jouissance d'une plénitude sans vibration, sans différence, me paraît être à la fois le mythe de la métaphysique—et de la mort. . . . Dans la jouissance vivante, plurielle, différentielle, l'autre est appelé . . .

When the voice trembles . . . it makes itself heard *because* the point of utterance is not fixed . . . pure differential vibration . . . a pleasure that would be the pleasure of plenitude without vibration, without difference, seems to me to be at once the myth of metaphysics—and of death. . . . In lively, plural, differential pleasure, the other is called . . .

—But then he isn't called by anything, not even his name. It is the voice alone, which says nothing, but which calls out?

—If voice says nothing, that doesn't mean that it doesn't name. Or at least, it doesn't mean that it doesn't clear the path for naming. The voice which calls, that is to say the voice which is a call, without articulating any language, opens the name of the other, opens the other to his name, which is my voice thrown in his direction.

—But if there are still no names, no language. There is nothing to stabilize the call.

—Yes there is, the voice calls the other only there, where as other, he can come. In the wilderness.

—But who comes to the wilderness, other than the nomads who cross it?

—Precisely, the voice calls the other nomad, or else calls him to become a nomad. It throws out the name of a nomad, which is a precession of his proper name. Which prompts him to leave himself, to give his voice in turn. Voice calls the other to come out in his own voice. Listen.

(A man of the desert lifts the veil from his face and reads aloud from Deleuze.)

La musique, c'est d'abord une déterritorialisation de la voix, qui devient de moins en moins langage. . . . La voix est très en avance sur le visage, très en avant. . . . Machiner la voix est la première opération musicale. . . . Il faut que la voix atteigne elle-même à un devenir-femme ou à un devenir-enfant. Et c'est là le prodigieux contenu de la musique. . . . C'est la voix musicale qui devient elle-même enfant, mais en même temps l'enfant devient sonore, purement sonore . . .

Music is first and foremost a deterritorialization of voice, which becomes less and less language. . . . Voice is far ahead of the face, far ahead. . . . To devise a voice is the first step in music. . . . Voice must of itself attain to a being-woman or a being-child. And that is the prodigious content of music. . . . The musical voice itself becomes child, but at the same time the child becomes vocal, purely vocal . . .

—The other is called forth to where there is neither subject nor signification. It is the wilderness of pleasure, or of joy. It is not desolate even if it is arid. It is neither desolate nor consoled. It is beyond either laughter or tears.

—But still, don't you have to concede—and you seemed to have done so at one point—that voice is first uttered in tears?

—That's true, that's the birth of tragedy. But what comes before that birth is the delivery of voice and it is not yet tragic. Those are tears and cries which know nothing of tragedy or comedy.

—Am I to make of that that they know nothing of their own utterance, their own effusion, of a body that opens and exhales, of a soul stretching itself?

—Yes, an open plain—*partes extra partes*—which vibrates—*partes contra partes*. It doesn't speak, it calls on the other to speak. Voice calls on the other to speak, to laugh, or to cry—even already in me. I would not speak if my voice, which is not me and which is not in me, even if it is absolutely mine, didn't call on me, didn't ask of me to speak, laugh, or cry, that other in me who can do such things.

(Montaigne, sitting at his desk, and while he writes:)

Le branle mesme de ma voix tire plus de mon esprit, que je n'y trouve lors que je le sonde et employe à part moy.

The very impetus of my voice draws more from my mind than I find there when I sound and make use of it on my own.

—Valéry said *(he pulls a book from his pocket and reads aloud)*: "*Language* issues from *voice*, rather than *voice* from *language*."

—And that is why he could say: "voice defines pure poetry."

—So poetry would then not speak?

—Yes, it speaks, but it speaks with that speech that is not executed by any language and from which, by contrast, voice issues and a language is born. Voice is the precession of language, the very immanence of language in the wilderness where the soul is still alone.

—You were saying that it made the other come there!

—Of course, that is how the soul is alone: not solitary, but with another, within calling distance of the other, and alone with respect to discourse, to operations, to occupations.

—And the other to which the soul cries out, that is then still the same soul?

—It is the soul itself which the voice calls forth from the other. That is how it frays the path for the subject, but it doesn't let it settle in yet. On the contrary, it avoids the subject. It does not call on the soul to hear itself, or even to hear any discourse. It simply calls, which is to say that it makes the soul tremble, arouses it. The soul arouses the other within itself. That is voice.

TRANSLATED BY NATHALIA KING

§ Menstruum Universale

Tell me, oh tell! what kind of thing is Wit,
Thou who *Master* art of it;
For the *First matter* loves Variety less;
Less Women lov't, either in *Love* or *Dress*.
A thousand diff'rent shapes it bears
Comely in thousand shapes appears;
Yonder we saw it plain, and here 'tis now,
Like Spirits in a Place, we know not *How*.
—Cowley, "Ode to Wit"

Witz as a principle of affinities is at the same time
the *menstruum universale.*
—Novalis

I

We are about to examine a subject that has been virtually neglected in the history of literature and philosophy, a subject that up to this point has never really been given its due in either of these histories, namely Wit, or in German, the language to which it belongs (while English literature, from Sterne to Joyce, is its favorite playing field), *Witz*. *Witz* is barely, or only tangentially, a part of literature: it is neither genre nor style, nor even a figure of rhetoric. Nor does it belong to philosophy, being neither concept, nor judgment, nor argument. It could nonetheless play all these roles, but in a derisive manner.

Yet it can also occupy strategically decisive positions in all seriousness: on rare but noteworthy occasions in history *Witz* has, in fact, appeared in such crucial positions. In his preface to *Tristram Shandy*, Sterne argues against Locke in the name of Wit, and in doing so ascribes to it the essential property of the entire philosophical genre. The founders of German Romanticism—the Schlegels, Novalis, Bernhardi, along with Jean Paul and later Solger—made *Witz* a dominant motif, indeed made it the principle of a theory that claimed to be aesthetic, literary, metaphysical, even social and political, all at the same time. Finally, Freud's first work devoted to aesthetics was on *Witz* and established what would remain to the very end of his work his definition of aesthetic pleasure.

But such is the nature of these occurrences [*apparitions*] that, on every occasion, it is their disappearance that seems remarkable. Sterne himself admitted that his arguments against Locke are so trifling that neither philosophy nor theory can "really" deal with them. In the theory of the Romantics of Jena, *Witz*, even more than other motifs, is confined to the transitory existence that characterizes this theoretical moment. It is limited to a handful of fragmentary texts, almost completely unproductive of literary works, and easily replaced by what is usually called "Romanticism." As for Freud, despite the importance of many of the questions he addressed in *Der Witz*, he never again took up either the theme or the work itself after 1905 (except for fleeting allusions), in contrast to the frequent reworkings of *The Interpretation of Dreams* and *Three Essays on Sexuality*.[1]

Witz does not *hold* the positions that theory—any theory whatsoever—might want it to occupy. It does occupy them—in Romanticism it even ventures to occupy, at one stroke, the position of a metaphysical Absolute ("The essence of truth is to be *Witz*; for all science is a *Witz* of the intellect, all art is a *Witz* of fantasy, any witticism [*Pointe*] is *witzig* only insofar as it evokes the *Witz* of truth," says Bernhardi in 1803 in his *Theory of Language*)—but it does not settle in them. It does not constitute, or it barely constitutes, a system; it does not constitute, or it barely constitutes, a school; it somehow avoids becoming a work as it avoids becoming thought. Its constructions are as stunning as they are unstable.

Why consider a subject that is almost totally neglected, unsubstantial, inconsequential? Why concern ourselves with this minute category—hardly a category really, indistinct and inconstant—usually no more than a witticism? Certainly not to enjoy the now fashionable pleasure of saving yet another of history's Cinderellas, nor to dazzle the world by showing the major importance of what everyone had thought insignificant.

Our intention is all the less likely to be this because today nearly everyone agrees that *Witz* has a decisive importance. Never set forth per se, this near-consensus is evidenced by the respect—at times even veneration—accorded to *Witz* as an indispensable element of the psychoanalytic apparatus as well as an equally indispensable element of literature that claims to be modern (always at least in part inseparable from a Joycean "tradition," whether in the European *nouveau roman*, in Faulkner, in Burroughs, or even in Borges, to limit the references arbitrarily). Such recognition verges on the religious: it is almost tacitly agreed that the aesthetic and *theoretical* virtues of *Witz* are without equal.[2]

The question that must be asked is exceedingly simple: how can insignificance assume such importance, and what are the implications of this operation? From this first standpoint, at least, it is not the insignificance of *Witz* but its "fullness of meaning" that must concern us, in its literary and philosophical history.

This immediately implies a second question: If the "fullness of meaning" of *Witz* can never be maintained, if it is always vanishing or slowly disappearing, in what way are we implicated in *Witz*, where does it lead us? This is the point at which the insignificance of *Witz* should—if it can be said—interest us. But then it will no longer be possible simply to transcend and establish its insignificance as has previously been done.

In other words, if Novalis—for reasons and in a context that remain to be defined—could call *Witz* the *menstruum universale*, meaning "universal solvent" in the vocabulary of alchemy, then it is in the end (but could it bring about an end?) dissolution *itself*, in *Witz* and of *Witz* itself, with which we inevitably have to deal. But nothing can be done with dissolution—perhaps it is not even possible to develop a discourse on "it."

But nothing can be precisely done with this either: should our own discourse dissolve, we can neither decide it, nor foresee it, nor wish it, nor master it. And this, on principle, even though all discourse—this one as well as others—can take no other form than the project of such mastery and its calculation. We must, therefore, cut off our introduction as abruptly as possible: our purpose as such, what we *propose*, can only be to attempt to master as completely as possible a subject known under the name of *Witz*.

I I

What is meant by *Witz*? Several things in any case, sometimes interrelated, sometimes distinct, depending upon the period and the context. At the same time then and separately, *Witz* is:

§ the particular kind of utterance [*énoncé*] named wordplay, witticisms of all the various types this category can include (from puns to plays on pure logic);

§ a procedure of this sort extended to the realm of literature and art but of a different nature than a strict utterance (e.g., the black page that appears in *Tristram*);

§ the psychological faculty capable of such productions, especially what is known as English *wit* and French *esprit* (*esprit de finesse*, subtlety, *esprit ingénieux*, ingeniousness, etc.);

§ the concept of the most general form assumed by these productions: always an association or combination that is unexpected, surprising, or not sanctioned by ordinary rules. In the state in which it came the closest to being a true concept—with the Romantics—*Witz* most generally designated the union, the mélange (or the dissolution) of heterogeneous elements.[3]

It is not a question of choosing between these accepted meanings, nor of organizing them in order to study them one by one. Neither are these the distinct meanings, or successive meanings, of the same term. Up to a point, each one is inseparable from all others: *Witz* is the "structure" of a production, *Witz*, which requires a faculty, *Witz*. Which means, furthermore, that "Witz" is in some way inseparable even in its semantic determination, from the expression "to make a *Witz*." This is to say that *Witz* in general (if such "generality" can be determined)—or some *Witz*—is inseparable from the form and the nature of utterance [*énoncé*], from an utterance that is, in its turn, inseparable from what utters it (from *Witz*, the utterer), thus also from the act of utterance and, by an inescapable contiguity, from the context, the occasion, the circum-

stances, or the situation of the act of utterance. *Witz* is inextricably—we shall prove it—a logical, semiotic, semantic, psychological,
philosophical, sociological notion. Cowley's "Ode to Wit"—an
excerpt of which we used as our epigraph—attests to this fact. We
quote from a text of the same period no doubt still pertinent today,
which approaches *Witz* in a manner completely different from but
as legitimate as ours: "Few people of distinction trouble themselves
about the name of Wit, fewer understand it, and hardly any have
honored it with their example. In the next class of people it seems
best known, most admired, and most frequently practiced; but
their stations in life are not eminent enough to dazzle us into
imitation."[4]

To find our bearings in the space or the play determined by this
word, we begin with what the simple history of the word offers us
(its German history, since we use the German term; but the history
of English "Wit" is for the most part homologous to it).

Witz acquired rather late the meanings we now attribute to it.
Witzi, in Old and Middle High German, designates an intellectual
faculty, if not *the* faculty of intelligence—intelligence as sagacity, as
the natural power of discernment. In retracing its etymological
path, we come upon the whole primitive family of *savoir*, to know,
in the sense of *voir*, to see: the Sanskrit *Veda*, the Greek *eidos* (the
Platonic Idea), the Latin-Cartesian *evidentia*; but instead of spreading out, like organic growth from a primary root, the history of this
word family, with its *Witz*, leads us away from the proper sense of
knowledge [*savoir*]. *Witzi* is knowledge linked to *List*: this word,
which later will only mean "cunning," signifies *savoir-faire*, technical skill, especially in the art of magic and in war. *Witzi*, then, is the
knowledge of skills, of calculation, of strategy. Thus it accounts for
Wissen—knowledge one possesses which can be systematized and
accounted for—and will remain closer to its twin, "Wise," a concept of aristocratic and courtly culture, and of knowledge understood as refinement. *Weisheit*, wisdom, will come later. *Witz* itself
will always remain closer to sagacity, to the perspicacity of a keen
mind that is discerning and nimble, and consequently to the
intelligence that nature is presumed to bestow and that cannot be

taught: the Latin *ingenium*, the capacity of the mind that is innate rather than acquired.

The first *Witz*, then, is knowledge that cannot be acquired, that is unprovable (as opposed to *mathemata*), knowledge that perceives [*savoir-voir*], that grasps the *idea* at a glance and distinguishes with lucidity.

The word *Witz* retains the meaning of the faculty of sight until the seventeenth century. Up to this point its gender is feminine. Later it will become masculine, and its sense will be displaced—not transformed, but endowed with a new position and a new function. The sex change and displacement do not simply occur within the German language. In a strange way the intervention of foreign languages is needed to accomplish it. English "Wit"—we shall meet it again—already occupies part of the future domain of *Witz*. But on the Continent, as a result of the cultural privilege claimed by the French language—and the consequent ignorance of all things foreign—*esprit* assumes this role. In reality, *esprit* in the sense of *avoir de l'esprit*, to be witty, falls far short of the scope of *Witz*. Yet the Germans cannot translate this word; in German the expression is "*esprit*, as the French say." And in France one hears and reads that the Germans lack *esprit*.[5] A German poet (Christian Wernicke) counters that German has *Witz* in its very language. But the poet's mother was English.

Witz itself, if one can speak in these terms, in the language where its entire concept will be formulated, is thus the product of a peculiar nationalist quarrel. Various cultures and languages presenting themselves as identities and claiming for themselves a particular *ingenium*, boast of their own *Witz* or despise themselves for not having any. Those that have none cannot acquire it by importation—*Witz* is neither transportable nor translatable—but it turns out that by chance or fate they already possessed it without being aware of it. In time, Kant will be able to write in his *Anthropologie* that the German language has the advantage of possessing two distinct terms, *Witz* and *Geist*, whereas French, less fortunate, has only the word *esprit* . . . But where did *esprit* come from?[6]

III

We shall try to describe the origin of *esprit*, of *Witz*, or more precisely what we might call the *generation* of *Witz* in a double sense: both the genesis or the engenderment of *Witz* and—as we say in the expression the "beat generation," the age or the era of *Witz*. *Witz* appears matter of factly and characterizes an entire era almost unexpectedly—and at the same time it corresponds to a process of permanent engenderment in the history of literature and philosophy. Neither a pure genesis nor a pure event, *Witz* is continually born and reborn like its hero, Tristram Shandy, whose identity is the identity of a *Witz*: although born from the normal generative process, Tristram owes his birth to an accident—his mother disturbing his father at the crucial moment by reminding him to wind the clock—and, as explained by Tristram, by an "unhappy association of ideas which have no connection in nature." This causes him immediately to evoke Locke, long before the preface, at the beginning of the story: "which strange combination of ideas, the sagacious Locke, who certainly understood the nature of these things better than most men, affirms to have produced more wry actions than all other sources or prejudice whatsoever."[7]

Tristram's birth is the uncontrolled birth of Wit, of a Wit—the parodic birth of the hero who caricatures or parodies philosophy, the birth of literature in philosophy, of literature as the *Witz* of philosophy, or of the *Witz* "literature and philosophy," or else of the dissolving union of these heterogeneous elements.

All these formulas must remain provisional and open to question, until the generation of *Witz* has been established. However, Tristram's birth indicates immediately the difficulty of such an endeavor. It would, in fact, require assuming *at the same time* a division of literature and philosophy that has *always already* taken place in the history of the West, *and* the emergence, from within philosophy, of the generation of literature, that is, the age of Tristram, our age.

The first direction compels us to go back to the first known forms of grotesque and carnivalesque literature, beyond the Latin *satura* and its mixture of genres and prosodies, beyond the scraps of texts of the Cynics, with their witty sayings and their parodies of philosophy, beyond the wordplays sprinkled throughout Plato's dialogues, beyond the very genre of the dialogue, a sophistic genre and the favorite haunt of "witticisms"[8]—and thus as far back as the first mimes and the birth of comedy *and* tragedy, as far as the *Witz* of their "strange combination" . . .

The lesson is clear: in such an endeavor we could never reach an origin, or we would reach it as a *Witz*, by a genesis taking the form of vicious circles—but at the same time we would have lost *Witz*, by extending its specifically modern character to all kinds of literature and philosophy.

In a way, it is the lesson of *Witz*; the uncontrolled and uncontrollable birth, the jumbling of genres, or of what one is tempted to call *the Western genre*, literature and philosophy, neither literature nor philosophy, literature or philosophy. In short, literary dissolution—where "literary" only means the domain of letters, of writing in general.

But even this—literary dissolution—has *also* occurred once before in history. *Witz* appeared, dissolution *occurred again* under the name and in the strictly modern form of *Witz*. (*Witz* in its strictest sense has absolutely no equivalent in ancient languages.) It is this recurrence and this emergence that we must trace; they are situated within philosophy, in the philosophical rebirth of literary dissolution.

We must go back again to the question: where did *esprit*, in the seventeenth-century French sense, come from?

In schematizing as much as it is possible without distortion[9] we will say this: *esprit* is the specific, modern outgrowth of the philosophical crisis of *judgment*.

What we designate as the "philosophical crisis of judgment" is the modern recurrence of a "crisis" constitutive of philosophical discourse: to be exact, of the crisis of the Greek *krisis*. In philosophy, *krisis, krinein*—judgment, appreciation, decision—has meant from the outset (from the *Poem* of Parmenides on) the act of choice, of decision, and of that decision's execution, an act exterior to the *logos,* and necessary in order for the (proper) *logos* to be sustained. Outside of the *logos, krisis* produces a *tonos* that is not limited by it. Thus *krisis* marks the element or the structure of "undecidability" of the "logical" decision itself.

Moreover, *krisis* and words of the same family, such as *judicium,* source of "judgment," are words of a practical or pragmatic origin in the fields of medicine, of judicial practice and of political action.

Stoic seminology designates *krisis* as the decision that relates the sign to the thing. If it is true, it posits the *idioma* of the thing; if it is false, it conveys only a troubling and dangerous *phantasma.* Therefore *judgment* is the act proper to *compositio,* the combination of signs with things and the combination of the signs among themselves. One has to have recourse to *compositio* when there is no *conceptio,* that is to say when there is no immediate auto-adequation (or simultaneous production) of the thing and its *concept. Compositio* is a deficiency in conception, a deflection or deferred engenderment, a birth uncertain of its control.

Long before scholasticism formulated, under the name of *critica,* a specific discipline of judgment, *critica* was already established as the particular study or discipline—being neither science nor art— that examines, comments upon, and judges texts. It was literary criticism before the fact, the exercise of judgment in its most "proper" domain: the domain of works not dependent on pure "logic" that do not give rise to any pure "conception." The theory of judgment and literary criticism go hand in hand: they are—and exchange indefinitely—the orders of the sign, of combination, and of their own interaction, as well as the order of the act that determines these relations. Thus they share—and even intersect at the location of—the indispensable *subject* of this act, a subject not to be taken in the sense of *sub-jectum,* the substratum (Aristotle's *hypokeimenon*), but rather as the author and performer of the decision, the author or performer of the idiom or phantasm.

Such a subject—let's call it the critical subject—is not the "impersonal" subjectivity of *the* Subject. On the contrary, it exists only in the inequality of subjects: if reason is distributed equally in everyone (except for madmen), judgment is distributed unequally.

We are all endowed with sound judgment (by nature, God, or chance) to a greater or lesser degree.

It is precisely from the already scholastic division of *ratio* and *judicium* that the modern metaphysics of subjectivity and "the generation of *Witz*" are formulated together.

The method of Descartes consists of ascribing being and truth to the subject of decision itself, not in the sense that the subject judges, but rather that it *conceives itself*, and even that it conceives itself in the act of conceiving. In a way the *cogito* formulates the (re)conquest of substantiality by the subject-performer of the decision. (But apart from the certainty of the *cogito*, all else is judgment, which must be guided, enlightened, guaranteed or rectified by that unique certainty.)

In fact, the Cartesian *act* of the *cogito* splits itself in two[10] and produces its own double: *l'homme d'esprit*, the man of wit. Instead of being unique and unitary like the *cogito*, the double proliferates and immediately becomes a multiplicity of figures. The courtier (Castiglione's or Graciàn's, to mention the best-known treatises), the man of taste, the man of the "salon," and the woman as well, the woman of taste, the woman of *esprit*, all these constitute the polymorphous character of the subject of judgment who finds his certainty within himself. He differs from his double in that he does not find this certainty by the light of intuition, but in the penumbra that is the product of a natural gift; in that he does not discover it as the truth, but only as an entity as precise as a glance or strategy can guarantee; in that he does not establish it as a substance, but cultivates it as an exercise of his talent; in that he does not link the deductions of a science to it, but derives works of political calculation, love strategies, and circumspect wisdom from it; finally, in that he does not propose any *Meditations*, but rather works of the genre "miscellany," where, by means of dialogue, fable, or aphorism, the saying [*sentence*] always reigns supreme.

Discourse yields (or wants to yield) the way to the truth it presents; the saying is "true" only by the force of its style and the extremity of its point. Discourse causes conception, the saying plays with the *concetto*. Discourse develops in terms of the me-

thodical order of science; the saying, through mixture and fragmentation, tends at any given moment to produce a *maxim*, that
is, the *maxima sententia*, the greatest thought possible. The man
of discourse considers himself to be only mind [*esprit*], the man
of wit [*l'homme d'esprit*], can see himself as part of the play of
representation.[11]

That the former is necessarily limited to the representation of his
substance, and that the latter considers his play to be the very being
of the subject, is perhaps what everyone admits secretly to himself,
but must deny publicly. The former re-invents philosophy, the latter re-invents literature—the man of thought and the man of wit.
They are one and the same, but the history of judgment is the history that divides them *and* links them irremediably to each other.

I V

Esprit, wit, *Witz* will henceforth—through the incessant modifications of their figure, their sex, their genre, their aspect—manipulate *belles*-lettres and *beaux*-arts (and the art of their criticism).
They are the doubles of judgment insofar as judgment has already,
through the logic of discourse, excluded itself from conception.
They are the doubles of the first *lack* in thought, and therefore
doubly lacking in thought.

From the seventeenth to the nineteenth century, philosophy
could not be severe enough toward *Witz*: *Witz* is found to be uncertain, confused, too obscure or too brilliant, limp, effeminate, de-
ceptive, and to offer phantasms of literature as its idioms. Hobbes
and Locke are the first to decree its exclusion without appeal: it is
dangerous.

But precisely this exclusion brings about the definition of *Witz*.
In 1689, Locke writes:

> For *wit* lying most in the assemblage of ideas, and putting those
> together with quickness and variety, wherein can be found any resem-
> blance or congruity, thereby to make up pleasant pictures and agree-
> able visions in the fancy; judgment, on the contrary, lies quite on the

other side, in separating carefully, one from another, ideas wherein can be found the least difference.[12]

Thus *Witz* receives its concept from philosophy—the concept that unites all of its diversified and dispersive manifestations. While the witty analysts of wit always equated it with the ultimate "propriety" of a *je ne sais quoi*, to use an expression that flowered in the seventeenth century,[13] rational analysts ascribe to it a specific function; none other than *compositio*, because Locke's wit assembles only things that are fairly similar to one another—but in its practice already then, and soon after in its theory, *Witz* consists in inventing the similarity of things dissimilar, that is, in bringing about the necessary synthesis of those things whose disparity is limited to discovering. *Thus Witz, at the moment of its exclusion, receives the primary qualification of judgment.* "Judgment" itself would tendentially be defined as an organization of conceptions . . .

Philosophy banishes *Witz*—it banishes literature as elegance, enjoyment, invention, ingenuity, and as the composition of figures and imagination. But by the same token philosophy baptizes them.

And thus most importantly, philosophy reinstates *Witz* within itself at the very moment of its banishment, because philosophy cannot cut itself off from judgment without at the same time excluding itself from discourse. Indeed, whenever it is not dedicated to finding a "well-formed language," a "characteristic" of Leibniz, or a "language of calculations" in the manner of Condillac, all of eighteenth-century philosophy could be described as the attempt to transfer the resources of *Witz* to the account of knowledge and truth. Thereafter truth will have to be embellished or adorned in order to be made intelligible. On the one hand, the help of rhetoric and fiction must be sought;[14] on the other hand, truth itself, henceforth mankind's truth, the truth of the subject whose *cogito* did not last any longer than the Cartesian moment, this truth also has to be found in the unstable and non-assignable functions of *taste, talent,* the faculty of *inventing, combining,* and *creating.* Aesthetics arises from philosophy as the project for a science of *Witz,* a science of art and literature—a science of the

Other that had been excluded—and since this exclusion is impossible, a science of *the sameness of the Other and of the same which excludes it*: philosophy wishes to become the *Witz* that is knowledgeable in philosophy and in *Witz*.[15]

But literature can claim no less. The preface to *Tristram Shandy*, which brings together all the essentials of the "defense and illustration" of *Witz*[16] begun more than a century before, must be read both as a parody of philosophy, as a debate with philosophy, *and* at the same time as a philosophical debate. Sterne insists on placing wit, in terms of rank, dignity, radiance, and necessity, on the same level as judgment. Thus Sterne claims that all of *Tristram Shandy* is the indispensable supplement to the philosophical pact and treatise—making up for its lack and perfecting its presentation. Furthermore, this preface, set down as it was in the middle of the novel, as in its heart or center, points to the literary self-production of the theory of literature, thus indicating *at the very least* that literary theory (or criticism) is the most proper supplement to philosophy, and *at the most* that literature with its own theory suffices to insure the knowledge or the idea of the identity of philosophy and literature—and can therefore do without philosophy.

Thus arises the specifically modern possibility that literature and/or literary theory (criticism, poetics, etc.) conceive themselves or are conceived to be the locus of truth—and reciprocally the possibility that philosophy will henceforth conceive itself in terms of the question of its own staging of the truth, in short, of its aptitude for literary composition and thus for *Witz*—this double possibility has emerged from the schism and the chiasmus that *Witz* effects simultaneously, from the *crisis* of *Witz*.

V

The foregoing does not mean that we are dealing with a simple exchange of roles, or with a simple split in identity. *Witz* has no doubt gained an identity from its definition as the combination of heterogeneous elements—and in a way this is the identity literature wants to produce, or to be, in exactly the same way as philosophy.

This identity, we might add, is nothing but *identity* itself, in so far as it can be posited, or thought, only by mediation of the non-identical: therein lies what defines the fundamental "dialectic" of all Western thought, as characterized by Heidegger.[17] In that case *Witz* would be nothing more than the dialectic thinking of identity, and primarily the thought of the *identity of "esprit" itself,* in the dialectic of the *je ne sais quoi* and of reason, of "phantastic" construction and demonstration, of "witticism" and discourse, of *compositio* and *conceptio.* We may even for the sake of rigor have to conclude that the total separation and opposition of *Witz* and Reason occurred only for the purpose of *facilitating* the functioning of this dialectic. Literature has been opposed to philosophy only the better to insure mastery over their partition.

The Jena group of German Romanticism represents, in its initial aspect, the thought of this identity.[18] Romanticism (if we may be allowed so to refer to *this* Romanticism, to save space) wanted to be, so to speak, the thought of the novel, or the novel as thought: thought in and as the mélange of genres, generalized *Satura,* and not only literary genres but genres of the mind [*esprit*] in general, if we may venture to say so; hence the thought of a superior fusion of philosophy, art, science, literature and society. Without further comment we quote some of F. Schlegel's fragments:[19]

> *Witz* is the principle and the organ of universal philosophy . . . the science of all sciences perpetually mingling with each other and separating, a logical chemistry.

> Language is poetical, writing is philosophical, *Witz* links them to each other.

> The supreme *Witz* would be the true *lingua caracteristica universalis* and at the same time *ars combinatoria.*

> *Witz,* perhaps the pure principle of philosophy, ethics, and poetry.

For this thought *Witz* must then also reconquer spiritual unity, wipe out the difference between mind and *esprit*: "What was *Witz* originally, then, if not the most intimate mélange and interpenetration of reason and fantasy?" (F. Schlegel).

Thus *Witz* came to occupy the supreme position of the mind [*esprit*] in relation to philosophy as well as to literature: "*Witz* is creative, it produces resemblances" (Novalis, *Blütenstaub*).

It would be too easy and too naive to label these formulas "unbridled idealism" or "wild romanticism." We hope to have shown to what extent they are the logical outcome of the *crisis* constitutive of the entire modern era. Romanticism, then, is the closure of the crisis: "*Witz* is the point of indifference where everything is saturated," wrote F. Schlegel, in transposing onto *Witz* the first principle of Schelling's metaphysics.[20]

Conversely, we must consider how this romanticism can at the same time be the "radicalization" of the same crisis.

Schematically, the crisis can be recognized by three features, which must be enumerated separately before they can be interpreted together:

1. Considered from the point of view of *Witz*, the work of the Jena Romantics is characterized by its . . . absence of works.[21] As far as theory is concerned, the theory of *Witz* is somehow summed up in the reiteration of the absolute affirmation of *Witz*, and in the circle which decrees that *Witz* can be posited, explained, and justified only by or in terms of *Witz*: "Language and *Witz* belong to metaphysics; a metaphysics which is not *witzig* is useless." (F. Schlegel). Ultimately, all is based upon the magic of one word, in the same manner that "The innermost essence of *Witz* can be explained only by the magic of ideas" (ibid.). As far as the theory of literature is concerned, *Witz* authorizes nothing but *Witz*—which remains at the level of a wish: "A theory of the novel should itself be a novel." Finally, as literature, the Romantic *Witz* is more or less limited to the production of the two unfinished novels of Novalis and Schlegel.[22]

2. Although in principle only one *Witz* exists ("*Witz* is the principle of the novel, of mythology, and of the encyclopaedia," F. Schlegel), there remains nonetheless an irreducible multiplicity and above all a hierarchy of *Witz*. The Romantics thereby repeat a critical gesture belonging to the whole history of *Witz*, which we have so far neglected: the condemnation of vulgar *Witz*, "low"

Witz, the simple pun (in the text quoted above Bernhardi adds that what he says should not be taken for a verbal pirouette, for *witzeln* . . .). Since the seventeenth century, the celebration of *Witz* has always consisted in *separating* good from bad *Witz*—and especially in *criticizing* aggressive, cynical, and obscene *Witz*.[23] There exists a vulgarization of *Witz* one must guard against: "*Witz* as an instrument of revenge is as ignoble as art as a means of sensual titillation" (F. Schlegel). That is why the fertile works of *Witz*, those of Sterne and Jean Paul, are acknowledged by the Romantics only with the precautions imposed by the criticism of their *poor taste*, their "morbid" (Schlegel) excesses in the grotesque. But it must be noted how Sterne and Jean Paul themselves, at the risk of self-criticism and self-mockery, insist on distinguishing a "great" *Witz* from a minor, inconsistent or even ignoble one.

3. Finally, a last aspect we have so far left aside. Since Shakespeare's famous "maxim" in *Hamlet* (constantly repeated even by Freud), "brevity is the soul of wit," the only "genre" or the only "form" always recognized as the property of *Witz*, as peculiar to all *Witz*, is succinctness, the swiftness of the utterance that carries the *point*. The Romantics were to express it by means of the much reiterated German *Witz*: *Witz ist ein Blitz*; wit is a flash of lightning. Flash, lightning, explosion are the forms of the *cogito*'s double insofar as it is *instantaneous*. But as much as the quickness of *Witz* is recognized as essential to its "being" and to *pleasure* and inseparable from them,[24] this same quickness dismays and staggers the thought of *Witz*: "In *Witz* there occur sudden petrifaction, dread, and coagulation:" (F. Schlegel). Lightning blinds, an explosion deafens, pleasure benumbs. *Witz gorgonizes* the thought of *Witz*—and thereby topples this thought from the supreme unity where it was lodged: "*Witz* is the proper form of our consciousness, insofar as we are potential organic beings who are *chaotic*."

This last feature allows us to understand all three traits together: *Witz*, in keeping with the disassociation to which it owes its birth, never corresponds to the necessary *organicism* of a synthesis or a completed work, and even less to the superior organism consisting of the synthesis of the (philosophical) synthesis and the (literary) work. It merely causes such a synthesis to fulgurate like chaos. That is why Novalis calls it *menstruum universale* as well as the "principle of affinities." This fragment, of course, is in itself the synthesis of a *Witz*: total affinity is the same thing as total dissolution. But obstinately, in the (petrified) heart of romanticism, it remains necessary for the utterance of this synthesis to dissolve somehow upon itself, since it is incapable of controlling the synthesis it utters by means other than *Witz*.

Yet *Witz* does not *control*: that is why philosophy began by excluding it. *Witz* effects combinations without *knowledge*; it remains heterogeneous to the assemblages of heterogeneous elements it produces; it seduces without proving; it couples without impregnating; it merits all our fears as much as all our hopes; it can literally do anything . . . As soon as there is a literary project or purpose, literary elegance, which remains "elegance" even when it mixes with debased forms, is a protection against this "anything," against chaos—just as philosophical reasoning remains "reasoning" even when it uses the resources of a fulgurating *Witz*.

Vulgarity, chitchat, femininity, and the inconsistency of witticisms have always corroded and threatened the works of *Witz* from below, even though these works had also derived from such humble sources their very matter and justification. Indeed, it is always possible to control *Witz*, to dispose it for the production of knowledge and of works that have always assured the finality of *judgment*. But because they reached the culmination of this mastery, the Romantics also saw it dissolve in their hands, in a flash. In their attempt to generate everything by means of *Witz* there recurred what most properly constitutes *Witz*, or rather what never constitutes *Witz*, but a *Witz*, what can never be appropriated in any way, what can never be injected into any work (not even, especially not, into *Tristram Shandy*): its uncontrolled birth.

The whole Romantic "quest" for *Witz*, its whole crisis, are perhaps summed up in Schlegel's fragment: "One should have *Witz* but not want to have it, lest it become *Witzelei*, the Alexandrian style of *Witz*."[25]

If all the differences between *cogito* and *esprit* were obliterated in speculative *Witz*, only one difference would remain: one cannot will *Witz*. But what cannot be *willed*, and what *not-to-will* is, philosophy has never been able to think nor literature to practice.

Unless, at this point, we give in to accepting their own dissolution, and only retain something which is still without a name in philosophy as well as in literature—something which could not bear any name *in all seriousness*, not even the laughable name of *Witz*: something having the non-assignable form and nature of this posthumous fragment of Novalis, not *intended* as a fragment but a note sketched for the unfinished sequel to his novel, a note sufficient even in its fragmented state for the execution of that part of the program it notes—of what ought to be the program of the *menstruum universale* if it could be or produce such a program, but being unable to do so,[26] can only be resolved or dissolved in this remark, which must remain incomplete: "*Dissolution of a poet in his song*: he will be sacrificed among savages."[27]

TRANSLATED BY PAULA MODDEL

§ Noli Me Frangere

—coauthored with Philippe Lacoue-Labarthe

Of the fragment, little should be written. It is not an object or a genre, it does not form a work. (Friedrich Schlegel's fragmentary *will* is the very will to the Work, and enough has been said about that. But what Blanchot calls the fragmentary *exigency* exceeds the work, because that exigency exceeds the will.)

Fragment: the text is fragile. It's nothing but. It breaks and yet it doesn't break, in the same place. Where? Someplace, always someplace, an unassignable, incalculable place.

It is a mistake, then, to write in fragments on the fragment (that goes for Blanchot, too). But what else is there to do? Write about something else entirely—or about nothing—and let oneself be fragmented.

"That goes for Blanchot, too": nevertheless, it was the publication of *The Writing of the Disaster*, in July 1980, that came along to interrupt the composition of a completely different text, which I could now call, having abandoned it, a supplementary dialectic of the fragment. Blanchot's exigency was its guide. Blanchot's text interrupted it. I quote that text:

The fragment, as fragments, tends to dissolve the totality that it presupposes and that it carries off toward the dissolution from which (strictly speaking) it does not form itself, but to which it exposes itself in order, disappearing (all identity disappearing along with it), to maintain itself as the energy of disappearing.

A supplementary dialectic of the fragment was therefore at work in that text as well. Perhaps it would not be wrong to call it a negative dialectic and to search for secret correspondences between Blanchot and Adorno. But that still means the dialectic—discourse—is indestructible. *Noli me frangere*, it orders in every text, and in the fragmentary text as well, and in the discourse in fragments on the fragment. Don't shatter me, don't fragment me.

This is not merely the effect of a will to self-protection, no more than the *Noli me tangere* of the Scriptures is. Don't touch me, says Christ arisen, because you couldn't, because you wouldn't know what you were touching, and because you would think you knew. You can't know anything or will anything about what is called a glorious body.

Above all, we must not believe that we could know how to fragment, that we could know ourselves in fragments, that we actually could fragment. No one fragments, unless perhaps it is that *Noli me frangere* that all writing utters: don't fragment me, don't wish to fragment me—fragmentation goes on, and I'm fragmented enough; anyway, it's not up to you.

All this is written in Blanchot's fragmentary writing. There's nothing to add, nothing to take away. Nothing to dialecticize, nothing to fragment. Above all, one mustn't fall into the double trap of overdialecticization and overfragmentation. Blanchot upholds to the point of exhaustion—to the point of no longer being able to bear it—the hazardous exigency of writing *right* between these twin traps. Thus his writing too (not just his discourse) declares: *Noli me frangere*. Don't shatter my insistence, my murmuring. You wouldn't be getting any closer to the fragment: it has already preceded my gesture and yours, and it will follow them forever.

Don't speak, don't write about the fragment. Or ever so little.

Finally, it is the fragment (fragments, the fragmentary exigency) that says *Noli me frangere*—thereby preserving no pure atom, no indivisible work, but, very simply, remaining unrelated to any operation, in any sense. The fragment is indestructible, which is to say that destruction is assured and that this assurance is not assurance—not, in any case, for any knowledge, any subject.

Someone writes, someone reads, people talk, something takes shape, makes sense, completes itself in a work or in fragments—in a work, that is, in fragments. And it's indestructible: a conversation every bit as much as a poem. What is indestructible is *fragility* itself, more attenuated, more tremulous, more untenable, unbearable, than any fragmentation, the fragility that dwells in speaking or in writing, in opening your mouth, in tracing a word. There and then it shatters—nowhere else, at no other time. The fragility of a glorious body (neither transcendent nor immanent, neither yours nor mine, neither body nor mind) shatters a throat or a hand. There arises a word, a discourse, a chant, a writing. The glorious body will never stop repeating this order as fragile as a plea: *Noli me frangere.*

. . . .

—Well?

—I'm torn, I'm hesitating . . . *Noli me frangere*—all right. But it's a bit . . . "Don't touch it, it's broken"—and then it has this speculative, Sully Prudhomme aspect . . .

—Let's not exaggerate.

—No, of course not. Because, at the same time, it's the non-ironic pole—or, even more, the "ironic" pole—of my *Schweben*, so I certainly recognize something there. What strikes me, I guess, is how closely the fragment is tied to an emotion of thought.

—Meaning . . . ?

—It's difficult. Obviously, I'm thinking about the "sentimental," both in the trivial sense and in Schiller's sense, which also contains the trivial sense. Therefore, I'm also thinking about the "subjective," about the thought-subject, whose body (writing) trembles from and is moved by its fragility, who is like the child that childhood abandons at the moment when the child opens its mouth to speak, to lament this abandonment. It's your final "plea."

—Or the "*chant romantique*," as Barthes defined it: the subject abandoned. Maybe the fragment isn't so far removed from the *Lied*. But in the Romantics, of course (and already in Schiller) there's something else. The Sentimental is what we tried to anaylze in *The Literary Absolute* as the process of infinitization: it's the matrix of the speculative dialectic, but it's also the movement of excess. The subjective never stops going beyond itself.

—Music, too, at least for me . . .

—And your *émoi*, which would be better here anyway than "emotion."

—No doubt. As long as you keep to the strict sense, loss of means—or keep to *Witz*, *é-moi*, out of the ego. But it musn't be *Et moi*!—and me!

—Precisely, *Witz* . . .

—Yes, just a moment ago, that's what I was also thinking about: the fragment as a spasm of thought. Today, naturally, we would immediately speak of *jouissance*, pleasure, orgasm.

—And why not?

—Yes, after all, why not? In the loss that *jouissance* entails, there is certainly an irrepressible movement of pleading. But the plea is contradictory: both "Touch me (undo me)" and "Don't touch me (help me, protect me)."

—The fragment, then, would be a moment of *jouissance* in thought. But "moment," when you think of the dialectical use of the word . . .

—Exactly: if your *Noli me frangere* is right—and I think it is—it's still what makes *jouissance* a "moment." In fact, from the outset, that's where I hesitated. I have the impression that these fragments consolidate, paradoxically, a speculation on the fragment.

—It's quite possible. I myself had a somewhat similar feeling. But vaguely. You'll have to explain.

—That can't be improvised.

—Then write it! We decided to sign this text together. Why not follow the fragments with a dialogue, in the style of the *Gespräch,* only shorter?

—That's it. We'll dance on the edge of the abyss!

—Well, where we stand now . . .

—Really, who knows? It may not be the worst way to spring the specular trap.

—Well, then, my dear Lothario! To your pen! Cover one or two of those tiny sheets you like so much with your divine scrawl. I'll give myself the pleasure—and duty—of answering you.

—We can always try.

LOTHARIO: I find it quite difficult, dear Ludovico, not to see in your series of fragments a veritable discourse in miniature—with its own composition, its introduction, its well-articulated demonstration, its ringing conclusion (as the genre demands). You cleverly conceal a powerful rhetoric—that is, in this case, a powerful dialectic. You conceal it by noticing it—and in such a way that, as you may agree, these fragments on (impossible) fragmentation are, properly speaking, a discourse on discourse, on the "indestructible" dialectic.

Far be it from me to reproach you: I know as well as you do the extreme vigilance needed in these matters. (There are so many weak repetitions of Romantic writing in our day, so many weak mimetic speculations!) And besides, I'm grateful that you give Blanchot credit for having avoided (or *known how* to avoid?) the "twin traps" of "overdialecticization" and "overfragmentation." But a dialectic, even supplementary, even negative, remains a dialectic—that is, an economy. Mainly, I don't understand Blanchot's phrase very well, the one you're basing your remarks on. If I follow you, this phrase seems to you the best translation of "fragmentary exigency" (as opposed to the "fragmentary will" of the Romantics). What I don't understand very well is the phrase "to maintain itself as the energy of disappearing"—that sort of negative sublation that would be senseless if it were not precisely an *energy* that was *maintained,* put to work. There is still a will there (can one be avoided, in any case?), and therefore probably calculation as well, the guile of an ultimate calculation: that of the incalculable. It's your indestructible dialectic that utters the *Noli me frangere* . . . For my part, I'd wonder (more baldly) whether it isn't the energy itself, the will to the work, that gives rise to fragmentation, the unrelenting passion toward the work. That would be, in an exemplary way, but *short of* his "fragmentary will," what happens in Schlegel, and in all those who have simply *suffered* fragmentation—a fragmentation they did not will.

LUDOVICO: You have read me very well, Lothario, every bit as well as you may have misunderstood one of my intentions, and for the same reason. It is indeed true that my fragments are a discourse. I will add that the *mise en abîme* (so tempting, so insidious and urgent) of the fragment ought, in my opinion, to display the irresistible reconstitution of discourse, from which the fragmentary *will* does not escape—and, even more, to which it yields beforehand, without knowing. But it's also in this respect that Blanchot surprised me and interrupted a first draft in which I was expressly trying to discourse. For I was finding, in passages like the one I've quoted, a singular dialectical resurgence, and—very precisely, as you say—the *maintenance* of an *aim* toward the *work*. Like the Hegelian Spirit, the energy of the work—if you'll forgive me that redundant expression—is what seems to maintain itself here in fragmentary death. That Blanchot, in that case, should write *right* alongside the dialectic also signifies precisely that he repeats, if you will, its external contours. And it means that, in this way, we all ask not to be shattered.

But at the same time, I was trying to read or to hear the same dialectic as the admission (and not the will) of a fragility of discourse, which discourse admits even as it begs to be spared. "Energy" is such a strange word in this context that it is no doubt necessary *also* to give it the meaning (if it is a "meaning") of a renunciation of energy. I wanted to speak of a "negative dialectic" in the sense in which Adorno writes: "The dialectic is the rigorous consciousness of non-identity." Adorno's book too, in its way, is written in fragments—without a visible *will* to fragment, but through the effect, it seems to me, of an extreme, almost unbearable, attention to the acute opposition, in Hegel, between the dialectic and the "viewpoint of consciousness," which brings back to its identity everything that differs from itself. Adorno attempts (I don't say he succeeds; that would make no sense) not to *maintain* the contradiction but to *bear* its rupture. The *negative* in Adorno and the *fragment* in Blanchot attempt to convert themselves from mastery to ordeal. In spite of everything. As if there were a space beyond Hegel and the Romantic absolute, *our* beyond—(not) one step beyond [*pas au-delà*], as you well know—where nothing more is willed, but where it is a question of experiencing non-identity. Of bearing in this way the weight of thought and writing. And that space begins, paradoxically, at the heart of identity, where discourse and consciousness plead *Noli me frangere* and thus admit that there is already fragmentation, that an interruption or a suspension has occurred, which did not involve a totality, and which did not shatter a unity, since unity is never achieved. A fragment that fragments—nothing. But I don't know whether I understand this ordeal in the same way that you understand the fact of "suffering" fragmentation . . .

LOTHARIO: "To suffer," as I understand the term, gestures toward "passivity." But the word that you yourself use, "ordeal," suits me perfectly; and everything you suggest about such an ordeal, I believe I could make my own—not just subscribe to. I believe I know—with no "knowledge" whatsoever—what it is to bear non-identity, to be doomed to this suspension, to this rupture or caesura that has always already happened (as what has never happened). I recognize this as the "difficult," the "impracticable"— as pain. In my pathos, which is not always so far removed from your own, I will say: write, think—*nothing* happens.

That, it seems to me, is how the disconnection is produced (without *production*). Adorno again: I'm thinking of the extreme acuity of his analysis of *parataxis* in the late poetry of Hölderlin— who in no way sought the rupture, even though, in full consciousness, he refused dialectical (conceptual) synthesis. When I spoke of "suffering fragmentation," I was actually thinking of him.

But the strange thing in all this is that you have often reproached me—or at least you have often been amazed, mischievously so, by what you call my tendency to mysticism. And you, my dear friend? What about this "admission," this "pleading," this "spare me"? When I myself no longer dared to tell you how upsetting I found Benjamin's way of appropriating Malebranche's proposition on attentiveness and inflecting it to describe writing or thought as "a form of prayer."

So there is certainly a misunderstanding between us. It is in the place you're pointing to, but it's not just there. And, to take the ball back on the rebound, I would prefer to speak, while we're at it, of malaise. You see, what really bothers me—and maybe it would have been better to say so right from the start—is your reference to the "glorious body." I find the resurrection, in whatever register—mystical, speculative—completely impenetrable. I have never found anything in Christianity more scandalous. That's why my mysticism, if that's what it is (which I greatly and deeply doubt), has little to do with the type of "negative theology" that you seem to be deploying there and whose absolute positivity I can't help suspecting. What bothers me, finally, is that, with an extra twist of logic or rhetoric, as if carried along by a movement of what would today be called "maximalization," you reinforce the mysticism of the fragment under the pretext of combatting it. If we find no solution to fragmentation—and here I quite agree with you—this is not because of the silent (and terribly eloquent) injunction of writing's "glorious body." Indecision is a *poor* experience.

LUDOVICO: A poor experience . . . I really have to grant you that. Or rather, I have nothing to "grant" you here, as if it were a question of matching thesis against thesis. You're talking about something in which or through which all theses and all positions of discourse collapse, but silently—or with a persistent murmur— concealing even the event of this collapse. Blanchot, writing about writing and about thought, has never stopped haunting these regions. The collapse is felt, and can hardly be expressed, much less justified. That is what happens: there is an exhaustion of discourse—an exhaustion of language—that can never be known or recognized, although it must still be said that the failure to recognize it dooms discourse to futility. This is not a mysticism of the ineffable, for it contains no secret of a hidden sense, of a Word beyond words. Instead, it is a mysticism of the fragility through which alone is disclosed what you will pardon me for calling, in spite of everything, a truth in human speech. (There is no other truth.) As you see, I don't reject the word "mysticism." On the contrary, I will place it—to echo your *prayer*—under the patronage of a mystical teaching, that of Meister Eckhart: "Let us pray God to be free and quit of God."

If that still reeks too strongly of negative theology (and since the articulation, in discourse, of negative theology's very real difference from mysticism would surely be an infinite task), then I must make a confession to you, Lothario, about my "glorious body." I did not deduce the discourse of these fragments from the thought of a glorious body. On the contrary, the phrase from the Gospels came first, alone, to my ear. *Noli me tangere*, in that Latin suffused with the ancient sonorities of the Church, in a tone of psalmody and holy recitation. I couldn't tell you why. (Could it be that *The Writing of the Disaster*, having interrupted my work, having *touched* me in the complex way that I've been telling you about, made me say, "Don't touch me?" I don't know.) But this phrase imposed itself, along with the dim memory of a narrative, of which I will now remind you: Mary Magdalene goes to the tomb and, seeing Jesus, on his feet, does not recognize him. Jesus says to her, "Mary!" Turning around, she says to him, in Hebrew, "Rabboni!," which means "Teacher!" Jesus says to her, "Do not touch me, for I have not yet ascended to my Father; but go unto my brethren."

You can feel how much this story—which John is the only one to relate—is made up entirely of an extreme, chaste fragility. It's an ordeal, a joy, and a disappearance all at once. And the glorious body that disturbs you shines here with a glory so poor that it is neither recognized nor named as such. I admit that I didn't reject what a fragile phrase, a fragment of sound and sense, thus brought me. But the glorious body, as I have written, offers nothing to know or touch. It's there, and it slips away. It's not so much that I wanted to create an allegory of writing as that I felt how this phrase and this story, their spiritual meaning and fleeting emotion, were suspended, fragmented, instantly. And the idea of "glory," of an invisible brightness . . . I believe that one always writes not only for glory but also *in* this hidden glory. I spoke to you just now about the weight of thought: in the Hebrew word that expresses Biblical "glory" there is the idea of a weight, a heaviness . . .

LOTHARIO: This "corpus," if I dare say so, is not very familiar to me. You know that: I really have forgotten quite a lot. Except, however, this figure of Mary Magdalene, who, for all sorts of reasons (some less admissible than others), has always been—how shall I put this?—very *close* to me. It's strange, besides—I didn't know she was implicated in this business of *Noli me tangere*— strange and, from a certain angle, troubling, suggestive. Perhaps that strangeness comes from the fact that, for me, she is first of all a secret, enigmatic figure from paintings. Or, if you like, the image of woman associated—memory immemorial—with La Tour's light. In fact, she's my image of love, or of the beautiful itself.

But, as you suspect, that has nothing to do with "glory," with splendor, which for me is inseparable—you'll laugh—from the Counter-Reformation, the Baroque. Ever since Plato, the beautiful has been a burst of light. But there are two kinds of such bursts, and ostentation (which is one of the meanings of the Latin *gloria*) puts me off a bit.

LUDOVICO: Do I dare say that it doesn't put me off? I must say so, at my own risk. I don't defend it, and I don't raise it in opposition to the restrained, vanishing, wholly interior burst of light that you seem to mean. I'll say instead that, for me, fragmentation is linked to this: that there is no (or no more) interiority.

And, consequently, it is indeed linked to something of the Baroque. The passivity that we are both talking about can be concentrated or dispersed. Perhaps I'm incapable of letting it be concentrated, and so I see it dispersing in the Baroque fragmentation that Benjamin knew how to talk about, the Benjamin of *The Origin of German Tragic Drama* (Romanticism no doubt having mixed, in variable proportions, the two kinds of fragmentation). The Baroque emerges from the loss of organic totality as interiority and gives itself up to the "incomplete, shattered character of sensible, beautiful physis." Of course, in rupture itself and in its intervals, in brusque immobilizations and in surprising simultaneities, in the play of mirrors and of shimmering surfaces, writing also finds itself "preoccupied, in all willingness, with developing its own energy." I'll claim for writing (not for "myself," but for "literature") nothing less than the risking of this willingness and the hazarding that writing may shatter, *burst* apart. There is certainly something of *Witz* here. *Witz* (play, chance discovery, encounters with the incongruous) is very close to the dialectic, as we have written. (You'll also remember that Heidegger, in his *Schelling*, speaks of a "Romantic transposition of the idealist dialectic.") But *Witz* isn't absent from writing. It's simply that it can't be ordered around—and on that, I believe, we agree. A conspicuous failure of the will, or of the project, *makes* fragmentation—or writing. It gives me up to a kind of devastation, indeed a brilliant one, from which play is not shut out, the play of ridicule or of rejoicing. You seem to me, at this point, to fall into contemplation, and I must admit that contemplation is what I have forgotten, or have never known. And this, no doubt, is only a sign of the times . . . I can't, finally, dissociate the fragment from the closure of the modern world.

. . . .

—So, there it is. I have the feeling we'd best just leave it at that. And, curiously enough, I think that with this method I ended up saying exactly what I wanted to say.

—And the posthumous fragment from Schlegel that you mentioned—didn't you do anything with that?

—No, fitting it in right would have taken me too far afield, and this is already long enough as it is.

—What did that fragment say? We can still put it into the little dialogue at the end.

—Here it is.

— "The activity whereby consciousness best reveals itself as fragment . . ."

—It's *Bruchstück*, piece. He doesn't say "fragment" . . .

— " . . . is *Witz*, whose essence consists precisely in its being torn. . . ." It's good, but . . .

—But?

—But the dialectic has struck again.

—Yes and no.

—Anyway, in your text, it works. But when I think that, right there at the end, you hit me with interiority, with contemplation! And what if I'd hit you back, with piety? I restrained myself from elaborating on an *Ad majorem scriptionis* (or *cogitationis*) *gloriam* . . . But let's be serious. I don't know if that's what you were really trying to say, but when you speak of the fragment as a sign of the "closure of the modern world," it seems to me that you're touching on something true.

—I meant to say that the fragment, even in Blanchot, is too much the mark of the modern. It's impossible to tear it free from modernity . . .

—From Nietzsche, for example, who plays a large role in the origins of Blanchot's "fragmentary writing." In short, if you mean there's nothing to be done with the fragment as such (that is, ultimately, with the fragment as *genre*) . . .

—Yes, but not with fragmentation . . .

—Then I understand perfectly. No, the fragment as genre is still the will to fragment, with everything that entails: *literature*, in its very delimitation; the letter of the subject. In Barthes, it's striking: Montaigne, the recurrence of self-portraiture. And as for Blanchot's anonymity and self-effacement . . .

—That's something else again. How could we reduce anonymity to self-portraiture, even to the self-portrait of the subject of literature?

—There's literature and there's literature, and someday we'll have to make up our minds to distinguish them a bit more rigorously.

—Absolutely!

We talked much more about this question—that day, and later on as well.

TRANSLATED BY BRIAN HOLMES

§ Exergues

Poetry and Truth: Whence does this come to us? What is the origin of this phrase that is not a sentence and makes no sense?

It does not come to us from the too-famous title of the great Counselor Aulique's Memoirs. He himself had already borrowed it: from an old uneasiness of truth's, from an old obsession of poetry's.

Am I true? Truth wonders. Is there anything truer than I who am truth itself? She answers: there is something truer than truth, something that tells the truth about truth and reduces the skeptic's strongest arguments to silence. She calls it "poetry," truer than truth, exact without measure, powerful without proof. This truth is manifest in and of itself.

Am I true? Poetry wonders. Is there anything truer than my splendor, my profundity, my chant? There is something truer: there is what neither chants nor enchants, what need not shine and thus could never become obscure, measure itself, proof, fidelity, and faith. This truth is manifest in and of itself.

So it was a waste of time, great Counselor Aulique . . . But it's true that you had, by a completely different path, found the secret of the distinction: "I devoted the first hours of the morning to poetry. The middle of the day belonged to business."

The Hatred of Poetry: He who risked this hostile and complicitous title overstepped his own dare. It betrays his resentment,

279

his feverish desire for the power of poetry. Not a will to power, but a will to chance, he wrote. Thus, not will, but a receptiveness. This receptiveness is what makes poetry: the infinite welcoming of finite chance offered in the instant of utterance.

He hated the codes and beliefs of poetry. The codes: abundance or restraint, images or their effacement, and all the rules of narcissistic tongues, complacent to the splendor of words—and the beliefs: to name the unnameable, to seize the instant, to convoke the gods.

But he did not, could not, hate letting his mouth receive a declaration. For poetry is speaking without will.

Remembrance of Things Past: He had never gone to bed without a kiss from his mother, and this made up one phrase, interminable and endlessly resumed, the sinuous, uncertain, and yet invariable line of his mother's trajectory to his room, to his bed, a slow and obstinate declaration that opened the child's lips without unclenching them, while other, equally silent, lips—proferring what blessing, fervent or distracted?—came to touch his forehead or his cheek, with the infinitesimal movement of a kiss, not enough to form a word, yet too much for the lips to be simply mute, moved, on the contrary, by the same imperceptible articulation, by the same parting, not even murmuring, the long, desperate discourse of which, unknown to him, came to part his own lips before abandoning him to the night, to the absence of signs, to the insistence of linked phrases.

Finnegan's Wake: You find the book again without willing it. He had wanted . . . Now you can open it, anywhere, and close it—above all, close it . . . Having opened it, you've closed it: it won't say anything, won't let anything out. It is not unreadable—on the contrary—but it is not to be read. In closing it, you open it: this agitation of jaws, of lips, of tongues, it is poetry, a strange strangling. Shut its trap. (It laughs, surrenders itself at last.)

A Season in Hell: There is no more hell, there is no more poetry. The poet will go off no more, will be feverish no more. We move away from the annals of the poem. No longer will we turn our pain into elegies. We will no longer capitalize on our losses. And yet we will make the journey, right here. We will know the anguish of departure and the worry of return, of repetition.

Why this distress in times of poets?

Meditations on First Philosophy: Having thought it through . . . it could have turned out that I didn't exist, but I say that I am, so this must necessarily be true. Because I say it. I declare: "I am," thus this very thing is true, that I am the one who says that he is. I couldn't, if I weren't, say that I was without, at the heart of my non-being, being in that instant. I am nothing, no thing, if not something which says that it is. What thing? An existence, a poem, a surprise, a declaration. Having thought it through, without thinking, I don't think, I am. "I" is all thought thoughtful of this being.—You, you are the existence that I am not, the truth.

XXX: To write, she wrote, is to blind oneself to everything else, to everything that is not the present object of the writing. Poetry should be writing without blindness. It wouldn't forget anything, wouldn't suspend anything. Not that it would say everything. Poetry would be fragmentary, multiple—but it wouldn't blind itself to everything else. It wouldn't be clairvoyant. But the light would not be limited.—She added: I wouldn't be forsaken anymore.

Being and Time: The existent, whose being is put into play in its very being, has a proper name. His being is to be gambled, risked, in his very being, and to be wagered on nothing but his future. He *is* to have yet to arrive or disappear. That is why he has a proper name, he is the only one to have it, he has nothing else. Or rather, he is nothing but this name.

It is not said, for it cannot be discussed. It is a secret lesson. It can only be a call. This existent must be called, each time the one who is no other, each time singular and singularly named. "Martin," "Georges," "Marie": each time the proper name is without propriety. It only calls him, calls him to come forward.

The Psalms of David: From the depths I cry out to you . . .
Listen to my prayer . . . I cry out to you . . . Listen . . . How
long?—But with you is grace, the abundance of few words, an
obscure reserve. (He psalmodizes, he touches the chords one by
one, pulling them and letting them go according to order and
measure.)

The Tropic of Cancer: Naked and cracked, off limits, it defies
intimacy. It will always be more intimate than the closest closeness,
farther away than extreme enmity. It will always overflow, within as
without. It is a mouth, which the lips open and close, proferring
intimacy, offering and exposing the indescribable: a mouth kissed,
a cadence, a gripping of the heart, a discharge.
Here words are no longer signs, nor appellations. They only
touch the page and pierce the writing. Here it is forced, turned
away, tempered, unoccupied. Literature is fucked. There is nothing
more to describe, and nothing to name. Obscenities have no
meaning. Poetry must not deliver obscenity; neither must it deliver
us from it.

The Iliad: . . . the hideous and mortal, glorious and warlike
anger that you were asked to sing, goddess, this anger still burns in
us. It is an impatience for the Greeks' cause: their memory punctuates ours. But it is an infinite pity for the ramparts of the other side.
For it is Ilion, and not the Greeks, that we have lost.

The Executioner's Song: How he recorded everything, how he
investigated and had people investigate, searched for people, consulted archives, files, a whole arsenal of tape recorders, telephones,
notes, typewriters, trips in airplanes and cars, a whole administration of memoirs, testimonies, fidelities, private documents, a whole
machinery for consignment, detection, decipherment, confrontation, verification, gap filling. How this was recorded—mixed-up
voices, mutilated discourses, fragments strewn along highways, in
motels, television stations, and a long, continuous, indisputable
declaration of distress and endless love, of space without direction,

blinking neons, sweating bodies, little houses of wood, men of the law. How the policemen talked into their radios, and how he called her "Baby." The end of fiction, the beginning of poetry.

The Phenomenology of Mind: Past the phrase, past the discourse, there is not silence.

The pure element of thought is not thought, is not cognition. It is simply receiving immediate knowledge of what is immediately. This knowledge is not knowledge—nor science, nor theory, nor intelligence—it is itself the reception of what is, of what is offered. We must be receptive to it, and change nothing of it as it is offered.—We hold out our hands, our lips, in a desperate grammar.

XXX: He told her the truth, told her that it was the truth, and that he couldn't take telling it anymore, not being able to tell it, not being able to make it come, to let it come, to make of it the truth that would impose itself by itself. He told her that it was the truth, that he couldn't let it do what it would, let it undo itself.

TRANSLATED BY EMILY MCVARISH

§ To Possess Truth in One Soul and One Body

—et il me sera loisible de *posséder la vérité dans une âme et un corps.*[1]

Who is speaking? Who stops speaking in this manner? We know it is Arthur Rimbaud, with the last line of his *A Season in Hell.* Rimbaud writes: "it will be permissible for me to *possess truth in one soul and one body.*" The italics are his. Having written and emphasized these words, he had only to follow them with "April–August, 1873," to be finished with writing, to be finished with poetry.

This is, at least, the version that I will hold to, leaving aside the problem of exact dates, not wishing to know if certain texts from *Illuminations* might be posterior to these last words. Rimbaud says "adieu" to Rimbaud with these words. The last text of *A Season in Hell* is entitled "Adieu." To say "adieu," "farewell," is to express an irreversible and irrevocable separation. One must "hold the stride gained" [*tenir le pas gagné*] as the text tells us, a few lines before the one just quoted.[2] This *step* is the "adieu." When the step is made there is no going back. There is but a tenacious holding-on. Just a "stride," a step, and no more; but one that is complete, accomplished, from which there is no return.

I choose to remain in this limit, on this line where something ends. One can do no less with Rimbaud. Perhaps one can do no less—and nothing else—with poetry itself, than to stand on the borderline. The stride in poetry made by Rimbaud, for us, up to and including us, is irrevocable. How is it made? How is it held?

284

What is its truth, or more precisely, as the last words lead us to ask, why and how will this step in poetry offer an access to truth? And in what future, if there is nothing more to do than to "hold the stride gained"?

~

In the same text, "Adieu," this "stride gained" is responding to the imperative "One must be absolutely modern." To be modern, and to be so absolutely, is not the same thing as being fashionable, neither is it an avant-garde, foreseeing and clearing the way for all tomorrows, which, in turn, would be "modern" or "postmodern." "To be absolutely modern" consists in "holding the stride gained." That is, in staying at the limit, the point where time is coming, and is only this "coming."

At this point, time does not cross over the borderline. It is the very tension of arriving at the limit where something will come, and consequently, has not come at all. This is an immanence, but held in tension, sustained, indefinitely retained in its coming. Modern is the time *ahead* of all past, present, or passing time, or what passes and precedes itself in this passing. (Is it in this sense that Rimbaud wrote to Démeny: poetry "will be ahead"?)[3] This is time, the moment or the place of the "ahead" that exposes itself to the *yet to come* but itself does not advance.

Being at this limit, in this state of tension, one speaks in the future tense: "it *will be* permissible for me to possess truth . . ." Nothing is being said about a truth of the future nor about a truth in the future that could be appropriated by anticipation in the present. The future comes from a place devoid of time (which is not a place). Nothing can reach us from there because it is yet to come, and this is especially so with truth.

Nothing can be transmitted or communicated to us from the future. This means that what is said in the future tense, and what is said about the future, cannot, for us, *already* have a meaning. This is told to us from an absence of place whence nothing can be said. (Rimbaud, in another text, calls this "eternity.") Holding the stride gained, the stride of poetry [*le pas de poésie*], is first of all keeping oneself exposed to the truth, of which there is no present, presentable, truth. But thus truth is presented: I *shall be* allowed to possess it.

"Rimbaud" is the name that presents what will face the truth of this eternal future. Who sees it coming. Who sees only this: that he sees it coming ("it will be permissible for me . . ."), and that he does not see what is coming ("truth"). Poetry's step is made with the eyes open in an absence of regard. To say "adieu," in the future tense, to the future. The present of this "adieu": *no* poetry.

It is necessary, for this, that the future tense of language not be transformed into real anticipated time: a time rendered prophetic, somehow knowing the future that is still unknown. A "prophecy," understood in this way, is a vision of the future. Nevertheless, it is to *vision*, all vision, that the *Season* says "adieu." Rimbaud writes, earlier in the text, that he is "richer" than "poets and visionaries." Rimbaud is the one who ends up writing without seeing. This is, after all, writing, and holding poetry's stride gained.

No vision, then, no message from the future: we cannot know the meaning of "to possess truth in one soul and one body," yet this is, nevertheless, what we need to know in order to be absolutely modern. We need to know the meaning of what comes from an absence of speech, from an absence of vision and an absence of poetry. To have the word of the last words.

What is dawning here is history after poetry, the story of what comes to poetry after poetry. No doubt, this history will not have a direction, a "sense of history," as the philosophy of Rimbaud's era proposed (this was a philosophy that he shared: he named the poet the "multiplier of progress"). Such a "sense" of history cancels out history in its prediction, in its expectation [*prévision*]. What is coming cannot have such a sense. It can only have the sense of being yet to come and of coming. That is, truth's sense as *in advance*, or truth's sense as what precedes. Rimbaud knew that truth has nothing to expect from the future, and that it is, on the contrary, this: to be exposed to the coming of the yet to come.

Above all, the last words are saying this, and it is a history, it is our history, and it is to us that this has not ceased to happen. We must still be absolutely modern.

~

Let us consider the *stride gained* as the "adieu" to poetry: the future must necessarily, must essentially, come from the point where, from here on, from now on, poetry will have been abandoned. Nothing to see, nothing to "envision," and nothing then to write: but this, right up until the end, up until the last words.

We are well aware that it is nothing new to say that Rimbaud breaks with poetry, but this itself must not be poeticized. Along with Rimbaud and with the stride gained, one must hold to a wager that is as untenable as it is necessary: *putting an end to poetry with last words that are still poetry.* It is necessary to insist, then, that it is no less improper to look for the feverish or sordid double of the poet in Rimbaud the adventurer or the merchant (as has so often been the case) than it is to try to capture in poetry what he ended, to try to make the moment of its interruption come back or resurface. Still, this moment must not be effaced from the writing to which it belongs. "To possess truth in one soul and one body" are the last words of poetry, and in this completion and *as* this completion must we read them.

The truth: effacing what must not be effaced, and must be read as yet to come.

Without a doubt, poetry is always ending: it is the essence of poetry to do so. Perhaps Rimbaud is saying nothing other than that. A poem, in its "constricted singularity," as Blanchot puts it, is always closing itself up, doing nothing but closing itself up. Always, therefore, opening itself up to silence. But this silence is usually understood as the fulfillment and the assumption of poetic speech, as an infinitely held vibration of its harmonies. (And, in point of fact, the poet of *Illuminations* writes: "I am the master of silence."[4]) Thus is understood the troubling and singular silence, so heavy, of Rimbaud after 1873. But the abandonment of the work and the rupture of the "adieu" are not the same thing as a sovereign entry into a silence that still proposes itself as a reserve and a possibility of speech (that is, as its highest possibility, as Heidegger, for example, would wish it). Bataille was able to write, as a poem, the following:

The alcohol
of poetry
is dead
silence.

But it is precisely here that Rimbaud renounces all drunkenness, and all silence, and all dialectic of "dead silence." The future: "it will be permissible for me . . ." is speaking from no place of speech, but it does not proffer a silence. To put it very simply, but in a less trivial way than it perhaps appears, there is no *sigh* in these last words.

Rimbaud's last words do not link up with silence. What links is always, in one way or another, discourse. There is no poetic discourse here. On the contrary, all discourse of, in, and by poetry is cut short. Poetry, unfinished, is interrupted. Not even expired, and impossible to embalm. "In one soul and one body" seems to resemble a formula for beyond the grave, but there is no such thing here. Neither death nor resurrection, and nothing but the truth of the "adieu."

Rimbaud writes, "No hymns! Hold the stride gained." No hymns means no religion, but also, at the same time, no chants. No religious chanting, no religion of the chant. Art ends with religion, or, as perhaps would be the case for Hegel, art ends with its religious service. That is, it ends with the service of presenting or representing truth. Religion is a presentation of truth: it offers a way to see, to feel, and to share truth. This leads to "mystical *élans*" that Rimbaud renounces (in a rough draft of the *Season*). There, one shares in the "supernatural powers" that are declared illusory in "Adieu." It is not the "power" that is illusory—Rimbaud never denied the power of poetic magic or the "alchemy of the word" ("Delirium," II, p. 49). It is because this power exists, it is because it is possible to believe in poetry and to poeticize all belief, that it is necessary to break with the effects of this power, with the illusory supernatural. In other words, this is trafficking in an absent presence in which truth lets itself be taken in by the sublime bonds of a song. If "art is foolishness," as another rough draft says, it is because it lends itself to this trafficking, to this manipulation.

The truth "possessed in one soul and one body" will not be, then, the truth that the poet attains by mystery or in a vision— "new flowers, new stars, new flesh, new tongues," to which Rimbaud here says "adieu" (p. 87). We do not know what this truth is, what it *will be*, but we know that it will not, in any way, be this poetic truth of the "new" by which it seems all truth must, for us, distinguish itself. Newness, the sudden appearance of the original, and the transfiguration of things received, always form, for us, the poetry proper to all scientific, religious, political, or metaphysical truth. It is to the poetry and the *poiesis* of the truth that Rimbaud says "adieu."

But we also know that this will not be one poetry pitted against another. It is a matter of poetry as a whole: "*No more words,*" as Rimbaud writes in the *Season* ("Bad Blood," p. 19), emphasizing these words. These are surely the last words of poetry. After them there will be no others. From then on, the possibility is open for what Bataille calls "the hatred of poetry" and what leads him to write, for example, "Poetic delirium has its place *in* nature. It justifies it, agreeing to embellish it. The refusal belongs to clear consciousness, measuring what happens to it." This is Rimbaud's refusal (of which, by the way, Bataille is thinking in this passage). And what happens is truth. Artaud will later write: "In the forms of the human Verb there is some sort of rapacious operation, some predatory self-devouring in which the poet, restricting himself to an object, sees himself eaten by this object." The devouring object is Bataille's "embellished nature," it is the effusion of newness, Rimbaud's "new flowers, new tongues."

"Hatred" and "revolt" are doubtless only half-measures: they include their reverse side, love. Beyond Bataille and Artaud, beyond us, something else may still open up. But for the moment, the stride gained must be held, and this must be said: "What happens" to "clear consciousness" is truth itself, truth that does not let itself be justified or embellished, but does not devour itself either. It is truth that denies and destroys "embellishments," and perhaps all aesthetics, truth that ruins self-devouring and its self-satisfaction. The name of what is refused is exactly the word repeated in "Adieu" and throughout the *Season*: the "lie." "At last, I shall ask forgiveness for having fed on lies. And now let's go" ("Adieu," p. 87).

~

Well then, let's go: let's not avoid a very simple question. If the denunciation of poetry as a lie is the most consistent movement in philosophy, from Plato to at least Hegel, does Rimbaud repeat such a gesture? Does the poet pronounce anew the philosopher's verdict?

How can the answer not be "yes"? At an early stage, at least, it is inevitable. Assuredly, Rimbaud breaks with poetry—or he breaks poetry—with a truly philosophical rupture, perhaps the philosophical rupture par excellence: one that demands the truth *in person*, the naked truth itself, soul and body, in opposition to all its representations, which it ruins, in opposition to all mimesis, which it discredits. What started with Plato burning his own poems is accomplished with Rimbaud: "Well! I must bury my imagination and my memories! An artist's and storyteller's precious fame flung away!" (This is in "Adieu" [p. 87], and it is the "adieu" itself.)

Here again, concessions must not be made. Just as we must not poeticize Rimbaud's entrance into life without poetry, so, in a symmetrical manner, we must not ignore any of the evidence proving that Rimbaud reproduces, on his own account, the philosophical exclusion of poetry.

For example, and to remain in "Adieu": "We are embarked on the discovery of divine light" (p. 85). There is no reading, no interpretation, that could exempt these words from carrying their strongest and most constant metaphysical burden. This is so as long as there remain questions of interpreting and deciphering the meaning or meanings of what cannot not, in spite of and/or because of "poetry" itself, be taken as meaningful discourse. If the objection arises that this is, after all, "only poetry," the response would have to be that poetry could not be anything but the fulfilled desire of philosophy. Because philosophy, since Plato, has wanted only one thing: to become *true* poetry, poetry of truth without the lie, poetry of divine light and, at the same time, the truth of poetry, of all poetry. (Finally, the name "Plato" names only that.)

In this case, "to possess truth in one soul and one body," these last words of poetry, compose the first words of the philosophical poem: they tell of the total appropriation of truth, its objective and subjective appropriation, which thus raises itself beyond this distinction to the absolute self-presence of truth. Hegel says of thought, as contrasted with poetry: "Thought, even while apprehending real things in their essential particularity and in their real existence, raises, nonetheless, this particular to the level of the general and ideal element in which only thought is by itself."

Is it possible to translate, to interpret, Rimbaud out of Hegel? Without a doubt. It is even indispensable. Indispensable, because the one and the other have, necessarily, the same *concept* of poetry (to the degree that it is a matter of concept—and how could it be otherwise?). That is, the concept of an incomparably rich and sensual representation of truth, but one whose richness nonetheless collapses in the pure identity of thought to which it tends, as to its truth, as to *the* truth. This collapse does not necessarily represent the "lie" of poetry, but it does at least represent this: thought gathers and sublimates poetry's beautiful presentation into itself. Even more: poetry gathers and sublimates itself in its truth (of) thought. (That, in the final reading, things are not quite so simple for Hegel himself is a matter with which I will not concern myself here.) It matters little that some, like Rimbaud, following the Romantics and in general after them, called this identity of thought and in thought "poetry": it is still the same concept and the same Idea of Truth. It will suffice to reread, in the *lettre du voyant*, what is properly philosophical, speculative, and, in a sense, Platonico-Hegelian: "The first study for a man who wants to be a poet is the knowledge of himself, complete. He looks for his soul, inspects it, puts it to the test, learns it. . . . He consumes all the poisons in him, and keeps only their quintessences. . . . He becomes . . . the supreme Savant!"[5]

~

But it is precisely to the "Science" of the *voyant* that the *Season* says adieu. And, in an equal measure, to a vision of a Knowledge.

Furthermore, what says adieu to this knowledge and its vision is, identically, what says adieu to poetry. In the farewell, poetry is not elevated, sublimated, into a higher philosophical truth. There, poetry does not become more true: it is posed, left, abandoned on this edge, on this limit, whence a future possession is only named, almost brutally only named, as the indiscernible, unforeseeable, unsignifiable yet-to-come of poetry's last words.

At this point, Rimbaud does not abandon poetry in order to open, beyond it, the pure path of philosophy as the truth of poetry returning into itself. To the contrary, this is exactly what he refuses, even though in these few words the refusal is indiscernible from its contrary. Discernible nevertheless, because these are the last words. What is refused is philosophy, the vision of truth, or what the letter calls "poetry." This is poetry according to philosophy, which is to say, the poetry that thinks itself and poeticizes itself as the presentation of the true, as the true presentation of the true.

However, this does not constitute a particular kind of poetry. It is the whole idea, and doubtless, every possible idea of poetry that is at stake. This is all that poetry is as long as we have an *idea* of poetry, even one opposed to a philosophical idea: because in such an opposition, an opposition that can only proceed from philosophy, both elements are accessories to the same will to present truth, to the same trafficking in truth, and therefore they are accomplices in the same lie. This means that poetry is at stake as long as there is a "concept," a "genre," and a "meaning" of poetry—and even as long as there is the word "poetry." The writer of the *Season* is not a poet: he says that he is "a thousand times richer" than "poets and visionaries."

Then, if concept, genre, meaning, poetry's name, and the poet to create it no longer exist, what will remain?—*Adieu* . . .

In fact, nothing will remain from the future of which the *Season* speaks, especially from where the end of the *Season* speaks. These are surely poetry's last words, and through these last words "poetry" has already lost its meaning. All meaning, along with all words ("*No more words.*") are thrown in the indiscernible face of what comes after poetry. The *Season*, or: How to project meaning into meaning's tomorrow. "This is the eve. . . . And, in the dawn . . . we shall enter magnificent cities" ("Adieu," p. 89). The night that one must pass through is a night where nothing will be guarded, whence nothing will be kept. Poetry: after.

This is not a dialectic, and this passing to the future but not getting through, holding oneself here, saving oneself for the yet to come (letting it come), is not a passage to another meaning, into another word, the meaning and the word of "thought" or of "philosophy." It is *as philosophy* that poetry is abandoned, and it is abandoned *as poetry* as well. Beyond this (but this is not *a* beyond), there will be something entirely different. Beyond this, "clear consciousness" will keep the "stride gained," confronted with "what happens to it." What? Something, in any case, which comes from farther away than any meaning that philosophy or poetry could assign.

~

Rimbaud indicates it himself: he also says *adieu* to philosophy, and philosophy, in a symmetrical way, is denounced as poetry. He writes in the *Season*: "Philosophers: The world has no age. Humanity simply changes place. You are in the Occident, but free to live in your Orient, as ancient as you please, and to live well. Don't admit defeat. Philosophers, you are of your Occident" ("The Impossible," pp. 73–74). What, then, is philosophy saying? It is denying history, it is denying that anything at all *happens*. It even goes so far as to deny that the West is a limit and it is ready to furnish an East, to manufacture origins and purities as a place to which one can flee and take refuge. This philosophy engages in poetic trafficking: vision and evasion. Rimbaud "slams the door," there is no escape and he terminates philosophy's lie: "Philosophers, you are of your Occident." You are of the world of "outdated poetics."

Earlier in the *Season* Rimbaud writes: "Oh! Science! Everything has been revised. For the body and for the soul,—the viaticum,—there are medicine and philosophy,—old wives' remedies and arrangements of popular songs" ("Bad Blood," p. 11). Arrangements of songs, the composition of nonsense (or the "alchemy of the verb," which also trafficked in common "naïveté" . . .). Arrangements, which is to say world *visions*. The *voyant*'s vision goes hand in hand with philosophical vision, which is itself like a medicine, a "grandmother's remedy," itself also arranged so as to work more or less, to make us believe it works.

"Viaticum": provisions for the journey, for the passage of the soul to the body, and—holy viaticum—of the body to the soul, supernatural, hallucinated life, poetic truth. Healing at the price of blindness. But "Adieu" is saying something else: it opens our eyes in order to do away with visions, it names these "millions of dead souls and dead bodies, *and which will be judged!*" Right alongside poetico-philosophical truth in its theological version, the judgment of this truth is announced. Here the last judgment is the stopping-point of all traffic in mediations, in visions, in arrangements. The future is the implacable exposition of the truth of souls *and* bodies, such as they here are, separated, dispersed, without mediation.

In "Adieu," it is not a matter of passing over to somewhere else. "I am returned to the soil with a duty to seek and rough reality to embrace! . . . Arduous night! The dried blood smokes on my face, and I have nothing behind me. . . . " And nothing "in front of me" except the same earth. The "stride gained" reaches no new shore, it stays in the same place. After all, the truth is so close, "the truth that may even now surround us with her weeping angels!" ("The Impossible," p. 75).

The angels of truth weep because the judgment is hard. "Yes, the new hour is at least very severe. . . . But the vision of justice is the pleasure of God alone" ("Adieu," pp. 88–89). The judgment is hard, like the night, because it pronounces this and only this: that truth surrounds us, that it is here and nowhere else, and that its future is its coming here itself. But here is not poetry. Truth is there, but it does not depend on a vision or on an alchemy. Neither is it, then, invisible (the invisible depends in reality on a higher vision: the invisible is always the matter of poetry, of philosophy). Truth is there, in the words that speak of its coming, in the yet-to-come of words, but these words are the last ones, returned to earth. And they say that the crucial point, what it *will be*, is not seeing truth, but *possessing* it: "To possess truth in one soul and one body."

The last words are still awaiting their due. They are waiting for us to give them, anew, the sense that they need, as words, but which cannot make sense for a new vision or for a new science. They are waiting for their ultimate sense of words, at the limit of all the words of poetry and of philosophy. "Soul" and "body": in what better way could one reassemble, articulate and sing, but also annul all the words of philosophy, of poetry?

~

It was stated above that philosophy is for the soul. To be in philosophy is to be in the context of the duality between soul and body. The last words are "one soul and one body." They expose this duality. What they do to this duality—what they *do* to it as the last words, rather than what they *say*—is of extreme violence. Being words themselves, heavy with such a metaphysical and poetic burden (one must say, heavy with *the* metaphysical/poetic burden), thrown at the end, offered to the future and coming from the future, these words do violence to the system of their duality. "In one soul and one body," this denies that one and the other exist in a relation of pure exteriority. It must be a matter of the one *and* the other. This is prerequisite to *possessing* the truth. But, at the same time, this also says that there are two places for this possession. This neither says two nor one. There is no word here for what would be the one *and* the other, or neither the one nor the other. This expresses neither a union nor a system of the two. No mediation, no system of whatever kind, no "systasis," no substantial union, and no pre-established harmony. "*In* one soul *and* one body": there can only be one "within," one identical closeness, identical in its difference and as difference.

"In one soul and one body": this expression, so simple at first glance, puts in suspension the signification of the two terms—at the edge of the end, last words before not saying, or knowing, or singing what the "soul" and "body" are. The expression suspends the signification of the words and their copula. It holds them in suspense while bringing them to their highest intensity. There are no words more naked that could convey the nakedness of the soul *and* the body, with no vision or mediation of the two, and consequently, that could pronounce them as two terms united but without rapport. Here there is no relation of content to container, of form to matter, of signified to signifier—or, finally, of soul to body . . . They do not copulate.

If the "soul" and the "body," in good philosophy and in good poetry, do not mean anything but their relation (and this as a relation of truth, of adequation), then these last words no longer say what they mean to say. But they are only thrown, smacked against the limit of their signification—"rough reality to embrace."

The body, here, does not clothe the soul (it clothes *the bones*, says a text in *Illuminations*). The body is not an envelope, decipherable or indecipherable (tearable or untearable). It is not a system of signs of the soul, nor is the soul the principle of the body's animation and meaning. If it were not so, how would it be possible to possess truth in the one *and* the other?

Words are not an envelope of truth, and truth is not the inexpressible that haunts them. In this sense: no more words! But it is here that truth is to be possessed, in naked words, in each word *and* each word, at the edge of words, without any more words.

"One soul and one body": each time it is *one*, each time singular, and each time it is *and*, each time tied together by a conjunction that contains its own disjunction. One is neither the meaning nor the truth of the other. The ONE is not the sense of the two. But the truth is to be possessed in each one in turn, *and* there where the one and the other belong to one another while separating. The fact that they separate does not imply that there are two "substances" that were previously independent. Nor does *the* truth refer to two rival instances of presentation, that of philosophy and that of poetry. Because truth is one, and alone. Philosophy is not the soul of poetry. Poetry is not the body of philosophy (and yet this is what is proposed in every idea of poetry, and of philosophy). Rather, soul *and* body: it is the unity that accomplishes itself through not presenting itself, neither by itself nor in any other way.

This does not present itself, and yet this never stops coming into presence, ceaselessly arriving to "clear consciousness." It occurs to clear consciousness that "soul" and "body" are devoid of sense, neither together nor apart: but together *and* apart, they constitute the limits of sense and of all the senses. The body is not an incarnation: it does not follow the major motif of the onto-theology of the West, which is also the major "poetological" motif, up to and including the "alchemy of the word," as well as this "poetic language accessible some day to all the senses" ("Delirium," II, p. 51), to which Rimbaud says adieu, in saying *adieu* to "outdated poetics."

It is not a matter of incarnation because it is not a matter of a mediation of the "spiritual" by the "sensual." There is, rather, a double immediacy, or a double "immediation," of both the soul and the body. This is why souls and bodies, in millions of identical and dispersed destinies, *will be judged.* Then, the pleasure of justice will be the pleasure that cannot be measured by any other, this joy beyond joy that comes when justice is rendered to the difference where the assumption is suspended, along with the vision and consummation of unity.

To say "the truth in one soul and one body" is to repeat—while interrupting, however, its essential mediation—the entire poetico-philosophical program of the aesthetic and the erotic as it has been developed from Plato to us. Soul and body are no longer the double name of the essential relation of signification, of expression, of presentation. What they name is the absence of relation, or an infinite relation.

∼

The soul and the body: Rimbaud likes this syntagma, this association, this dissociation. He often writes about it, and it is no accident that he makes these his last words. Rimbaud, in a text from *Illuminations* ("Morning of Drunkenness"), facilitates our understanding when he writes: "Our created body and soul." Body and soul are created being as such. Created being is the being of finiteness. It is the being of this life, of this existence for which "true life is absent." But the experience of the *Season* is the experience that leads to the future: "I will bless this life." It is the experience of recognizing truth *in* finite life, what no mediation accomplishes or signifies.

(This experience, this thought, is the only one that can fill the gap between the last words of poetry and Rimbaud's death. He will have spent all this time putting to the test this truth: that life has no access to a vision of its truth. Among the multitude of possible quotations from his letters, these: "Ultimately, our life is misery, unending misery. Why, then, do we exist?" "It is fortunate that this life is the only one, and that this is obvious, since we cannot imagine another life with a boredom as great as this one." "Those who repeat that life is hard should come spend some time here, to learn philosophy!")

The soul and the body as created-being, that is, nothing *but* created-being, does not refer to creation. It refers to the absence of a creator: there is only what is "created." In the *lettre du voyant*, Rimbaud writes: "author, creator, poet, *that* man never existed."[6] During this period he wanted that man to exist—the creator, the poet, the god. But by the time of "Adieu," he renounces this wish. The creator sees the soul in the body he fashions for it, and thus it is always something of himself that he sees, and it is always the sublime identity of his creative force that is grasped as truth. It is creation, *poiesis* itself, the absolute making of the absolute "work," that sees and conceives itself in truth—which is the truth. Created being, to the contrary, knows itself in dependence, a dependence which reveals nothing of what it depends on—or rather, which reveals that it depends on *nothing*. It is an errant dependence. "But no friendly hand! And where turn for help?" ("Adieu," p. 87). Created being knows itself as the erratic and opaque adjoining of a soul and a body that occasion no vision or meaning for each other, but "rough reality to embrace."

Infinite truth attained, as its highest possibility, the dissociation of soul and body, the dismemberment of the beautiful presentation: this is not death, or this is not only, or first of all, death. There is nothing less morbid, nothing more *lively*, than Rimbaud's language, than his tongue. This is the sharp liveliness, and the vigor ("let us receive the influx of vigor and of real tenderness"; "Adieu," p. 89) of the strangeness to the self that states that finite existence *is* infinitely. There is no reduction of this strangeness and there are no "secrets for *changing life*" ("Delirium," I, p. 41). Neither in philosophy nor in poetry, nor in this poetry of philosophy that has always presented itself as transfigured life. No more transfigurations: "dried blood smokes on my face." It is the blood of the words "soul and body," face to face.

From then on, there is the adieu and the future of its affirmation. Truth will be what it already is, unknown to itself, always in the midst of coming to itself: a soul *and* a body that do indeed comprise one existence, and "the only life," but which do not see each other and which do not speak to each other. No "mystery" here; simply an offered evidence, without mediation, offering itself as evidence, invisible, then, in the simple visibility and the simple readability of its words, soul and body. Or again, as is said in the "Sonnet" (poetry itself . . .), in *Illuminations* (in "Youth"), "brotherly and discrete humanity in the imageless universe."[7] The entire "Adieu" is already there, is still there.

~

How will this truth be possessed? Possessed and not presented. Neither represented nor, even less, put into images. Unpresentable, if you like, but not as a "beyond" presence: to the contrary, as what never ceases coming into presence and as what lets itself be possessed in this coming, what renders itself possessed in the yet to come of its possession. It will be possessed as one soul and one body are possessed in love. But this is not the same "love." Let us reread the entire ending of "Adieu": "What was I saying about a friendly hand! One fine advantage is that I can laugh at old lying loves and put to shame those deceitful couples,—I have seen the hell of women down there;—and it will be permissible for me to possess truth in one soul and one body" (p. 89).

The "old loves" are caught in the lie, along with poetry and philosophy. For one as for the other, for one through the other, love was always fulfillment, as well as knowledge, mediation, and dazzling vision. *Illuminations* concerns one who "wanted to see the truth, the moment of essential desire and gratification."[8] Here, though, there is no desire. The future is not the anxious anticipation of desire, but rather the warm reception of whatever comes, as a generosity, a grace, even as a surprise: "it will be permissible for me to possess truth . . ." This possession will not produce the "satisfaction" that responds to desire. No more than truth will be simply a "woman," as it always has been for philosophy and poetry, and as poetry itself has, most certainly, always been woman and body for the soul of philosophy.

This is not to say that the possession will be without pleasure [*jouissance*], nor that truth will be masculine. Furthermore, this does not mean that all is resolved in indifference. But in this possession sex, love, will be in each sex what it is before having been *a* sex: its own duality, its own division with itself, this "soul and body" that is "the" sex, this always-double sex that a text from *Illuminations* designates, with an evident semantic and sexual ambiguity, in the body of a young fawn: "Your blood pulses in that belly where sleeps the double sex."⁹ Where the double sleeps.

Love will be double, double as the place where finite truth is to be enjoyed: in one soul and one body. Love will be double, double as the place without place where soul and body touch each other. They touch each other, they do not unite, they do no signify each other. This is not the love that raises itself by mediation of the body to the level of the soul (in Plato and in all philosophy and in all poetry), and it is not, therefore, the love that comes back to itself and that takes pleasure in itself. "Love must be reinvented, that's obvious," as is written in the *Season* ("Delirium," I, p. 39). Truth will be possessed, but it will not possess *itself*. It will be possessed *in* one soul and one body, and it is of little importance whether this is my soul and body or someone else's—or which sex it is: because "me," the possessor, I will always end up being possessed. "I! I who called myself angel or seer, exempt from all morality, I am returned to the soil with a duty to seek and rough reality to embrace!" ("Adieu," p. 87). I will be possessed by truth, by the double strangeness of the soul and the body, without mediation, without knowledge, without images.

The possessor will enjoy, but he will be enjoyed: "Oh! the loins are being dug out, the heart groans, the breast burns, the head throbs, the night wheels in my eyes, to the Sun"—as a rough draft puts it. And "Adieu": "Arduous night! The dried blood smokes on my face. . . . Spiritual combat is as brutal as the battle of men" (p. 89).

Is there still a "poet" to enjoy words? There are words that get pleasure from him, the last words. Grasped in rough reality: truth does not return to itself, nor to any "I." But this "non-return" comes from the future, this infinite inappropriation is truth. It is the truth of "Adieu." The soul and the body, the lovers, the poet and the word, say adieu to each other, when the unique truth is possessed in each other. Such are the loves that will be "old" or "deceitful" no more.

And it is not death. ("Because love and death are the same thing," as philosophy and poetry have repeated since Ronsard.) "Death's friends" in "Adieu" are "damned" (p. 89). This is not death desired as an inscription of the impossible, as a satisfaction of unappeasable desire, and as mediating negativity. It is an affirmation and a joy, the joy of the future that is coming: "Meanwhile, this is the eve. Welcome, then, all the influx of vigor and real tenderness. And, in the dawn, armed with an ardent patience, we shall enter magnificent cities" ("Adieu," p. 89).

The cities are modern. The "peasant" "returned to the soil" (p. 87) will enter the cities. There, the soul and the body will be fire and mud, associated and dissociated, as the splendor and the besmirchment of the modern world ("the enormous city with its sky stained by fire and mud" ["Adieu," p. 85]; previously Rimbaud had written: "What can it matter to the whore Paris,/Your souls and your bodies, your poisons and your rags?"). Cities are modern, double, divided truth, and this is what offers itself, what is coming and what lets itself be possessed. Finite truth, infinitely finite, where the future dispossesses itself, not making anything known, giving nothing to be seen. To be modern is to be on the edge of this truth that carries with it no resolution.

This does not mean that it does not call for revolution. Just before the adieu, the question is posed: "When shall we go beyond the mountains and the shores, to greet the birth of new toil, of new wisdom, the flight of tyrants, of demons, the end of superstition, to adore—the first to adore!—Christmas on the earth?" ("Morn-ing," p. 83). Revolution, though, demands the adieu and the holding on, *pas gagné*, in a vigil that perceives nothing and knows nothing of its tomorrow, and that knows itself only as a stern vigil, where songs die out and where words reach their end. Tomorrow, the watchman will be enjoyed by the dawn, by the joy of finite existence that lets sense come to it, without "imagination" and without "memories."

~

But if I say that it is a joy, and if Rimbaud says it in rediscovering a word and a future from "The Drunken Boat" ("O countless golden birds, O Force to come"),[10] will it be necessary to say that the last words of poetry are still poetry? Earlier, the city itself had been "sacred supreme poetry." Will it have to be said that the lie extends into the future?

Obviously—logically—the words of adieu are words of poetry. How could it be otherwise? And just as obviously they are words of philosophy, as we have seen. If they were not, we would not have been able to interpret them. But here, interpretation touches upon this: that the soul and the body do not mutually interpret each other and that they have no "content" or "sense" save for absolute, future truth dissociated in them. The interpretation affects the words themselves.

Rimbaud (and doubtless, all great "poetry") does not defy inter-pretation by means of enigma or mystery (the romantic mode of philosophical overdetermination of the poetic). It defies it by words, taking it to the limit by a patient and brutal stripping bare of all words. "For I can say that victory is won: the gnashing of teeth, the hissings of fire, the pestilential sighs are abating. All the noisome memories are fading. . . . Spiritual combat is as brutal as the battle of men: but the vision of justice is the pleasure of God alone" ("Adieu," pp. 88, 89).

"The hallucination of words" in the "Alchemy of the Word" ("Delirium," II) and the "latent births" of "Vowels" confront justice: words are dead, poetry's life has left them, they are exposed and swallowed dead things and, henceforth, full of hard, live, unbearable presence, where, without holding, Rimbaud holds fast, with his words.

> *No more words.* I bury the dead in my belly. Shouts, drums, dance, dance, dance, dance! I cannot even see the time when, white men landing, I shall fall into nothingness.
>
> Hunger, thirst, shouts, dance, dance, dance, dance! ("Bad Blood," p. 19)

Finally soul and body, the limit-words that say the limit on which words, language in general, can be formed. Language is the mediation of soul and body. The last words suspend this mediation. Truth in the soul and the body is language's truth in that it no longer belongs to language. Truth no longer lets itself be poeticized. It is impossible language, snatched from language and from vision, exhausted language, dying, born exhausted, sentences that only articulate a language monster, a monstration of nothing but itself—its voice that does not speak. "My comrade, beggar-girl, monstrous child! how little you care about these unhappy women and these manoeuvrings, or my difficulties. Tie yourself to us with your impossible voice, your voice! the only hope of this vile despair."[11]

The limit of the last words—the adieu—this limit that they themselves assign to their powers, their magic, their sense as words, is the same as the limit where the soul and the body turn away from each other in touching. It is the same as the limit where poetry and philosophy reject each other while desiring each other and identifying with each other, and it is the same as the limit upon which the possibility of words, of *saying*, separates itself from what it says is yet to come: the truth.

The last words: let us stop trying to decide if they are poetry, philosophy, or both—they are not, in any case, from another language. They are *already* precisely what they will be: *no more words*. They are what they will be, that is, what they are not at all, and the words are, or perhaps will always be, something other than words. The last words are the words of the ultimate possibility of words, which is, at the same time, the last, the highest, and the smallest. They are words of the *yet to come*: the infinite, finite yet to come of an adieu, from which they come, coming at us, to let themselves be pronounced, interpreted, sung, and touched. "It is love, the measure perfect and reinvented, marvelous and unexpected reason, and eternity: beloved machine of the fatal powers."[12]

But *in* this future—in the eternity of this yet to come, truly eternal, for it comes outside of time, it comes to time outside of time, the outside of time from which time is woven—words have not already taken place. Words come from where words are not in use, neither as words of vision nor as words of signification. No more words: always more, never more.

> It is found!
> —What?—Eternity.
> It is the sun mixed
> With the sea.
>
> ("Ravings," II, p. 333)

There is no poetico-philosophical mystique of the ineffable in this. Nothing is ineffable. Rimbaud, above all, says nothing of the kind. Everything that is, comes to words, comes to the end of words. And this is why eternity is ceaselessly rediscovered in the adieu, as the adieu. Because this comes from the elsewhere that words speak of and, in saying it, cause to come each time from farther still. If "poetry" means the will to re-inscribe this exscription, it is necessary to say adieu to poetry.

But if poetry does not mean this, if it no longer *wishes* to say anything (without once more wishing to express mystery, the arcane, or whatever), and still speaks, pronouncing its last words, then it says: adieu.

～

"One soul and one body": this is the union, the system par excellence, that adjoins outside and inside, elsewhere and here; this is animation and incarnation in their perfect reciprocity. But it is, as well, each time, in the *and*, a punctuality where conjunction is suspended: deposed poetry.

Poetry and thought are, since the impartation [*partage*] of these words, since the beginning of their conjunction/disjunction, the infinite will to express each other, body and soul of one and the other in turn. The adieu immobilizes them at the point of impartation: the one and the other are at the edge of where they are coming from, ceaselessly coming, and never arriving except to this very edge. This is the edge of something that does not go beyond words, as would another type of superb and sublime language, nor adopt the manner of an ineffable silence, but is rather something like this *thing*—the "thing itself," why not?—that truth alone inhabits, and where it is to be possessed. This is no longer the business of poetry or of philosophy. This is another exposition of words. Poetry exposed.

"To possess truth in one soul and one body" are the most ample and most simple words, which contain, for us, all the secrets of language and of thought, of poetry and of philosophy, of art and of love. With these words, all is said. Rimbaud did not choose these last words as the definitive words of the adieu by chance. But he turns them to the future, he exposes them to their source, to the end of words, in a definitive manner.

"As for me, I can no more explain myself than beggar with his endless *Paters* and *Ave Marias. I can no longer speak!*" ("Morning," p. 81)—an inexplicable prayer.

To conclude, Rimbaud speaks, without speaking about it and no longer speaking, of what one can indiscriminately call the thing, the real, existence—of what we will not name and words exscribe. To say "soul and body" is to speak of this "real" in that it cannot be appropriated, even in its possession. Who enjoys the soul and the body? And which one of the two is enjoying the other? But to enjoy is to be fulfilled with the singular joy of their division.

The adieu is the adieu of words to words, and their exscription in this division. Words end as they began, and as they will begin: writing themselves outside of words, in things, the truth, the reverse side of their writing. That upon which writing, to conclude—and it is ceaselessly concluding, as it must, and "Rimbaud" is the knowledge of this necessity—returns and exscribes itself, by itself.

On the edge one hears the adieu. But the adieu has the sole task of transporting us to this edge, and never to another edge: there is nothing to pass over to. "Poetry" meant a passage to "new flowers, new stars, new flesh, new languages" ("Adieu," p. 87). On this edge, to the contrary, we are exposed to the coming of words, the same old words, which do not come from any word and which do not lead us to any other word. But they are coming from the future of finite existence, and with it, from this freedom thanks to which "it will be permissible for me to possess truth." This truth *is going*, in bringing to me the last words, the words that are always last, it is *going* to free me from speaking. *I can no longer speak*: this happens, this is still happening, an inexplicable prayer.

~

Last words written by Arthur Rimbaud (to the Director of Maritime Communications, Marseille, November 9, 1891): "I am completely paralyzed: therefore I wish to be embarked early. Tell me at what time I must be carried on board . . ."[13]

TRANSLATED BY RODNEY TRUMBLE

§ We need . . .

Imagine poetry. You are ill-equipped to talk about it. But I'm not asking you to talk about it, I'm asking you to imagine it.

There is no image. Or rather, there is but one: the image of divine goodness at work on its creation, at the task of making a world by the stark power of its verb. What penury and what power! But is this an image? Montaigne says of divine goodness that it must be imagined as being unimaginable. Do you want me to imagine unimaginable poetry? Or perhaps, with imagination dead, to imagine?

There is a rhythm of the phrase, a rhythm of declaration; there is a tone of address, a tone of destination; there is a timbre of elocution, a timbre of the voice. Of declaration, of destination, of voice, there is nothing to be imagined. One does not invent poetry.

It never was a human invention. It is not a procedure, not a technique. Nor is it literature, if literature is an invention of the modern world. Poetry is immemorial. It might be said to be older than man, if there were anything older than man. But man, if only as an animal, is older than man. (And what can be said of you? There is nothing to say, yet you are the one to be addressed;

however, we don't really know who is speaking.) Poetry is no older than man's work. It is born of exigent, exacting, exhausting work. This work cannot be learned, nor can it be improvised. It is not work, without being play, or magic.

Poetry is unimaginable, for it alone does not use words as images. Everywhere else, even in everyday language, words evoke images—more or less frequently, more or less knowingly, but they evoke images. Poetry is defined by its refusal or abandonment of images. When a literary piece extends credit to images, uses words as images, one can be certain, no matter how superb the work, that it is not poetry. This, then, is what Bataille calls "poetry's sticky temptation." It is the temptation to capture the inexpressible with the glue of images.

Yet the inexpressible is still an image. Poetry knows nothing of the representation or evocation of the inexpressible. It is thoroughly coextensive with the limits of language's entire area, which it nowhere overflows. It consists of none other than the task of measuring this area, of taking a complete reading of it, of locating and inscribing its bounds. The poet can be recognized by his surveyor's step, by his way of covering a territory of words, not in order to find something, or to plant a crop, or to build an edifice, but simply to measure it. Poetry is a cadastre, or else a geography.

Hence the inappropriateness here of the idea (image) of creation. To poetry the earth is given—an inheritance to be surveyed—and there is nothing but this to be noted: that the earth is given, that you are there, that I am there (elsewhere, always, inexorably), and that words exceed the earth and the places it assigns us, that words exceed and exhaust these places, and yet that at the same time, these very words falter before them. I remain there, you remain there, elsewhere. Words have charted our positions.

Poetry is made of the patience to bear both this excess and this faltering. Hence the infinite rarity of poetry. Such patience and such a trial are not at the level of everyday life—which, however, is precisely what poetry must take on in patience. But its rarity has nothing spectacular about it. Rather it takes the form of an effacement: a gesture which itself is, after all, commonplace, which indicates your place, mine, yet another's, and which withdraws.

History, or what we believed to be the modern history of humanity, or the existence of a historical humanity, has deprived us of poetry because this history has tried to pass for the absence of excess and faltering, for the powerful equalization of words and of nature, for the advent of a man who would be not a surveyor but a creator and whose gesture would be ineffaceable. Now the territory is strewn in bits by the works of these creators. Our places are blurred or ill determined. (Where are you now?) It is time for a new survey. We must cease to imagine that what we have to do is to create, or that an ancient power of creation has been lost. What we need is simply poetry, with justice.

TRANSLATED BY EMILY MCVARISH

§ Speaking Without Being Able To

—coauthored with Ann Smock

This conversation began in October 1989, when Jean-Luc Nancy and I (Ann Smock) were invited by Larry Gilmore to speak at Small Press Distribution, a Berkeley, California, bookstore. We were free to choose any topics we liked, but Mr. Gilmore hoped we would keep in mind the general subject of a series of events he'd organized at the bookstore that fall: Bataille's writing and ideas about communication, community. We decided to try a dialogue. It started off from comments by me on Blanchot's words "Il faut parler. Parler sans pouvoir" (You must speak—speak without the power to do so). Our conversation has continued since, somewhat haltingly and over a long distance. The following is its summer, 1990 stage.

A.S.: Blanchot explains that it's precisely when you're speechless that you have to speak. "Il faut parler," he writes, "Parler sans pouvoir." When another human being approaches and you are face to face with him, you must speak: you're under an obligation. You're under an obligation to respond to him, answering the demand, which his nearness is, that you should hear him—hear him and thus let him speak; make it so he can; let him come up close and be there, speaking.

But he *is* there, close by, speaking. His proximity is immediate—it's a given and indeed *the* given of this situation—and also it is remote, a stranger to the realm of possibility. Likewise speech. You must speak—in fact it is given you to do so—just as the power to speak departs from you.

The other who approaches speaks and asks you to make it so that he can speak: Blanchot says you hear him asking you to find the words with which he'll make you hear him. Isn't it just as if your duty were to answer for language in the absence of language—in the absence, that is, of any common usage, shared assumptions, or common ground to start out from?

In this situation there is nothing to start out from, nothing to base anything upon. You have to answer an utterance (an entreaty, a question, a command, who knows?) that you have never heard and that you won't have heard until you've answered. For if you *have* to answer ("Il faut parler"), it's so that *what*, or rather *whom*, you are obliged to answer might be heard. Thus you must speak without being able to—without knowing what the question is that you must answer or even if it is a question; you must answer without understanding for what or whom it is that you're accountable. Your whole attention is required but by exactly that which (or rather he, or she who) withdraws from your attention everything it needs to go on and renders your thoughts aimless. You must speak just as the power to speak departs from you—just as the world wherein speaking is a possibility and a thing you can do recedes and leaves you face to face with the other as if you two were the sole vestiges of a world long over with. Yet this is the beginning, the start of the world where people can approach, can hear and answer one another, speaking together. The obligation that speaking initially is ("Il faut parler") must be the duty of vouching for this world—the one where people recognize and acknowledge one another—when it is coming, precariously, unexpectedly, and implausibly, to be.

The other who draws near you does so, Blanchot says, by turning away, backing off out of your reach, out of your ken. He draws near withdrawing. This does not mean he doesn't come close; it does not mean he doesn't take you by the hand and speak to you; it means it's he who's come. Or she. Not "he-or-she," or "s/he"; rather, a singular being, incomparable, unmistakable. The woman who comes at night in poems by des Forêts—the woman who comes each night and stands among asters and roses saying that she has left the world—is "the dearest one," the one most loved. Her coming—to announce her absence—means that "it is she." "She is there." Likewise in Blanchot, that the other draws near withdrawing means that it is he, and that you are face to face now not with another object of attention, which you know how to face, or with another subject, whom you can hear and recognize, but with the friend. Who is way beyond you and way beyond anything or anyone you ever could be with.

He draws near you turning away and withdrawing, and by this sign, if you were ever in a position to perceive it, you would know him: you could greet the friend. But you aren't ever in such a position. There is no position from which to know what is happening when this happens. For no matter how many times he comes, even if he comes all the time, it's always without precedent. Even if he ceaselessly comes back to you—even if you can't forget him— never has he ever come before; he turns from you and leaves. The obligation that speech essentially is, is the duty to recognize without mistake and welcome him, or her, or what is in this way far beyond all recognition.

> It is she once again standing and smiling
> Amid the asters and the roses
> In the full radiance of her grace
> She is as proud now as she always was
> And never appears except in dreams
> Too lovely to lull suffering to sleep
> With such deceptive nocturnal reunions
> Each one attesting to her absence.[1]

She comes exclusively when and where it's perfectly clear she's not. She indulges in lies no more now than she ever did, but comes to say she hasn't come and that, standing and smiling in the garden, it isn't she. How to receive her visit? How to acknowledge her? Who else would be so true as to say "I am not with you; I haven't come?" It's she! There she is once again and as she always was, undeniably herself. Yet this is to deny exactly what it is so like her to convey (the truth, that she is gone)—and not to hear, or welcome her.

How to recognize someone who says she isn't there? How to understand her words—understand them to be hers? How to recognize her voice when she says *You do not hear me?*

She comes to say she hasn't come—she wants to disappoint. How not to misconstrue, and disappoint her? If you take her visits for delusions and turn away from the figure in the garden, you'll be disappointed, but mistaken, because your sadness means you haven't heard *her* say "I've gone," but only whom she isn't, saying it is she and that she's there. And if you did hear *her*, come each night to say "I've left you," you'd be consoled and turn gladly to her beauty in the flower garden: and instead of misunderstanding her, you'd once again misunderstand. You'd be consoled instead of disappointed: your happiness would mean you haven't heard her say "I'm *gone*, you do not hear me."

But perhaps between there's speaking without the ability to speak: speaking that just lets her be—different from herself, which is her proper, her unmistakable, her unrecognizable trait.

Maybe in between the communication of disappointment and the disappointment of communication, there is speaking—there where the voice breaks, where the words part and divide in two—in two misunderstandings—where one is able only by mistake to turn away and depart from speaking, failing the obligation that speaking is, but unable, after all, to do that either; unable even to do that; unable to do anything but let the differing of language be—its division, its splitting between two.

J.-L.N.: I must speak, without being able to, and first, here, because I speak such a poor English.

I must speak to you. But I don't know who *you* are, or who you *is*. For *you* is only the "I" of an utterance addressed to *me* (I mean, here, now, addressed to everybody, each of them as a me, a me/

you), who can only be an "I" when he/she is addressed by a "you," a "you" said by you, but said before you are able to recognize me— being yourself not able to recognize yourself. (Who is "Ann"?)

This may look like a joke, indeed, like the famous Jewish joke reported by Freud: "Why do you tell me you are going to Cracow, to make me believe you are going to Warsaw?" I could say, "Why do you call me 'you,' to make me believe that you know me, when you know neither me, nor what 'you' mean?"

You said: this is the disappointment of communication. This is true. Communication is always disappointing, because no subject of the utterance comes in touch with another subject. There is no subjectivity here; in this sense there is no self-recognizing of the utterance. It always speaks *before* becoming self-present. Moreover, if it speaks, it always goes instantly "behind" the subject who is speaking.

A.S.: "Behind." Behind and ahead. Blanchot says that nothing follows from the demand that the presence of an other is. So, whoever is subject to that demand just has to lead. When you hear another asking you to find the words with which he'll make you hear him—asking you to tell him what it is he wants to ask you— nothing follows. So you have to turn and walk away from friendship's infinite obligation; you must turn and walk ahead, not knowing if you're followed; and all the while you have to follow in the stranger's footprints as it were, retracing his steps through a trackless void—repeating his utterance before hearing it.

Isn't a conversation necessarily distant, separate from itself, and isn't it this parting? This separation or departure from itself? It pursues itself, both in the sense that it chases and seeks to catch or join itself (beginning, paradoxically, by getting left behind, or over, or by following in its own wake before there's any wake to follow in), and in the sense that it pursues nothing whatsoever but itself: it simply goes along and has no purpose other than to continue thus. It is, immediately, its end. It is inaccessible and right there (given). Between its presence and its absence there is no difference, but it is "itself" that difference, from itself. That interval.

It's unattainable, impossible, nothing prepares for it or foreshadows it—rather, everything (including it) puts it off, rendering it even more implausible and remote—and yet it's there, there it is, all the time, all the time unexpected, unanticipatable, new.

J.-L.N.: Speaking comes by surprise. Or by chance, as a chance. Therefore, the best "model" of speaking is the conversation, the loose conversation, where nobody knows what he or she will say before he or she has said it. This was a model for classical as well as for romantic aesthetics. The contrary of the "interview."

But you also said: this is the communication of disappointment. Then, communication takes place. But how?

Since at least part of this exchange is supposedly devoted to Bataille, I'll refer to him. ("You" play Blanchot; "I" play Bataille . . . Again, this is and is not a joke. The voice of a written text is not that of "Monsieur Blanchot." It is a voice asking to be recognized, you said, as impossible to recognize. One has only to let it be.)

For Bataille—as for Blanchot, as for you, as for all of us today, I assume—communication takes place as the communication of a disappointment, of a nonpossibility, of a withdrawal of communication itself.

On the one hand, this is tragedy. It is the tragedy of a world, a mankind, where there is no longer a substance, a subject giving the matter and the way of "communicating." That is, giving the element, the body of a "communion." Or at least, of real encounter, where there is a partaking of the same sense. (Even "encounters of the third kind" are the same: one has to understand a different way of telling the same. But can we imagine a language that would not be a language in the same sense? Does that even make sense?)

This tragedy implies its own comedy. Every attempt to communicate, to make present the link, the real linkage and exchange between two, is comedy: the words of lovers, but also "love making" itself, and philosophical dialectics, and religious sacrifice.

But finally, this implies also that communication communicates this withdrawal—communicates it, and through it, and as it.

You withdraw yourself and the communication by demanding

silently, "Speak, without being able to recognize me." I withdraw myself and the communication by answering, "I can't speak except by exposing that I can't do it, can't recognize you or make myself recognized."

But what is "withdrawal"? (At this point, I refer to Heidegger and Derrida as well.) Or better, what is it to be "withdrawn" (which is the position of the speaker)? This is first to be remote, isolated— also, modest, shy, also unresponsive. But it is also to be drawn—to be described, or inscribed, drafted, sketched, even portrayed. In French, a portrait was a *retrait*, like the Italian *ritratto*—which can be understood as "withdrawn" as well as "drawn again, a second time." In the withdrawal, something (or someone) is withdrawn and drawn again, drawn for a second time without any first time— without a model, a "first person." It—or she, or he—is drawn in its (her, his) disappearance. At the point of disappearance—as it were—some "presence" is drawn, not re-presented, but presented becoming absent.

To come, for Bataille, is the becoming-present of this becoming-absent. It is even becoming the present—the gift, the offering—of this withdrawal itself.

A.S.: "Presented becoming absent," you say, "the becoming-present of this becoming-absent." I think these expressions apply to the nocturnal visitor in des Forêts's poems whom I described and who comes to say she's gone. Such a coming and a saying—such a being there—seem impossible to understand and to acknowledge truly. I think they're *the* unrecognizable and, as such, the presentation of language (the gift of speech?): its presentation broken, like bread, yet also like a pitcher or something similar, which is utterly useless when no longer whole and one. I mean to suggest that the coming of which you speak is also the coming apart and coming to be—the coming to be dialogue—of language. And maybe the coming to be of the language you were imagining and wondering if it made any sense to imagine: the language "that would not be a language in the same sense." This language would be the element of communication and community in that it is not to be had by us in common and doesn't even have anything in common with itself, but only differs and departs. Are people together thanks to this parting rather than to anything more likely to join them—united by the speaking that speaking separates them from?

Joined by our separateness, we are perhaps divided by together-ness—the togetherness that remains, between us, to be reached. We are still together then—left together. Perhaps I could say we leave each other face to face and remain there all alone together, way beyond anywhere that any of us has ever been.

J.-L.N.: So the disappointment is also . . . an appointment—I mean, a "rendez-vous." A "rendez-vous" means "Be there; you promise to be there, at this time." Every speaking event is such an appointment: "Be there." The answer is "Let me be"; the promise is "Let me be there; I'll be there."

And this is community, as the possibility of being together there, presented to the "togetherness."

This is literature: an indefinite appointment with every reader, every reading. Would you agree?

A.S.: Your suggestion makes me think of Blanchot's description of literature: a sort of interruption in its own coming to be. It interferes, intervenes, and postpones itself, inasmuch—for example—as it can't be written until it's read. So everything literature is, is the deferral of all that into the future; it's as if literature were all in all a sort of appointment to be all that, ever so unexpectedly, it already is. But all it is, so far, is a divide between writing and reading, indeed, between a writer and a reader. A delay, interim, or interval. In this dividedness between *suddenly now!* and *never never quite yet*, between the most disarming surprise and the longest wait, between a gift beyond anything that could ever be hoped for and dis-appointment, we confusedly feel, perhaps, how literature is shared.

J.-L.N.: It's because of the interval that everything is possible and impossible. In it we begin to speak, and it is what remains when we've finished. If it weren't for the interval, there would be neither "together" nor "apart."

The interval makes speech possible—and necessary. But speech, ultimately, just designates the interval, nothing else.

This is not a failure. On the contrary. By designating the interval, speech designates all of reality: when reality is thus altogether designated, "together" itself is designated. Little by little, nothing less than all humanity, inasmuch as humanity "is together" (which is not to say that all together it forms a totality).

The interval, the space between us—which makes "us" possible—is all that remains when there is no more God. God filled the intervals; he was himself without interval. The "death of God" signifies the opening of space and access to the inaccessible reality of "together" or of "in-common" as the reality of our being. If we have neither one common being nor beings that are utterly distinct, this is because we have—because we divide between us—the being of the interval, or . . . the scant being of the interval.

But this scant being is our whole reality, our most concrete, most existing, most "in the world" reality. We are in the world thanks to this scant being. And it's the scant being of our being—or our sharing—that calls for so much speaking. Little being = lots of speaking, for you never get done designating the interval. You never finish speaking—which explains the ever so singular, obstinate murmur of every variety of literature (although everything has already been said, if you will, for a long time now). But one speaks so that the abundance of speech—every instant, or as often as possible—lets the scanty being, our existence, show through.

§ Exscription

Two texts are joined here, but the second alone can explain their common title. Eleven years separate these two texts, and the reader will sense this distance.[1] The writing of the second one brought me back, however, and unexpectedly, to the first. A continuity was inescapable: that of a community with Bataille that goes beyond and can do without theoretical debate (a vivid, though not harsh debate I could imagine on the subject of what might be called Bataille's tragic religion). Therefore, this community also goes beyond the commentary, exegesis, or interpretation of Bataille. It is not without distance or reservations; but these are, precisely, theoretical. It is a community in that Bataille immediately communicates to me the pain and the pleasure that result from the impossibility of communicating anything at all without touching the limit where all meaning [*sens*] spills out of itself, like a simple ink stain on a word, on the word "meaning."[2]

This spilling and this ink are the ruin of theories of "communication," of the conventional chatter that attempts to promote reasonable exchange and serves only to obscure violence, betrayal, and lies, leaving no possibility of measuring oneself against powerful follies. But the reality of community, where nothing is shared without *also* being removed from this kind of "communication," has already, always, revealed the vanity of such discourses. They communicate only the postulation of the communication of a "meaning," and of the meaning of "communication." Bataille, beyond and sometimes apart from what he says, communicates community itself—that is, naked existence, naked writing, and the silent, haunting referral of the one to the other, which makes us share meaning's nakedness: neither gods nor thoughts, but the *us* that is imperceptibly and insuperably *exscribed*. Today there is something of a need to say this, and to say it again: we exist, we write, only "for" this staggering spillage of meaning. More than a few years are repeated in this way: it is our whole tradition that must reappropriate its experience. "Je ferai un vers de vrai rien... J'ai fait le vers, ne sais sur quoi" [I'll make a verse of true nothing . . . I made the verse, about I know not what], writes Guillaume de Poitiers, around the year 1100.[3]

Reasons to Write

WRITING, ON THE BOOK

In a certain sense—very certain, in fact—it is no doubt nearly impossible today to *rien écrire* on the book. This peculiarity in the French usage of the word *rien* obliges us to understand at the same time that it is no longer possible to write anything whatsoever on the subject of the book, and that it is no longer possible to avoid writing on the book.

It is no longer possible to write anything whatsoever on the subject of the book: if the issue must indeed be "the question of the book," to borrow an expression from one of the texts that form the horizon of this impossibility ("Edmond Jabès et la question du livre," by Jacques Derrida), then we must posit at once that this question has now been fully treated (although it has not been, nor can it ever be, the object of any treatise). A wish today to advance, to invent, anything about it can spring only from ignorance or from naïveté, real or feigned. Something definitive has been accomplished, with respect to this question, by a group, a network, or whatever we wish to call it, of texts that cannot be avoided, texts bearing the names Mallarmé, Proust, Joyce, Kafka, Bataille,

Borges, Blanchot, Laporte, Derrida. A list that is no doubt incomplete and perhaps unjust—it is nevertheless certain that we must not only pass through these texts but also *stay with them.* Which is not at all fetishistic, idolatrous, or conservative—quite the contrary, as should be clear. It is time to affirm that the question of the book is *there*, already. Reactionary pietism consists of the exact opposite, of calling on these same texts indefinitely, zealously or voraciously, so as to extract from them and reopen in a thousand more or less declared ways, by gloss, imitation, or exploitation, a question of the book in the form of speculation, *mise en abîme*, staging, fragmentation, denunciation, or enunciation of the book, stretching as far as the eye can read.

I, for my part, would have liked to content myself with patiently recopying those texts here. Nothing can assure me that I should not have done so.

But—at the same time, by the same categorical imperative—it is no longer possible to avoid writing on the book.

This question is not a question, is not a subject that we can consider to be completely or incompletely explored—much less exhausted. Exhaustion—an undefined exhaustion—instead forms the subject that we must face, here as elsewhere.

As for the book (Mallarmé's title and program), something has now been knotted in our history. The strength of this knot is not due to the "genius" of these "authors," but signals the historical, and more than historical, power and necessity by which the writing of the book had to get all knotted up in itself. Since the West—what Heidegger made us think of as the West—decided, as far back as human memory goes, to consign to books the knowledge of a truth deciphered in a Book (of the World, of God, indeed of the Id) that was nevertheless impossible to read or write, the West is knotted up with writer's cramp. This, in sum, is the primary motif of what we must incessantly reread in these texts.

And of what we must rewrite—on condition that we do not follow current fashion, forgetting the implacable lesson of Pierre Ménard and allowing the concept of *réécriture* to sink to the level of "rewriting."

According to a law that all these texts contain and articulate, and whose rigor needs no demonstration, this history stricken with writer's cramp can end only by repeating itself. Never taken up, the question of the book marks the resurgence of repetition. Not of its *own* [*propre*] repetition, because it is, insofar as it is, the question of what remains without property (such is the question of literary property and literary communism). Repetition is the form, the substance, of what does not have its identity imprinted once and for all (or more than once) in the untranscribable Book. For whoever happens to be deprived of this identity—for everyone in the West—repetition forms the question of the book, the question which must be written in order that something be dissolved in its writing—but what?

In order—but the gesture of writing is never satisfied with a teleology—to dissolve—but in a dissolution itself dissociated from the values of solution always conferred on it by metaphysics—not only the ideal identity inscribed in the blinding whiteness of the Book (for in the depth of eternal light, everything scattered throughout the universe is reunited, as if bound by love, into a single book; Dante) but to dissolve even the privation, which also forms the privatization, of this identity, to dissolve even the Book itself, and even the privation, the privatization, of the Book. The Book is there—in each book occurs the virgin refolding of the book (Mallarmé)—and we must *write on it*, make it a palimpsest, overload it, muddy its pages with added lines to the point of the utter confusion of signs and of writings: we must, in short, fulfill its original unreadability, crumpling it into the shapeless exhaustion of cramp.

What for? We certainly must take the risk: we must write on the book *for the sake of deliverance*. Which has very little to do with Freedom (I mean with that subjective, subject, subjugated Freedom that the God or the Spirit of metaphysics automatically confers on itself). Writing ought to slip through the crack in the strange *liber/liber* homonomy, into the everyday ambiguity of *livraison* [delivery].

Writing? Twisting off one's fingernails, quite vainly hoping for the moment of deliverance? (Bataille)

—and the sentence that follows in the same *Story of Rats*:
My reason for writing is to reach B.
    B. is the woman in this story, but her initial and the sentence
itself make us read woman, this woman, a woman, a man, and B.:
Bataille himself, and a place and a book and a thought and deliverance "itself," in person, with no allegorism.
    Such repetition: resumption, rewriting of the petition, of the
effort to reach and join, of the request, of the demand, of the desire,
of the claim, of the supplication. Rewriting on the book is the
renewed clamor or murmur of a demand, of a pressing call. If the
texts that I have mentioned will *remain* henceforth in our history,
it is because they have not taken up any question but have knotted
up this call in one and many throats of writing: a grand glottal
spasm.
    They have knotted up the ethical, more than ethical, call of a
deliverance, to a deliverance. The imperative is not to answer this
call (. . . the neutral, writes Blanchot, naming the literary act,
which, entailing a *problem* with no *answer*, has the closure of an
aliquid to which no question would correspond)—or, rather, it
would be indispensable to distinguish, with all possible care, between two incommensurable concepts: the answer to a question,
and the response to a call.
    It may be that one responds to the call only by repeating the
call—as night watchmen do. It may be that the imperative is not
the response, but only the *obligation* to respond, which is called
responsibility. How, in the book, can the issue be responsibility?
Eluding it is no longer possible, any more than avoiding this: how,
in writing where the Voice is absent (a voice without writing is at
once absolutely alive and absolutely dead; Derrida), can there be a
call to be heard, how can there be any question of vocation,
invocation, or advocation? How, in general, can the book's complete otherness be delivered?
    All these texts have exhausted the theme, the theory, the practice,
the metamorphosis, the future, the fugue, or the cut of the book for
no other reason than to repeat this call.
    I myself had something else to write, longer and for more than

one person. Long in the writing. This would have been a book as long as *The Thousand and One Nights*, perhaps, but quite another one. (Proust)

REPETITIONS

Still, it is certainly better to dot the *i*'s in repetition, at the risk of repeating oneself somewhat.

The reduplication of the book at its own heart, the self-representation of literature, each work's story of its own birth—of its own delivery—its self-analysis, the involution of its message in the exhibition of its code, the figuration of its process in the narrative or demonstrative procedure of its figuration, the putting into play of its rules according to the rules of its play, everything that I will call, in a word, autobibliography, all of it dates from the invention of the book. Everything on which our modernity has amassed entire libraries—and it had to be done, it was necessary, through the very necessity of the book that no written text escapes (this useless and prolix epistle I am writing already exists in one of the thirty volumes on the five bookshelves in one of the innumerable hexagons, and so does its refutation. Borges, "The Library of Babel")—all of it makes up the self-repetition that unavoidably constitutes the book from birth. My reason for writing is to reach B.: Babel, Bible, bibliology, bibliomancy, bibliomania, bibliophilia, bibliotheca.

This is what the book more characteristically came to recite and rehash in the age of its material and technological invention: in the age of printing, the age of the true book, the age of the fully developed subject and of communication. Printing satisfied the need for relationship in an ideal mode. (Hegel) Since then, everything has been going on as if the ideal content of communication consisted entirely of autobibliography. Every book displays the being or the law of the book: from the beginning, the book has no other object than itself, and this satisfaction. I am writing to you, dear daughter, with pleasure, even though I have no news to tell you. (Mme. de Sévigné)

Everything has been said, and we have been coming too late, in the more than seven thousand years that there have been thinking men; that is how the first chapter, on books, of a book entitled *Characters* must begin. The exhaustion of the material imposes the infinite possible ways of forming its signs. It is the history of this world where we now visit, the goddess tells him: it is the book of its destinies. They pass into another room, and here is another world, another book—somewhere in there you will also find the Essays of theodicy where that is written, and here you will read that Borges never wrote anything but a thought of Leibniz's that Lichtenberg had already copied out: the libraries will be cities. No place will be free of books, even if there should be some lack of them. You are quite right, sir, there is a whole chapter missing here, leaving a hole of at least ten pages in the book, writes Tristram, the author who also recounts his own birth. Nor will any book be free of books, for, not content to inscribe our names on anonymous thoughts by a single author, we appropriate those of thousands of individuals, of epochs, and of entire libraries, and we steal even from plagiarists, writes Jean Paul, plagiarizing himself one more time. The textual anthology—the choicest blooms from books, the book's choice to arrange in each book the bouquet of its literariness—continues unabated up to our own day.

All this repetition *en abîme* of the book constitutes its redundancy—native and, more than is usually thought, naïve. Redundancy is the overflow, the excess of the wave: the Book has always been thought to be the endlessly spraying foam of an inexhaustible ocean—a jet of grandeur, of thought or of emotion, considerable, a sentence pursued in large type spaced out to one line a page, wouldn't that keep the reader breathless for the whole book. (Mallarmé) Reverberation, the crashing and recurling of the wave: should this repetition properly be called composition? To compose [*rédiger*] is to regroup, reintegrate, return, reduce. Each book returns the Book's redundancy to a space whose boundaries are set by an inscription. In each of its temples, autobibliography worships itself—

—on condition that it know nothing of the other repetition whose reprise or remuneration it actually is. The age of printing is indeed the age of the subject—there is no book that is not the book of an "I," and "I" repeats itself, can be recognized because of that.

I have no more made my book than my book has made me, a book consubstantial with its author. The subject sets itself up as a Book, and it is only this erection that has ever secured the substance of a subject—whose frank dissimulation lets its desire be read like an open book: thus, reader, I am myself the material of my book; you would be foolish to spend your leisure on so frivolous and vain a subject. I am not raising a statue here to erect at the town crossroads; this is for the corner of a library, and to amuse a neighbor. Others mold man; I tell of him, and portray a particular one, very badly made. I want people to see my natural, ordinary gait, however offtrack. My reason for writing is to reach B.: to reach myself, to reach in her my society, her solitude, to reach the one who, he or she, says "I"—an (un)natural, (extra)ordinary gait [*pas naturel, pas ordinaire*].

"I" repeats its desire to itself—but can that desire be anything but offtrack? That the "I" may display itself is not enough to make it visible. Someone gets irremediably lost in the matter of his book— someone who will not stop repeating to himself: "the matter of my experience, which will be the matter of my book," and this time it's Proust. Lost in every book, someone—who is and is not the one who says "I"—repeats himself. Through the *abîme* of autobibliography and in spite of this *abîme*, an autograph walks into the abyss. Its errant movement begins at the same crossroads as its erection.

The autograph is he who takes a singular leave at the very opening of his book. Farewell, then—Montaigne, this first day of March, fifteen hundred and eighty. Signature of place, signature of name, signature of farewell, it enters its own book as if this were a tomb. It is the sameness that, altering its identity and its singularity, divides the seal. (Derrida)

Literal, literary repetition belongs to the one who gets lost in his own footprints—in the speeches of his own wake, like Finnegan's, signs are on of a mere by token that wills still to be becoming upon this there once a here was: an exodus has begun again, here, and someone has entered into the history of its diaspora. The call that repeats itself comes always from him. It is the call of a solitude predating all isolation, the invocation of a community neither contained nor preceded by any society. How to deliver the complete otherness common to all books? someone asks, a writing whoever, an "I" who is called.

> bent over the book open to the same page
> what he hears are the songs from
> the other side where the others are
> —*Jacqueline Risset*

THE STORY HE WRITES HIMSELF ABOUT THE BOOK

is a story in keeping with his desire and his exodus. Writing, he says, everywhere marks the end of communism. That is, of what he has never known, because he was born with writing.

But he writes in his books—and he writes in all his books—about what communism was, the absence of the book. The book never aspires to anything less than the retracing of what exceeds it. The question of the book's origin will never belong to any book (Derrida)—and yet, O memory! you who have written what I have seen, here will be seen your nobility. (Dante) And so he writes about the world of the bard, the storyteller, the sacred singer. The first poet, who took this step to set himself free, through imagination, from the common herd, knows how to return in real life. He goes among the herd and relates the deeds that his imagination imputes to the hero. At bottom, this hero is no one but himself. But the audience, which encompasses the poet, can identify with the hero. (Freud) This pure autopoiesis in pure community continually haunts all of literature: and it is a man of the here, a man of the now, who is his own narrator, at last. (Robbe-Grillet)

It was, he says, the world of a mime who had no examples and will have no imitators, the world of the brilliant improviser, of the dancer drunk on god, of the drumbeats, the blows, the whistling of an unwritten music, the world of prayers, supplications, invocations. It's the tribe with its words and its dirges, the chanting cry of the primitive commune around its hearth—silent graph of a fire so bright that it tears itself apart without leaving a trace. (Laporte)

What follows, in the story we tell ourselves, is the society of the writing that is not the book but the engraving of sacred characters, the inscription of the Laws on tablets of stone or of metal, on columns, pilasters, pediments, and mouldings, hard writing and the erection everywhere of stelae setting forth the Order and the Arrangement, the Structure and the Model—giving them to be read by no one and thus by everyone: this is monumental communism, architectural writing, and hieroglyphic monarchy. All its words must have a character of depth or prominence, of engraving or sculpture, as the writer of maxims (Joubert) says of sacred writing. And every book tends uncontrollably toward the maxim: *maxima sententia*, the greatest thought . . .

Last comes—from nowhere and everywhere, from Egypt, Ionia, Caanan—the book; last come *ta biblia*, the irremediably plural Bible, the Law, the Prophets, the Scripture as it divides itself, arranges itself, puts itself *en abîme*, and disseminates itself. It is and it is not the book of only one—author or people.

Last comes the very belated, very ancient religion of books, and all the exoduses begin. Egypt, Ionia, Caanan move, constantly scattering communes crossing the desert.

The history of books begins by losing itself in the book of history. Nothing in it tells us who wrote the very first pact, or even if it was written, the pact that is nevertheless called the Book of the Covenant (*Exodus* 24:7). It is the history of the pact, a pact of deliverance—broken, kept, betrayed, still offered—and of the renewed call to sign it once again. Scarcely graven before they were broken, the Tablets are never erected, they wander in the Ark with the wandering tribes. The Scrolls unroll, and the volume of history swells until it reaches us: the book is inseparable from the story, history from the novel [*roman*]: the age of the book is Romanticism. In our writings, thought seems to proceed with the movements of a man who walks straight ahead. In the writings of the ancients, on the contrary, it seems to proceed with the movement of a bird that soars and wheels as it goes forward. (Joubert)

Who does not see that I have taken a road along which I shall go, ceaselessly and without struggling, as long as there is ink and paper in the world?

Books begin with their repetition: two stories of genesis mingle, overlap, repeat, and contradict each other. Books are copied, they are reproduced, they are *published* because they are not in themselves public, neither in the manner of a song nor in that of an obelisk; we transmit them, translate them—seventy-two Jews, six from each tribe, in seventy-two days, on the island of Pharos, make the Bible Greek—we betray them, we counterfeit them, imitate them, recopy, recite, and cite them. He who says "I" confuses, in his book, books and signatures: In the reasonings and inventions that I transplant into my soil and confound with my own, I have sometimes deliberately not indicated the author, to bridle the temerity of those hasty condemnations that are thrown at all sorts of writings. Here the reiterated repetition begins again.

Books are a corruptible matter. Books are made of wood: *biblos, liber, codex, Buch,* it's always bark or tree. The book burns, it rots, it decomposes, it's erased, it falls to the gnawing criticism of mice. Bibliophila, as much as philosophy, is an impossible love, its objects discolored, faded, worn out, cut up, full of holes. The book is miserable, hateful. Descartes hates the craft of making books. The subject—the other, the same, he who says "I (think)"—finds nothing for himself in those "huge tomes," nothing but a loss of time, a life uselessly consumed in reading the scraps of a science that I myself can found. There should be some legal restraint aimed against inept and useless writers, as there is against vagabonds and idlers. I as well as a hundred others would be banished from the hands of our people. This is no jest. Scribbling seems to be a sort of symptom of an unruly age. When did we write so much as since our dissensions began?—since the dissension of our writing began.

He who says "I" *must* nevertheless write, and the proof is inexorable: thinking through the problem of the ego and the alter ego, of the originary coupling and the human community, Husserl writes: In all this there are essential laws or an *essential style,* the root of which lies first in the transcendental ego, and then in the transcendental intersubjectivity that the ego discovers there, and consequently in the essential structures of transcendental motivation and constitution. Success in elucidating them would in itself give this aprioristic style a supremely honorable explanation: final transcendental intelligibility. Husserl writes what he does not want—to write. He writes that the originary alteration of the ego, the community of men, forms or deforms style, writing, even intelligibility, whose ultimate success it irremediably tears apart.

Thus did supplication through the book begin at the same time as the persecution of books. Writing is bound to a cruel simulacrum of torture. (Laporte) And now, through the glass, everyone can see the inscription being etched on the body of the prisoner. A simple writing cannot be used, obviously, it must not kill on the spot, but within twelve hours, on the average. (Kafka, "The Penal Colony")

The officer in charge of the machine executes himself, at the end of the story, by engraving on his own body the law that he has violated: *Be just!* But only the mad machine is left to apply the law, savagely—the communism and the capitalism of writing machines [*machines à écrire*, typewriters]. Yet it's the same call: How to deliver the book's full otherness?

APOCALYPSE

And what if books always announced, always provoked, the resumption in our history (or in our *story*) of what does not take place there? And what if we understood why it is that, when we speak and write today, we must always speak *several times at the same time*, speaking according to the logic of discourse and therefore under the nostalgia of the theological logos, also speaking to make possible a communication of speech that can be decided only on the basis of a communism of relations of exchange and therefore of production—yet also not speaking, but writing in rupture with all language of speech and writing? (Blanchot)

At the end of books, there is the Apocalypse. This is prophecy's essentially written genre—that is, the call's. It is the book of the end of the world, the book of the new beginning. Its writer says "I" and

says his name—John—and names his place of exile, the island of
Patmos. This book is a letter to the scattered churches, to the community deprived of its communion. In this letter, a letter is addressed to each of the churches, to each of the assemblies. The letter is repeated, divided, transformed: To the Angel of the Church
of Epheseus, write: Thus speaks he who holds the seven stars
(*Revelation*). To them in Ysat Loka. Hearing. The urb it orbs.
Then's now with now's then in tense continuant. Heard. Who
having has he shall have had. Hear! (Joyce)

In this book, John writes the visions it is given him to see: but he
writes only because the visions command him to write. The Angel
speaks to him, holding the Book, but John does not copy it out: he
writes what the Angel dictates. What is revealed is neither the
Angel nor the Book: it is man's writing. He who is announced
through the revelation, who in turn says who he is, is he who *says*—
he of whom John writes that he says he is the alpha and the omega.
He is the Book, of course, but he is also nothing but the final count
of the characters of writing—nothing more is revealed about the
seven broken seals of the book of the slaughtered Lamb. It is the
end of religion.

John writes all his visions of writings. But, in the middle, he is
forbidden to write the words of the seven thunderclaps. No book
delivers unheard, inaudible, deafening speech—the primitive tu-
mult to whose sound the mystical community's exaltation would
have taken place. But the book knows about the dispersion of the
fellowship—it is its inscription, and it communicates its call: Let
the listener say "Come!" *Come!* punctuates the apocalypse—and
our books on books. Come, and restore to us the comeliness of
what disappears—the movement of a heart. (Blanchot, quoted by
Derrida) It's up to you to take the step of (not) meaning [*faire le pas
de sens*]. There is no chance of deciding, no future in deciding, in
whatever language, what comes in "Come." (Derrida)

It is not a call to communication, but the propagation of the
repetition of the call, of the order and the demand, which carry,
produce, convey, teach nothing—*come*—which call not for a response but for the simple obligation to respond, the responsibility

to write again with the twenty-five letters that contain no revelation but only their own exhaustion.

Here, the exhaustion is initial: my reason for writing is to reach B.—to go from the first to the second letter, to trace letters linked to one another, which is called writing, which calls writing, which calls a woman, a man, a book, a history, and always, like B. in the story, an impossible, unsustainable nakedness.

Far beyond and far short of what any speech can unveil of the true—far short and far beyond anyOne Book—the apocalypse remains to be discovered, the discovery that unsettles all books: that the book and communion are stripped naked, dis-covered, in all books. The Book's absence is the absence of Communion—our communion or share of one for all and all for one. (Mallarmé) But it is also the presence—always instantly swallowed up—of the book. John must swallow a little book. I took the book and swallowed it; in my mouth it had the sweetness of honey, but when I had eaten it, it filled my bowels with bitterness.

What communicates, what is taken in communion, is nothing and yet not nothing, nothing but bitterness but still a call; another communism—still to come, but not the culmination of history—a communism of exodus and repetition would mean nothing (but, asks Blanchot, *besides* whatever they mean, what do these words want: relations of exchange, and therefore of production?), but this communism would write the deliverance of books, in books. Deliverance, vain so long as it is bookish (Montaigne coined that last word, *livresque*)—and how could it not be vain, even here?—will also no doubt be bookish so long as it is vain, so long as writing, still and again, is not nakedly at risk in it.

I repeat: The reasons for writing a book can be reduced to the desire to modify the relations that exist between a man and his fellows. These relations are judged unacceptable and are perceived as a dreadful misery. (Bataille)

Far calls. Coming, far! End here. Us then. (Joyce)

April 1977

Reasons to Read

It is becoming urgent to cease commenting on Bataille (even though commentary on him is still rather scanty). We ought to know that, and Blanchot, fittingly, has given us hints, refusing to comment on this refusal of commentary. Therefore, I have no intention of commenting on Bataille in his stead. (But Blanchot so often does nothing but "comment on" Bataille: thinking with him, conversing with him endlessly. Thus he writes: "How had he come to wish for the interruption of discourse? And not the legitimate pause that permits the give-and-take of conversations . . . What he had wanted was something completely different, a cold interruption, the rupture of the circle. And at once it had happened: the heart ceasing to beat, the eternal talking drive stopping."[4])

Moreover, there can be no question of a "refusal." There has never been and will never be anything simply reprehensible or simply false in the fact of commenting on what, by venturing into writing, has already presented itself for commentary and has really already begun to comment on itself.

But such is the ambiguity of Bataille. He involved himself in discourse, and in writing, deeply enough to submit himself to the full necessity of commentary—and thus to its servility. He advanced his thought so far that its seriousness deprived him of that divine, capricious, evanescent sovereignty which nevertheless remained his only "object." (A heartrending limit, sorrowful, joyous, and relieved, a deliverance of thought that does not abdicate— quite the contrary—but that no longer has reason to be, or does not yet have reason to be. A freedom preceding all thought, and which by no means can be made into either object or subject.)

But when he stole away from the gestures, the propositions, the positions of a thinker, a philosopher, a writer (and he continually stole away, not finishing his texts, still less the "summa" or the "system" of his thought, occasionally not even finishing his sentences, or relentlessly obstructing, with an eccentric, disorienting syntax, the logic or the purpose of a linear sequence of thought—

when he stole away, he also stole away our hope of access to what he was communicating.

"Ambiguity": is that the word? Perhaps, if it is the ambiguity of an act, of a simulacrum—which we must not *also* hesitate to ascribe to him. Bataille always *played* at being unable to finish, *acted out* the excess, stretched to the breaking point of writing, of what makes writing: that is, what simultaneously inscribes and exscribes it. It was a game and an act, for he never stopped writing, always writing the exhaustion of his writing. He both said and wrote this game, this comedy. He wrote of his own guilt for talking about the glass of alcohol instead of drinking it and getting drunk. He got drunk on words and pages, to express and at the same time drown the immense futile guilt of the game. Perhaps he also protected himself that way, if you will, always too sure of finding salvation in the game itself—and thus not detaching himself from a too visibly Christian theater of confession, absolution, relapse into sin, and renewed abandon to forgiveness. (Christianity as theater: the repair of the irreparable. Bataille himself knew how much theater there is in sacrifice. But the issue is not one of opposing to it the abyss of a "purely irreparable." What must rid us of the dominating spirit of catastrophe is a higher freedom, perhaps more terrible but in quite another way.)

This theater is ours as well: a sacrifice of writing, by writing, which writing redeems. Some, no doubt, have put on quite a show by comparison with what was, in spite of everything, Bataille's restraint and sobriety. Too much has been made, no doubt, of the fingernails ripped from the writer's hand, or of his suffocation in underground vaults of literature and philosophy. Still others, of course, have rushed to reconstruct his sequences of thought, filling in the gaps with ideas (commentary, in both cases). This is not to encourage any critique of the commentaries on Bataille (otherwise, I too would be implicated). There are some powerful and important ones, and without them we could not even pose the question of commentary on Bataille.

But, after all, Bataille wrote: "I want to arouse the greatest mistrust against myself. I speak only of lived experiences; I do not confine myself to cerebrations" (6: 21).[5]

How can we not be affected by this mistrust? How can we simply go on reading and then close the book, or make notes in its margins? If I underline only this one passage and quote it as I have just done, then already I betray it, I reduce it to a "state of intellection" (as Bataille says elsewhere). Yet it was already reduced to something that intellection, surely, does not fully exhaust, but whose staging it nevertheless surveys. Still elsewhere, Bataille writes that writing is the "mask" of a cry and a non-knowledge. What, then, is done by the writing that writes that very thing? How could it not mask what, in an instant, it unveils? And how, finally, could it not mask the very mask it states itself to be, which it says it applies to a "screaming silence"? The blow cannot be parried, the machinery or machination of discourse is implacable. Far from rising to deafen us, the cry (or the silence) has been stolen away in its nomination or in its designation, under a mask all the harder to spot for its supposedly having been shown and named in turn, in order for it to be denounced.

Ambiguity is therefore inevitable, insurmountable. It is nothing other than the ambiguity of *meaning* itself. Meaning should signify itself, but what makes meaning—or, if you like, the meaning of meaning—is really nothing but "this empty freedom, this infinite transparence of what, in the end, no longer bears the burden [*charge*] of having a meaning" (6: 76). Bataille never ceased to fight this burden and wrote only to unburden himself of it—to reach freedom, to let it reach him—but writing, speaking, all he could do was once again accept the burden of some signification. "Dedicating oneself on principle to this silence, and then continuing to philosophize, to speak, is always a murky business: the slippage without which the exercise could not be is then the very movement of thought" (11: 286). The ambiguity lies in emptying experience of thought, through thought: this is philosophy, this is literature. And yet emptied experience is not stupidity—even if it contains an element of stupor.

The slightest commentary on Bataille involves him in a direction of meaning, leading to univocality. Bataille himself, therefore, when he wanted to write *on* the thought with which he had most in common, wrote *On Nietzsche*, in a move essentially devoted to not commenting *on* Nietzsche, not writing *on* him. "Nietzsche wrote 'with his blood'—whoever criticizes him, or better, *experiences him*, can do so only by bleeding in turn." "*Let no one doubt for an instant*: you haven't understood a word of Nietzsche if you haven't *lived* this dissolution bursting into totality" (6: 15, 22).

But the same goes for all commentary, on any author, on any text whatsoever. In a writer's text, and in a commentator's text (which every text in turn is, more or less), what counts, what thinks (at the very limit of thought, if necessary), is what does not completely lend itself to univocality or, for that matter, to plurivocality, but strains against the burden of meaning and throws it off balance. Bataille never stops exposing this. Alongside all the themes he deals with, through all the questions he debates, "Bataille" is *nothing but* a protest against the signification of his own discourse. If one wishes to read him, and if this reading rebels right away against the commentary that it is and against the *comprehension* that it must be, then one must read in each line the work or the play of a writing *against* meaning.

This has nothing to do with nonsense or with the absurd, nor has it anything to do with a mystical, philosophical, or poetic esotericism. It is—paradoxically—a manner of weighing, in the very sentence, in the very words and syntax; it is a way, often clumsy or lopsided, removed as much as possible, in any case, from the operation of a "style" ("in the acoustico-decorative sense of the term," as Borges says), a manner of weighing on meaning itself, on given and recognizable meaning, a way of hampering or oppressing the communication of this meaning—not first of all to us, but to meaning itself. And reading in turn must remain weighty, hampered, and, without ceasing to decode, must stay just this side of decoding. Such a reading remains caught in the odd materiality of language. It attunes itself to the singular communication carried on not just by meaning but by language itself or, rather, to a communication that is only the communication of language to itself, without abstracting any meaning, in a fragile, repeated suspension of meaning. True reading advances unknowing, it is always as an unjustifiable cut in the supposed continuum of meaning that it opens a book. It must lose its way in this breach.

This reading—which is first of all *reading* itself, all reading, inevitably given over to the sudden, flashing, slipping movement of a writing that precedes it and that it will rejoin only by reinscribing it elsewhere and otherwise, by ex-scribing it outside itself—this reading does not yet comment. This is a *beginning* reading, an *incipit* that is always begun again: it is neither equal to interpretation nor in a position to force any signification. Rather, it is an abandoning to the abandonment to language where the writer is exposed. "There is no pure and simple communication; what is communicated has a sense [*sens*] and a color" (2: 315) (and here *sens* means movement, advance). It doesn't know where it is going, and it doesn't have to know. No other reading is possible without it, and every "reading" (in the sense of commentary, exegesis, interpretation) must come back to it.

But in this way Bataille and his reader are already displaced with respect to ambiguity. There is not, on the one hand, the ambiguity of meaning—of all possible meanings, the ambiguity of univocalities multiplied by all the "acts of intellection"—or, on the other, the "ambiguity" of meaning that jettisons all possible meaning. Something quite different is finally in question, which Bataille knew: it is perhaps even what he "knew" before everything else, "*knowing nothing.*" It is not a question of that necessary and derisory machinery of meaning that puts itself forward as it steals away, or that masks itself by signifying itself. To leave it at what condemns writing without appeal (certainly this condemnation haunted Bataille), and condemns to ridicule or untenability the will to affirm a writing removed from intellection and identical to life ("I have always put into my writings my whole life and my whole person, I know nothing about purely intellectual problems" [6: 261]). For this is still, and always, a discourse full of meaning, which steals away the "life" *of which it speaks.*

There is something else, without the "knowledge" of which Bataille would not have written, any more than anyone else would, and it is this: "ambiguity" does not truly exist, or it exists only so long as thought considers meaning. But there is no ambiguity, once it is clear (and it necessarily is, before any consideration of meaning) that writing *exscribes* meaning every bit as much as it inscribes significations. It exscribes meaning or, in other words, it shows that what matters—the thing itself, Bataille's "life" or "cry," and, finally, the existence of everything that is "in question" in the text (including, most remarkably, writing's own existence)—is *outside* the text, takes place outside writing.

At the same time, this "outside" is not that of a referent that signification would reflect (something like Bataille's "real" life, signified by the words "my life"). The referent does not present itself as such except in signification. But this "outside"—wholly *exscribed within* the text—is the infinite withdrawal of meaning by which each existence exists. Not the raw, material, concrete datum, supposed to be outside meaning, which meaning represents, but the "empty freedom" by which existence comes into presence—and absence. This freedom is not empty in the sense of being vain. It is certainly not directed toward a project, a meaning, or a work. But it passes through the work of meaning to expose, to offer in its nakedness, the unemployable, unexploitable, unintelligible, ungroundable *being* of being-in-the-world. *The "fact" that there is being*—or some being, or even beings, and particularly the fact that *we* are, as community (of reading-writing): this is what provokes all possible meanings, this is the very place of meaning, but it *has* no meaning.

To write, and to read, is to be exposed, to expose oneself, to this not-having (to this non-knowledge) and thus to "exscription." The exscribed is exscribed from the very first word, not as an "inexpressible" or as an "uninscribable" but, on the contrary, as writing's opening, within itself, *to* itself, to its own inscription as the infinite discharge of meaning—in all the senses in which we must understand the expression. Writing, reading, I exscribe the "thing itself"—"existence," the "real"—which *is* only when it is exscribed, and whose *being* alone is what is at stake in inscription. By inscribing significations, we exscribe the presence of what withdraws from all significations, being itself (life, passion, matter . . .). The being of existence is not unpresentable: it presents itself exscribed. Bataille's cry is neither masked nor stifled: it makes itself heard *as the cry that is not heard.* In writing, the real is not represented; it presents unheard-of violence and restraint, the surprise and freedom of being in exscription, where writing at every instant discharges itself, unburdens itself, empties itself of itself.

But "exscribed" is not a word in our language, and one cannot invent it (as I have done here) and remain unscathed by its barbarism. The word "exscribed" exscribes nothing and writes nothing; it makes a clumsy gesture to indicate what can only be written, in the always uncertain thought of language. "There remains the nakedness of the word 'write,' " writes Blanchot,[6] who compares this nakedness to Madame Edwarda's.

There remains Bataille's nakedness, his naked writing, exposing the nakedness of all writing. As ambiguous and clear as a skin, as a pleasure, as a fear. But comparisons are not enough. The nakedness of writing *is* the nakedness of existence. Writing is naked because it "exscribes"; existence is naked because it is "exscribed."

From one to the other passes the light, violent tension of the suspension of meaning that forms all "meaning": a *jouissance* so absolute that it arrives at its own joy only by losing itself in it, spilling into it, so absolute that it presents itself as the absent heart (the absence that beats like a heart) of presence. The heart of things: that is what we exscribe.

In one sense, Bataille is necessarily present to us, with a presence that holds signification off but is still communication. Not an assembled body of work made communicable, interpretable (his complete works, so precious, so necessary, still provoke unease: they communicate as complete what was written only in pieces and by chance), but the stumbling insistence, now completed, of an inscription of finitude. Here is discharged an infinite *jouissance*, a pain and a pleasure so real that touching them (reading them exscripted) immediately convinces us of the absolute meaning of their non-signification.

In still another sense, this is Bataille himself, dead. In other words, it is the exasperation of reading: every moment brings the certainty that the man who wrote this did once exist, as well as the confounding evidence that the meaning of his work and the meaning of his life are this same nakedness, this same denuding of meaning that distances a work from a life—with all the distance of an exscribing writing, an *é(x)criture*.

The dead Bataille, and his books offered as his writing leaves them behind: they are the same thing, the same interdiction of commentary and comprehension (the same interdiction of murder). This is the implacable, joyous counterblow that must be struck against all hermeneutics, so that writing (and) existence once more can expose themselves: in the singularity, in the reality, in the freedom of "the common destiny of men" (11: 311).

Reflecting on Bataille's death, Blanchot wrote: "The reading of books must open us to the need for that disappearance into which they withdraw. Books themselves refer to an existence."[7]

August 1988

TRANSLATED BY KATHERINE LYDON

§ On Painting (and) Presence

I

Let's get it over with right away (some days of the *Semainier*,* he told me, he would dip his paintbrush in the water left from the night before and paint a few strokes *to get it over with right away*): there is an incapacity, an infirmity, an impossibility inherent to writing about painting, to writing in the face of painting, for which every text on painting must account. There is nothing new about this realization. Or rather: writing is not obliged to account for its incapacity (such an account would only—and in vain—provoke discourse on discourse, discourse to put an end to discourse), but it

---

*This text was written in 1988 in conjunction with the exhibition of a work by the Parisian painter François Martin entitled *Le Semainier*. The work was presented in fifty-two panels composed of six sheets of drawing paper, each of which bore a different painting or drawing. For a year, François Martin had made himself paint one sheet of paper a day in addition to his usual work. Every Sunday, he mounted the six sheets of the past week on panels. The succession of motifs, colors, and degrees of elaboration of each painting responded to an imperative of rapidity, of submission to the daily present of the obligation—as opposed to work done in duration.

It was impossible to reproduce the work here. But the text was not written as an illustration of it. Rather, it seeks to retrace a gesture of Painting that does not belong to any painting in particular.

341

is obliged to take into account the fact that it will never account for
it. Never. Purely and simply. Not even by striving to write this
"never" and to modulate from it, to mold all of its implications.
One cannot dip one's pen in last night's water. Ink is always fresh.
Sentences leave no trace or deposit in it. Everything must be started
over; one can never begin to get it over with, unless it be by getting
it over with before starting. And for that, as you see, it's already too
late. All of this is known and written and has been for a long time,
forever, for as long as there have been painting and writing (with
regard to which, we may still ask ourselves which is the chicken and
which the egg—but, of course, there is neither egg nor chicken in
this case: more like dog and cat). All of this, for as long as there has
been something like "art," or the "beaux arts"—and who can say
how long that is?

In its way—in its way of getting-it-over-with-right-away every
day for a year—the *Semainier* says this: forever. This is not, however, to deny that there is, for us, an era of art (that of the Western
world) and even, within this, an era of the fine arts (that of the
modern Western world) and even, in/after this, an era of art *as
such*, which leaves behind the "fine" (here we are! stop right away!
let's get it over with!) and addresses itself to its own end, heads for
the extreme: our time, the time of a rare, uncertain measure of
time, counted day after day and week by week—the era without an
era. The seven days of Creation that have enough to do just
following one after the other. Painting that wants nothing more
than to get it over with every morning and, each morning, is done
wanting and simply exposes itself: exposes itself to itself, that is, to
you. This is not denied. By any means. On the contrary. The
Semainier is not here to proclaim a nontemporal value of art. For
that matter, it doesn't proclaim anything. There isn't even a shadow
or a trace or the painting, here, of any manifesto. Not even something like the very beautiful, very pure, and very classical "technical
manifesto" of Lucio Fontana, or the 1946 group's "White Man-
isfesto." No more manifestos and no more "manifestations of
being," as they used to say, with such rapid reasoning. (They would
say: speed is henceforth a fundamental element, and there is no

such thing as a tranquil, calm, peaceful life anymore. The *Se-mainier* proves them right and wrong: calm and hurried, tranquilly precipitate, successive-simultaneous).

It is *manifest* enough as it is. What? That there is, because it is repeated from one day to the next, because Martin repeats it day after day, that there is something the very name "art" already disguises and diverts (disenchants and turns back?). Something that has never mixed with the sacred, nor been complacent in decoration. (Forever: since the immemorial, since that of which memory is not the place, *of which memory is not the memory*—and, in the *Semainier*, since woman bore a tiger, since woman has been naked, since the rise of the breasts, since the moon, since the shell, since the beginning of the week . . .).

About the world of the sacred, as about that of ornament—and about the world of sacred ornament—discourse knows how to speak. Or thinks it knows how. One might even say that these two worlds, whatever their relationship or lack thereof (the chicken and the egg again?), are already worlds of discourse. Sacred, ornament: a long palaver . . . What is called "art" would, on the contrary, be defined, or at least posited, deposited, marked out, by a limit of discourse (even within the arts of language, or perhaps starting with them). This is why the name itself—"art"—remains suspect, being a term of discourse, laden with discourse (let's get it over with! let's get it over with! dip your pen in the painter's leftover water, and say no more!). But if we say, as we say, "painting" (and we say it, otherwise we wouldn't be here, neither you nor I), and if we say it without asking ourselves if painting is a part of art, one of the arts, or a paradigm for art (at least pretend not to ask yourself: that will suffice for the moment—"Sufficient unto the day its pain, also its painting," the painter seems to say), we are no longer simply within this discourse. We remain at an elementary, designative level of language, which is not encumbered by the polysemia of the word "painting." We take "painting" as a practice, "painting" as a product ("work," "canvas," or "piece"), and "paint(ing)" [*peinture*] as a colored substance. With it, we mix the idea of something that has its place in an uncertain classification between (on, under, to the right or left of?) music, architecture, dance, sculpture, poetry. This is naïve, certainly. But it is not inane. The *Semainier* presents us with painting, presents itself as painting, and everyone knows what that means. We see it every day. The *Semainier* presents all these days to us: not a painting of the "everyday," but the "everyday" of painting: each day, each time, painting again, each time one time, "once upon a time, there was painting," singular, coming back without linking, linking without following, each time an advancement without progression, moving along a one-way sense without developing a meaning. In short, the dis-course of painting—for it has its discourse, of course. Nothing is simple, and discourse has its painting, and the one wouldn't stand up without the other, nor without music, poetry, and so on. Nothing is simple. The ideas of "discourse" and of "painting" are false ideas, caricatures of Ideas. On the other hand, something resists, something like "brush *versus* pen" . . . Let's let everything happen, let's watch it come. That's what Martin has done with this painting. At the end of the week, on God's day, the mounting is done, as it comes.

François Martin has painted: each piece of the *Semainier* repeats this. Three hundred and twelve times, a year without its Sundays (the mounting!), he has painted. He will have painted. Each day, he painted. At least once a day, he would paint. As many times, he suspended discourse—and especially, the discourse of these days, of this year, this sequence, the discursivity of time. What is here is, decidedly, incommensurable, inassimilable to a journal or a narrative, or a chronicle, or to a meditation on time, or to the logic of a process. Sequence without consequence. A dis-course of time at once suspended and passing, passing by its suspension, suspending its passage (its flight [*vol*], as they say), but here, another theft [*vol*], penetration by breaking into time, time made off with: the painter, a stealer of time, of each instant of time, of his present; the painter, a stealer of the present given him each day, the present of the present day—how can one steal what is given? It's a painter's secret.

As many times presence has given itself back, the simple rendering present of something that at first cut the thread of discourse: time, each day in dis-course, open in space, making space, opening a place, spaced, incised. This has given itself, again and again, and taken itself back, hidden, flown, withdrawn into the cut of this incision as many times.

This cut is not only, nor, perhaps above all, that of a figurality slicing into a discursivity. What has just been suggested, what François Martin's *Semainier* suggests, is that figure and discourse, the plastic and language, while cutting into each other, also belong to the same *plasticity*: but how is this plasticity the same, by what spacing of itself, by what distance between painting and discourse, is this very distancing of the plastic to plastify, to figure, and/or to speak? That is the question, and more than the question: that is, here, now, in this text, the primal given, about which everything has already been said for a long time, and which nothing will finish saying. But the cut is perhaps first that of "each time": each time, this, this drawing, this stroke, this splash, this color. Each time unique, irrepeatable, irreplaceable: what the signs of discourse cannot be. And yet, like these signs, repeatable from one time to the next, substitutable. Paintings functioning as asignificant signs, with plastified significance, and in the face of them, signs writing "plastic," writing tracing "painting" and plastifying itself in this word . . .

"To speak"—here, to write—if I wish to do so (and why would I want to or should I? To what does this respond? And what does it ask? A thousand things, everything and nothing. Everything and nothing from the same thing, from the very sameness of painting and writing, from their plastic spacing)—to speak, here, means first to be exposed to what constitutes the *discretion* of painting, first in the mathematical sense of the word: the discontinuity of stroke-by-stroke. Each time, this painting is unique, absolutely different, heterogeneous, and yet it forms a sequence, a suite, a series, a discourse. Head, moon, panther, spiral, soup bowl, Monday, Tuesday, Thursday, cactus, fan, spots, boat, lines, Sunday, but also oil, gouache, acrylic, Friday, Saturday, coffee, pool-cue chalk, Sunday, and pink, intense green, black and red, imbibed or marked paper, thick lacquer, impalpable film. Each time singularly.

~

   Alarm signal: in the face of discretion, in all senses of the word, in the face of these discrete[1] presences, discourse is intimidated, even speechless, but it may also feel authorized to say anything at all. The most difficult is related to the easiest. The absolute gap between painting and writing allows ten incoherent or contradictory texts to be written about the same work, each of which is nonetheless convincing, and none of which is more appropriate than another. This happens all the time, and it should serve as a lesson. The easy option is perhaps not foreign to the "common" plasticity in question, and one is perhaps *also* right to abandon oneself to it. But we should start with extreme reserve, another and like form of discretion, a deliberate difficulty that lets painting come, approach, and dictate the gesture of writing, which it will never dictate. Not dictate it then, but rather . . . hinder, hamper as it solicits it, shackle as it touches it, plastify it. Another temptation may offer itself at the same time: to imitate painting, to "render" the pictorial by word choice (grain, spot, puddle, flow, trail, mass, crust, glaze, crest, filament, flattening, etc.), by the will of a language that would make itself, materially, into its object. This is undoubtedly a necessary extremity of language, but an extremity where language loses itself. And if it doesn't lose itself, it contorts itself in vain. Even Baudelaire: "Delacroix, lac de sang" [Delacroix, lake of blood][2]— the splash of the assonance gets no further than a school exercise. Even Artaud: "le point de la pointe du pinceau vrillée à même la couleur, chahutée, et qui gicle en flammèches" [the period of the point of the brush itself screwed right onto the hearty color that spurts forth in forks of fire[3]]—there is still too much intention. I don't mean to imply that there is a solution. By definition, there is none. "In any event, good painting will be that about which, always trying to speak, we will never say anything satisfying," writes Ponge (in *Tome premier*). But perhaps one should measure oneself by this dissatisfaction, perhaps one should disembark there, and perhaps one should get irritated by it to the point of anger.

And it is *also* fitting that one hit all the dead ends, drive language mad, starve it, paint it in all the colors of the rainbow, reserve it, chastise it, and renounce all intention. This renunciation is perhaps, in the end, what is least foreign to painting, *and* to writing. It would thus reside in their common plasticity. The rule of the *Semainier*, "a painting a day, no matter what," is an intention to renounce intention, a discipline of discretion: rigorously to let come whatever presents itself. Anything, *but only* the presence of something. This would be plasticity, the one that is relentlessly at work in Plato's plastic *chora*.

I I

Of course, texts are also discrete. Wherever a work happens, this discretion operates. In the so-called plastic work, it is dealt out all at once: a painting is, each time, the entirety of its own discretion, and of the discretion of painting. A painting pushes aside all others and presents its distance from them. And if the same goes for works of writing, music, etc., it can only be said and shown by starting with the plastic, with what is plastic in these works, or with the general and generative plasticity of all the "arts." Their constituent painting, or their archi-painting . . . Discreteness *is* plastic: stroke against stroke, color against color, stroke against color. (And when speaking of fragments, of fragmentary discreteness, for example, one necessarily speaks of sculpture.)

The *Semainier* presents this 312 times and once, at once, just as it enumerates 312 days simultaneously. Simultaneous succession, discreteness as continuity and as totality, do not constitute a contradiction, but compose the paradoxical logic of presence. The presence of something, not its substance or its being, but its being *there*, in front, offered, exposed, the fact of its presence, is, each time, the discreteness of its singularity, *and* the effacement of this discreteness by its position in the in-discrete world of the present and of being-in-presence. But there is a trace of this very effacement. The edge of the painting, and the slightest of its strokes, re-traces the fact that this so present presence comes out of discretion. Presence comes out of discretion, and its coming is discretion, effaced and retraced in its coming into presence. This painting, here, and each of its component paintings, comes of separation, of a retrenchment of itself and of all the paintings into the archi-plastic. We'll say: like every thing, it comes of the retrenchment of every other thing and of itself, of its sameness, which becomes discreteness in its presence. But this general law is painting's to expose. Painting presents presence and always, saying nothing, says: here is this thing, and here is its presence, and here is presence, absolute, never general, always singular. Presence which comes, the coming into presence, the coming-and-going, ceaselessly coming and going from its own discreteness to the discreteness of every time that is "proper" to it. "There is no such thing as presence proper, there is only the coming and going of presence," repeats the *Semainier*.

The discretion of presence is what the thing does not appropriate in its presentation, what withdraws from presentation, and in presentation. It is—insofar as one can say "is"—the very thing that painting . . . how shall say it? . . . doesn't present, but *paints*. That is to say, first in the most banal sense, reproduces and, in another banal sense, colors.

The painter reproduces the discretion of presence because he imitates it, because he repeats it, and because these two gestures are one and the same. Of presence in general (e.g., of what was formerly called "nature," but everything in the *Semainier* still comes from "nature"—parrot, foot, or boat), it imitates the line drawn by withdrawal, the silent coming and going in which presence exchanges itself ceaselessly with its own disappearance, leaving and coming back ceaselessly from farther away, from farther back, from the bottomless region, from the space of *chora*, where the pure separation of forms and colors would be rigorously equal to the total indistinction of a single material mass. Coming and going: the infinite in the finite, or rather, the infinite of the finite. Alternation as simultaneity. Departure in arrival. The movement of the immobile. The syncopation of time. The syncopation of enjoying. In a sense, one cannot say that the painter imitates this: he makes it, he paints it. But "this," this coming and going, is what imitates itself, a presence that mimes itself in coming and going from its discretion to its discretion, from far behind itself to far beyond itself. Where imitation very singularly tends infinitely toward zero, without any proper and inimitable presence taking its place.

This region from which presence comes and to which it goes, overflowing itself, ebbing within itself, is where transcendence and immanence would come to be confused in the very impossibility of their confusion. In this place, which is at once without place and in a hundred places (312, to be exact), *the transcendent and the immanent would imitate each other*, in an impossible and tenacious imitation. Pure opening and intact adherence, the gush of painting and its naked substance.

This region is François Martin's blank [*blanc*], the white left blank on the paper (here as in the majority of his work), which is not only the "background" from which "forms" and "colors" rise, but which is also the reserve of all the forms and colors, and the reserve where forms "and" colors belong mutually to one another in a flat burst, an unlimited precision, a vanished tenderness, a motionless acidity. This white does not have exactly the value of Mallarmé's blanks: it does not simply assume the importance and the "central purity" of "some transparence like ether," but it drowns everything, bathes everything, it carries everything to the inapparent appearing of a profusion that is materially incorporated in everything. It is not the determination of an essence—for that matter, see how dirty it is in places, and dirty white is not a color, but still white—it is the coming of an existence, the coming to existence, singular and fabulous (*look* at the panther born out of the white of the woman's womb), and this is what the "essence" would be here, and painting would be the "essence" of presence, that is to say, its coming.

The white is not the background: it is the division of colors and forms, of form-colors and of color-forms, the discretion of their separation, the presence, ever more discrete, ever more separate proportionally as it is more indiscreet, more insistent on being offered on the surface of the paper. What the painter reproduces is

the offering of presence: not the gift, but the discreet gesture that
offers the gift and holds it retained, suspended in this coming that
disposes itself according to the freedom of your gaze, and the gaze
of your freedom. It is, properly, this that the painter steals, and that
he steals in order to offer it to you.

Because it is not given but offered, presence only comes in the
repetition of its coming. Retained in itself, the offering repeats
itself. Organs offered, vulvas of velvet, cracked triangles: take me,
touch me, again. (But also: don't touch, turn your eyes, again.)
"Once and for all" is identical, here, to a thousand times, to 312
times. What the painter reproduces is the reproduction of the
unique presence, is this: that the unique, the irrepeatable, the inimitable repeats and imitates itself (woman/woman, woman/pan-
ther, panther/panther, or boats/knives/cakes [*bateaux/ couteaux/
gâteaux*] . . .), never stops coming to light, offering itself and
exposing itself to the eyes, from a night composed of slightly,
furtively soiled whiteness where all presence presses toward—or
against—existence. Imitation, birth, both mixed into each other,
one saying to the other: touch me, take me, again, don't touch,
don't look, again. "To paint is to love again." (Henry Miller)

INTERLUDE: INTERPOSITION

An old story, all this . . . So many repetitions . . . Painting has
known all this for a long time and repeats it . . . It repeats it in/by
painting . . . To paint is to paint again, and to love is to love
again . . . The painter says nothing about it, by definition, by
profession, by painting, by love . . . But for him, the art historian
and the aesthetician say it. Secure in their certain and delicate
knowledge, they say:

—But what are you saying there? All of that is well known.
Painters have never done anything else. You're knocking down
museum doors that are already open. And already painted open on
canvasses. Not only is that not new, but it loses what novelty, what
freshness of paint it has by being thus poured into infinite philosophical commentary . . . As if this "presence" business were put
in order because you're talking about it! On the contrary, it is put

out of order. All this discourse doesn't give us an ounce of painting, and whatever you try to maintain, there will still be discourse. But an ounce of Z's or G's (great classical names here) painting gives us what we need. And we don't need you. Let us savor painting in peace.

—Fine, fine, ladies and gentlemen (old style—it has to be), you're quite right! Who claimed to tell painting what it did, what it painted, what it should paint? Pardon me, but I see neither writer nor philosopher in this role . . .

—But you claim to state a truth about painting . . .

—Certainly! The truth in painting, as a friend of mine said . . . But we claim that the truth in painting is such that its truth defies all of our discourses on truth . . .

—Good apostles! You only say that the better to trick us. In the end, it's just another way of attracting the eye to your discourse and away from painting.

—You may be right, since later we'll say that painting is not to be seen . . .

—That does it—your clowning is tiresome . . .

—I'm sure it is. But your obstinence in taking painting as an object, as an object of knowledge and an object of taste, is no less tiresome to me. You manipulate it with delicate instruments, no doubt, you make a profession of respecting its silence, but what a bore . . . Why don't you rub up against a little wet paint: actually, your suit *could* use some color.

III

"Painting brings its lighting with it wherever it goes" (as opposed to sculpture), said Da Vinci. The painter doesn't paint things in light but the light of things, their luminous presence. Light is nothing but the discretion of their presence. Light is the discretion that offers presence in the indiscretion of the things presented (figures, meanings, objects: here a funnel, here a baboon—they impose themselves, to the point of uneasiness). Color is thus indissociable from reproduction. Coloration is not applied to things or their forms: there is nothing beneath the color, unless it be more color. But color is the presence of the thing and of its form, color comes and goes like presence itself, from "beneath" to "upon," delving again into its own bottomless thickness.

François Martin does not treat colors as values, but as an absolute of presence, unique each time. In this way, he resolutely follows the later Picasso—white goats and green nymphs, red and white muske-teers. From this Picasso, as thinker of presence, maker of presence—just as, let's say, Bacon or Fontana, Motherwell or Twombly—light-years to the "problems of representation." If painting, since then, has come back to trampling through these problems (including the cry "Back to painting!" in "Zeitgeist" or "Transavantgarde" style), if painting chats with materials and symbols instead of conceiving (making-thinking) presence, Martin is one of those who persist simply, calmly, in this conception of presence, repeating to us that this has always been painting's issue (and that questions of "repre-sentation" have been suspended from it whenever they have pre-sented themselves).

Color is always the color of "each time": each time, in each place, *local* color, literally. This green is not that other green, nor that ocre, nor that dirty blue. But this does not happen according to the differential continuity of a spectrum (though the latter is always there somewhere, surfacing in the white: the color spectrum, the model of infinite discretion). It happens as a unique, instantaneous stroke: flame, ice, knife blade, desire. Now there is only *this* green, *this* vermilion, all of the color is there, the unique color repeated. He is the painter of a single color: the one that repeats itself, inimitable. *Mimesis*, here, means that this green is *like* it is, and *like* this brown, too, and like the white—and more, it is like the form (angel, clover, house, fish, spiral, pistol). The form is a stroke [*trait*]—a spot, a passage, a spurt—of color, the color as trait, as traction, drawn from white onto white, discretely. An arrow, a shot that hits itself as target: rose arbors collapsing pink into pink, amid white.

Yet color and stroke do not mix, don't simply pass into each other. Here and there, there is a visible *stir* between them: the patch and the line do not coincide, but demarcate themselves (see these women sitting, these vases, these fans). The thing moves away from itself. It repeats its irrepeatable unicity. It overflows itself. It comes out of the sign that it is, and that it never stops being (shoe: this is a shoe; angel: this is an angel; and not "this is not a pipe," as the representative of representation said). It has "a meaning beyond itself," as Proust tries to say about things in the paintings of his painter Elstir. But this beyond is not meaning anymore, nor, in reality, is it beyond. Rather, it is this infinitely intimate stirring of the thing in itself, on itself, this repetition of the thing itself, analogous to what happens if you repeat the same word a number of times, whose meaning starts to tremble, to become dissociated, to become a thing: skull, skull, skull, skull; or painting, painting, painting, painting (312 times) . . .

Again, it is a coming into presence: how the thing becomes thing, how it exists *as* the thing that it is: contour/color, not a form cut out of matter, nor a material that fills a form, but this rising, this lifting—the plasticity—this coming of that in relation to which "form" and "matter" are abstractions, just as "drawing" and "color" are: roses, roses, forms of color, banalities of painting, all things are roses, and "the rose grows without reason" (Angelus Silesius). Each time, *one* thing, an "object," a "being," a being, *this* existent, *such* a thing *in itself*, such as it comes to be posited, deposited, offered to presence. The "thing in itself" is not some transcendent super-reality that haunts another, bloodless world. No, it is the thing itself, as it comes plastically to the world, as it is entrusted to this world, its own; there is no other. It is "in itself" because it is all given over to its presence, all coming to its presence: there is no scene in the *Semainier* except one, that of coming into the world. It is not "in itself" as if returned to an interior. The thing that comes into presence has no interiority. All of its intimacy is its exposition to presence: in other words, its being painted, its being thrown, abandoned to the canvas. The bearing of Martin's gesture, his casting: carelessness, impatience, violence; he is pursued by this casting off, by this abandon; and what he does is never enough to obey it— but tenderly, composedly, for it is the pose of the thing. Its position, its pause—as a coming of dizzying speed. There is no intimacy beyond what is exposed—or else, there is no intimacy, there is only inexhaustible discourse, chatter on the interior of the interior, the buried depth, secretly given to itself. Intimacy is not its own, is not beside itself. It is love and its simple obscenity. Painting paints this.

Look again at the sexes of the *Semainier*. When you notice them, among the dogs, the heads, and the clover, you isolate them, or rather, your gaze is isolated by them, is drawn, attracted, discreetly, indiscreetly. (It is not a question of voyeurism; on the contrary: the gaze of painting is definitely not perverse; it does not pry; it is all on the surface; it strips everything naked.) Your gaze is attracted into the impossible vision of intimacy. Impossible but possible, in any case, certain: it's there to be seen, almost like a painful disappearance of the image into the image. It is not an image, it is the thing offered, it is the offering of the thing, the coming and going of its presence that beats on the blank white, the blank that itself beats, between the strokes of the cracked triangle. There are breasts, too, and buttocks, and desire on its hind legs—and rightly, as always in painting, no hint of eroticism, nor even, here, of what was called the "nude" (in the sense it had as the pleasure source of princes, popes, and the bourgeois): we are withdrawn from nudity. Nudity is presence given (the famous truth), but here it is the gift itself that is in question, or the offering, and the coming—and the going—of what could, for an instant, be the nude as a veil between two strangers. It is intimacy, the intimation and the intimidation of intimacy.

It is not "sexual"—notice, for that matter, how discreet it is. (The word "sex" is indiscretion itself. It makes no distinction, it doesn't mark the difference—what, while dividing the sexes, divides each sex in itself as well, infinitely.) It is something that corresponds to the whole series, to all the sequences and all the pauses of the *Semainier*: the intimacy, the exposition, the coming into presence of the thing, its very *reality*. The real: what bears, what demands, what arrests all meaning. What, consequently, only bears it by its own default and only demands it in refusing it. Plasticity, once again.

François Martin is, above all, a painter of the real. There are other paintings; some of them are paintings of meaning, some of the imaginary, some of sensation, some of concept, each having its excellence, all of which *are* painting. Here, a painting of the real: a painting of the reality or of the *existence* of things, of the effectivity of their existence. Shell, penis, bowl, spot, cow. The cow as spot, the spot as cow: this is not a representation (stylized, symbolic, subjective, etc.) of the cow, and it is not the cow either, nor the spot, as pretext for a calculation of values, for an internal harmony of the painting. It is only, uniquely, desperately, *the cow* or *the spot*, absolutely. It is as old as painting is old, as new as it is new. Repetition of the same, each time different, abandon to the thing, all things rose, coming without reason into presence. The *Semainier*: a daily return of that thing. Painting's return, coming back from so far, going so far away: the history of painting, in this year of the *Semainier*, does not repeat itself, does not recapitulate itself, it reopens, with discretion, it recalls precisely that there is something to do besides reciting the history of painting.

I V

Consequently, no *scene*. This painting does not propose a stage before which to seat ourselves or on which to climb. Not a theater of representation but, at most, of presentation. (But isn't this the truth of the theater as well? Martin has painted for the stage on several occasions.) Notice that the *Semainier* has as exclusive "genres" the *nature morte* and the "portrait"—or shall we say a mixture of the two that the German expression *stilleben* (or the English "still life") could help to designate: the calm, silent life, the simple coming into presence—not imposing or noisy, narrating presence. Once again, the lineage—without lineage—of Picasso, the lineage, without direct line, of Chardin, of Cézanne, of Nicolas de Staël, equidistant from the dramatizations of what is called, on the one hand, abstraction, and on the other, expressionism. (There is no evaluation here, obviously. There will be only when I say that I'll leave aside, regretfully, Braque or Klee, or some others, overly mastered, cautionary, self-staged painting.)

No memory (which is another stage), either. This painter is not harboring something that comes to deposit or gather itself. He forgets, he repeats, he changes tone, subject, each time, at the same time. The "same time" of the exposed *Semainier* undoes the chronology by which it is ordered. There is only the present time. François Martin says: "I'm making, I'm making myself, I'm making you a present of time." Time as coming and not as retention of images.

But these images, what are they? They are themselves "a bit of time in its pure state" (Jean Magnan—staged by Anne Torrès, with sets by François Martin, at the Théâtre de la Bastille, Paris, in 1987). That is, each time, a bit of coming, a bit of beginning, coming to light, rising to the surface, coming into the world, coming and going, a passage of the real that does not lodge itself in the imaginary. The surface of the image, the surface that the image is, where a "rising," an "emergence" happens, but emerging from nowhere, from no depth, and going toward no height. Emerging as the very depth, which does not stay at the bottom, and rising as the very height, which rests on the plane. The deep and the high *surface*. Just as their only necessity is that of each day of the week repeated fifty-two times, these images' only freedom is the strict place of the plane, of the white. Light, humorous, tender, it is, at the same time, a rather severe painting: a discipline of the image, which is not there to pose as image but to be what it is, laid out, aligned, image by image. (Just as color is not there "to be colorful," which would, in a traditional register, means as flesh, warmth, sensuality, makeup, but it is posed there as a skin—of paint—that does not seduce but provokes one to the exactitude of a touch and of its agitation.)

Yet it is a painting of images, a picture painting—is there any other?—and it is a picture book:

—yes, it is: see the parrot? It was painted for a child who didn't like other versions of parrots—

—and it's also a picture book of painting: the woman in the armchair, the head crowned with laurel, the angels and devils, maternity, roses, and skulls—

—and it's also a picture book of bric-à-brac, of everyday, and less than everyday, junk: in prints from Epinal, people used to look at pigeonholes filled with heteroclitic objects solely for the pleasure of seeing them drawn and colored well, for the pleasure of seeing how many disparate things there are in our world (anything at all: discreteness itself, Manet's bunch of asparagus)—

—but also a disenchantment: it's always the same things that come back with the same days, the same wearing away of the same world, so slight, so repetitive, a severe and joyous painting—

—and it's a book of forbidden pictures, and a coloring book, and like all picture books, it is not a book, it has neither beginning nor end. It can be taken in any direction. It is not read.

This painting of images has nothing to do with the imagination: nothing of the prestige of absence, still less of illusion, shines here. (Yet, consider this canonical definition of the imagination: "the representation of a thing in its absence." Usually we take it to mean "while the thing is absent, is elsewhere." But what if we were to understand: the presentation of a thing *within* its absence, going to the heart of this absence, penetrating into, and abandoning itself unto the infinite hollow of presence whence presence comes?)

"Image," here, means rather the emotion of a coming into presence, coming from no presence, going to no presence. Like a love tryst (but then perhaps any meeting, whatever its purpose, inasmuch as one comes, goes to it, shows up as planned and promised, but also as one might never have come—perhaps any meeting merely replays a well-hidden love scene). Please, let the other come! And when the other comes/is present, what presents itself is precisely this: that it's the other, here, immensely far from here, since it's the other, always infinitely improbable, unattainable, having been capable of not coming, having been able to break the promise, to forsake love.

The *Semainier*: a daily meeting, a few hundred meetings with . . . painting? No, "painting" doesn't exist. But with images, not knowing which one will show up or, of course, if there will even be one.

And as at a tryst, it's all or nothing: the instant before, the other wasn't there; the instant after, the other is there. Between the two, vertigo, anxiety—even slight—which makes one think one sees the other appear every instant before he or she arrives: this is the imaginary, the as-if-there-were-an-image. And there is nothing— just the open space from which the image might come, from which it has promised to come. But when the image comes, it is every- thing, it takes up the whole place, it is wholly there. Nothing is left behind it, nothing lingers behind its coming—unless it be the very withdrawal of its presence into its coming, its becoming the other again when it comes. And this withdrawal is so withdrawn— discretion itself—that it can't even be designated. Martin paints with nothing left over, no background in which to obscure an origin (always white), no ulterior motive.

Can we say that there is thought in this work? In what sense? In a sense that no meaning of the word "thought" can approach. Or should we say that there is only "thought" in the sense, so evasive, so discreet, of "thinking of . . .": he *thought of*—that morning—a moon, a stairway, painting. Each of these thoughts-of is revealing, surely, and if we wanted to find Martin's vulture, akin to the one Freud found in da Vinci, we would be sure to find it in them. But then it wouldn't be painting. Each of these thoughts-of, and all of them together, their calculated or random composition, re- veals . . . revelation itself: that it creates an image, that it comes in as an image, that it thinks images, that the painter is someone to whose encounter it comes. (And when it didn't come, when he couldn't wait, he got it over with right away, in three strokes of wa- tery color, marking the day and place of the tryst—which couldn't be said to be broken, since painting never promised him anything.)

It also means: this thinking-of is made of taste, a taste for hats, for panthers, for spots, or for women. It is "taste," of which there are no "concepts" available to one's judgment, fragile and fallible, and yet which judges absolutely and infallibly. ("There is no perfec- tion in art. He who feels it and loves it has perfect taste." La Bruyère) But it is not the tyrannical, arrogant "taste" illustrated by modern subjectivity and aestheticism. It is not an indignant de- fiance in the face of necessity and of the common order, nor the

taste that tastes itself rather than its object. Rather, it is the taste
that the image awakens and ravishes, coming from nowhere, going
nowhere but to the image itself, with grace and discretion, with
humility. The primitive—always primitive—taste of art, the one we
think ourselves touched by at Lascaux, on its first date.

Or with no date. Chance encounters of lingering glances that
search vaguely or merely let others come. A pickup of the eye—if,
indeed, it is the eye, which is not even certain. "Vision" is out of
place here. Another sense, perhaps—one that touches and draws
and colors first. A sense unknown to the catalog of senses. A sense
that picks up images.

<h2 style="text-align:center">V</h2>

"Painting, art of the visible," or "of the invisible, of vision, of
visibility" . . . it's true, but in the end it's false. You see, maybe
there's nothing to *see* here. To chew, to feel, to calculate, or to think
would perhaps be no less appropriate . . .

There's nothing to see, you see, nor to penetrate, in the invisible
or in the buried concept of vision or of visibility, or of the two at
once. All of this has been said, and rightly, but it is not enough. It
doesn't *stand up* before Martin's painting, which has so much to do
with this haunting presence and with its coming, and which
exhausts itself in providing its rhythm.

A whole discourse on painting has been developed, from which I
have not failed to borrow a few elements here. It is a multiple and
differentiated discourse, certainly, but which nevertheless exercises
a sort of unitary hegemony (coming from afar—as, for example, da
Vinci's aforementioned phrase shows—but which has only really
blossomed in our time), and which can be reduced to the proposition that painting is extravasated light. That is, light in itself—
the invisible and unseeing absolute, the diaphanous concentration
of the world in its pure possibility of appearing, the phenomenon
of the phenomenon—would be extracted from its own being-
concentrated-in-itself, and itself offered, as such, brought to light
for us, in painting.

Once again, this is not false. But there is something else, you see. When we *see* this painting, or when we see painting as this, we are cross-eyed. One eye on painting, the other on the discourse of extravasated light. One eye empirical, the other theoretical. One eye on the exhibition wall, the other on the text of the catalog. This cross-eyed vision is important. It teaches us a great deal. It leads us out of a simply ignorant nonvision or a vision reduced to the charm of impressions. But really this divergent exercise is only possible if we have first seen painting. Not seen it as another object of perception (upon which we almost always look cross-eyed, having other things to do with these objects than just to perceive them), nor as vision itself, seen in the element of the light that crosses it. But seen it as painting. That is—pardon the truism—*gazed* at it.

What happens when one gazes? A gaze dissolves vision. I see the *Semainier*, that is, I perceive it, I "situate it in my field of vision," I recognize that it is—painting, a series of paintings, in which I can also see each painting and situate it, recognize its subject and its construction, and so on. The discourses of analysis, of interpretation, that I could formulate come out of this vision; they prolong it; they lend it more and better sight; they double it—we have entered cross-eyedness. But if I gaze, let's say, at *this* boat, soon I no longer see. I am beyond vision or beneath it, somewhere in the image, in a line here, a sweep of color there, in the form of a boat (in the "subject") and in the material, which is neither boat nor trapezoid, and in an imagery of transatlantic steamers, and in each trace, mark, streak, scratch, trail, touch, pore, and skin of paint. I gaze into the plastic, and my gaze is itself plastic. I am "inside," but there is no inside. Similarly, it is the "outside" which comes "into" me. But I am emptied of an "inside" by it: I am this boat, this drawing, this blue-gray. I am like Condillac's hollow statue, which becomes the smell of a rose as it approaches the flower. I become painting, and it is not visual. It is rather a hollow of the eyes that becomes an image (and this has nothing to do with a projection on the retina). Neither is it intellectual. This "I am" is not an "ego sum." No *cogito*: that's just it—the cogito eclipses itself. (Hence Descartes' need to suppose that there was nothing to see in order to arrive at the cogito.) In the gaze, "I" am absorbed, as they say. To the point of going astray. The gaze strays, necessarily. If it fixes itself on something, it wavers and disappears. Thus, it slips or it jumps from place to place, but there are no "places," there are no "details" for the gaze, as there are for vision (the reproduction of a detail, in a work of painting, is an act of vision, of analysis, of theory). No places, since the image itself, as a place, is total, unique, indivisible. And yet, without unity: these images of Martin's slip over themselves, hardly attached to the white background, just barely resting on it, suspended over bottomlessness. Ever-imminent slippage. Very slow, constant displacement of what is only still when it skids. An image is never immobile, never a "fixed view." The gaze never ceases to be dislodged from its place. It skids, gets stuck, trips, gets up, comes back to vision, loses painting, lets it come back, slips on its smooth surface, goes astray again.

What is there in the "media" of painting—here, oil, gouache, lacquer, or watercolor, charcoal, ink, lead, acrylic, or coffee? Always something elementary, on the order of a fluid or a powder. Elementary plasticity. It is more or less thick, more or less watery or viscous, more or less finely grained, granulated, pulverized—but it is always slippery, it comes by polishing and rubbing, fluids and powders wherein vision decomposes, becoming polishing and rubbing. The gaze polishes and rubs the eye until it leaves only something like a very thin blade of a glassy substance, straying on the image, in the image.

It is no longer a question of light. It is no longer a question of daylight (or of night, and not of chiaroscuro either: we don't think enough about what is at stake in the disappearance, throughout contemporary painting, of Classical, Baroque, and Romantic delicacies of chiaroscuro); it's only a question of days plucked and gathered together in the *Semainier*, by its smooth, wearing insistence without progress, discrete displacements of almost nothing onto almost nothing—is it even a question of presence, of coming, of comings and goings, of intimacy, as I said? All of this, for all its validity, says too much. All of this lends too much body, or too much soul, to this painting. It is held together by a mere thread,

from whiteness to whiteness, from one day to the next, and it is this
thread of time that retains nothing, that leaves nothing in presence,
and that draws itself out and withdraws, the thread of Ariadne and
of the Fates, the lost thread of a fabric that isn't woven, the white
thread that goes from a glass to a vase, from a funnel to a spiral,
from a woman's bosom to a man's head.

With discretion, the painting would say: painting is already past,
with the passing of time. Not in order to hand us the prefab idea of
the "end of art" once again, not to stage "the whole history of
painting" again (which would be the same thing). But to say:
painting has passed by, there where you're looking, and there is
nothing left to see, nothing but this passage, this passing, mobile-
immobile, coming and going, barely existence, birth—the birth of
the tiger or the panther, the birth of the streak or the spot—and so
perfectly real ("there is a point of perfection . . ."). You see, you'd
have to know how to do nothing but realize this (to realize in the
sense of understand and of effect).

This what? Realize what? The reality of the passage of the image,
in the image. The reality of the image (which is utterly, infinitely
different from the image of reality, and which is neither its opposite, nor its reversal). The very simple, very clear, very white
reality of Martin's images—enigmatic solely in their clarity, real
solely in their enigma. (An absolutely classical art . . .)

What enigma are we talking about? The one by virtue of which
these things, these creatures, these women, these spirals could so
clearly, so intensely and so discreetly want to be painted, could seek
to discover and appropriate their own plasticity, and offer themselves to painting, day after day, week after week, according to
Martin's intention, without his intention, by the repetition, neither
forced nor ritualistic, of a gesture so light, so brief, and so precise.
Each time, this painting, here, this clover, this devil or dog, each
time this, each time this time here, this time, unique and already
repeated, this accident, this case, this event of painting. Each time,
the whole painting drawn into itself and thrown out with a touch, a
stroke, abandoned to its event, abandoned to being painting.

Minimal obstinateness of the painting's event, of the painting-event . . . unwearying to the point of weariness . . . taste to the point of distastefulness. Not painting as event: something is undone here, shakes off the character of ostentatious manifestation, of ostensorium, of designated mystery, that the "tableau" so often presents (rightly so, no doubt, and without complacency). Painting as an art of glory in all senses of the word—including the pictorial and the sacred. The "tableau" presents its own glory and the glory of its specificity, the glory of its advent, the triumph of its achievement: orderly in the very burst of its appearance. Here, the glory is the slightly soiled whiteness, the discretion.

"Ephemeral immortal so clear before my eyes!" (Valéry)—yes, that's it, or rather, that was it an instant ago . . . but it's Narcissus speaking . . . the glory of appearing to oneself . . . the immediate painter, who doesn't wait, doesn't allow time for . . . doesn't let a thing desire to be painted . . . that's it, if you like, but in a discreet reading, not glorious, not sovereign . . . more ephemeral . . . more immortal . . . and my eyes, here they are, taken in by the gaze . . .

The painting-event (or advent—which would be a triumphant coming . . .)—the trait by which painting is also the closest thing to the "work of art" in general, in the most sustained, the most glorious sense, that this expression practically imposes—the painting-event yields under the repeated, daily, weekly pressure of the painting's event. The stroke, the line, the randomness of a jar, of a pencil, the dreamy imperative of a subject: today, this black chest, this blue moon . . . The coming of this day today, but as a rigid and sober discipline, and like a worry that knows it will never find rest, since the comings and goings of presence know none.

The event of painting, the surprising and surprised coming—stark, slight, held back—held and let go—thus slips fairly far from the "work of art" in general and from discourse. Because of its discourse. Art is withheld: it is this withholding that makes art. Withheld as abandon. Which abandons itself to the limits of the Western world: these images precede us to places we may never get to, beyond the West, but where others . . . who won't even know the meaning of "Western" nor what "art" represents . . .

Art is withheld: it is this withholding that, from now on (if it hasn't always) makes art as a reserve on our limit, a promised reserve on a date with a coming that will come, not in proportion to our expectation, but to our surprise.

Art is withheld: it is this withholding that makes art. Withheld as abandon. As a joy—violent and tender, drunken, sober, debauched, secret. Perhaps these discrete events—those that we look at here and a few others—are announcing a withholding of art that has always guided it and yet still precedes it. A withholding in the work of its own inauguration—and its replacement into the flow of days. A withholding of presence in its coming, bringing, gently bringing back to the insignificance that we are—or a pure significance, delivered from the ties of meaning. Baboon, cactus, fan, and roses, archways of roses—too significant, insignificant roses, and then again spots and lines, dots, stains, births that will never take place, birth places, birth of places . . . A withholding of ourselves in ourselves, outside ourselves, and of an event so past, so future that the heart capsizes in it; the emotion is too simple, the gaze gets lost in it, in a trail of color, the color of a trace, the color of an erasure—which is almost white.

POSTSCRIPT

1. "Let the same thing happen now which occurs in the case of the painters. They set forth their wooden tablets, draw white lines around them, and trace in outline the royal images before they daub on the true colors. They are perfectly free to erase the sketch and substitute another instead, correcting mistakes and changing what turned out badly. But after they go ahead and daub on the pigments, they can no longer erase again and substitute, since they injure the beauty of the image by doing so, and it becomes a matter for reproach."[4]

2. "Post scriptum," after the written, after the writing—does this exist? Is there ever such a thing? Does this after ever come? Even the painter still writes, on the canvas, on the back, post-pictum he writes his name, the title, the days and weeks . . . Yes, yes, writing

is never over. Painting finishes right away. Each instant, it finishes, gets it over with. It starts and finishes where writing never finishes finishing. Writing endures, painting hardens.

After the written, after the writing, what's left to write? Drawings, colors, but that's not writing. There is neither drawing nor color in writing. Text without color or form. Amorphous achromy. After the fact, after the week, and the year. Beyond the link, in the void. The void in which I am held, contained, condemned and also sustained by your painting. Your.

Your painting itself. Day after day. Post diem. Scriptum post scriptum. Week: weekend after weekend. It painting self your— Stop!

3. Again, the gaze returns. It slides, catches, and passes. Goes back. From one to the other. What? Again: hat, rose, bust, woman in an armchair, boat, vulva, dirt clod, parrot, parrot, flow, vase, mud. What? Subjects: it was called the subject of a painting. The theory of the subjects of the *Semainier*: "theory" means, first, spectacle, a great celebration, with procession, shows, and games. A theory of the subject in the *Semainier*: a great celebration of subjects, a progression, a cavalcade, it's all there—the fabricated, the natural, the trivial, the almost nothing. Let everything present itself. Each day is a day of presence. Each presence is its own celebration, its own discrete procession.

Undone as soon as it arrives: "there, heaven with its harmonies overhanging thee, when in the free air thou didst disclose thyself."[5]

Everything presents itself. Everything. What else? Nothing, there is nothing that does not come into presence. Nothing if not nothing. There is no such thing as the unpresentable.

Everything comes to the skin. *Chroma*, skin, carnation, color. *Chrozein*, to touch, to skim, to color. *Graphein*, to scratch, to flay, to engrave, to draw, to paint. Painter chromographer, flayer of color, colorer of the flayed.

This tender cut is not a wound. And yet to the quick: *nature morte, nature vive*, portrait, self-portrait, angels and beasts. Autochromography, heterochromography.

Paintings, their techniques, technologies. Eveything touching skins, epidermises, pigments, reactions, grazings, moistenings, dryings, hardenings, flayings, splayings, applications, soakings, passages, brushings, micrometries, thermodynamics, moleculographies. The science of time, of measure, of thresholds, frequencies, intensities, spectrums, sporads (not monads). Knowledge, pleasures. But the cut of pleasure is not a wound. Kiss it.

4. Such disappointment he experiences in rereading this sentence, "We should start with . . . a deliberate difficulty that lets painting come, approach, and dictate the gesture of writing, which it will never dictate" (in the end, the whole preceding text seems only to have betrayed this sentence, to have failed it) . . . a difficulty that awakens the anxiety of not having let painting approach. And that awakens the desire to paint—could you paint the desire to paint belonging to one who doesn't paint, who doesn't know how, can't, and perhaps doesn't want to, but who desires it as soon as his writing represents to itself the unavowable, the impossible design of touching painting?

You weren't asked to talk about the writer, but about the painter, or rather, painting. Not about yourself but about Martin.

It's true, though, that the latter will only be discussed if I succeed in making the former talk. And the former will only talk if he talks about what paints within him, on his part, on his end. Yet what paints on his end is only the desire to paint. It cannot reach its end. It will only lead him to exasperation. There is no passage from words to images, all the less since already in the word "image" the reality of the image consumes itself, amorphous, achromous. Might there be a chance that indefinitely adding amorphous to amorphous, achromous to achromous would catch something and paint the desire to paint? None. There is no such chance in the postscript.

The writer's desire to paint is a nerve-racking restraint, a twinge, an infinitesimal, inapparent, unappearing muscular contraction that presses on something (the thing itself) in his hand, in his arm, his stomach, and through a whole network in the machinery of synapses. A rush presses to get the tracing of words over with, to get it over with and liberate this trace, finally deliver it unto itself. Such that, in a blow, in a single blow, it no longer rests on the page, but occupies it, scratches it, throws itself upon it, tightens the page like the skin of a drum . . . And let rhythm come.

The writing hand would be handed over to painting by means of another hand, striking flatly, held out, tense, the hard skin of big African drums. (Sometimes the skin of the hand cracks, and the skin of the *djembé* is colored with blood.)

5. Have I let painting, that of F. Martin, that of the *Semainier*, approach?

But this question mustn't be asked.

Writing undoubtedly approaches in some way, even if it doesn't "progress." It gives the impression of approaching a truth . . . It's not false . . . But with painting, it is truth itself that approaches—the thing itself. Painting stays on the wall, catches, does not approach. But truth approaches it. Each day. Each day, a little more, a little less white, a little more touching the skin.

6. The above, too, to be crossed out. Scratch, graph. Crossed out, leave it exposed, naked on the page. (Mallarmé, "À la nue accablante tu")

Leave it aligned, nothing more. *Nullus dies sine lines.*

Colors, once and for all: eternity. Gone with the sun.

Life always discolors. Colors are not life. Rather the inverse. *Glacis lavis.* Rather a fixity of bursts. Breast. Each day. No continuity. Discretion. Hat. Each day the transfixation of a color. Coloring of a fixity. Rose. Approximation of presence. Panther. Almost amorphous, achromous—but color, painting. Coming. All coming. Coming and going.

Week.

Approach.

TRANSLATED BY EMILY MCVARISH

§ Laughter, Presence

I

Is it possible to be in the presence of laughter? Does laughter have a presence? That is: laughter itself, not the person laughing, nor the object of his/her laughter. Laughter always bursts—and loses itself in its peals. As soon as it bursts out, it is lost to all appropriation, to all presentation. This loss is neither funny nor sad; it is not serious, and it is not a joke. We always *make* too much of laughter, we overload it with meaning or nonsense, we take it to the point of tears or to the revelation of nothingness. But laughter bursts—laughter, which is never *one*, never an essence of laughter, nor the laughter of an essence.

Perhaps it is always a woman's laugh and—who knows?—a woman-laugh?—laughter as this presence we would like to call: a woman's. The "laughing man" would be forever frozen in his grimace, whose range runs from the comic to the ironic and sardonic. But a woman would be the presence of a burst of laughter, the presence of laughter in peals. A presence that no present captures, and that no being-present can identify. Let's not make too much of it. If possible, let's let it present—lose—itself.

We will make very little of it here. We will simply read this poem in prose by Baudelaire:

LE DÉSIR DE PEINDRE

Malheureux peut-être l'homme, mais heureux l'artiste que le désir déchire!

Je brûle de peindre celle qui m'est apparue si rarement et qui a fui si vite, comme une belle chose regrettable derrière le voyager emporté dans la nuit. Comme il y a longtemps déjà qu'elle a disparu!

Elle est belle, et plus que belle; elle est surprenante. En elle le noir abonde: et tout ce qu'elle inspire est nocturne et profond. Ses yeux sont deux antres où scintille vaguement le mystère, et son regard illumine comme l'éclair: c'est une explosion dans les ténèbres.

Je la comparerais à un soleil noir, si l'on pouvait concevoir un astre noir versant la lumière et le bonheur. Mais elle fait plus volontiers penser à la lune, qui sans doute l'a marquée de sa redoutable influence; non pas la lune blanche des idylles, qui ressemble à une froide mariée, mais la lune sinistre et enivrante, suspendue au fond d'une nuit orageuse et bousculée par les nuées qui courent; non pas la lune paisible et discrète visitant le sommeil des hommes purs, mais la lune arrachée du ciel, vaincue et révoltée, que les Sorcières thessaliennes contraignent durement à danser sur l'herbe terrifiée!

Dans son petit front habitent la volonté tenace et l'amour de la proie. Cependant, au bas de ce visage inquiétant, où des narines mobiles aspirent l'inconnu et l'impossible, éclate, avec une grâce inexprimable, le rire d'une grande bouche, rouge et blanche, et délicieuse, qui fait rêver au miracle d'une suberbe fleur éclose dans un terrain volcanique.

Il y a des femmes qui inspirent l'envie de les vaincre et de jouir d'elles; mais celle-ci donne de désir de mourir lentement sous son regard.[1]

THE DESIRE TO PAINT

Unhappy perhaps is the man, but happy the artist that desire tears apart!

I burn with the desire to paint her who appeared to me so rarely and who so quickly fled, like a beautiful regretted thing the voyager leaves behind as he is carried away into the night. How long it is now, since she disappeared!

She is beautiful and more than beautiful; she is surprising. Darkness in her abounds, and all that she inspires is nocturnal and profound. Her eyes are two caverns where mystery dimly glistens, and like a lightning flash, her glance illuminates: it is an explosion in the dark.

I would compare her to a black sun, if one could imagine a black star pouring out light and happiness. But she makes one think rather of the moon, which has surely marked her with its portentous influence; not the white moon of idylls which resembles a frigid bride, but the sinister and intoxicating moon that hangs deep in a stormy night, jostled by the driven clouds; not the discreet and peaceful moon that visits the sleep of pure men, but the moon ripped from the sky, the conquered and indignant moon that the Thessalian Witches cruelly compel to dance on the frightened grass!

That little forehead is inhabited by a tenacious will and a love of prey. Yet, in the lower part of this disturbing countenance, where quivering nostrils breathe the unknown and the impossible, bursts, with inexpressible grace, the laughter of a wide mouth, red and white and alluring, that makes one dream of the miracle of a superb flower blooming on a volcanic soil.

There are women who inspire you with the urge to conquer them and to take your pleasure of them; but this one fills you only with the desire to slowly die beneath her gaze.[2]

We read this poem in prose as a presentation of laughter, and as nothing but this presentation—or: we read it as a presence of laughter, as a poem, the poetry of which, in its prose, is composed according to the bursting presence of the laughter of this wide mouth red and white, which the poem longs to paint. We read the poem as composed according to this laughter; we read it as being, itself, this laughter—and we read laughter as the presentation of the poem itself (it offers itself, and the desire it is, in this laughter), inasmuch as a laugh can be said to be "legible"—an assertion that remains in doubt. Perhaps our desire to read has, unbeknownst to us, already disappeared in peals of laughter. But perhaps, too, *the desire to paint*, which the poem offers to be read as its title and thus as its text, attains to nothing but the burst of a laugh in which it is lost. To read the laugh of a desire could be . . . divine. But what if the laugh had, like the gods, and with them, already turned away from us?

Yet we have already read the text of the poem, and we have already received its laughter. We have not even deciphered the meaning, or the several meanings, of the word "laughter" in this text, but this word has made our reading laugh or smile; it has given a specific tone to our pleasure. The pleasure of the poem has also been the pleasure of a laugh. What is the relationship between the two? Between aesthetic pleasure and the pleasure of laughter? Is there an aesthetic of laughter (which wouldn't be any aesthetics of the comic, for it is clear that what we've read here is not a comedy—or at least, that is not all we've read)? And is there a laugh of aesthetics (as we begin, most unexpectedly, to suspect when faced with the discreet but continuous insistence of a laugh, of a smile, of a joy, in the *Aesthetics* where the philosophy of art and of beauty was fully realized, that of Hegel)? Or is laughter, after all, before or beyond any "aesthetic"? Where does laughter come into this text? Where is the laughter of this text? What or whom does it touch? What desire or pleasure? What presence? We know from the start, from the first reading, that the question here is not What is the woman laughing about? Nor Why is she laughing? Rather, the question would be "What is this poem laughing?"—but to this impracticable question, there is perhaps no art of reading that can respond (without laughing).

As for the complementary question "What does laughter poetize or poematize?", there is perhaps no poetic or philosophical art that can answer it. That Aristotle (or another, it makes no difference: it was a Greek) should define man as an "animal endowed with laughter" and that the part of the *Poetics* in which laughter was supposed to appear should have been lost—this background is full of instruction: in that we learn nothing from it.

Yet we attempt to read. What the poem communicates to us is simple. It is about the joy of the artist who longs to present or represent beauty—Beauty itself and consequently, as is just, something or someone who is "more than beautiful." That is to say, it is about the artist, absolutely, whose desire as such, inasmuch as it "burns" him, inasmuch as it is a desire for the "impossible," procures the strange and extreme pleasure of disappearing in the face of Beauty. The work's desire is satisfied in the artist's consumption. At the same time, and by the same logic, the unpresentable Beauty is presented; it is presented as unpresentable, or its impossibility comes into presence. It is "painted" by the desire itself, or more precisely, it is painted by the painting executed by the poem, whose *subject* (in the two senses of the word) is none other than *the desire to paint*: painting of the desire, impossible painting of the lack of the object (or of the subject), painting of the impossible. Its runaway presence becomes the "cavern" and the "darkness" into which the one who made it appear disappears. It vanishes in its own presentation, plunging into its obscurity the one who presents it.

The poem is thus an excellent summary of the main program of philosophical aesthetics from Plato to (at least) Baudelaire himself. Specifically: the aesthetic program containing presentation of the infinite desire for an impossible Beauty *as* the presentation of Beauty itself. The beautiful offered, not as a substance or as a form, but in the very desire for the beautiful. The philosophical eroticism of aesthetics, and the sublime aesthetics of eroticism.

(Baudelaire is Platonic, as we know. Is Plato Baudelairean? When he wished to paint the philosopher Thales, with his eyes turned toward the stars and falling into a pit, he made a Thracian servant laugh. It isn't far from Thrace to Thessaly, and once they were one and the same people. From the servile to the sovereign laugh, the distance must be infinite, but in what sense should it be taken? And from philosophy to poetry? And to painting?)

However, the program says nothing of laughter. And this is not in the least surprising, since laughter has never really found its place in the erotico-aesthetic dialectic of philosophy. I mean, laughter "itself," and not the comic, humor, or irony. For the comic, humor, and irony have their place—even if it is confined and awkward—within this dialectic. But laughter "as such," the laughter that passes through all aesthetic, psychological, or meta-

physical categories without yielding to any of them, the laughter
that takes on anguish and joy alike—this laughter remains in
the margins. Clearly, "The Desire to Paint" culminates in a burst
of laughter detached from all categories—if not from an "inexpressible grace," whereby beauty is eclipsed in the surprise of an
offering.

What happens here by way of laughter? What happens to the
philosophical and aesthetic program where laughter is concerned?
What happens, if the poem contains at once the program and what
is not in the program—or if, in one stroke, it accomplishes the
program and exceeds it, in the same laugh?

Perhaps nothing very important happens: as I've said, let us not
make too much of it. Nothing but this: beauty presents itself in a
laugh, recognizable and unexpected, bursting and in peals. What
mode of presence or of presentation is this? What comes into
presence and how? What is meant by *come*, if it is laughter that is
coming—the joy, the pleasure of laughter? Which beauty comes—
and how does it come—in the "wide," "alluring" mouth? It is
beauty *itself*, and its pleasure, and yet it isn't; beauty is not given to
be enjoyed. We are trying to read the minuscule, infinite difference
between beauty and its presentation.

I I

Upon first glance at the poem—at its bifocal ellipse: the burst of
the eyes, the burst of laughter, which together make up the "gaze"
in which it ends—upon a first reading (which is the right one),
nothing is more visible than the passage from one desire to the
other. The poem is written for this purpose: to bring us from the
"desire to paint" that is its title to the "desire to die" that its last
sentence declares. The poem goes from one desire to the other, or it
is the metamorphosis of one into the other, or again, it proposes
each one as the truth of the other. Or there is but one desire—as
there is but one word for it, which the text is careful to distinguish
from "urge" [*envie*]—a single desire and two objects, to paint and to
die, which are transformed, one into the other. To paint the "flash"

and the "burst" of beauty will be to die. To die will be to offer
oneself to "her gaze"—in which painting is fulfilled. But this gaze is
laughter: it is by laughing that the desire to paint will have penetrated "into the darkness" of its object, only to discover itself to be
the desire to die.

The only, the absolute desire, which has no "object" but which is
the "subject" of art, opens the poem in its first sentence. "Happy
the artist that desire tears apart!" ("Heureux l'artiste que le désir
déchire!"): it is also the first verse of this poem without verse. "Le
désir déchire" provides the internal rhythm and rhyme of this
"poetic, musical prose without rhythm or rhyme," of which Baudelaire speaks in his famous preface. The poem ends on the rhythm
and rhyme of "désir de mourir" [desire to die]—which *jouir* [enjoy]
echoes. This fundamental note will be carried by "inspire" and
"aspire"—and by *le rire* [laughter]. Laughter is the only sonority
"painted" in the poem: it lends the poem its tone. Laughter, at first,
has no comic value: it is the sound of the poem, it makes the poem
heard. Desire, tear, inspiration, and death, these are first heard in a
laugh—or they are painted by a laugh.

"Le désir déchire" lends the poem its cadence as well as its theme,
and this desire, as the desire to paint, finds its note of truth in *le rire*.
Music, poetry, painting, the holy trinity of the arts proposes and
composes itself here. Does everything, then, become confused and
fused in laughter? Is laughter, then, the generic art of the three
major arts? But there is no art of laughter, or rather, there is no
laughter as art, and there is no generic art. Laughter bursts right
between the arts. Before the poetic desire to paint, the absent rises
musically: art itself. What then is art, if there are only several arts,
and if its place is that of a burst of laughter?

But let us not read too quickly. Desire tears apart: it leads to
death because its object remains impossible, or more precisely,
because its object, here, is clearly the impossible itself. Desire tears
apart—and herein lies the artist's joy—to the point of presenting
death as its true object. But if death can become such an object, it is
because it comes into presence here, or becomes the present action
of a subject. Not submission to death but the act of dying fulfills

the desire. But this presence of dying, the presence of this objective action to the consciousness of the subject (the artist at the peak of his joy), which is the presence of the abolition of the subject himself, is made possible only by mediation. This mediation consists of a woman's "gaze" "beneath" which the artist dies—or longs to die. It is in this gaze that death presents itself, as dying.

The gaze is the main object of the painting of the woman proposed by the poem. It is the main object of the painting of the beautiful. The woman is not presented as a body. Before getting a glimpse of the three parts of her face, which don't even constitute a physiognomy (the forehead, the nostrils, and the wide mouth: lairs and caverns, all of them), we've seen only her eyes and their "illumination." The desire, which "burns" to paint, paints only the "explosion" of this gaze—and is, indeed, consumed therein. What is painted is not a seeing gaze, but, above all, a gaze that "pours out light and happiness" (albeit "like a sinister and intoxicating moon").

This light, "ripped from the sky," does not shed light on the woman, who is herself the illumination, withdrawn into her "nocturnal and profound" foyer. But she illuminates the artist who dies. To die beneath the illuminating gaze of one's own painting (which is not one's own portrait, but which is at least the painting of one's own inability to paint Beauty: a self-portrait of a desire that "burns"), that is, to place one's death—or, more precisely, one's "dying slowly"—in such a light, is to *see* oneself die (this slowness is the time required for such a view, the time to convert a flash into vision, the cadence of an appropriation of the burst). Nothing other than the impossible par excellence, or the possibility of penetrating this impossibility, of coming into its presence and of making it come into presence.

The immortality of the one who sees himself die is the outcome of this death, and of desire, and of the poem. Has there ever been an art without the purpose of immortality? This dying [*mourir*], opposed here to "enjoying" [*jouir*], would seem only to refer to the pleasure of the woman who illuminates and sees it. But in its immortal slowness, this dying enjoys itself. Renouncing the enjoyment of Beauty (of painting it), the artist enjoys, incomparably, dissolving in its light, appropriating it or identifying with it.

What is laughter doing in this dying? The woman's laugh is *visibly* at the center or at the heart of her gaze. It is itself the visibility of this gaze. The light of darkness is made visible in the burst of this laughter: it is the latter that lends a color, an accent, and even a splendor, to the invisible gaze. It is as if light only shone, only came out of darkness in laughter—illumination made flesh. The laughing mouth, the mouth whose mere "width" is already bursting in her face, out of her face, is the veritable illumination of her face, is its "flower," makes her face into a flower, the blooming of the flower in a pure coming: blooming out of the petrified explosion of a "volcanic soil."

What is this laugh laughing about—or what is it taking pleasure in? What is the woman, beauty, laughing at and enjoying? She is laughing at the artist who is dying and who takes pleasure in dying beyond enjoyment. She is laughing because she knows all about death (all that she is, all that she knows, participates in the nocturnal "mystery"). She knows about immortality, of which she herself is the illumination. She knows how immortality *comes*: never being given to presence nor to the present. Or: she knows that she herself is immortality: the very immortality of death. ("How long it is now, since she disappeared!") Her laughter is simply her knowledge; her knowledge is simply her laughter.

This laughter—this knowledge—is not derision in the face of the tragedy of death, and of art. It is a gaze brought to bear on tragedy itself, in its tragic truth: namely, that immortality only comes with death, and as death itself. The laughter is a knowledge of this truth. But it doesn't know this truth as a content of knowledge. It is in laughing that it is known, it is in laughing that laughter *is* this truth. The one bursts with the other and from the same burst, truth withdraws into laughter, into "the dim glistening of the mystery." That is why the laughter remains mysterious—more, it is the exposition of a mystery. The burst of laughter reveals that the structure of its truth is to be hidden. Unless its mouth were painted (precisely . . .), the laughing head could be a skull's—and it must be: the text of the poem describes nothing else. The skull is not laughing *at* anything (one need only free it from its religious or moral functions—and this is exactly what the poem does, depicting it as simply "beautiful, more than beautiful"); rather it should be stated in the transitive mode: the skull laughs immortality, it confers upon immortality the burst of a presence that slips away from it. Darkness laughs darkness—such is the impossible "black sun."

Unless its mouth were painted . . . Here, although painting only reaches what will not let itself be painted, still the poem paints the very locus of this impossible painting. Painting's only real place, in the text, is that of the "wide mouth, red and white" "that makes one dream of the miracle of a suberb flower blooming on a volcanic soil." The only color of the text is here—just as it is here that its only sonority resounds—and thus it is here, indeed, that the *desire to paint* is satisfied: in the painting of the laugh. But this laughter laughs the painting that paints it (as much as it laughs it off). At the same place, at the same instant, on this same mouth, the desired painting is executed and flies apart. It *bursts itself* into laughter, the truth of immortality, the truth of death, the truth of truth itself—truth offered beyond any realization, any assignation of truth, and thus, the truth of art. Art as truth—this is what the poem (once again, after so many others, and in keeping with the program . . . give or take a laugh . . .) paints; this is what the poem poematizes and puts to music. All the arts together (the total work of art . . . give or take a scene . . .) as a divine laugh of artistic immortality. The desire to paint paints art, absolutely. And this would, in the end, be banal, if the painting weren't laughing.

The painting is the poem, and it is into the painting that the artist sinks—and is fulfilled. The poem here is thus no longer a painting as image or representation. It is rather representation passing beyond itself, to its truth, which cannot be represented. But this truth is presented: it is the presentation of the artist's desire, which knows itself to be the desire to die in the presence of what surpasses all representation. Such a truth is none other than what tradition has called the "sublime": presentation of the impossible presence, beauty beyond beauty. Not something like "sublime painting," but painting of the sublime itself.

Here again, nothing but banality—and this banality can marshall laughter to its orders, if laughter is, here, the painting of the sublime and the fulfillment of the erotico-aesthetic program. With its joy and its pain, with the pain of its pleasure and the pleasure of its pain, laughter reveals itself—it does nothing but reveal itself—as the sublime flower of the impossible and the painting of the unpresentable. Laughter as pure presentation: it is an extremity that art has rarely reached. Yet it will have done so, if only in this poem. An extremity—but one that purely perfects the whole desire of art, that is, the whole metaphysics of art. The laughter of sublime beauty is pure presentation. The poem of this laughter is the art of pure presentation: art, absolutely, and as the truth of all other truths. A truth beyond language and, appropriately, a truth-woman.

The program is fulfilled. Laughter carries art and the artist into the mystery of a beauty that is "more than beautiful," beyond all painting. Laughter states the impossible statement of beauty beyond all representation, and it presents the impossible immortality of death as the life of the gaze that laughs as it looks, that looks through laughter. The painter is *seen* in the laughter and by it the desire to paint is brought into view, in the perspective of its ultimate truth. The vision of the one who sees, the vision of and by light, bursting in laughter: *theory*. The philosophical theory of art is faultlessly fulfilled here.

But from this perspective, in the end, all that is left of laughter is the absolute purity of its *burst*, shedding the light of theory. In it, beauty itself can be seen—*theomenos auto to kalon*, such was the goal that Diotimus assigned to the eroticism of beauty as "what is most worthy of being lived." Diotimus, who himself was known to burst into laughter . . .

In the end, the poem will have sublated woman into a gaze and laughter into theory. The artist "who is torn apart by desire" will have sublated himself to the rank of philosopher—the desire-philosopher present unto himself in the immortality of his own tearing apart.

III

Let's start our reading over. There is never a single reading—just as there is never a single laugh in laughter.

This is a painting. It is the painting of a woman—inasmuch as she is not painted in the painting and cannot be painted there. She "fled," she "disappeared" a long time ago. This is, in fact, the painting of her disappearance or of her disappearing. If it is possible to long to paint her, it is because she has "appeared"—but "so rarely," and "so quickly fled." What creates the desire and remains to be painted is the trace of a rare appearance in an infinite disappearance. Or rather, it is the disappearance itself—"caverns," "mystery," "the unknown"—as the only testimony and the only trace, slowly being effaced, of her appearance.

But the painting of her disappearing is nothing other than the disappearing of the artist. It is he, not she, who finds himself "carried away into the night"—and into his desire. As for her, she is the night itself, as well as the very beauty for which the night nurtures a regret. She is not the beauty of the night—which is "stormy," "jostled by the driven clouds"—but the night of Beauty. She does more than just disappear (as if she merely slipped away): she is the disappearance into which the artist is carried, she is the disappearing by which he himself disappears. Far from slipping away, she offers herself in her flight.

This painting paints the night of disappearance that is Beauty itself—and more than beauty. But this night of disappearance is none other than the night into which the voyager is carried. He is carried by his desire—his voyage is his desire. The night is full of this desire for the night: or it is the night of desire? The painting of the night paints nothing but desire. It paints how "I burn" to paint—it paints a nocturnal flame, and the consumption of the painter.

(And what if art were to be understood as the capitalization of consumption? Couldn't that be a definition for art, at least according to the philosophical program of aesthetics and its eroticism? Create a work out of desire, out of its failure, capitalize on the expenditure . . . What if it were at this, too, that the poem were laughing—perhaps despite itself? An art of consumption, of the consumption of consumption: "sinister and intoxicating moon," "Thessalian Witches," "the frightened grass"—a whole aesthetic modernism claiming also to imitate antiquity, imitation of imitations in a chain stretching from the burning of Troy to the slashed eyes of Oedipus . . . imitation of the night, and the night of imitation . . . art consuming itself in the imitation of what offers nothing for imitation . . . art consuming itself and offering itself for consumption as the imitation of the inimitable that devours it with sublime and derisory excesses. So, a burst of laughter. A pre-recorded laugh, resounding infinitely in the night, more ancient than art, younger than it, perhaps, but itself also caught in the program, as the very laughter of failure, and the irony that capitalizes on it . . .)

The artist paints his desire, paints himself desiring, torn apart, happy to be torn. He paints the desire to paint inasmuch as this desire is the subject to be painted par excellence, the inimitable subject of painting, absolutely. As if painting itself were something like desire: less desirable than desiring (and as such, infinitely heartbreaking—and desirable). What is painted here is representation as desire: not the desire to represent, but the representation itself, the painting, the image itself as desire.

It is as if the image were no longer the result or the product of a desire to paint, not representation achieved, but just a desire. An image-desire, which would thus no longer be an image-representation. (Which would imply, perhaps, that the desire is no longer to be constructed upon the representation of its object . . .) Just a desire, just the desire "itself," which no longer longs to render something present, or to render the presence of something—and consequently, to represent something—but which longs to desire. Desire that is, in and of itself, already pleasure: the pleasure, heartrending and happy, of going endlessly toward pleasure, of *coming* to pleasure, and not of having reached it. Something, thus, which would resemble the "fore-pleasure" that Freud considers to be the order proper of aesthetic pleasure—in art as in sex—which is none other than the pleasure of desire, and which remains, as he confesses, so mysterious to him. (He discovers it for the first time in his work on jokes, in the region of laughter: in fact, laughter is, for him, the first form assumed by "fore-pleasure.")

The desire to paint is the desire to paint endlessly. It is not the urge to conquer an image and to enjoy it, but it infinitely longs to not cease to be, to come into the coming of the image. It is the imagination, but in a sense that strips from this word all undertones of representation. It is the imagination of becoming-image: not to become an image, but to be the image that comes, inasmuch as it comes, to be the very plasticity of its fictioning—of its modeling. That is to say, the emergence of the visible as visible, the place, the time, and the gesture of light as it mixes with the birth of the forms it illuminates—like the moon, here, with the dance of a shadow. It is the desire to become, not the appearance, but the apparition, not the phenomenon, but the phenomenonalization, its *phainestai*. It is the desire to become the "surprise" that the poem presents as the essence of sublime beauty—the surprise that the woman *is*, that surprises the artist, that disconcerts his art, but in which his whole art becomes one of letting oneself be caught.

The desire to paint becomes art's desire to let itself be surprised—surprised by a painting that will not have been executed as a canvas, but which will have come from the depths of the visible. A painting come from the depths of painting, from a place where nothing is painted, but where everything is in the process of blooming into the miracle of its own apparition. The place and the moment of this surprise are, here, those of laughter.

In this laughter, the presence (of the woman, of the artist, of beauty) desires itself in its surprising apparition—and surprises itself in its coming to presence. The woman's face is painted inasmuch as it does not compose a face but surprises itself, is the visibility outside itself where all faces (and their desire and their pleasure) burst. What is painted is the pleasure of painting, which surprises and disconcerts, which foils all desire for representation. Perhaps the painting of this laughter—this laughter of the painting—is nothing but the rendering in an image (in a poem) of these lines by Diderot: "What torture for the painter is the human face, this stirring canvas that moves, stretches, relaxes, becomes flushed or somber, in keeping with the infinite changing of that light and mobile spirit we call the soul! . . . Does a woman have the same complexion in the expectation of pleasure, in its arms, coming out of its arms? Oh, my friend, what an art is that of painting!" ("Essai sur la peinture"). The soul of pleasure, the soul as pleasure, is what desires itself here, what imagines itself unimaginable, and laughs.

The desire to paint does not long to represent—it only longs to . . . present itself: *the desire to paint*—this is what the title presents, and it only presents this title. But at the heart of its presence unto itself, in the *ego sum, ego existo* of the artist and of art, it only offers itself as a laugh—and the laugh [*rire*] only offers itself as a rhyme for the desire [*désir*] that tears one apart [*déchire*], a desire for her who inspires one to take pleasure [*jouir*] and die [*mourir*]. What, then, is rhyme? There will be no answer: this prose is devoid of it. Laughter makes the rhyme and refuses to answer it.

Laughter does not answer to poetry, or for poetry—no more than it answers to representation or for representation. It answers the desire to paint as a desire to present the disappearance of the thing of art in its very presence. It is the desire for a presentation that disappears in presence, and the reciprocal desire for a presence that disappears in its presentation. It is no longer presence beyond representation, as its model and its truth. It is presence as it presents itself, as it comes—coming from far short of any presence, going far beyond, and retaining these distances in the heart of its presentation: yet these cannot be retained; they are only distant in their flight.

Just one thing, in this prose, comes to presence and is not content to plunge into absence: "yet, in the lower part of this disturbing countenance . . . bursts, with inexpressible grace, the laughter of a wide mouth, red and white and alluring. . . ." The text pivots around "yet"—the disturbance does not disappear, but awaits—another rhythm, another rhyme are heard [*une grande bouche, rouge et blanche*)—the painting finally appears: red and white, which are not so much two colors as they are color itself, the colored (coloring) essence of color—the woman has painting right within herself; she *is* the being-right-within of painting, the stroke as the very ground that could define painting, the red and white right within the mouth, which *are* the mouth and which open it to itself as if at the groundless ground where, whence, laughter comes—unless laughter itself is the abyss and the coming of this groundless ground. Painting is always the "miracle of a superb flower blooming on a volcanic soil."

Painting offers itself in laughter, and as laughter. It is not a painted laugh: laughter "itself" is nothing—nothing at the center of the flower, and nothing but the blooming of the flower. Painting bursts into laughter. Laughter is the explosion of painting, the unpainted essence of painting as presentation of a presence in its own disappearance. Not only does the portrait disappear in the "wide mouth" of laughter, but painting itself withdraws as it offers itself absolutely: pure color and pure blooming, the pure pleasure of a pure stroke right there at the untouchable. But poetry also disappears, the poetry that painting, here, was only to "represent": laughter carries away the rhythm and the rhyme, and all language— yet without attaining a musical value.

Laughter is thus neither a presence nor an absence. It is the offering of a presence in its own disappearance. It is not given but offered: suspended on the limit of its own presentation. It is the surprise of this "surprising" woman—it offers and withdraws her— she offers herself in it, and withdraws into it. She comes into it, and does nothing but come and come back to it. The poem suspends itself on this laughter, as the artist's dying is slowly suspended beneath her gaze. It completes without completing, it offers the completion—the woman presented, the pleasure, art—without giving it. It is the gift that is not carried out as a gift, that is not simply inscribed in the economy that assigns mutually exclusive values to "giving" and "holding back." This is not to say that it is "pure expenditure." It bursts on a limit where nothing lets itself be purely spent, or purely saved. There, desire casts itself happily away, without pleasure taking any fee. For presence is no longer the object of this desire, not the grasping of presence—not even the desire's own presence unto itself—but just the *coming* preceding all presence, beyond all presence. The burst of a presentation or its offering. In the end, there is no more object of desire, and consequently, no more subject; it is no longer a desire: it is something that burns, and it is a joy.

No one knows why the woman is laughing, or at whom or what (if indeed it is she who is laughing—the poem does not say: it is the laughter of "a wide mouth" . . .). It could be irony, mockery, derision, amusement, gaiety, drunkenness, nervous exhaustion after the cruel dance . . . It could be all of these things at once—or none of them. Laughter bursts without presenting or representing its reasons or intentions. It bursts only in its own repetition: what, then, is laughter—if it "is"—what is it if not repetition? What it presents (which can consist of a multitude of meanings, all possible and actual at the same time) is not presented by signification, but somehow purely, immediately—yet as the repetition that it is. The "burst" of laughter is not a single burst, a detached fragment, nor is it the essence of a burst—it is the repetition of the bursting—and the bursting of the repetition. It is the multiplicity of meanings as multiplicity and not as meaning or intention of meaning. Intention is abolished in laughter, it explodes there, and the pieces into which it bursts are what laughter laughs—laughter, in which there is always more than one laugh.

It is thus that presence laughs: it laughs at coming into presence without intention and consequently without presentation other than its coming, preceding all presence, beyond all presence. Such is the "inexpressible grace" of the offering. Nothing in it is seized as a given, as a given being or meaning. One is simply seized by its grace. It is, indeed, death that seizes here, in the surprise of a gracious laugh—death at which the "unhappy" man can never laugh. The artist would thus be the one who is happy to let death laugh—just to let it laugh and repeat its laugh—at the edge of art, at its limit, where painting flees but where art will not capitalize on this flight, or on its own consumption of desire. An art abandoned to laughter: the end of the erotico-aesthetic, the opening of grace.

I V

By all appearances, painting in this poem represents poetry. Poetry thereby represents itself and art in general—by the detour of a poetic representation of painting that itself is a pictorial representation of poetry. "To paint" is a common metaphor—actually, a catachresis—for "to represent" in general, in language, in music, and so on. Painting is the catachresis of all the arts, inasmuch as it is their task to represent. "To paint" represents representation in general (despite *or with* the ambiguity of "to paint": to render the image of, or to cover with paint).

Poetry presents itself here as the desire to represent beauty, sublime and ultimate beauty. It longs to produce beauty's true or truthful representation, to be the *poiesis* of its *mimesis*, and to respond thereby to the essential aim of poetry, which has always been considered, not just to be the primary art, but also to be the fulfillment or the presentation of the essence of art—if this essence can be found in the play of these two axioms, *poiesis* of the *mimesis*, and *mimesis* of the *poiesis*. Hence it follows that "poetry" (and the "poem" that offers it to us here) represents all the arts and/or art in general. This is why the poem gives only the name, "artist," without further specification. (Thus, poetry is not even named here: but it is already here, before any reading, since it is given to be read—the desire to paint is offered to a reading.) Even painting must be poetic to be what it is—an art or a piece of art. But poetry must be pictorial to be what it is: true representation. Each of them is thus the model for the other. *Ut pictura . . . ut poesis . . .*: what counts is not so much the order of the arts as the *ut*, the "as, just as, in imitation of." The arts are not only, essentially, mimetic (of nature, of beauty, or of poiesis, or of all of these at once): they must also be mimetic of one another.

(Between painting and poetry, in the between-the-two that is, precisely, the space, the time, of the poem, there is music. Poetry has represented itself here as "musical prose"—and "dance"; the only movement of the poem as laughter is its only sonority, seems to offer itself at the intersection of music and painting. Music, too, is a model for the arts and for art in general, as we know. Let us not forget this—we will come back to it.)

The mark of poetry in this poem without poetry, the mark of poetry in this poetry that longs to imitate music better than poetry (whatever is not prose) is, as we know, the rhythm and rhyme of "le désir déchire . . . le désir de mourir"—it is by these that poetry is inspired to renounce "pleasure," to take pleasure beyond pleasure, in the act of dying exposed to laughter, poetry beyond the poetic, poetry that paints its own surpassing—*art itself,* in truth— as the interminable transformation of its desire.

Poetry presents itself as desire and it is thus, as it knows, that it will be deadly beautiful. It fulfills itself *as* desire: the *poiesis* of poetry in a prose wherein dissolves all that would not yet be—not yet truly—the *mimesis* of the infinite desire to be the *poiesis* of what has fled, of its flight, in truth, of the truth of its flight *as* "explosion" of dark light, and *as* the "inexpressible grace" of a mouth that says nothing, but that does not remain silent. Poetry becomes an infinite movement from the desire for presence to the presence of desire, from the pleasure of dying to the dying of pleasure, and from the laugh that tears apart to the tearing apart that laughs, poetry "inspired" inasmuch as it is absorbed [*aspiré*] in "the unknown and the impossible" of its own painting. (All of this constitutes, and does not constitute, a dialectic, indefinitely . . .) It is laughter that decides this permanent indecision: but it neither settles nor resolves anything; rather it offers indecision as such, bursting from a laugh that is a laughing multiplicity. There is a laugh that laughs at failure, at the consumption of the artist in his desire (which neither derives pleasure from, nor takes pleasure in, the presence of painting)—and there is a laugh that laughs painting itself, where painting *is* laughter, and where the artist who takes no pleasure in his art is himself *enjoyed.*

Poetry falls short of imitating pictorial imitation: painting is thus the perfect imitation. But why? Precisely because painting, here, is not the reproduction of a model. The model has fled, and this is what provides the model, this is what offers it to be desired by the desire for imitation. The model comes from before all models, and it goes beyond them. This is what poetry, in the single gesture of this poem, both manages and fails to imitate.

If painting itself is the model for artistic representation—and if "I burn to paint" means both "I burn to execute the poem of this woman" and "I burn to transform the poem into painting," a double meaning that itself burns up and yet forms a singular—it is because painting does not offer itself as the reproduction of a model, but rather as the *presentation* of the unpresentable flight of the model and as the presentation of the exemplary, and more than exemplary, night from which the model comes, because it disappears there. Painting is not understood as imitation but as . . . the modelization of the model. (Less the drawing than the tracing, and less the tracing than the color, and less the color than the pigment itself, the flesh or skin of painting: a wide red and white mouth.) Painting models the model, lends a form to its own original—or lends itself form as a model (the model and flight of the model, the desire for this flight, a model for desire, thus modeling itself infinitely . . .). Painting models the absent body and face of the woman, models this absence.

This "modeling" is itself the "becoming-model" of the model, what makes it a model and presents it as such: in the inaccessibility of its flight and its surprise. This modeling is not based on another model (how could there be a model *of* a beauty that is "more than beautiful"?) But neither does it simply happen without a model, as a pure auto-formation. It is neither heterogeneous nor autogeneous. On the one hand, it is given as a model, on the other, this model itself is not given to be represented. It is neither a figure nor an Idea. It is neither anything visible, nor anything that has an invisible form, nor the form of the invisible. It does not fit into the logic of visibility and invisibility—and thus not into the logic of representability and unrepresentability. The modeling has neither a model nor itself as model. The desire to paint burns between the desire to enjoy the woman (in representation) and the desire to present oneself to oneself in the eternity of death. The woman is not represented, but in the slow dying it is her gaze that presents (itself). It is a presence that comes of no other primitive presence, nor from a pure absence. It is the presence that comes in disappearance, *as* disappearance, as the appearance of disappearance. It is the pleasure that comes without having been there before (there was only desire), and yet without having been absent—a pleasure of before and after pleasure.

This happens (this pleasure, this modeling) where painting comes in: in the red and white mouth (white, the color of innocence, Kant reminds us, and red, the color of sublimity). It is here that painting models, and models itself as the model of art. It does not paint a figure—and the poem does not paint a meaning. It disappears in the laughter of the painted mouth. The mouth bursts: it is the explosion of painting, the blooming of color. Painting comes here, arrives at its pleasure, at the modeling of its pleasure—but it is not a painting, not a portrait.

Laughter is what models itself here without another model, and without itself as model. An art of before and after all the arts, an art without art or any essence of art in general. Laughter is the coming of the model of art, of all the models of the arts: thus of painting, and of poetry, and of music. It is the laughter of their reciprocal exemplarity and of their circular *mimesis*, which has no closure. It laughs at the fact that painting bursts into sonority and that poetry bursts into painting, which itself . . .

There remains sound (but inaudible: this is not music, it is the dissolution of musical prose itself). Laughter is the sound of a voice that is not a voice, that is not the voice it is. It is the material and the timbre of the voice, and it is not the voice. It is between the *color* of the voice, its *modulation* (or its modeledness) and its *articulation*. Laughter laughs a voice without the qualities of a voice. It is *like* the very substance of the voice, indeed, like its subject, but a substance that disappears in presenting itself.

Laughter is the substance of art, the subject of art (and the subject, in every sense, of this poem), disappearing in its coming. In laughter, the essence of art bursts—presents itself—as the "art" of making each of the arts disappear in its own essence, in its own absence of essence. Laughter of infinite mockery, of derision, and irony: the subject of art sees itself there *as* what bursts, explodes, is consumed, and disappears. But also, the laughter and smile of an "inexpressible grace," of the grace with which "art" slips away, and each art disappears into another only to bloom there again, a superb flower but impossible to recognize, to relate to its model—on the volcanic soil where there is never anything *like* art, where all essence is petrified.

Laughter slips art away from any identification—and the poem, which longs only to present art as itself, presents this infinite slipping away in laughter. In the same way, it longs only to present or represent each of the arts by way of another, and in laughter it exposes their common slipping away from this representation. (One could, on the other hand, demonstrate how all philosophy of art, including the one in this poem, seeks only to efface, to sublate, or to sublimate the differences between the arts.)

The arts cannot be represented one by way of another—and they never cease to pass into each other, to present themselves in place of one another. For none of them represents anything. Each of the arts is merely the coming into presence of *some* presence, which thereby models itself. Not of presence in general, nor of the essence of presence. Presence is without essence: this might be what, for want of being said, is laughed by the poem. Some presence, some presences: multiple singularities, which are only present for being singular, and thus multiple, which don't come from any empyrean of presence. Presence "itself" only takes place in the difference of its presences—and each of them only stems from a singular *coming* into presence, a passage through which presence disappears in offering itself.

The singularities are none other than those of the senses, and of language. The transcendental condition of the arts is this material *fact*: that there are several senses and not one common sense, and that there is not a community of sense between the senses and language.

(No doubt, a long detour should be made here. What of the sharing [*partage*] of the senses?—and what if it were exemplary of sharing in general and, singularly, of the sharing of voices, and of the sharing of being together: the sharing of communication, the

communication of such sharing and thereby, a community that is a
priori diffracted?—How are the senses related to one another,
supposing we could even maintain their usual distribution? Can
they be felt? Do they feel that they can't be?—Is there a purity of
each sense, or would there be no vision without a trace of touch, no
touch without a trace of taste, and so on?—Is there a language
without a trace of one or the other? But then: how are the senses
shared with regard to art? How could one fail to observe that the
three senses devoid of art "proper"—touch, smell, and taste—are
also "most properly" the senses of sensual love?—And the "wide
mouth, red and white," so close to the nostrils, is it not, precisely,
their locus in the poem? . . .)

Laughter bursts at the multiple limit of the senses and of language, uncertain of the sense to which it is offered—to the sight of
color, to the touch of the mouth, to the hearing of the burst, and to
the sense without meaning of its own voice. Laughter is the joy of
the senses, and of sense, at their limit. In this joy, the senses touch
each other and touch language, the tongue in the mouth. But this
touch itself puts space between them. They do not penetrate one
another, there is no "art," still less a "total" art. But neither is there
"laughter," as a sublime truth withdrawn from art itself. There are
only peals of laughter.

V

This "wide mouth, red and white," which is not that of a "frigid
bride," has the splendor of the "sinister and intoxicating" moon
"ripped from the sky." Its "mystery" is not that of the gods: it is
rather that of their departure, of their absence, or of their turning
away. With the gods has fled the inextinguishable laugh of their
serenity—the "Homeric" laugh, the laugh of the original Poem.
There would remain the evil laugh, the laugh that takes pleasure in
"a tenacious will and a love of prey." All of the comic, perhaps all of
what we call the comic (or of what Baudelaire calls "the significant
comic") would find its place here—and this poem would also be a
version of the other poem that tells how the poet lost his halo in the

gutter. The loss of the aura, the loss of art in its mystery: the very modernity of aesthetics.

But the laughter of this woman, of this mouth, the splendor of this moon and the miracle of this flower, too, form the aura of the poem—the "inexpressible grace." What is this grace if it is no longer divine or if, at least, its splendor, torn from the sky, retains nothing of the gods that is not marked by this ripping, the tearing apart?

This grace is vulgar. The laughter that takes pleasure in the artist exhausted by his own desire and the mouth that devours him as its prey can only be vulgar. At the end of art, if it is not "thought" itself that arises (as, for Hegel, it had to be). What else could it be but vulgarity? "Woman is . . . vulgar," writes Baudelaire.[3] This wide, red and white mouth can only be vulgar: it is the mouth of a tart, a *fille*, to use Baudelaire's word.

Yet she is not the prostitute: he is. "To worship is to sacrifice oneself and to prostitute oneself. Therefore all love is prostitution. . . . The most prostituted being of all is the ultimate being— that is, God—since he is . . . the . . . inexhaustible reservoir of love."[4] Art here is prostituted like God, in imitation of God, and in the absence of all gods. Art is sacrificed to vulgarity, it dies slowly beneath its gaze—and its laughter. Laughter is vulgar; man certainly knows no laughter which is not vulgar and prostituted.

And what if it were the vulgarity of art that was sacrificed here? The vulgarity of representation, and the vulgarity of the pretension of the unique thing, the dense ideal, "art" or "beauty"? This woman, this tart with her painted mouth, is "more than beautiful." If she is vulgar, she is not so—not simply, at least, not only—with the base, trivial, and resentful vulgarity that laughs at the loss of art. Nor is she of the symmetrical vulgarity—which, actually, provokes the former—where "Art" is thought of, desired, as what should be present, presentable, and consumable with profit, as imitation of the inimitable and appeasement of infinite desire: art that takes pleasure without joy.

But the laughter of this painted mouth, the laugh, here, of painting—and the laughter of painting, of music, of dance, and of poetry touching each other and changing places—is the "vulgar" laughter of the senses, which no doubt is what laughter always is. The joy of the senses laughs at the fact that they touch one another and touch language, this other sense, without ever achieving *a* sense or *a* face—without ever achieving a painting that could pass for the representation of all representation, and for its model. If this painting were executed—instead of the single stroke that forms the mouth and its laugh—everything would be presented (God would be replaced), and nothing more would have to come into presence, or come for anyone. There would be no more comings into the world, because there would be no more world and no more sense in being in the world, or for being in the world. The "vulgar" is also, is first and foremost, "the common among men" and what is common to men; what they share before anything else—and in which they are shared out—is being in the world by way of the difference of the senses, the differences of sense. Being in the world by strokes, by bursts, by shakes of rhythm and dispersion of rhymes, by a harsh dance and the delicacies of lava—by a certain death, an inconceivable star, and the grace of a tart shaking with laughter.

TRANSLATED BY EMILY MCVARISH

§ Psyche

"Psyche ist ausgedehnt, weiss nicht davon." This is a post-humous note of Freud's. The psyche is outstretched, without knowing it. Everything ends, thus, with this brief melody:

Psyche ist ausgedehnt, weiss nicht davon.

Psyche is outstretched, *partes extra partes*; she is but a dispersion of infinitely parcelled out places in locations that divide themselves and never penetrate each other. No encasement, no overlap; everything is outside another outside—anyone can calculate their order and demonstrate their relationships. Psyche alone knows nothing of this; for her, there is no relationship between these places, these locations, these bits of a plane.

Psyche is outstretched in the shade of a walnut tree, as evening falls. She is resting; the slight movements of sleep have partly uncovered her chest. Eros contemplates her, with both emotion and malice. Psyche knows nothing of this. Her sleep is so deep that it has taken from her even the abandon of her pose.

Psyche is outstretched in her coffin. Soon it will be closed. Among those present, some hide their faces, others keep their eyes desperately fixed on Psyche's body. She knows nothing of this—and that is what everyone around her knows, with such exact and cruel knowledge.

TRANSLATED BY EMILY MCVARISH

Notes

Identity and Trembling

NOTE: This essay was originally published in M. Borch-Jacobsen, E. Michaud, and J.-L. Nancy, eds., *Hypnoses* (Editions Galilée, Paris: 1984).

1. G. W. F. Hegel, *Hegel's Logic* (Oxford, 1975), ed. J. N. Findlay, tr. W. Wallace, §115, p. 168. Hereafter all references to Hegel's *Encyclopedia of the Philosophical Sciences* (of which the *Logic* forms the first part) will be noted by section number, using the symbol §. For the other two parts of the *Encyclopedia*, I have used J. M. Petry's translation *Hegel's Philosophy of Nature* (London, 1970, 3 vols.), and his bilingual edition *Hegel's Philosophy of Subjective Spirit* (Dordrecht, 1978, 3 vols.). The translations of Hegel have occasionally been modified: for instance, I have followed current French usage in rendering *Begriff* as "concept" rather than as "*Notion*." All following source citations in this essay are mine.—Trans.

2. What comes into play from this point on does not interest me here, nor does analysis in itself. I note the exclusion of hypnosis and retrace its philosophical provenance and implications. But analysis—in accord, moreover, with this provenance—does not limit itself to this simple exclusion. To demonstrate this would require another study. [The volume in which this essay originally appeared, *Hypnoses*, does contain a study by Mikkel Borch-Jacobsen that focuses on the themes of hypnosis and awakening in Freudian psychoanalysis.—Trans.]

3. *Encyclopedia*, addition to §115.

4. Hegel, *The Phenomenology of Mind* (New York, 1967), tr. J. B. Baillie, p. 93.

5. *Encyclopedia,* §376.

6. *Phenomenology,* p. 75.

7. *Encyclopedia,* §386.

8. René Descartes, *Principes de la philosophie,* in *Oeuvres de Descartes* (Paris, 1972), ed. C. Adam and P. Tannery, p. 3; my translation.

9. *Encyclopedia,* §398. Unless otherwise indicated, all further quotations are taken from §396–406 of the *Encyclopedia.* Some quotations have been slightly modified.

10. The term "impartation" should be taken as a sharing out that bestows a content always broached, or "parted," by the very movement that brings it forth. This translation of *partage* does not invalidate the translation "sharing," which has been used elsewhere in this essay and this book. Rather, it accents an originary offering, an incessant parting that persists in all sharing, precluding any fusional communion, as well as any "shareholding" or commerce in indivisible shares.—Trans.

11. *Encyclopedia,* §387.

12. Nancy's use of the idiom *à même,* as it recurs throughout this volume, puts etymological pressure on the *an* of German *an sich.* Usually translated "in itself," this term means literally "at itself," with *an* having the force of Latin *ad* in "adjacent." No single English phrase can convey this sense—the semantic domain overlaps with English "just at," "right with," "in the very," and even just "in," in the baggy sense not of "within," carrying its ghost of some nesting transcendence, but of "inseparable from, yet not identical to." The term conveys the emphasis on exteriority, on the naked givenness of the existent to what cannot safely be encased within itself, of such terms as the *exposition* of objects, or their *exscription.* A moving gloss is given by the author himself, in a letter written while suffering a rejection after a heart transplant: "To what extent is this heart, which the rest of my body tries to reject, *à même* my body?"—Trans.

13. See *Encyclopedia,* §380.

14. Again, see ibid.

15. Ibid., §379.

16. See ibid., §164.

17. "Clairvoyance" translates *Hellsehen,* which at the time designated the power, attributed to magnetized individuals, of seeing through bodies, as well as into themselves or into the past and the future.

18. Which, according to the Platonic affinities, should also mean a poet and a rhapsode, a *hermeneut,* in whom the "divine logos" is imparted and communicated. Plato's *Ion* presents *hermeneia* through the image of

(mineral) magnetism. See my "Sharing Voices," in Gayle L. Ormiston and Allan D. Schrift, eds., *Transforming the Hermeneutic Context: From Nietzsche to Nancy* (Albany, N.Y., 1990), pp. 211–59.

19. *Encyclopedia*, §17.
20. See ibid., §392.
21. Ibid., §349.

Abandoned Being

N O T E : This essay first appeared in French in *Argiles*, no. 23–24 (1981); it was later included in *L'Impératif catégorique* (Paris: Flammarion, 1983).

1. French uses only one word to express the ideas of "abandon," or joyous surrender of inhibitions, and "abandonment," or the condition of being forsaken. Although I will more frequently employ "abandonment," the ambiguity of the original French term should be borne in mind. This and all following notes are mine.—Trans.

2. *Le disponible*—the open—could also be translated as "the ready-to-hand," "the available," "the receptive," or even "the free." It refers to Heidegger's notion of *Schicklichkeit* and perhaps more particularly to the adjective *geschicklich*, which has elsewhere been translated as "fateful." See "Logos," in *Early Greek Thinking*, tr. D. F. Krell and F. A. Capuzzi (New York, 1984).

3. "My formula for greatness in a human being is *amor fati*: that one wants nothing to be different, not forward, not backward, not in all eternity. Not merely bear what is necessary, still less conceal it—all idealism is mendaciousness in the face of what is necessary—but *love* it." (Friedrich Nietzsche, *Ecce Homo*, in *On the Genealogy of Morals and Ecce Homo*, tr. and ed. Walter Kaufmann [New York, 1967], "Why I Am So Clever," 10, p. 258.)

4. Michel Deutsch, *Le chanteur/L'Amour du théâtre* (Paris, 1979), p. 46.

5. Bertolt Brecht, "A Little Organum for the Theater," *Accent: A Quarterly of New Literature* 11, no. 1 (winter 1951), p. 15.

Dei Paralysis Progressiva

N O T E : This essay first appeared in English in Thomas Harrison, ed., *Nietzsche in Italy* (Saratoga, Calif., 1988), pp. 199–207.

1. Friedrich Nietzsche, *The Will to Power*, trans. Walter Kaufmann and R. J. Hollingdale (New York, 1967), no. 582, p. 312.

2. Theodor Adorno, *Negative Dialectics*, trans. E. B. Ashton (New York, 1973), p. 371.

3. Letter to Jacob Burckhardt, January 6, 1889, in *The Portable Nietzsche*, tr. Walter Kaufmann (New York, 1968), p. 686.

4. G. W. F. Hegel, *The Phenomenology of Mind*, tr. J. B. Baillie (New York, 1967), p. 93.

5. Ibid., p. 94.

6. Ibid., p. 93.

7. Letter to Peter Gast, January 4, 1889, in *The Portable Nietzsche*, p. 685.

Hyperion's Joy

NOTE: In French, this essay first appeared in *Les Etudes philosophiques*, no. 2 (1983), pp. 177–94. It was republished in Jean-François Courtine, ed., *Hölderlin, Cahiers de l'Herne* (Paris, 1990).

1. Friedrich Hölderlin, "In lieblicher Blaue . . . ," in *Poems and Fragments*, trans. Michael Hamburger (Ann Arbor, Mich., 1967), p. 603. Unless another author's name is given, Hölderlin is the author of all the works cited. This and all following notes are ours.—Trans.

2. *Hyperion*, trans. Willard R. Trask (New York, 1965), p. 54.

3. Ibid., p. 169.

4. Untitled fragment, in *Hölderlin Werke und Briefe* (Frankfurt, 1969), I: 244. Where an English translation has not been cited, translations are our own. We are grateful to David E. Wellbery for checking and correcting these translations.

5. Immanuel Kant, first Introduction to *The Critique of Judgment*, trans. Werner S. Pluhar (Indianapolis, 1987), p. 397.

6. *Hyperion*, p. 93.

7. Ibid., p. 23.

8. Ibid., p. 170.

9. "An Zimmern" (To Zimmer), in *Poems*, p. 589.

10. *Hyperion*, p. 54.

11. "Der Einzige" (The only one) (3d version), in *Sämtliche Werke und Briefe*, ed. Gunter Mieth (Munich, 1970), I: 378.

12. Kant, *Critique of Judgment*, p. 111. Translation slightly modified.

13. *Hyperion*, p. 53.

14. Kant, *Critique of Judgment*, p. 113.

15. Kant, *The Critique of Pure Reason*, trans. Norman Kemp Smith (New York, 1965), p. 353.

16. *Hyperion*, in *Hyperion and Selected Poems*, ed. Eric L. Santner (New York, 1990), p. 40.

17. Jacques Derrida, "Living On: Border Lines," trans. James Hulbert, in Harold Bloom et al., *Deconstruction and Criticism* (New York, 1979), p. 108.

18. "Über Religion," in *Werke und Briefe*, II: 638.

19. Epigraph, fragment of Ignatius of Loyola's epitaph, in *Hyperion*, p. xix.

20. "Der Wanderer" (2d version), in *Sämtliche Werke*, I: 293.

21. "Mnemosyne" (2d version), in *Werke* (Tübingen, n.d.), p. 463.

22. "Anmerkungen zum Ödipus" (Notes on Oedipus), in *Sämtliche Werke*, II: 395–96.

23. *Hyperion*, p. 55.

24. Ibid., pp. 96–97.

25. "Über die Verfahrungsweise des poetischen Geistes" (On the workings of the poetic spirit), in *Sämtliche Werke*, I: 865.

26. "Anmerkungen zum Ödipus," in ibid., II: 396.

27. Kant, *Critique of Pure Reason*, p. 353.

28. "Das Werden im Vergehen," in ibid., I: 900.

29. Ibid., I: 901–2.

30. Ibid., I: 902, 903.

31. Kant, *Critique of Pure Reason*, p. 353.

32. "An den Äther" (preliminary version), in *Sämtlich Werke*, I: 200.

33. In *Werke und Briefe*, II: 512.

34. "Brod und Wein" (Bread and wine), in *Poems*, p. 245.

35. "Urteil und Sein" (Judgment and being), in *Sämtliche Werke*, I: 841.

36. "Über die Verfahrungsweise des poetischen Geistes," in ibid., I: 866.

37. *Hyperion*, p. 131m 129.

38. Ibid., p. 131.

39. "Über das Gesetz der Freiheit" (On the law of freedom), in *Sämtliche Werke*, I: 836.

40. "Heimkunft" (Homecoming); "Der Einzige" (1st version), and "Wie wenn am Feiertage . . ." (As on a holiday . . .), in *Poems*, pp. 261, 453, and 375.

41. *Hyperion*, pp. 60, 61.

42. "Reflexion," in *Werke und Briefe*, II: 604.

43. *Hyperion*, vol. II, book 2, antepenultimate letter.

The Decision of Existence

N O T E : This essay first appeared in French in *Être et temps de M. Heidegger* (Marseilles: Sud, 1989); it was subsequently incorporated in *Une pensée finie* (Paris: Galilée, 1990).

1. Specific remarks on certain problems of translation will be made as the need arises. They are necessary and sometimes essential—as, for instance, when it is a question of retaining a visible link between *Erschlossenheit* and *Entschlossenheit*, or of respecting the value of *Eigentlichkeit*. Still, nothing can be decided by the endless exercise of approximating a meaning, when it is a question of the movement of thought and of the gestures (no doubt the most secret ones) of that thought's decision. Questions of semantics—which have overburdened debates surrounding the translation of *Being and Time*—should yield to the syntactics of thought or should be inscribed in it. For the rest, we have used the translation of Emmanuel Martineau (Paris, 1985)—modifying it at times, and also consulting that of François Vézin (Paris, 1986). For convenience, we have indicated the German pagination [*Sein und Zeit*, Tübingen, 1926]. [In this, the English, translation, quotations from *Being and Time* are based on the translation by John Macquarrie and Edward Robinson (New York, 1962); page numbers of this translation follow the German pages, in italics. Some modifications have been required to convey the author's sense of the original. In particular, "decision" and "decisiveness" replace terms like "resolution" and "resoluteness." "Decision," in Heidegger, is not a choice between distinct alternatives but an *existentiell* operation that precedes any possible agency; as such, it is at once transitive and reflexive. Given the wordplay in the shared root of *Erschlossenheit* and *Entschlossenheit*, the precise quality of "decisiveness" could be unpacked, perhaps, in some phrase like "openedness that decides (itself)." What is at issue in this question of translation, this rejection of "resolution," is the consequences of the tenor of a thought for how that thought plays itself out. "Resoluteness," like "authenticity" (see below, n. 45) carries an air of the exceptional, the great, the heroic; "decision" seeks to convey something more everyday, more open and opened. All translations from sources other than Being and Time are mine.—Trans.]

2. The formula is taken from an earlier essay, where this philosophical

question was already raised; see "Fragments de la bêtise," in *Le Temps de la réflexion* (Paris, 1988), vol. 9. Emmanuel Levinas expresses himself similarly in "Mourir pour . . .": "*Eigentlichkeit*—emergence from the 'they'—is gained by a shaking-up within the everyday existence of the 'they.' " See *Heidegger: Questions ouvertes* (Paris, 1988), p. 261.

3. Throughout this essay the authorial "we" is used to translate the French impersonal pronoun *on*, though *on* is also equivalent to Heidegger's *das Man*, the "they." The disjunctive union of being-in-common toward which this double meaning points should be kept in mind throughout the essay.—Trans.

4. The political stakes are therefore clear, at least insofar as it is a question of holding in check, from within *Being and Time*, a certain style of political "decisionism" (whose virtuality can also be glimpsed in *Being and Time* itself, as we shall see farther on, and which would bring us back to Heidegger's relation to the thought of Carl Schmitt). That does not mean, however, that we will oppose to this decisionism a politics of everyday banality (management of interests + ideology of values), which is not a politics. In no way will we attempt to propose "a (correct) politics drawn from Heidegger." We will attempt only to demonstrate the relation in which the thought of *Being and Time* invites us to place praxis and thought itself, and to demonstrate that this relation does not permit us simply to "draw" a politics from a way of thinking. Nor will we attempt to evaluate whether, or to what degree, Heidegger himself may later have misunderstood this relation.

5. §2, p. 5; *25*.

6. §4, p. 13; *34*. We cannot linger here over the motif (which the end of this essay will reapproach) of the *existentiell* decisions or of the "factual ideal" (§62, p. 310; *358*) underlying "the ontological Interpretation of Dasein." Likewise, the decision to continue elaborating the existential analytic, for example—that is, to decide the course of a philosophical inquiry on the basis of *this* particular thought (from *this* Heidegger, if you will)—presupposes an *existentiell* gesture that in turn would have to be grasped as such (politically and ethically, but also according to philosophy's own *existentiell*). Nevertheless, philosophy may not have the capacity to grasp itself in its entirety, in the midst of its own decision. Otherwise, it would be infinite thought and, by the same token, complete. We would like to note, on this occasion, a certain proximity to, or affinity with, the manner and tone in which François Laruelle envisages what he calls the "irreflective affect" of the "philosophical Decision"—for

example, "in the end, we *know* why we philosophize; perhaps we know it in a simply irreflective, non-objective way, but we know it with a knowledge or a gnosis that is our very life, *our most intimate subjectivity as humans, rather than as philosophers.*" See "Théorie de la décision philosophique" in Cahier 3 of *Pourquoi pas la philosophie?* (Paris, 1984).

7. It would be as impossible to exaggerate the scope of these axioms or premises of all exercise of thought as to linger over the formulations of them given here or there, without seeking immediately to transform them, displace them, reinscribe them: that is, to relentlessly put writing to the test of their intractable character. Indeed, a type of flaccid practice of thought or discourse is becoming widespread these days, and it immediately represses thought, insofar as thought is decision, existence, and, consequently, writing. This discourse does not, first of all, bring its own decided-Being into play. It does not expose itself to the *existentiell* that it *exscribes* (as we will explain farther on), but rather contents itself with intoning values, models, or ends. (One of the homilies most in favor, one that is in the air these days, is the one about "communication," about a communicational rationality and sociality. The discourse of this communication is abundantly communicated, but what might play in the communication of thought—that is, in thought itself—is scarcely ever examined). These discourses are content to place existence in relation to this or that ideal floating far above it (although the ideal may well be modest and reasonable, as befits the times, and may be presented in its most concrete, practical, or pragmatic aspects). As we will see here, with Heidegger, the ontological structure of the decision is precisely what destroys this type of relation to the ideal.

8. §60, p. 298; *345.*

9. §9, p. 42; *67.* In this study, we deliberately leave aside any interrogation of restricting to Dasein the traits that are proper to existence, or any interrogation of restricting to *man* the traits proper to Dasein. There are other questions to pose on this subject, sketched out in my *L'Expérience de la liberté* (Paris, 1988) or, with respect to animals, in Jacques Derrida's *De l'esprit* (Paris, 1987). [Both are translated, as *The Experience of Freedom* (Stanford, forthcoming) and *Of Spirit: Heidegger and the Question* (Chicago, 1989)—Trans.]

10. This motif of "passibility" to sense has already been discussed in my *L'Oubli de la philosophie* (Paris, 1987). [See also "The Heart of Things" in the present volume, specifically the definition of "passibility" given in note 2 of that essay.—Trans.]

11. Heidegger, "Seminar in Zähringen 1973," in *Gesamtausqabe*, ed. C. Ochwadt (Frankfurt am Main, 1986), 15: 399.

12. A highly singular "systematicity," weighted "against" philosophical systematicity: it is unnecessary to explore this here at any greater length. While speaking of "systems," however, we also wish to indicate the continued importance, beyond *Being and Time*, of a motif wherein "decision" disappears in favor of *Ereignis*. But this occurs in accordance with a deeper continuity (which could be uncovered by certain precise analyses, among them an analysis of *Beiträge*).

13. *On-tique* conflates the ontical with the *on*, the "they."—Trans.

14. §34, p. 166; *210*. See also p. 160; *202–3*.

15. §31, pp. 142–3; *182*.

16. For the translation of *Auslegung* as "clarification" [*explicitation*] rather than as "interpretation," see my "Sharing Voices" in Gayle L. Ormiston and Alan D. Schrift, eds., *Transforming the Hermeneutic Context: From Nietzsche to Nancy* (Albany, N.Y., 1990), pp. 219–22.

17. §34, p. 161; *203*.

18. §34, pp. 166–7; *210*.

19. See §34, p. 167; *210–11*. Heidegger hastens to emphasize that the analysis beginning here "is purely ontological in its aims, and is far removed from any moralizing critique of everyday Dasein." Thus it will not be necessary for us to decide on a value for the "they," and we must not yield to any appearance, any suspicion, of a decision of this sort, even if the text appears to lend itself to one, and even if it does so lend itself at times, as we will point out later. Heidegger puts us on guard, we might say, against a too *on-tique* reading of his own statements. We must not think, in the "they," of anything but the givens and the conditions of disclosedness. But these should be thought of as onticality itself, in its totality.

20. §35, p. 168; *212*.

21. *Bavardage* is therefore not a good translation; but isn't (un)translatability an element or aspect of *Gerede*? François Vézin translates it, provocatively, as the *on-dit* [the "they-say"].

22. The word is constructed like *Gerede* (with the help of the globalizing prefix *ge*), and its pejorative nuance is undeniable; but this makes memory of the warnings against disparaging the "they" all the more necessary.

23. And not to *littérature*, as Martineau translates it—unless one were to propose a total re-elaboration of the idea of "literature" (which would

certainly be possible). Vézin translates this as *le "c'est écrit"* [the "it is written"], whose imperative connotation is foreign to the text.

24. What is read passively, mechanically, with no real understanding.

25. §34, pp. 168–69; *212*.

26. §34, p. 163; *206*.

27. The "sharing" of Being in the communication of the assertion was analyzed in §33, p. 155; *196–97*.

28. To use this word in passing; we will come back to it.

29. It is, on the contrary, quite remarkable that "poetic" discourse alone should have been privileged, a few pages earlier, as the discourse in which "the communication of the existential possibilities of one's state-of-mind can become an aim in itself" (§34, p. 162; *205*). We will not inquire here into this privilege, which remains without explanation or clarification in *Being and Time*. We will only note that there can be absolutely no question of conferring, without any further deliberation, an ontological privilege of any kind on *any* form of speech or communication, each of these forms being under the power of the "they" and subject to the hearing of the "they." Section 27 (p. 127; *164–65*) asserts, "We take pleasure and enjoy ourselves as *they* take pleasure; we read, see, and judge about literature and art as *they* see and judge; likewise we shrink back from the 'great mass' as *they* shrink back." We could then ask with what mode of "privilege" or "separation" *Rede* must have been invested, later, in the *Rektoratsrede*, in this discourse proposed, without mediation, to the communal sharing of the originary, in this discourse immediately proposing decision. How was the unappropriable decision appropriated there? How, at that time, was it both strictly faithful and strictly unfaithful to its essence? How was it both opened and closed off to its own understanding? We have said that we will not attempt to answer these questions here. We wish only to indicate that it is from the standpoint provided by Heidegger himself that these questions are to be posed.

30. §36, p. 172; *216*.

31. §36, p. 170; *214*.

32. §35, p. 170; *214*.

33. §33, p. 156; *199*.

34. "Et c'est là qu'il (se) décide": Nancy uses parentheses here to indicate the simultaneity of a transitive and reflexive act, both a decision on some matter and the movement whereby decisiveness (or "resolution," in the terminology of Macquarrie and Robinson) is attained.

Throughout, I have rendered the reflexive sense with the formula "to reach its decision."—Trans.

35. §38, p. 177; *221.*

36. §38, p. 179; *222.*

37. The reader will have noticed the repeated use of this word—*echt*, *Echtheit*—with an obviously critical or ironic value, as opposed to the value of *eigentlich*, "own." We will return to this presently. [In this passage, Nancy renders *echt* and *Echtheit* as *authentique* and *authenticité*, a choice preserved in this translation.—Trans.]

38. §38, p. 179; *224.*

39. Nancy renders *eigen* and its cousins by a series of terms based on the common French word *propre*. I reproduce his emphasis with a series based on the common English word "own" (which, in fact, is etymologically related to *eigen*). Nevertheless, I do occasionally use "proper" and its variations—as appropriate.—Trans.

40. The authentic calls up something on the order of "racial purity."

41. §9, p. 43; *68.* The context clearly shows (p. 42; *67–68*) that the possibility of being *eigentlich* is the possibility of being "something of its own"—*sich zueigen*. Vézin translates this as *propriété* and *propre*. See also Giorgio Agamben (note 47, below).

42. §60, p. 297; *343.*

43. Heidegger, *Beiträge*, in *Gesamtausgabe*, ed. C. Ochwadt (Frankfurt am Main, 1986), sec. 1, no. 44.

44. And existence no doubt entertains a very intimate relation to Descartes's *ego sum*, although we cannot analyze it here.

45. Therefore, we distance ourselves deliberately, decidedly, from an entire stratum of meaning that is uncontestably present in *Being and Time*, one that, in spite of everything, lowers and denigrates the world of the "they" and makes it, or at least tends to make it, a world of "inauthenticity." Without seeking to explain this in greater detail, we will say that in Heidegger there is an *existentiell* prejudice (quite *banal* itself, moreover, and typical of an attachment to the representations and values of the exceptional, greatness, heroism, even the originary and ownness themselves), which the text does not acknowledge, and whose mediocre character it does not perceive. We will come back to this. That having been said: (1) we must not forget that the same text is what allows us to bring this prejudice to light, nor must we forget that the same text designates its own relation to the originary as undecidable for the ("average") understanding, and therefore puts us on guard against belief in a

sort of philosophical performativity that would make ownness exist by naming it. Despite this prejudice, there is perhaps no other philosophical text that refers us more forcefully than this one does to the exteriority of the experience that it attempts to analyze. As we will try to make clear later, experience (the decision of existence) is *exscribed* here rather than "inscribed." (2) We will not undertake—in a reversal of the text's naïve prejudice—any valorization of banality, to the detriment of the exceptional. That would be ridiculous. Instead, we will try to extract ourselves from all gestures of valorization and from their prejudices or presuppositions, not to flaunt a space of indifference or nihilism, but rather to let decision open even more to existence, from which can and should proceed all affirmations of "values"—which is to say, first of all, the affirmation of that invaluable value, exceeding all value, which can be called, with the term Kant opposes to "value," the *dignity* of existence as such. *Being and Time* should be read as a book of this dignity, the sense or the sentiment of which forms *the other* "prejudice" (or the "factual ideal"; see note 6, above) of the same book.

46. Which is also to say, *freed for*. "Freedom"—a singular freedom, which is the most inalienable ownness of the most inassimilable ownlessness—is directly and essentially in play in decision, as decision. See *L'Expérience de la liberté*.

47. Such is the *sense* of Derridean *différance*. It differs/defers (the Being of) Being's difference-of-Being; or it differs/defers (the Being of) the difference-of-Being of existence and its action.

48. §60, p. 298; *345*. We will simply say "factual" for *faktisch* so as to preserve the value of the mundane, material, carnal, existential *fact*, which is what matters. But we have not forgotten the singularity of the "fact" that Heidegger thus seeks to designate and distinguish from *Tatsächlichkeit*, or the immediate, raw "state of things." (We would like to ask, however, whether there is ever anything so "raw.") In this respect, we must refer to the remarkable analysis carried out by Giorgio Agamben; see "La passion de la facticité," in *Heidegger: Questions ouvertes* (Paris, 1988). This text also replies, in many respects, to what we attempt to say here about ownness, ownlessness, and the maintenance of the one by the other and in the other.

49. §60, p. 298; *344*.

50. §60, p. 298; *345*.

51. Here, we will make use of an expediency of translation for *schuldig*: it can have neither simply the sense of "guilt," which is too moral, nor

simply that of "debt," which is too economic. But in guilt as well as in debt, one is *responsible*. It is precisely a question here of *responding to the call of a friendly voice*, which is the voice of Dasein's difference from itself. We will say, therefore, "responsible"—with the obligation to return elsewhere to that for which we have taken this risk and this responsibility.

52. §57, p. 278; *323*.

53. Ibid.

54. §60, p. 300; *347*. That everything from this point on in Heidegger should imply "death," and the "ahead-of-itself" of existence in or toward death, is certainly of the greatest importance. We will excuse ourselves, however, from speaking about this in the limited scope of this essay. Anyway, a too exclusively "mortal" mood is not necessary for an understanding of what is in play: "death" is only the ownness of "possibility" as such, that is, the ownness of essential ownlessness. And that is just as well said and understood, if not better said and understood, in a mood that is resolutely affirmative of existence.

55. §62, p. 310; *358*.

56. Ibid. It is remarkable that Heidegger, having named these moods, goes on to declare that their analysis would transgress the limits of the analytic. This declaration greatly resembles an evasion—more precisely, an evasion of *joy*, since anxiety constitutes the object of a long existential investigation. But isn't the knot of anxiety and joy what *makes* the decision itself—the decision of existence? And, in this knot, if anxiety forms the "knotted" aspect of a passivity that lets itself be abandoned and opened, doesn't joy form the "knotting," or rather the "unknotting"— that is, the "cutting-through"—of decision, all the knots of existence being Gordian knots? But here, the sword that cuts would not be military or imperial but strangely passive. In any case, we would like to suggest briefly, in conclusion, that this is so, and thus suggest a "Spinozan" reading, or rewriting, of *Being and Time*.

57. §62, p. 310; *358*. The word *gerüstet*, which Martineau translates as "vigoreux" (and which Vézin only very indirectly translates, as "la joie d'être à la mesure de cette possibilité"), gives joy a heroic, almost warlike, overtone (*gerüstet*: equipped from head to toe, outfitted for), in which we cannot fail to note the ethical-political harmonics proper to a climate of "conservative revolution." We will therefore dispense with this word here, keeping "joy" without any attribute—and thinking of Spinoza. All the "violence" of the interpretation that we have proposed can perhaps be reduced to this: drawing this *gerüstet* away from the *Entschlossenheit*.

How could we think that joy can be "equipped" and "harnessed," if it gains its firmness and lightheartedness only from abandoning itself to the openedness of disclosure?

58. §59, p. 295; *341.*

The Jurisdiction of the Hegelian Monarch

NOTE: This translation first appeared in *Social Research* 49, no. 2 (summer 1982), pp. 481–516.

1. G. W. F. Hegel, *Hegel's Philosophy of Right,* trans. T. M. Knox (Oxford, 1952), §347, p. 217. Other references to this work will be made in the text by paragraph number. The translation has occasionally been modified.—Trans.

2. Cf. *Le Collège de sociologie* (Paris, 1979), p. 533.

3. Eugène Fleishmann, *La Science universelle ou la logique de Hegel* (Paris, 1968); Eric Weil, *Hegel et la philosophie du droit* (Paris, 1979); Bernard Bourgeois, "Le Prince hegelien," in *Hegel et la philosophie du droit* (Paris, 1979).

4. Theodor W. Adorno, *Trois Études sur Hegel* (Paris, 1979).

5. Eric Weil, *Hegel et l'etat* (Paris, 1974), p. 60.

6. Hegel, *The Phenomenology of Mind,* trans. J. B. Baillie (New York, 1967), p. 804.—Trans.

7. See the text edited by G. Planty-Bonjour, Presses Universitaires de France, p. 144.

8. See p. 110 of the Taminiaux translation, published by Payot.

9. Ibid., p. 199.

10. Hegel, *Der Geist des Christentums,* ed. Werner Hamacher (Ullstein, 1978), p. 362. The translation is ours.—Trans.

11. Ilting edition, 3: 679.

12. Hegel, *The Scientific Ways of Treating Law,* trans. T. M. Knox (Philadelphia), pp. 123–24.—Trans.

13. Ilting edition, p. 678.

14. *Phenomenology,* p. 154—Trans.

15. Ibid., p. 155, translation modified—Trans.

Finite History

NOTE: This essay first appeared in David Carroll, ed., *The States of "Theory": History, Art, and Critical Discourse* (New York, 1990), pp. 149–72; © Columbia University Press, New York. Used by permission.

1. Marx never accepted the representation of history as a subject. He always insisted that history is "the activity of man." In this sense—not to mention the additional analysis of Marx that would be necessary—I am attempting here nothing other than a reelaboration, in a quite different historico-philosophical context, of this indication. I take the occasion of this first note to apologize for my poor English, which makes not only the language poor, but also the discourse rough. But I express my gratitude to those who helped me to make, at least, this experience possible: Elizabeth Bloomfield, Brian Holmes.

2. Else Morante, *History: A Novel*, trans. William Weaver (New York, 1977).

3. G. W. F. Hegel, "Introduction," in *The Philosophy of History*, trans. J. Sibree (New York, 1956), p. 21.

4. Theodor W. Adorno, *Negative Dialectics*, trans. E. B. Ashton (New York, 1983), p. 129.

5. Karl Marx, *The Holy Family*, in *Writings of the Young Marx on Philosophy and Society*, trans. Loyd D. Easton and Kurt H. Guddat (New York, 1967), pp. 385, 382.

6. Jean-François Lyotard, *L'Enthousiasme* (Paris, 1986), p. 77.

7. Jacques Derrida, *Writing and Difference*, trans. Allan Bass (Chicago, 1978), p. 291 (translation modified); idem, *Dissemination*, trans. Barbara Johnson (Chicago, 1981), p. 184. Similar remarks can already be found in *The Origin of Geometry*.

8. Marx, *Grundrisse: Introduction to the Critique of Political Economy*, trans. Martin Nicolaus (New York, 1973), p. 109.

9. Martin Heidegger, "Art and Space," trans. Charles H. Seibert, in *Man and World* 6 (1973): 5; translation modified.

10. Marx, *Grundrisse*, p. 100.

11. See Heidegger, *Being and Time*, trans. John Macquarrie and Edward Robinson (New York, 1962); Derrida, *Writing and Difference*, p. 114; and Christopher Fynsk, *Heidegger: Thought and Historicity* (Ithaca, 1986), p. 47.

12. Heidegger, *Being and Time*, §74, p. 386, *438*; translation modified.

13. See ibid., §84, and the commentary by Paul Ricoeur in vol. 3 of *Time and Narrative*, trans. Kathleen Blamey and David Pellauer (Chicago, 1988).

14. Cf. my *L'Expérience de la liberté* (Paris, 1988).

15. Suzanne Gearhart, "The Critical Moment of (the Philosophy of) History," manuscript.

16. Werner Hamacher, "Ueber einige Unterschiede zwischen der Ge-

schichte literarischer und der Geschichte phänomenaler Ereignisse." *Akten der 7en Internationalen Germanisher Kongress* (Göttingen, 1985), vol. II.

17. As Lyotard claims in *L'Enthousiasme,* pp. 45–46.

18. Hannah Arendt, "The Concept of History," appears in *Between Past and Future* (New York, 1968).

19. Walter Benjamin, "Theses on the Philosophy of History," appears in *Illuminations,* trans. Harry Zohn (New York, 1969).

20. Benjamin, "Theses on the Philosophy of History," Thesis 14, in *Illuminations,* p. 261; translation modified.

21. Henri Birault, *Heidegger et l'expérience de la pensée* (Paris, 1979), p. 545.

The Heart of Things

NOTE: This essay appeared in French in *Alea,* no. 9 (1989); it was subsequently incorporated into *Une pensée finie* (Paris: Galilée, 1990).

1. Patrice Loraux, "Une phrase risquée," in *L'Ecrit du temps,* no. 18 (Paris, 1988). [All translations from French sources will be our own unless an English edition is indicated.—Trans.]

2. "Passibility" is defined, in the *Oxford English Dictionary,* as the "capability of suffering, or of receiving, impressions from external agents." We should note, however, that its French cognate also conveys the sense of the English word "liability."—Trans.

3. "What does *there is* mean (to say) as soon as what there is is removed out of reach of the *it is,* the *this is,* the *c'est,* the *ceci est,* out of reach of the *ostention* of all presence?" Jacques Derrida, *Glas,* trans. J. P. Leavey, Jr., and R. Rand (Lincoln, Nebraska, 1986), p. 167 (translation modified).

4. See Pierre Alféri's analysis of the relation of the sign to Ockham's "ultimate singular being," in *Guillaume d'Ockham: Le Singulier* (Paris, 1989).

5. See "Exscription," in this volume. This motif of the impossibility of naming ties in with some of the motifs pursued by Jacques Derrida concerning the *khôra;* see "*Dénégations,*" in *Psyché* (Paris, 1987), pp. 535–96.

6. Alexandre García-Düttmann, *La Parole donnée* (Paris, 1990).

7. "The Thing," in Martin Heidegger, *Poetry, Language, Thought* trans. A. Hofstadter (New York, 1971), pp. 181–82 (translation modified).

8. Malcom Lowry, *Under the Volcano,* quoted by Clement Rosset,

"Reality and the Untheorizable," in Thomas M. Kavanagh, ed., *The Limits of Theory* (Stanford, 1989), p. 95; Jacques Roubaud, *Quelque chose noir* (Paris, 1986), p. 76; and also "the *idion* of the thing, which dictates according to its muteness, in other words singularly, a description of itself," Jacques Derrida, *Signéponge/Signsponge*, trans. R. Rand (New York, 1984), p. 46.

9. John Cage, *Pour les oiseaux*, interview with Daniel Charles (Paris, 1976).

10. Rémi Brague, *Aristote et la question du monde* (Paris, 1988), p. 313.

11. Heidegger, *What Is a Thing?* (Chicago, 1967), trans. W. Barton and V. Deutsch, pp. 14–15.

12. Doubtless another version of the ontology that Alféri garners from Ockham: "poor," "reduced to but little," "indebted" to a reason that is neither cause nor principle.

13. Maurice Blanchot, *The Writing of the Disaster*, trans. A. Smock (Lincoln, Nebraska, 1986), pp. 5–6.

14. But "consciousness" could in turn be the very thing of mediation, or mediation as thing—and would then be brusquely torn from the pure relationship of mediation that seems to constitute it, for Hegel in particular. It goes without saying that consciousness thus given as a thing would have nothing to do with the object of a psychology. It would coincide with the point of consciousness without self-consciousness that lies at the heart of consciousness and that the latter knows only as the hard, nocturnal point from which it proceeds and to which, in the end, it penetrates.

15. Here it would be necessary to analyze at length "things" as *vorhanden* and *zuhanden* in Heidegger's *Being and Time* (trans. J. Macquarrie and E. Robinson [New York, 1962]). For the moment, provisionally, we will retain only the tone—for example, of this sentence from section 27, treating the mode of "they": "But because the phenomenon of the world itself gets passed over in this absorption in the world, its place gets taken by what is present-at-hand within-the-world, namely, Things" (p. 163). This classically modern suspicion of "things" is obviously insufficient for the ontology of *Dasein*.

16. That is, *a* principle is needed for what, in principle, does not allow itself to be returned to a unity. Or rather, *a knowledge* must be implied for what Badiou calls "the multiple without any other predicate than its multiplicity," or "the inconsistent multiple of whatever situation." In these conditions, "emptiness" itself, to continue following Badiou—this

"emptiness" that I would designate as the absent space of the discretion of things—"is multiple, is the first multiple." See *L'Être et l'événement* (Paris, 1988), pp. 31, 36, 72.

17. This withdrawal of the cause into the thing, determining the characteristic mode of a *fact* of freedom, is discussed in my *L'Expérience de la liberté* (Paris, 1988).

18. *Causa*: an affair where interests are at stake, from which the "cause" is derived, either as the good reason supporting a litigant or as the occasion, the event, by which some affair comes about.

Corpus

NOTE: This essay was written to be presented at the 1990 meeting of the International Association for Philosophy and Literature held at the University of California, Irvine; the overall topic of that meeting was "the body." We are very grateful to Juliet Flower MacCannell and Avital Ronell for extensive suggestions that helped shape the final translation.

1. *Entree* is being used here both in the sense of a dictionary entry and in that of the openings, or orifices, of the body.—Trans.

2. Bernard of Clairvaux, *De Diversis*, sermo 74, *Patrologia Latina* 193, c; 695.

3. See the formula Origen uses to designate Christ as "visible image of the invisible God." Christ, the "new Adam," whose "glorified body" is the singular property beyond death, has not always been thought of as a savior. His incarnation has also been thought of, especially in the high Middle Ages, as pure manifestation, as the radiance of God in his creation, or as the supplement that perfects creation.

4. Plato, *Phaedo*, 82e; *Gorgias*, 493a.

5. In Merleau-Ponty, the same obsession characterizes the thought of "the joint property between feeling and being felt" ("L'oeil et l'esprit," *Temps modernes*, no. 184–85 [1961], p. 187), or that of the "body [that] belongs to the order of things in the same way that the world is universal flesh" (*Le visible et l'invisible* [Paris, 1964], p. 181), or that of the flesh as "an *internally* shaped mass" (emphasis mine; ibid., p. 193). For the body in Hegel, see *The Phenomenology of Mind*, trans. J. B. Baillie (New York, 1967), pp. 337–72.

6. Merleau-Ponty, *Résumés de cours* (Paris, 1968), p. 177.

7. Roland Barthes, *Essais critiques* (Paris, 1982), p. 143.

8. How is this played back in the other areas of art? According to

which identity and which difference? This would have to be investigated elsewhere.

9. St. Thomas Aquinas, *Summa Theologica*, Ia, qu. 91, 3.

10. Merleau-Ponty, *Le Visible et l'invisible* (Paris, 1959), p. 192.

11. See n. 4 above and also Valéry: "There is no name to designate our sense of the substance of our presence, our actions and feelings, not only in their actuality, but also in an imminent, deferred, or purely potential state—something more remote and yet less intimate than our secret thoughts" ("Some Simple Reflections on the Body," trans. Ralph Mannheim in *The Collected Works of Paul Valéry* (New York, 1964), 13: 36.

12. Derrida has analyzed the insidious return of the "spirit" in Heidegger after his setting aside Spirit in *Being and Time* (*De l'esprit* [Paris, 1988]). One could also investigate the absence, in *Being and Time*, of an analysis of the body, which Heidegger considers extraneous to his project (p. 108 of the German edition). Heidegger keeps certain references to the phenomenology of the "body proper" and to Scheler, but their status is not clear.

13. See my *L'Insacrifiable*, forthcoming.

14. Marcel Henaff, *Sade, l'invention du corps libertin* [Paris, 1978], p. 322.

15. Elaine Scarry, *The Body in Pain: The Making and Unmaking of the World* [New York, 1985], pp. 35, 45.

16. The author is playing here on *ravaler ses mots*, "to retract one's words," but literally to "swallow" them—Trans.

17. Gilles Deleuze and Félix Guattari, "How Do You Make Yourself a Body Without Organs?," in *A Thousand Plateaux: Capitalism and Schizophrenia*, trans. Brian Massumi (Minneapolis, 1987), pp. 149–66.

18. The author uses the idiom *se réjouir*, "to look forward to something," in its literal sense "enjoy oneself again"—Trans.

19. Al Lingis, "L'ivresse des profondeurs," trans. N. and D. Janicaud, *Poësie* 51 (1989).

In Statu Nascendi

1. Jean-François Lyotard, in particular, has already contributed; see "Principales tendances actuelles de l'étude psychanalytique des expressions artistiques et littéraires," in *Dérive à partir de Marx et Freud* (Paris, 1973), and "Freud selon Cézanne," in *Des dispositifs pulsionnels* (Paris, 1973). It appears that, since this time, the question has not been taken up

extensively; instead, it has been covered over by other matters concerning psychoanalysis. The present text dates from 1977, and I have not tried to "update" it, since its question still appears quite new, if I may say so.

2. None of the common English expressions—"form and matter," "form and ground," "form and content"—are perfectly able to render the opposition of *forme et fond* developed here. Therefore, "fundament" will be used to designate the stubborn belief in an underlying element that functions as the repository of essential realities, divorced from merely accidental forms.—Trans.

3. *Jokes and Their Relation to the Unconscious*, in *The Standard Edition of the Complete Psychological Works of Sigmund Freud* (London, 1960), ed. and trans. J. Strachey (henceforth *SE*), 8: 179; further references to this text will be indicated by page numbers in parentheses in the text. Certain small modifications have been made in the translations of the *SE*, notably for the words *Verlockungsprämie* and *Tendenz*, which are rendered as "premium of pleasure" and "tendency." Throughout, the German word *Witz* has been retained in place of *joke*; see "Menstruum Universalis," below, for the definition and history of this word.—Trans.

4. The French word *sens* denotes both "direction" and "meaning."—Trans.

5. Theodor Reik, "Künsterisches Schaffen und Witzarbeit," in *Lust und Leid im Witz* (Vienna, 1929).—Trans.

6. On the primitivity of representation in general in Freud's work, see Philippe Lacoue-Labarthe, "Theatrum analyticum," in *Glyph* 2 (1977): 122–43.

7. This point was raised by Jean Baudrillard in *L'Echange symbolique et la mort* (Paris, 1976), p. 332.

8. *Delusions and Dreams in Jensen's Gradiva*, *SE*, 9: 84.—Trans.

9. *Three Essays on the Theory of Sexuality*, in *SE*, 7: 207; further references to this text will be indicated by page numbers in parentheses in the text.—Trans.

10. See Freud, "On Narcissism: An Introduction," in *SE*, 14: 78: "The individual himself regards sexuality as one of his own ends; whereas from another point of view he is an appendage to his germ-plasm, at whose disposal he puts his energies in return for a bonus of pleasure [*Lustprämie*]."—Trans.

11. Freud, *Thalassa: A Theory of Genitality* (New York, 1938), trans. H. A. Bunker, p. 41.—Trans.

12. *Introductory Lectures on Psycho-Analysis*, *SE*, 16: 396.—Trans.

13. *Group Psychology and the Analysis of the Ego*, in *SE*, 18: 124. For a model of sociality opposed to the one implied by the "absolute Narcissus," see Jean-Luc Nancy and Philippe Lacoue-Labarthe, "The Unconscious Is Not Structured like an Affect," *Stanford Literature Review* 6, no. 2 (fall 1989), pp. 191–240.—Trans.

14. In the first version of this text, written in 1977, there was no allusion to Lacan's dissolution of the Ecole Freudienne de Paris. The changes made since then have not concerned this notion. But, retroactively, all readings are possible. It is also necessary to point out that J. Derrida's *La Carte postale* (Paris, 1980) has introduced a major displacement in the analysis of the "pleasure principle," of which it would now be necessary to take account. I will simply note that this reading of *Beyond the Pleasure Principle* and the one I propose of *Der Witz* and *Three Essays* confirm each other in many respects.

Vox Clamans in Deserto

N O T E : This translation first appeared in *Notebooks in Cultural Analysis* 3 (1986): 3–14.

Menstruum Universale

N O T E : The text that follows formed part of a seminar presented in the Department of French and Italian at the University of California, Irvine, in the fall quarter of 1976. It is not possible in this limited space to publish the entire series of lectures as they were given (besides, a writing down after the fact distorts and deforms even the order of an oral presentation). We have tried to summarize the main passages and only mention in passing or footnote those we had to omit. A comment regarding the word central to this work; we were compelled to use German *Witz* rather than English "Wit," as it is only in German language and theory that this term has acquired all the values and functions whose system we propose to disassemble. The essay was first published in *SubStance*, no. 21 (1978), pp. 21–35. All quotations from Schlegel are from the "Fragments" published in the journal *Athenaeum*. Because these texts have much more to offer about *Witz*, this unique, global citation is an invitation to take the whole as the true context of reference.

1. The question of *Witz* in Freud must be omitted from these pages. In

the lectures we undertook a preliminary analysis which will be developed elsewhere. Let us simply note that a study of *Witz before* Freud, along the lines we suggest, seems absolutely indispensable to any study of Freud. Even though Freud himself, intentionally or not, barely refers to the previous history of *Witz*, his work on *Witz* and all that it entails concerning psychoanalysis in general depends in a complex manner on that history. We would also like to mention Jeffrey Mehlmann's article "How to Read Freud on the Joke," in *New Literary History*, Winter 1975, and Samuel Weber's essay, "The Divaricator: Remarks on Freud's Witz," *Glyph* I, 1977, which could be shown to justify our reasoning in so far as it concerns the relations between *Witz* and thought.

2. This is the place to show how, in their style, in their puns (good or bad), *in the very construction of* their "problematic," a number of contemporary theoretical discourses (on literature, psychoanalysis, criticism, or science) derive key resources from *Witz*. To note this fact by no means implies that one can contest simply or fully its legitimacy. But this question should be asked: to what extent is the use of *Witz* inevitably linked to the repetition of what *Witz* has *already* put into play in our history and especially in Romanticism? In other words, an outline of the history of *Witz* should raise these questions: to what extent are we still Romantic? Can we still be Romantic without knowing it: Plainly and simply, can we still be Romantic?

3. Thus once again, and in many different ways, we find the union of the sexes, which obeys in every respect the entire "logic" of *Witz*. This aspect of the sexuality of *Witz*, which obviously needs to be linked to what we shall later say of its *pleasure*, will not be developed here.

4. Anonymous essay on wit in *The Weekly Register*, London, July 22, 1732, no. 119. We will show further on that a particular *commonness* [*bassesse*] of *Witz* is always rejected, even by the partisans of *Witz*. The fact that this commonness also corresponds to the social conditions of those who have no part in literature or philosophy is surely not without significance.

5. Père Bouhours, for example, in *Entretiens d'Ariste et d'Eugène* (1671). The same reproach will reappear much later, e.g., in 1740 in the *Lettres françaises et germaniques* of Mauvillon. To be exact, this reproach continued to be expressed even in Germany. According to F. Schlegel and Jean Paul, the Germans lack *Witz*. This "guilty conscience," felt neither by the English nor the French, characterizes those who make *Witz* into a

supreme principle: as if this high rank could be granted only when *Witz* vanishes, or at least *feels* that it is vanishing.

6. We know that this motif of the genius proper to language will become a truly philosophical motif with Kant, Herder, the Romantics, and later Hegel and (more politically than speculatively) with Fichte. *Witz* is the symptom or the symbol of the metaphysical assignation of thought in language, in the origination and the living identity of a language, of the presentation of sense *itself* in words. It is even its matrix; because it is always as a *game* and as a gathering of heterogeneous elements that sense appears directly in words (and not behind them). Thus, when Hegel sees the proximity of truth in language, i.e., the presence of the *thing in thought*, he hears the assonance of the words *Ding-Denken* (thing-thought). To question metaphysics on this point— as was done in an essential and complex manner by Heidegger and later by Derrida—is to question *Witz*.

7. Lawrence Sterne, *Tristram Shandy* (Harmondsworth, 1967), chap. 4, p. 39.

8. Therefore beyond what the age of literature has at times wanted to resuscitate and at other times considered as the origin of the genre that combines all genres within itself: the novel. In this context we refer the reader to the essay we published with Philippe Lacoue-Labarthe, "Le Dialogue des genres," in *Poétique*, no. 21 (1975).

9. Here we must cut and summarize considerably the properly philosophical exposé on the question of judgment. What follows should be regarded as a synopsis.

10. Since even before Descartes: here Renaissance Italy, Spain, and England should be explored. But we know that the *cogito* also implied "antecedents" in the same period: cf. L. Blanchet, *Les Antécédents historiques de "Je pense donc je suis,"* (Paris, 1920).

11. It is not possible here to cite and analyze all the texts where this debate occupies the foreground. As a whole they can be symbolized by the juxtaposition of two titles: *La Logique ou l'art de penser* (Logic or the art of thinking; the famous "logic" of Port-Royal, entirely devoted to judgment), and *La Manière de bien penser* (The proper way to think), by Père Bouhours. But we would first have to consider Castiglione, Gracian, Cervantes, Shakespeare, Malebranche, Shaftesbury, La Rochefoucauld, etc. And we would have to analyze the constellation of terms that surround *l'esprit* (1758), which admirably represents the annexation of the

values of *Witz* to philosophy (to a philosophy striving to be anti-Cartesian): genius (the invention of combinations), imagination, sentiment, *esprit* itself as an "assembling of ideas and new combination"—but also the renewed distrust of the philosopher whose judgment distinguishes and qualifies as good or bad *l'esprit fin* (delicate wit), *l'esprit fort* (the free thinker), *l'esprit de lumière* (the enlightened mind), *l'esprit étendu* (the comprehensive mind), *l'esprit pénétrant* (the keen mind), *le goût* (taste), *le bel esprit* (the elegant mind, in the sense of speaking and writing well), *l'esprit du siècle* (the spirit of the times), and *l'esprit juste* (the sense to see things as they are) . . .

12. In the *Essay Concerning Human Understanding*, ed. Alexander Campbell Fraser (New York, 1959), bk. II, chap. ii, §2, p. 203.

13. Bouhours does not hesitate, or only pretends to hesitate, to see a divine element in the *je ne sais quoi*.

14. This is what should be understood throughout Leibniz's *New Essays*. It is in fact a question of making truth accessible—in a system where the absolute intuition of the *cogito* belongs only to God—and to give to this same truth a supplementary radiance. A supplement (in the sense Derrida gives to the word in his *Grammatology*) and beauty *must* henceforth intervene in the presentation of the truth.

15. Here we must deliberately leave aside all that concerns Kant. For if he belongs—as he surely does—to this logic, he also raises the question of the existence of such a logic as a fundamental question. The Kantian *Critique* is the thought of thought *without conception*; that is why it is a *critique*, and its only object is *judgment*. That is also why it treats *Witz* rather ambiguously (this problem is examined in *Le Discours de la syncope I, Logodaedalus* [Paris, 1976]).

16. Essentially that of the novel, from the English novel to the Goethean novel (mutatis mutandis), and according to a movement along a path whose detours and returns on itself could be traced up to the contemporary novel. But it is also the aesthetics of Romantic drama, particularly Hugo's (here the preface to *Cromwell* should be reread). As a counterproof it could be shown how, from this point on in literature, an *other* literature—which to express it very briefly would go from Flaubert, Baudelaire, Mallarmé, Rilke, Valéry, to Eliot—branches off from *Witz*, or the willful choice of *Witz*, and thus maintains an entirely different relationship with philosophy.

17. In Schelling's *Abhandlund über das Wesen der menschlichen Freiheit* (Tubingen, 1971), p. 98–99: "In all philosophy, decisive propositions are

always 'dialectic'; we give this expression a very broad but decisive sense, namely that a thing, when it is essential, can be truly conceived only through its changing into another thing," and further "Friedrich Schlegel says somewhere (*Athenaeum* 82): "a definition that is not *witzig* is worth nothing." Here we can see a romantic transposition of the idealist dialectic.

18. It is not possible in this space to give the desirable historical details on the few years' existence and activity of this group. In essence they concern the brothers Schlegel and Novalis, and the texts published in the journal founded by the Schlegels, *Athenaeum*, between 1798 and 1800. We shall quote only a few significant excerpts from these texts, which will not constitute a reading of the texts, but the outline of such a reading.

19. These are texts written as *fragments*, the fragment (according to the logic of the saying and the maxim mentioned above) being *the* genre of *Witz* for the romantics.

20. It would therefore (this is the essential part) be naive to ignore those elements in literature and philosophy—and in psychoanalysis—that even today reiterate this romanticism.

21. It is not by chance—though it is by *Witz*—that we go back to Maurice Blanchot's formula: the question of *désoeuvrement* ("unworkedness"), as he formulates it, is obscurely raised from romanticism on.

22. *Heinrich von Ofterdingen* and *Lucinde*. On the latter, cf. P. Lacoue-Labarthe, "L'Avortement de la littérature," in *Poétique*, no. 21.

23. Hence the essential functions Freud will attribute to *Witz*, all the while assigning them to this "logical" function.

24. That is to say, the pleasure of *surprise* (but is there a pleasure other than by surprise?) long recognized in *Witz*; e.g., "Wit is the qualifications of the Mind, that raises and enlivens cold sentiments and plain Propositions, by giving them an elegant and surprising turn" (Sir Richard Blackmore, *An Essay upon Wit*, 1716)—which does not prevent the same author from later condemning at great length the unseemly surprises of obscenity or aggressiveness. It should also be noted that, with the romantics, the swiftness of *Witz* refers to the *chemical* and alchemic analogies of *Witz* and *mélange* in general: dissolution, combination, precipitation, all have their equivalents in a chemistry intermediary between the organic and the inorganic. Cf. Peter Kapitza, *Die frühromantische Theorie der Mischung* (Munich, 1968).

25. Cf., on the permanence of the crisis, these words by Derrida: "When *Witz* is practiced, authorized, cultivated, there is always the

economical vulgarity (precisely the vulgarity of *our* era) that claims to condense *beforehand*—ideally in order to control them as cheaply as possible—appropriating and signing a blank check for what has even been thought of in the language: 'effects of sense' " (*Pas*, in *Gramma*, no. 3/4, 1976).

26. Which means that *there is no menstruum universale*, that instead universality is what dissolution excludes. Beyond the analysis of *Witz*, we would be led to the analysis of the very *particular* character of *menstruum*. And in particular to that of the singular *conception* at the origin of the word and the thing in alchemy: *menstrue* (masculine), the solvent, is named by analogy with *menstrue* (feminine), menstruation, supposedly endowed with the capability to dissolve. It is thus linked to the negative sign of fertility, but also to both a sexual taboo, which corresponds to this power of dissolution, and to one of the major differences between the sexes—more precisely, to the difference whose masculine counterpart Fliess, at the time of his connection with Freud, found in the "menstrual" swelling of the nose. Well, the *nose*, throughout the literature of grotesque *mélanges* (and particularly in some pages of Sterne and Jean Paul), brings us back to *Witz*: "The Romans knew that *Witz* possesses a prophetic faculty; they gave it the name of nose." (F. Schlegel) Cf. our *Rhinologia*, to be published.

27. Novalis, "Preparatory Note" to *Heinrich von Ofterdingen*; in his *Werke*, ed. P. Kluckhohn and R. Samuel (Stuttgart, 1965).

Noli Me Frangere

NOTE: "Noli Me Frangere" first appeared in German in the volume *Fragment unt Totalität* (Frankfurt am Main, 1982), ed. L. Dällenbach and C. L. Hart Nibbrig. It was later published in French in the *Revue des Sciences Humaines* no. 185 (1982).

At the authors' request, I have translated the majority of quotations directly from the French, so as not to disturb the flow of the phrasing. The following references can be consulted for more information; they do not always offer word-to-word correspondences with this text.

Theodor Adorno, *Negative Dialectics*, trans. E. B. Ashton (New York, 1973), p. 5.

Roland Barthes, *L'obvie et l'obtus* (Paris, 1982), pp. 253–58.

Walter Benjamin, *Illuminations*, trans. H. Zohn (New York,

1969), p. 134; *The Origin of German Tragic Drama*, trans. J. Osborne (London, 1977), p. 176.

Maurice Blanchot, *The Writing of the Disaster*, trans. A. Smock (Lincoln, Nebraska, 1986), pp. 60–61.

Meister Eckhart: A Modern Translation, trans. R. B. Blakney (New York, 1941), p. 231.

Martin Heidegger, *Schelling's Treatise on the Essence of Human Freedom*, trans. J. Stambaugh (Athens, Ohio, 1985), p. 82.

For the authors' previous reflections on the fragment and fragmentation, see *The Literary Absolute: The Theory of Literature in German Romanticism*, trans. P. Barnard and C. Lester (Albany, N.Y., 1988). —Trans.

Exergues

NOTE: First published in French in *Alea*, no. 5 (1984), pp. 23–26. [Georges Bataille wrote *La Haine de la poésie*; Norman Mailer, *Executioner's Song*. *XXX* stands as title for a book yet to be written . . .—Trans.]

To Possess Truth in One Soul and One Body

NOTE: This essay first appeared in *Poésie*, no. 50 (1989), pp. 113–27.

1. Arthur Rimbaud, *Un Saison en enfer*, "Adieu," in *Oeuvres complètes* (Paris, 1972), p. 117. The following translations of this work are taken from Rimbaud, *A Season in Hell and the Drunken Boat*, trans. Louise Varèse (New York, 1961); where necessary, the translation has been adapted to more closely reflect the French phrasing. This and all following notes are mine—Trans.

2. *Pas* often asks to be read as a negation; thus *pas de poésie* means both "stride of poetry" and "no poetry."

3. Letter to Paul Demeny, May 15, 1871, in Rimbaud, *Collected Poems*, trans. Oliver Bernard (Harmondsworth, Middlesex, 1962), p. 13.

4. *Illuminations*, "Enfance," in *Collected Poems*, p. 240.

5. Ibid., p. 11, translation modified.

6. Ibid., p. 10.

7. Ibid., "Sonnet," in *Collected Poems*, p. 293.

8. *Illuminations*, "Conte," in *Collected Poems*, p. 240.

9. Ibid., "Antique," pp. 243–44.

10. "The Drunken Boat," in *A Season in Hell and the Drunken Boat*, p. 101.

11. *Illuminations*, "Phrases," in *Collected Poems*, p. 252.

12. Ibid., "Genie," p. 290.

13. Letter to the Director of Maritime Communications, November 9, 1891, in *Collected Poems*, p. 42.

We need . . .

N O T E : This piece first appeared in *Po&sie*, no. 26 (1983), pp. 93–94.

Speaking Without Being Able To

1. L.-R. des Forêts, *Poèmes de Samuel Wood* (Paris, 1988), pp. 11–12. My translation (Ann Smock).

Exscription

N O T E : A version of this translation first appeared in *Yale French Studies* 78, "On Bataille," ed. Allan Stoekl (1990), pp. 47–65.

1. The first, in a slightly different version, was published in the anthology *Misère de la littérature* (Paris, 1977).

2. See my *The Inoperative Community*, ed. Peter Connor (Minneapolis, 1991).

3. The quotes from various authors woven into "Reasons to Write" will not be referenced, out of respect for the spirit of this first section of the article.—Trans.

4. Maurice Blanchot, *L'Entretien infini* (Paris, 1970), p. 26.

5. All quotations from Bataille are translated from the *Oeuvres complètes* (Paris, 1970) and are referenced in the text by volume and page numbers to that edition—Trans.

6. Blanchot, *Après-coup* (Paris, 1983), p. 91.

7. Blanchot, *L'Amitié* (Paris, 1973), p. 327.

On Painting (and) Presence

1. French *discret* means both "discrete" and "discreet"; *discrétion* means both "discreteness" and "discretion." Wherever possible, I have used the cognate "discretion" (with its shadow personification and hint of pro-

cess), but sometimes "discreteness" was mandated by context. The reader should bear in mind that in the semantic domain of the French words, the two always shade into each other. This and all following notes are mine.—Trans.

2. Charles Baudelaire, "Les Phares" (Beacons), in *The Flowers of Evil*, sel. and ed. Marthiel and Jackson Mathews (New York, 1955), pp. 12, 13. Translation modified.

3. Antonin Artaud, *Anthology*, tr. Mary Beach (San Francisco, 1965), p. 156.

4. St. John Chrysostom, baptismal instructions, 12th instruction, 23, in *Ancient Christian Writers*, no. 31 (Westminster, Md., 1963), pp. 179–80.

5. Dante, *Purgatorio*, trans. John D. Sinclair (New York, 1939), XXXI, ll. 144–45.

Laughter, Presence

NOTE: In French, this essay first appeared in *Critique*, no. 488–89 (January–February 1988), pp. 41–60.

1. Charles Baudelaire, *Oeuvres complètes* (Paris, 1975), 1: 34. All notes to this essay are mine.—Trans.

2. Trans. Louise Varèse (New York, 1947). Translation modified.

3. Baudelaire, *My Heart Laid Bare and Other Prose Writings*, ed. Peter Quennell (New York, 1975), p. 176.

4. Ibid., p. 190.

Psyche

NOTE: In French, this piece first appeared in *Première Livraison*, no. 16, 1977.

MERIDIAN

Crossing Aesthetics

Library of Congress
Cataloging-in-Publication Data

Nancy, Jean-Luc.
The birth to presence / Jean-Luc Nancy ;
translated by Brian Holmes, and others.
p.   cm.
Translated from French.
Includes bibliographical references.
ISBN 0-8047-2060-6
1. Ontology.   2. Criticism.   I. Title.
BD311.N36   1993
110—dc20
92-30596
CIP

⊗ This book is printed on acid-free paper.
It was typeset in Adobe Garamond and Lithos
by Keystone Typesetting, Inc.